Techniques of Demographic Analysis

K.B. PATHAK
Director, International Institute for Population Sciences,
Mumbai-88.

F. RAM
Reader, Department of Fertility Studies,
International Institute for Population Sciences,
Mumbai-88.

Himalaya Publishing House
ISO 9001:2015 CERTIFIED

First Edition : 1992
Second Revised Edition : 1998
Edition : 2013, 2015, 2017, 2019
Edition : 2020, 2021, 2022, 2023
Edition : 2024

Published by : Mrs. Meena Pandey
for **HIMALAYA PUBLISHING HOUSE PVT. LTD.,**
"Ramdoot", Dr. Bhalerao Marg, Girgaon, Mumbai - 400 004.
Phone: 022-23860170, 23863863; **Fax:** 022-23877178
E-mail: himpub@bharatmail.co.in; **Website:** www.himpub.com

Branch Offices :

New Delhi : "Pooja Apartments", 4-B, Murari Lal Street, Ansari Road, Darya Ganj, New Delhi - 110 002.
Phone: 011-23270392, 23278631; Fax: 011-23256286

Nagpur : Kundanlal Chandak Industrial Estate, Ghat Road, Nagpur - 440 018. Phone: 0712-2738731, 2721216

Bengaluru : Plot No. 91-33, 2nd Main Road Seshadripuram, Behind Nataraja Theatre, Bengaluru - 560 020.
Phone: 080-41138821; Mobile: 09379847017, 09379847005

Hyderabad : No. 3-4-184, Lingampally, Besides Raghavendra Swamy Matham, Kachiguda, Hyderabad - 500 027.
Phone: 040-27560041, 27550139

Chennai : No. 34/44, Motilal Street, T. Nagar, Chennai - 600 017.
Mobile: 09380460419

Pune : First Floor, "Laksha" Apartment, No. 527, Mehunpura, Shaniwar Peth (Near Prabhat Theatre), Pune - 411 030.
Phone: 020-24496323, 24496333; Mobile: 09370579333

Cuttack : Plot No 5F-755/4, Sector-9, CDA Market Nagar, Cuttack - 753 014, Odisha. Mobile: 09338746007

Kolkata : 3, S.M. Bose Road, Near Gate No. 5, Agarpara Railway Station, North 24 Parganas, West Bengal - 700109. Mobile: 09674536325

Printed at : Infinity Imaging System, New Delhi. On behalf of HPH.

PREFACE TO THE SECOND EDITION

Authors are thankful to Students, Researchers and Teachers in Population Studies all over India and abroad for appreciating first edition of this book published in 1992. We have learnt a lot from the readers' comments and personal letters for clarification about certain concepts which were, many times, very brief. In the present edition we have tried to remove the shortcomings of first edition and have added some topics on Popular Demand. In Appendix of this edition we have added Evaluation and Adjustment of Demographic Data. We have only included basic materials on Evaluation and Adjustment due to escalating cost of the book.

We have also included in Chapter 4 a Popular Method of Decomposition of TFR as proposed by Bongaarts. This was added because various variants of Bongaarts Model are being used in demographic analysis and evaluation of family planning programme. In the recent, it has been felt that P/F ratio method by Brass and other methods that are based on constant fertility and mortality assumptions are no more needed. But they have been retained keeping their historical and basic technical importance. During the last six years there are many new development in order to estimate abortion and maternal mortality ratio but they are not included here as we feel that there is need of more work on these techniques in order to make them perfect. We hope second edition would fulfil the requirements of Students, Teachers and Researchers in the field of Population Studies.

K.B. Pathak

F. Ram

PREFACE TO THE FIRST EDITION

This book is written with a view to appraise the post-graduate students with upto date knowledge of available tools for analysing demographic data obtained from surveys, censuses and vital registration system. In order to make analytical methods more suitable for the application, adequate number of illustrations and worked out examples are provided in each chapter. This has enhanced the usefulness of the book. In addition, a comprehensive bibliography is provided at the end. The book has been written after several years of teaching technical demography to the post-graduate students of International Institute for Population Sciences, Bombay. With the publication of this book, paucity of a standard text book on this subject will no more exist for quite some time to come. Needless to say, it is not possible to encompass all the dimensions of population studies in a book. This book is therefore basically devoted to present a discussion of all the mathematical procedures that measure population change and its underlying factors and help in visualizing the future prospects of population growth. It provides all the essential ingredients to the reader to comprehend the demographic process in depth and sharpen his analytical capabilities in the demographic analysis.

The book contains nine chapters namely (1) Measures of Population Growth and Distribution, (2) Mortality Analysis and Life Tables, (3) Construction of Life Tables, (4) Measures of Fertility and Reproduction, (5) Nuptiality (6) Migration, (7) Demographic Models, (8) Estimation of Vital Rates from Incomplete Data, (9) Population Estimation and Projection. Spatial distribution of population and growth are the important aspects of population and indicate the areal differences in economic development. Chapter I discusses the different measures of population growth and population distribution with suitable illustrations from India. Chapters II and III provide the basic measures of mortality and methods for construction of life tables. The most recent techniques of constructing life tables from the age distribution of two censuses are also discussed along with illustrations. The Chapter IV gives the basic measures of Fertility and Reproduction. Chapter V outlines the different measures of nuptiality and techniques for analysing the marital status data. It discusses the utility of marital status data in understanding the process of marriage and its dissolution. Chapter VI deals with migration, which forms as an important component of population growth. More emphasis is however, given on the analysis of internal migration. The international migration is only briefly discussed. Chapters VII and VIII are intrinsically linked. The demographic models discussed in Chapter VII help us in understanding the population dynamics and human reproduction process and in providing the measurement of the effectiveness of population control programmes and their evaluation. Due to non-availability of good quality data from the vital registration for most of the developing countries, the indirect methods of estimating vital rates become more important. Chapter VIII not only provides the estimation procedures but also the critical interpretations of results of different procedures. Chapter IX outlines procedure for population estimation and projection. It also provides discussion of the techniques of population projection at national as well as sub-national levels. In the recent past, the projection of population for the districts has gained greater attention because the district is being considered as the unit of planning and implementation of the development plans. We have therefore given more emphasis on projection of the population for the smaller areas and provided adequate number of illustrations to demonstrate their uses. We sincerely wish that this book be widely read by demographers to give us their comments and suggestions for further improvements.

At different stages of writing this book, a number of persons helped us in different ways. All the faculty members had participated in discussion on the organization of the book. The authors are thankful to them. We are highly indebted to Dr. K. Srinivasan, Director of the Institute, for his help and encouragement throughout the preparation of the book. Thanks are also due to Mr. B.S. Singh, M.D. Singh and Md. Fayazuddin for assisting us in working out the numerical examples. The Institute provided the initial financial help in preparing the first draft and getting it finally typed. Our thanks are due to all the typists of the IIPS. The last but not the least, authors would like to thank Library and Computer Staff of IIPS for their help, assistance and cooperation.

K.B. Pathak
F. Ram

CONTENTS

1

Measures of Population Change and Distribution

Demography is the study of population change over time and space, the various determinants of population change and the impact of such change on the world around us. Population change not only implies the change in its size but also in its internal composition and structure with respect to its various characteristics and spatial distribution. Before one envisages to study the implicatins of such change on various social, economic and eco-systems including the demographic processes, such as births, deaths and migration, one needs the measurement of such change so as to have assessment of the impact and comparision of the change potential in any two populations. It is needless to mention that population always refers to a fixed boundry area, such as a Country, State/Province or District or Village. size of the population in any area increases through births and inmigration and decreases through deaths and out migration.

The total population of an area may be determined by a census count in two ways. The easier way is the "de-facto" count in which all the persons are to be counted in a place where they are found at the time of enumeration irrespective of the fact that they belong to the place or not. This system has greater chance of counting the moving population and ensures maximum coverage of the population. It,however, fails to provide the exact areawise distribution of the population which is very much essential for not only administrative purposes but also for planning various welfare programmes in different areas and for analysing population trends. The other way in which census count is done is known as "de-jure" method in which persons are enumeratad on the basis of their place of usual residence. Most of the countries follow the dejure system of obtaining the total population of all the areas. The concept of "usual residence" is however vague and provides enough scope of misjudgement. This does not include foreigners and temporary visitors, though they may be substantial in number to affect the social and economic activities of the population. Most of the modern censuses therefore combine the two systems to derive the maximum information on the population.

1.1 RATE OF POPULATION CHANGE

Change in the total population of an area is measured by the rate of growth per annum. Any mathematical method of estimating the population change consists in expressing population at time t as a function of t. The simplest form of the assumption which can be made is that population is increasing by a constant number *i.e.*

$$\Delta P(t)=rP(o)$$

Where,

$$\Delta P(t)=P(t+1)-P(t)$$

The constant term is defined as annual increase or growth in the population. If we take t years from base year o to time t then number of persons added would be $r.t$ times of population $P(o)$. So the population at times t would equal

$$P(t)=P(o)+rt\ P(o)$$

$$=P(o)\ (1+rt) \qquad \ldots (1)$$

The equation (1) is known as arithmetic growth model. In this case, there is no compounding of the population after the base year.

Let us assume that the population is compounding annually with growth rate r. The population change during t to $t+1$ is then given by:

$$\triangle P(t)=r\,P(t)$$

where

$$\triangle P(t)=P(t+1)-P(t)$$

So,

$$P(t+1)=P(t)\,(1+r)$$

It means that the population size at the end of a year is $(1+r)$ times the population size at the beginning of the year. Following the above rule, we have

$$P(t)=P(t-1)(1+r)=P(o)(1+r)^t \qquad \ldots (2)$$

The above equation is known as the geometric law of population growth. Sometimes, population following such pattern of growth is called Malthusian population. If population size at two points of time are available, r can be estimated and with the help of equation (2) population at any point of time between o and t can be estimated. If some assumption about r is made for the future, population size can easily be projected into future.

In deriving equation (2), we assumed annual compounding. Let us assume that compounding takes place n times in a year then,

$$P(t)=P(o)\,\{(1+r/n)^n\}^t \qquad (2a)$$

In case $n\text{—>}\infty$ compounding takes place instantaneously then,

$$\lim_{n\to\infty}(1+r/n)^n=e^r$$

and,

$$p(t)=P(o)e^{rt} \qquad \ldots (3)$$

The equation (3) is known as the exponential form of the population growth and it is continuous form of discrete equation (2). We can also derive equation (3) by considering the instantaneous rate of change as:

$$\frac{1}{P(t)} \times \frac{d}{dt} \{P(t)\} = r \qquad \ldots (4)$$

or $\frac{d}{dt} \log \{P(t)\} = r$

By integrating both sides, we get,

$\log \{P(t)\} = r\,t + \log C$ so that

$P(t) = C\,e^{rt}$

When,

$t = o,\ C = P(o)$

So,

$P(t) = P(o)\,e^{rt}$

In the last three models, it is assumed that population would continue to grow but it is commonly known that the population can not continue to grow infinitely. In other words, there would be a time when population will cease to grow and would attain its maximum stationary population size at that time. Under such law, population growth follows a Logistic curve. The Logistic curve can be derived as:

$$\frac{d}{dt} \{P(t)\} = r\,P(t) \left\{ 1 - \frac{P(t)}{K} \right\} \qquad \ldots (5)$$

Where k is maximum population size and is known as upper asymptote. The above equation can also be written as;

$$\frac{K}{P(t)\,\{K - P(t)\}} \times \frac{d}{dt} \{P(t)\} = r$$

or,

$$\left\{ \frac{1}{P(t)} + \frac{1}{K - P(t)} \right\} \frac{d}{dt} \{P(t)\} = r \qquad \ldots (6)$$

By integrating both sides of equation (6),

we get

$$\log_e P(t) - \log_e \{K - P(t)\} = rt + c$$

Where c is the constant of integration,

thus we have,

$$\frac{P(t)}{K - P(t)} = e^{rt+c}$$

$$\text{or} \quad P(t) = \frac{K}{1 + e^{-(rt+c)}} \qquad \ldots (7)$$

The above equation may also be written as:

$$P(t) = \frac{K}{1 + e^{a+bt}} \qquad \ldots (8)$$

$$b < 0$$

For point of inflextion

$$\frac{d^2}{dt^2}\left\{P(t)\right\} = 0$$

which gives us

$$P(t) = \frac{K}{2}$$

and

$$t = -\frac{a}{b}$$

It means, this curve has increasing growth rate for $P(t) < \frac{K}{2}$. Equation (8) may also be written as

$$\frac{1}{P(t)} = \frac{1}{K} + \frac{1}{K} e^{a+bt} \qquad \ldots (9)$$

or,

$$Y_t = A + B\,C^t \qquad \ldots (10)$$

This is known as modified exponential curve,
where,

$$Y_t = \frac{1}{P(t)}$$

1.2 ESTIMATION OF THE PARAMETERS OF LOGISTIC CURVE

The procedure for estimation of the parameters of Logistic curve is similar to that for the modified exponential curve. There are two procedures to estimate the parameters namely (i) by choosing three selected points and (ii) by taking partial sum. Both the conceptually the same. Here we discuss the method of partial sum. Let us recall equation (10),

$$Y_t = A + BC^t$$

where,

$$Y_t = \frac{1}{P(t)}$$

$$A = \frac{1}{K}$$

or,

$$K = \frac{1}{A} \qquad \ldots (11)$$

$$B = \frac{e^a}{K}$$

or,

$$e^a = K\,B$$

$$a = \log_e (K\,B) \qquad \ldots (12)$$

and

$$C = e^b$$

or,

$$\log_e (C) = b \qquad \ldots (13)$$

In this procedure, the time series data is split up into three equal parts containing, say, n observations of $P(t)$.

$S_1 = 1, 2, 3 \ldots n$ for first group

$S_2=n+1, n+2, \ldots 2n$ for second group

$S_3=2n+1, 2n+2, \ldots 3n$ for third group

Let us assume S_1 S_2 and S_3 as the sums of the $Y(t)=\dfrac{1}{P(t)}$ in three sub-groups having equal number of observations, then

$$C^n=\frac{S_3-S_2}{S_2-S_1}=\frac{d_2}{d_1}$$

$$C=\left[\frac{d_2}{d_1}\right]^{\frac{1}{n}} \quad \ldots (14)$$

where,

$$d_1=S_2-S_1$$
$$d_2=S_3-S_2$$

$$B=\frac{(C-1)d_1^3}{C\,(d_2-d_1)^{\cdot 2}} \quad \ldots (15)$$

When t starts from zero, then C will not appear in the denominator of the equation (15).

$$A=\frac{1}{n}\left[S_1-\frac{B\times C\,(C-1)^n}{C-1}\right] \quad \ldots (16)$$

Once we get the estimates for A, B and C, we can fit the modified exponential curve or the logistic curve.

1.3 DOUBLING TIME FOR A POPULATION

The doubling time 't' years for a population may be obtained using the relation:

$$P_t=P_o\,(1+r)^t$$

Since,

$$P_t=2P$$

we have,

$$t=\frac{ln\ 2}{ln\ (1+r)}=\frac{0.693}{ln\ (1+r)}$$

Expanding the function $ln\,(1+r)$ in the denominater we get,

$$t=\frac{0.693}{r-r^2/2+r^3/3} \quad \ldots (17)$$

Since for most of the populations, $|r|$ lies between 0.00 to 0.04, $|r|<1$ and hence $t=\frac{0.693}{r}$,

If r is expressed as percentage we have t = 70/100r which implies that a population with $r=0.01$ will double in 70 years and with $r=0.02$ will double in 35 years. Of course if the population is decreasing, *i.e.*, r is negative, then t gives the timing of halfing of the population in place of doubling. The calculation of doubling time provides a quick perspective of change in different populations.

If r is defined as an annual rate compounded continuously, the equation for the doubling time t becomes

$e^{rt}=2$ whose solution is just $t=0.693/r$ or $69.3/100r$.

These equations to find doubling time are equally useful in calculating 'r' if t is known. If we know that population has doubled in $n=100$ years, it implies that r must be $0.693/100=0.00693$. In general $r=0.693/t$.

In the population closed to migration, the rate of increase of the population is called natural growth rate and it is caused due to excess of the birth rate (b) over death rate (d) *i.e.*

$$r=b-d$$

Let us consider the population of the world at the time of Augustus being 250 million. It increased to 545 million people by the mid seventeenth century, an increase of 2.18 time over a period of 1950 years. So that

$$2.18=e^{r(1650)}$$

or

$$r=\ln 2.18/1650=0.00047 \text{ (See, Keyfitz, 1977, p. 7).}$$

If death rate is 40.00 per thousand population, then birth rate (b) is given by 40.47.

Thus simple use of the exponential rate of growth of the population gives the idea of birth and death rates in the remote past. This idea may further be expanded to ascertain the change in birth rate over time.

1.4 POPULATION DISTRIBUTION

We require the population data not only for a nation but also for its geographic subdivisions and socio-economic categories. Census is the main source to provide the geographic distribution of the population by states and districts, urban and rural areas. Below we discuss some measures used to study the distribution of population in different areas.

1.4.1. Population Density

The density of population in any area is usually computed as number of persons per square km. or per square mile of land area. It is however a misleading index of population distribution since different areas are not uniformly inhabited. For example, the density of population living in Madhya Pradesh and Rajasthan is much less than those in Kerala and West Bengal.

The densities of urban areas are much higher than those of rural areas. Countries with vast areas under deserts, mountains, forests and icecaps etc. have low densities. The most thinly settled countries of all is the Antarctic Circle. Thus more meaningful density may be obtained by relating the population to the area of agricultural lands under use. However, this definition of density does not carry any sense in case of "City States" like Hong Kong, Singapore and Vatican etc.

Barclay (1958) has suggested another measure of density which relates to the "ratio between requirements of a population and the resourses made available to it by production in the area it occupies",

$$\text{Density} = \frac{NK}{SK^1}$$

Where,

N=Total population, K=the quantity of requirement per capita, S=area in square kilometers, and K^1=the quantity of resources produced per square kilometer.

Duncan (1957) gives the following classification of the different measures of population distribution:

Spatial Measures

(i) Number and density of inhabitants by geographic subdivisions
(ii) Measures of concentration
(iii) Measures of spacing
(iv) Centrographic measures
(v) Population Potential

Categorical Measures

(i) Rural—Urban and Metropolitan and non-metropolitan classification
(ii) Community size distribution
(iii) Concentration by proximity to centres or to designated sites

1.4.2 Percentage Distribution and Ranks

A simple method to study distribution of population is to compute the percentage distribution of population living in the geographic areas, such as states, change in percentage of population over two points may indicate the gain or loss in the share of the area depending on the fact that the difference is positive or negative.

We can also rank the states or areas according to the size of the population from highest to the lowest corresponding to consecutive censuses and then study the change in the rank of a state/area over the inter censal period. Geographers have shown interest in finding the 'median lines' which are the two orthogonal lines dividing the area into two parts such that each part has equal number of inhabitants. The median point is the intersection of these two lines. This method however describes the distribution of population rather than the concentration. It is mathematically more convenient to find out the centre of gravity of the population as below:

$$\overline{X}=\frac{\Sigma P_i x_i}{\Sigma P_i};\quad \overline{Y}=\frac{\Sigma P_i y_i}{\Sigma P_i}$$

Where P_i is the population at point *i* and x_i and y_i are its horizantal and vertical coordinates respectively.

Thus the mean point unlike the median point depends on the distance of a person from it. Ascertainment of both the median point and mean point of the population is not so elegant and depends largely on the number and size of geographical units.

Related to the concept of average distance of different populations from the central point, is the measure of dispersion of the distances. The standard distance is given below:

$$D=\sqrt{\sum_{i=1}^{n}\frac{(x_i-\overline{x})^2+(y_i-\overline{y})^2}{n}}$$

Where,

$\overline{x}$ and $\overline{y}$ are the coordinates of the centre and x_i and y_i are the coordinates of any area *i*. It may be mentioned that the distance of different states/may be measured from the capitals.

1.4.3 Population Potential

The concept of population potentiality means the accessibility to the population. The total potential of the population at a point (*G*) is the sum of the reciprocal of the distance of all individuals in the population from the point. Under the assumption that influence of any person on any place is inversely proportion to his distance at the point, we have

$$G=\sum_{i=1} P_i / D_i$$

Where,

P_i is the population of area *i* and D_i is the distance of the central point of the area *i* from that place.

Distribution of Population by Rural-Urban Category

One can use the percentage distribution of population in rural and urban areas for studying the concentration of the population. The common definition of urbanization in terms of percentage of total population living in the urban areas is not suitable where distribution of urban areas varies widely with respect to the size of their population. Gibbs (1966) gave two measures called "Scale of urbanization" (*Su*) and "Scale of population concentration" (*Sp*). If X_i is the proportion of the urban population in urban size class *i* and all size classes above it and Y_i is the proportion of the total population in urban size class (*i*) and all size classes above it then

$$S_u = \sum X_i Y_i \qquad \text{...(18)}$$

$$S_p = \sum Y_i$$

However, the scale of urbanization is not independent of the arbitrary population size used to define urban. It is highly dependent on number of categories in the distribution. Of the two measures, the scale of population concentration is superior.

1.4.4 Lorenz Curve and Gini Concentration Ratio

The concept of the lorenz curve was used basically to measure the distribution of income or wealth area. It was developed by Lorenz in 1905. But it can also be used to measure the degree of concentration of population by localities or any other characteristics of the population. Like other curves, we have to prepare a frequency distribution of units according to indepedent variates either individually or grouped in class intervals. For example, we take different size of the cities as independent variates and number of cities in each size (Y_i) and population (X_i) as frequencies. If there is no concentration of population, we would get straight line passing through origin when cumulative proportion of Y_i is plotted against cumulative proportion of X_i (figure 1.1).

Gini concentration ratio measures the area that lies between the straight line (diagonal) as expected in absence of concentra-

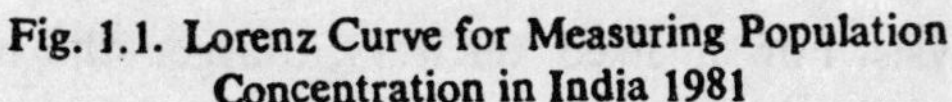

Fig. 1.1. Lorenz Curve for Measuring Population Concentration in India 1981

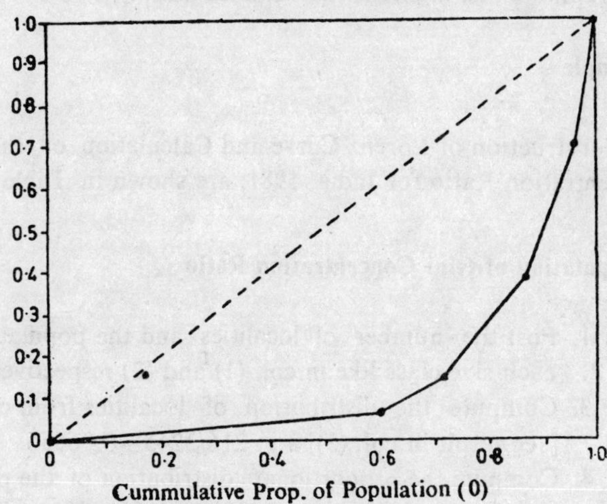

tion and the Lorenz Curve. The Gini Index can be calculated using the following formula;

$$\text{Gini Concentration Ratio} = \left[\sum_{i=1} X_i \, Y_{i+1}\right] - \left[\sum_{i=1} X_{i+1} \, Y_i\right]$$

$$= G_1 - G_2$$

Detailed discussion of the application of this concept is available in article by Duncan (1957).

In place of Gini Concentration Ratio, Duncan introduced index of concentration, which is calculated simply by per cent distribution of the units. The index of concentration is given as :

$$I.C. = \frac{1}{n} \sum_{i=1}^{n} \left[x_i - y_i \right]$$

Where x_i and y_i are just per cent distributions of the two variates. The above index is equivalent to the Index of Dissimilarity. Geometrically, it is the maximum vertical distance from the straight line (diogonal) to the Lorenz curve. The Index of concentration depends upon the set of geographic units used in the analysis. For a fixed territory, larger the number of geographic units, higher is the value of index.

Example

Construction of Lorenz Curve and Calculation of the Gini concentration Ratio for India, 1981, are shown in Table 1.1

Computation of Gini Concentration Ratio

Steps 1. and 2. Post the number of localities and the population for each size class like in col. (1) and (2) respectively.

Step 3. Compute the distribution of localities from col. (1) [see result in col. (3)] *e.g.* 216/3245=0.06656.

Step 4. Compute the proportionate distribution of the population from col. (2) *e.g.* 94293000/156185512=0.60371 [full result in col. (4)].

Step 5. Cumulate the proportions of col. (3) downwards *e.g.*, 0.067+0.083=0.150 [full result in col. (5)].

Step 6. Cumulate the proportion of col. (4) downward and result is given in col. (6).

Step 7. Multiply the first line in col. (6) by the second line in col. (5), the second line by the third line etc. to obtain col. (7).

Step 8. Multiply the first line in col. (5), by the second line in col. (6), the second line by the third line etc. to obtain col. (8).

Step 9. Sum of cols. (7) and (8) are 2.853 and 2.165 respectively.

Step 10. Subtract the total of col. (8) from the total of col. (7) to obtain which the Gini concentration Ratio.

1 4.5 Rank-Size Rule

It has been empirically observed that the product of city size by its rank tends to be constant. If p_i is the population size of the *i*th city and r_i is its rank, then

TABLE 1.1

Computation of Gini Concentration Ratio for Persans Living in Urban Localities in India in 1981

Class	Number of Towns	Population	Proportion		Cumulative Proportion		$X_1 \times Y_{j+1}$	$X_{i+1} \times Y_1$
			Localities	Population	Localities	Population		
	1	2	3	4	5 (X_1)	6 (Y_1)	7	8
Total	3,245	156128507	—	—	—	—	—	—
I	216	94292988	0.067	0.604	0.067	0.604	0.000	0.000
II	270	18191847	0.083	0.116	0.150	0.720	0.090	0.048
III	739	22413463	0.228	0.143	0.377	0.864	0.272	5.129
IV	1,048	14862211	0.323	0.095	0.700	0.959	0.605	0.362
V	742	5641505	0.229	0.036	0.929	0.995	0.891	0.697
VI	230	786483	0.071	0.005	1.000	1.000	0.995	0.929
Total							2.853	2.165

The Gini Concentration Ratio=2.853−2.165=0.688.

$$p_i \times r_i = \text{Constant (K)}$$

$$\text{or} \quad P_i = \frac{K}{r_i}$$

The constant K is the size for the largest city. The above concept has been elaborated in detail by Zipf (1941). Stewart (1947, p. 462) provided following general rank-size rule:

$$P_i = \frac{K}{r_i^n}$$

Where n is a positive constant. He evaluated n to lie between 0 and 1 for India and Japan. It has been observed in number of applications that this rule is not generally applicable. There may be number of cities which may be much larger than what is expected from the rank-size rule. The Primate cities may be simply the largest city in the country. So the size of other cities in the same country is related with the primate city. It has however, been found that the primate city urban structure does not always appear to be a function of the level of economic development, industrialization or urbanization.

1.5 ANALYSIS OF AGE DISTRIBUTION

The data on age-sex distribution of the population from census or survey are generally given in five year age groups like 0-4, 5-9 . . . . But in certain analysis, like school enrolment, labour force status at young ages, single year age data is required. One may even tabulate age data in pre-defined broad groups like 0-14 (children), 15-64 (labour force) and 65+(old age). In case of fertility analysis, we require 15—49 age group female population. The age data, may be analysed in different ways. Some of them are as follows:

(i) Per cent Distribution

(ii) Per cent Change by age

(a) Index of Relative Difference

(b) Index of Disimilarity

(iii) Measures of Central tendency and Dispersion

(iv) Graphic Representation.
(v) Measures of old age distribution and Aging of Population.

The calculation of per cent distribution by age of population is simple. But generally in tabulation we have a category in its ages not stated which in certain analysis has to be redistributed in all the ages on prorata basis.

1.5.1 Per cent Distribution

For comparison of different age distributions and the age distribution of any area over a period of time, it is necessary to convert the absolute age distribution into proportions. If Pi is the population in the ith age group; P is total population, the per cent or proportion can be given as:

Per cent of population in ith age group

$$C_i = \frac{P_i}{P} \times 100$$

The per cent distribut ion of the population is either calculated for 5-year age groups or for broad age groups (0-14, 15-64 and 65+). The distribution by 5-year age groups or other broad age groups is used in the graphic representation also.

1.5.2 Per cent Change in Distribution

The change in age distribution over a period of time can also be calculated as follows:

$$\text{Per cent Change of population in } i\text{th age group} = \frac{P_i^{t+10} - P_i^t}{P^t} \times 100$$

The above equation provides nothing but decadal linear change as discussed in case of arithmatic growth model. Instead of this one can use other some indices for comparison.

1.5.3 Index of Relative Difference (IRD)

Let us assume that C_{1i} and C_{2i} are two per cent distributions of ith age group at two points of time or of two Populations. For calculating IRD following formula can be used:

$$IRD=\frac{1}{2}\times\frac{\sum_{i=1}^{n}\left|\frac{C_{2i}}{C_{1i}}-1\right|}{n}$$

where n is the number of age groups.

1.5.4 Index of Disimilarity

The index is based on the absolute difference in two per cent age distributions of the population. Following formula is used in the calculation of this index:

$$ID=\frac{1}{2}\sum_{i=1}^{n}\left|C_{2i}-C_{1i}\right|$$

It must be mentioned that this index is also used in the analysis of the distribution of population of geographical units. The above two indices are affected by age groupings used and the difference between the two age distributions.

1.5.5 Measures of Central Tendency and Dispersion

Among all the measures of central tendency, median is the most appropriate being sensitive to changes in age distribution. The mean is less favoured because of the high skewness of the age distribution. Secondly, we have open ended interval which may affect the calculation of mean. For calculating dispersion (variance or sd) we need to calculate mean. For such calculation, one can use proportion or per cent distribution of the population.

1.6 Graphic Representation of Age Data

The graphic representation is generally done with per cent age distribution of the population by sex. This is done by two ways:

(a) Time series chart for each age group
(b) Population Pyramid

The time series chart can be drawn by taking broad age group but population Pyramid very effectively depicts not only the age-sex composition of the population but also the history of population dynamics. The population pyramid is nothing but drawing the histogram for each sex side by side. The age interval can be shown either on left or right or both sides of the Pyramid but it is generally put straddling in the central axis as shown in figures 1.2 and 1.3. In drawing Pyramid, age interval for both the sexes should be of the same size. The old age population is generally represented as one group (60+or 70+or 80+). The Pyramid of different populations or same population at different points of time or different groups of the population can be super imposed and represented in different colours. The Pramid may be either broad based (reflecting high fertility, low median age) or narrow based (low fertility, high median age). Figures 1.2 and 1.3 reflect the above two situations.

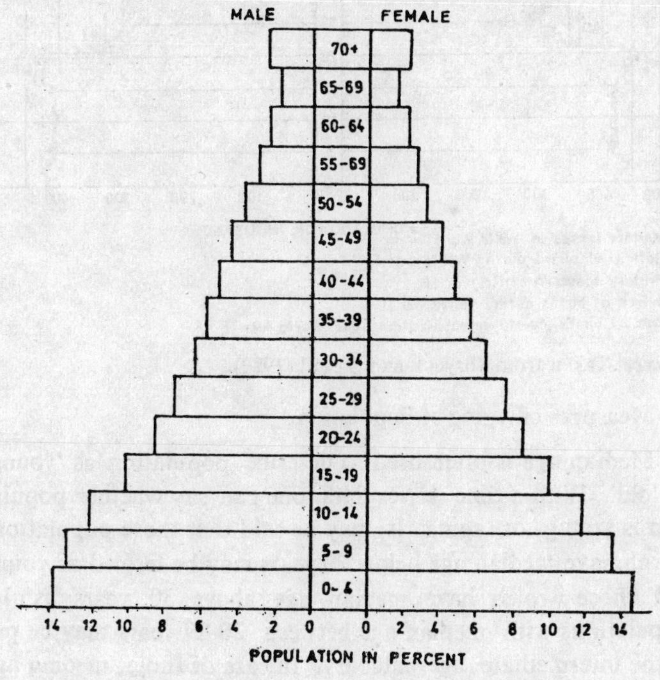

Fig. 1.2. Percentage of Age Distribution in India (1981)

Fig. 1.3. Population of France, by Age and Sex: January 1, 1967

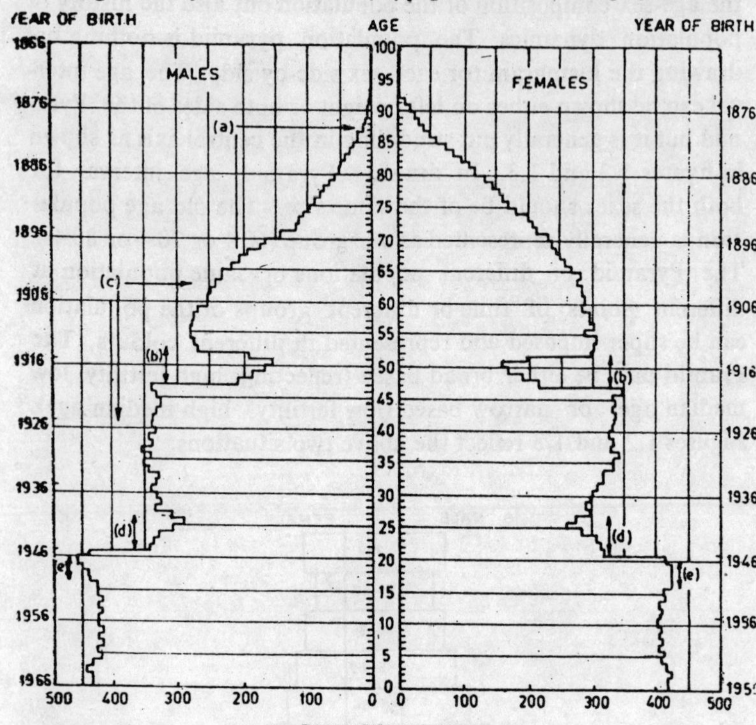

(a) Military losses in World War I
(b) Deficit of births during World war I
(c) Military losses in World war II
(d) Deficit of births during World war II
(e) Rise of births due to demobilization after World war II

Source: Taken from Shryock and Siegetl (1980).

1.7 Measures of Aging of Population

Median age is often used to describe population as 'young' or 'old'. With a time series data, one can say whether population is young or aging. It may be said that those populations which have median age below 20 years may be termed as young and those which have median age above 30 years as old. Populations with median age between 20-29 years may be put in the intermediate age category. In case of India, median age was around 20.5 in 1981. In addition to the median, we may calculate following measures to indicate the change:

(i) proportion of aged person
(ii) proportion of population below the age of 15
(iii) aged-child ratio
(iv) age-dependency ratio

The first two measures can be directly obtained from per cent or proportion age distribution of the population.

The aged-child ratio (ACR) is calculated as:

$$ACR = \frac{\text{Population above the age of 60 or 65}}{\text{Population below the age of 15}} \times 100$$

As the value of *ACR* increases we may say that population is aging. In case *ACR* is below 15, population may be termed as young. The population may be termed as old if *ACR* is above 30.

The Age-Dependency Ratio (*ADR*) is defined as:

$$ADR = \frac{P_{65+} + P_{0-14}}{P_{15-64}} \times 100$$

The two terms old age dependency (P_{65+}/P_{15-64}) and child dependency ratios (P_{0-14}/P_{15-64}) are generally defined as components of *ADR*. It may be clearly seen that *ADR*=Child Dependency Ratio+Old age Dependency ratio.

During the last 40 years various types of change have taken place in the age distribution and population of different countries. However, two distinctive trends have been clearly observed. The first is aging and second is a Juvenation of population. The aging of the population is a process in which the share of the older persons in the population increases and the share of children decreases. Due to this, median age increases. This process has been clearly felt in most of the developed countries where demographic transition is completed. The Juvenation of the population is a process in which the share of children increases and the share of older persons declines. Many countries of the less developed regions where the fertility and mortality were high and the population was already young experienced this process. Whenever there is decline in mortality of such population, the survival of infants and children increases leading to increase in proportions of the population below the age 15. Nevertheless, Juvenation was also observed in the developed countries in the 1950's and early 1960's due to post war baby boom. In the developed regions, the proportion of elderly persons increased from 11 per cent in 1950 to 16 per cent in 1985. At the same time, the median age rose from 28.2 in 1950 to 32.5 in year 1980.

In the developing countries, population has been younging until 1970. In this process, median age declined from 21 years in 1950 to 19 years in 1970 and again rose to 21 years in 1985. It is expected that in future aging would be the main feature of the population in the developing countries and the increase in elderly persons will be much faster than what was observed for the developing countries. The aging of the females is generally more than males. For details about the problems associated with aging, one can read the publication by U.N. (1988).

2

Mortality Analysis and Life Tables

The reduction in mortality, especially after World War II in most of the developing countries, has contributed to the rapid increase in their populations. Among the components of population change, mortality thus plays a vitat role of determining the size of population. It also exerts its influence on the age structure of the population though much smaller than fertility. Study of mortality is needed for the analysis of several other demographic phenomenon like nuptiality, fertility and migration; for public health administration and several other studies like projection of population in future, ascertaining changes in the characteristics of population, developing plans for housing and educational facilities; managing the social security programmes, providing various services like life insurance policies and commodities for various groups of the population. Local health authorities use mortality statistics to evaluate the effects of public health programmes in their areas. Mortality statistics are very much needed for the proof of death of the deceased persons and determining the heirs of the deceased persons.

Main source of the data on mortality is the vital registration system. The other alternative sources are national censuses and sample surveys. In addition to supplying direct data on number of deaths in a given period prior to the census or survey date, they provide age distributions of population at different points of time from which mortality can be inferred. Surveys provide some greater details about the deceased at the time of death including cause of death but for smaller areas only. The quality of data on deaths obtained from the vital registration is quite poor because of incomplete registration and inaccurate recording of cause of death, age, and other characteristics of the deceased. This puts serious limitations on the analysis of levels and trends of mortality in the developing countries.

Age and sex are the two important characteristics which form the basis of the detailed analysis of mortality. The other characteristics considered in mortality studies are, place of residence of the deceased, cause of death, marital status, occupation and family size. Any study of mortality reduces ultimately to ascertaining the 'risk of death' for different segments of a population characterised by certain characteristics, like age, sex, place of residence, occupation etc. The measurement of mortality risks is the main thrust of this chapter. We have discussed a number of techniques ranging from the conventional direct methods to the more innovative methods of indirect estimation.

2.1 MEASURES OF MORTALITY BASED ON DEATH STATISTICS

There exists a number of measures of mortality which are based on death statistics. They are being discussed below:

Crude Death Rate (CDR)

The crude death rate is defined as the number of deaths in a year per 1,000 average population in the year. It is the simplest and commonest measure of mortality level. If D is the number of deaths in a population during a given calender year, and P is the average number of persons living in the population during the year, then the CDR (*d*) is

$$d=\frac{D}{P}\times \mathrm{K}$$

Where K is a constant and is generally taken as 1,000. Normally population changes more or less uniformly during a year, hence it may be closely approximated by the average of the populations at the beginning and at the end of the year. Though crude death rates may be computed for any period, typically they are calculated for the calender year, or any convenient 12 months period in order to eliminate the effect of seasonal or monthly variations.

Since deaths are generally under registered, they should be adjusted for the under registration, if the satisfactory estimate of under registration is available. Similarly population should be adjusted for the under enumeration.

It has been found that the annual crude death rate fluctuate from year to year. In order to render the rates comparable and add stability to the rates based on small number, some times an annual average crude death rate covering data for two or three years is computed as follows:

$$\text{(i)}\quad \bar{d}=\left[\frac{D_1}{P_1}+\frac{D_2}{P_2}+\frac{D_3}{P_3}\right]\times 1000.$$

Where D_i and P_i refer to number of deaths and average population of the year i and $\bar{d}$ is the average CDR for years 1, 2 and 3.

$$\text{(ii)}\quad \bar{d}=\left[\frac{D_1+D_2+D_3}{P_1+P_2+P_3}\right]\times 1000$$

$$\text{(iii)}\quad \bar{d}=\left[\frac{D_1+D_2+D_3}{3P_2}\right]\times 1000$$

Unless there are wide fluctuations in tne size of the population, all the above methods give almost same result. Procedure (ii) is more exact but procedure (iii) is more convenient and hence commonly used.

CDR requires minimum data on mortality and is easy to interpret. Since the risk of death is not uniform for different segments of population (age, sex or other characteristics), CDR is a crude measure and hence cannot be used directly for comparing the levels of mortality in two or more countries.

Crude death rates so far reported have ranged between 5 to 55 per thousand population in normal conditions.

Specific Death Rates

A specific death rate may be computed for segments of the population specified by age, sex, race, marital status, occupation and other characteristics provided both D and P relate to the same segment. Since the risk of death is highly dependent upon age, any refined measure of mortality must necessarily take the age structure into account. A study of the age specific death rates would provide a detailed picture of mortality by age.

Age Specific Death Rates

If ${}_nD_x$ is the number of deaths between ages x and $x+n$ among the residents in a population during a year, and nPx is the average number of persons between agcs x and $x+n$ living in that population during the year, then the age specific death rate (*ASDR*) denoted by $n^m x$ is given by

$$n^m x = \frac{{}_nD_x}{{}_nP_x} \times 1{,}000.$$

Example 1: Singapore, 1979.

Deaths in age group 15-24,=442

Mid year population aged 15-24,=566000

$$ASDR\left(15\text{-}24\right) = {}_{10}m_{15} = \frac{442}{566000} \times 1000 = .781$$

However, age specific death rates are generally calculated separately for the two sexes and in that case both numerator and demoninator for the rate should refer to the same sex. Thus we can get age sex specific death rates. Table 2.1 gives the ASDRS by sex for India.

A study of the schedules of ASDRs indicates the typical pattern. The rates are high at the infancy, drop to minimum at about the ages 10-14 and rise almost gradually to a maximum at the every old age, surpassing the infant death rate in the

TABLE 2.1

Age-Specific Death Rates, India 1976.

Age	*Specific Death rate*	
	Male	*Female*
0—4	49.6	51.9
5—9	4.2	5.1
10—14	2.4	2.5
15—19	2.5	2.9
20—24	2.7	4.1
25—29	3.1	4.6
30—34	4.2	4.8
35—39	4.5	5.0
40—44	9.5	4.7
45—49	12.1	8.0
50—54	19.5	12.6
55—59	28.6	18.5
60—64	48.4	33.4
65—69	57.6	46 4
70+	114.6	85.5

Source: Office of R.G., Government of India. SRS Bulletin Vol. XIII, No. 2, December 1979, Table 5.

age range of 60 to 90. Age specific death rates are generally computed in 5 or 10 year age groups. However, separate death rates are calculated for the age groups under 1 and 1 to 4 due to high risk of death for the infants. In case of infant deaths, U.N. suggested tabulations to be made by days, that is mainly under 7 days, under 28 days and under 1 year. A crude death rate can be expressed as the weighted mean of the age specific death rates where the weights are the proportions of the total population at each age *i.e.*

$$\frac{D}{P}=\sum_{a=0}^{w}\frac{(D_a/P_a).\ P_a}{P}=\sum_{a=0}^{w}\ (ASDR_a).\ \frac{P_a}{P}$$

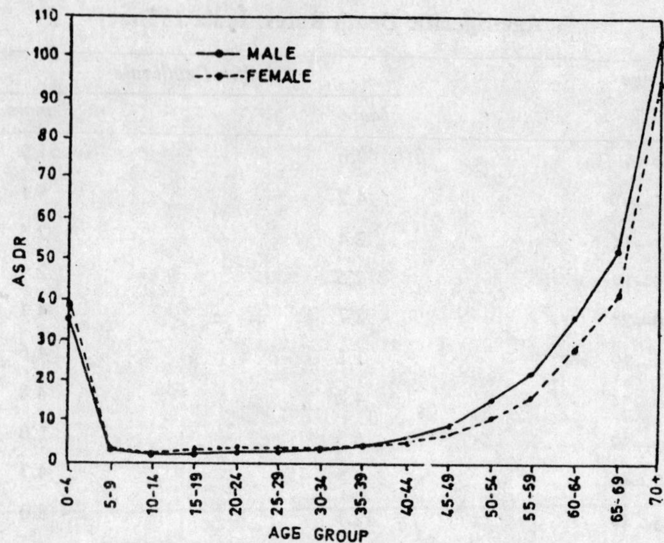

Fig. 2.1: ASDR (India 1983)

P_a/P denotes the proportion of population in age group *a*. This decomposition is quite useful in understanding the change in death rates over time. Change in death rate may be either due to change in age distribution of the population or due to change in age-specific death rates. Similarly death rates of two populations may be different because of difference in their age distributions as well as in the schedules of their age specific death rates. Death rates may be calculated specific to any other characteristics in addition to age and sex.

Cause Specific Death Rates and Ratios: are of special importance in mortality analysis. The classification of deaths according to cause of death in most of the countries is done according to the International classification of diseases as recommonded by the World Health Organisation. If D^i is the number of deaths due to cause *i*, then the crude death rate for this cause *i* is

$$m^i = \frac{D^i}{P} \times K$$

where K may be taken as 10,000 or 100,000 instead of 1,000 to make the value of m^i more easily comparable. Deaths due to cause i may be related to total deaths in a year to obtain a cause specific death ratio. Symbolically, it is calculated as

$$\frac{D^i}{D} \times K$$

K may be taken to be 100 to give the percentage of total deaths due to the specific cause i. The analysis of mortality by cause gives a more cohesive picture of 'mortality risks' prevailing in a community and the diseases can, therefore, be ranked according to their seriousness in causing deaths so that public health programmes may be undertaken to eliminate the major causes of deaths. Cause specific deaths can also be analysed specific for age and sex. Age and cause specific death rate is given by:

$$m_a^i = [D_a^i / P_a] \times K$$

where D_a^i is the number of deaths due to cause i at age a in a year and P_a is the number of persons aged a at the mid year. K can be conveniently taken as 100,000. Most of the deaths can be considered belonging to two broad classes of deaths, namely, endogenous and exogenous. Endogenous deaths are mainly the results of the genetic composition of the individual and the circumstances of prenatal life and the birth process. Deaths due to the degenerative diseases of old age *e.g.*, heart disease, cancer, diabetes etc are endogenous. Infant deaths occurred due to immaturity, birth injuries, postnatal asphyxia etc., are called endogeneous deaths. Exogenous deaths are those which are result of the impact of environment, such as infections and accidents. Unlike endogenous mortality which are biological in nature, the exogenous mortality is preventable. These groups are, however, somewhat arbitrary because accidents and infectious diseases help in degeneration of body and a worn out body is more liable to accidents and infectious diseases occurring due to external factors. In the developing countries, the leading causes of death are gastro-enteritis, influenza and pneumonia, accidents, heart disease and cancer. In developed countries, last two diseases surpass the prevalence of all other causes because of the aged population.

The mortality analysis, therefore, may be done by calculating separate rates for both endogenous and exogenous deaths by simply replacing the numerator in the rates so far discussed accordingly: *e.g.*

$$\text{Endogenous death rate} = m_{en} = \frac{D^{en}}{P} \times 1{,}000$$

$$\text{Exogenous death rate} = m_{ex} = \frac{D^{ex}}{P} \times 1{,}000$$

Where D^{en} and D^{ex} are the number of endogenous and exogenous deaths in a community in a year.

Death Rates Specific for Social and Economic Characteristics

Study of variations in mortality rates by different social and economic groups helps in understanding the effect of the physical and sociological factors on the health and hence help in planning of the public health and other welfare programmes. Death rates specific for marital status, age and sex are useful in studying of dissolution of marriages, in addition to the mortality analysis. Study of mortality according to occupation helps in measuring the effect of occupation upon mortality. In this case, however, age-specific death rates are to be calculated for the productive period of the worker by omitting retired persons who form a small number of the total. Occupational death rates may be used to identify specific hazardous occupations or to reflect the differential risks of mortality according to different occupations, income and educational level etc., Study of differentials in mortality due to occupation should be made with caution because of selectivity of occupations by persons, Persons in poor health and short statured will never be selected in army or some strenuous occupations. These rates have to be adjusted (as discussed later on).

2.2 SOME SPECIAL RATES OF MORTALITY

Infant Mortality Rate: Infant mortality rate measures the risk of dying during the first year of life. This measure gives a probability of dying for an infant within a year of its birth. Conventionally *Infant Mortality rate is defined* as the ratio of the number of infant deaths in a year to the number of births, multiplied by 1000 *i.e.*,

$$IMR = \frac{D_o}{B} \times 1000$$

Where D_o denotes the number of deaths of infants during a year and B denotes the total number of live births occurred during the year. Analysis of infant mortality has been generally done with the help of IMR than the infant death rate. Infant mortality rate is treated as the most sensitive indicator of general health and medical facilities available in a community. If mortality conditions improve, the IMR is immediately affected. IMR has also been used in many studies as an explanatory variable for studying the variation in the fertility levels.

The conventional measure of IMR does not provide accurately the risk of dying during the first year of life. The infant deaths during any year do not belong only to the babies born in that year. Infact, many of these dealhs are of the infants born in the preceding year. If the number of births does not change singnificantly from one calendar year to another, the conventional measure of IMR is quite reliable measure of mortality in infancy. In case, the births are changing rapidly between the years and within years, the conventional IMR will give distorted picture of both levels and trends of infant mortality. It is thus desirable to adjust the conventional measure of infant mortality to bring it closer to the true probability.

The infant deaths that occur during a year represent deaths among the infants born in that year and the preceding year. The situation is better presented in the Lexis diagram. Let B_1, B_2 and B_3 be the number of births observed during the years 1, 2 and 3 respectively. Let D_i^s and D_i^p be the infant deaths

occurrng in i^{th} year (i=1, 2, 5) among the infants born in the same year and previous year respectively.
Following diagram explains the data:

Year	*Live Births*	*Infant Deaths*	
1	B_1	D^s_1	D^p_1
2	B_2	D^s_2	D^p_2
3	B_3	D^s_3	D^p_3

From the above data, conventional measure of *IMR* for year 2 is:

1. $IMR_2 = \frac{D^s_2 + D^p_2}{B_2} \times 1{,}000$ where IMR_2 denotes *IMR* for the year 2. If there are no migrations*, the probability of dying for the cohort of births B_2 between ages 0 and 1 will be

2. $IMR_2 = \frac{D^s_2 + D^p_3}{B_2} \times 1{,}000$

The above measure of infant mortality involves the effect of two years' mortality conditions (namely years 2 and 3). However, if we assume no migration, we can obtain the probability of survivorship from the exact age 0 to 1 during year 2 as a product of (i) probablity of surviving of B_2 infants during the year 2 and (ii) the probability of surviving during the year 2 of the survivors of B_1 births at the begining of the year 2. If we denote this probability as p_0 then:

$$p_0 = \left(\frac{B_2 - D^s_2}{B_2}\right) * \left(\frac{B_1 - D^s_1 - D^p_2}{B_1 - D^s_1}\right)$$

*In case of migration, a corrected attrition probability can be computed (See Wunch and Termote, 1978).

Thus the probability of dying between birth and the exact age one during year 2 is equal to $1-p_0=IMR_2$ Thus

$$3.\quad IMR_2=\left[1-\left(\frac{B_2-D_2^s}{B_2}\right)\left(\frac{B_1-D_1^s-D_2^p}{B_1-D_1^s}\right)\right]*1000$$

While the above procedure incorporates the effects of mortality conditions prevailing in the calender year 2, it involves two birth cohorts. As an approximation to the procedure (3) following measure is found good and easy to compute:

$$4.\quad IMR_2=\left[\frac{D_2^p}{B_1}+\frac{D_2^s}{B_2}\right]\times 1{,}000$$

This measure is same as measure (2) if $\frac{D_3^p}{B_2}=\frac{D_2^p}{B_1}$

Also the relation (4) is equivalent to (3) if $B_2=B_1$ and $D_1^s=D_2^p$. However, the last condition is usually not met.

In case the infant deaths are not known by their age and birth cohort, the precedures (2) to (4) cannot be used for computing IMR. Some adjustment to either numerator or denominator of IMR can be made in order to derive an approximation to probability of dying within the first year of life for an infant. If f is the proportion of infant deaths within a calender year which occurs among the births of the preceding year then the adjusted IMR for the year 2 is given by

$$5.\quad IMR_2=\left[\frac{D_2(1-f)}{B_1}+\frac{fD_2}{B_1}\right]\times 1{,}000$$

Where $D_2=D^s{}_2+D^p{}_2$,

The above formula is similar to (4) if $D_2\ (1-f)=D_2^s$

and $f\,D_2=D_2^p$.

Thus $f=D_2^p/D_2$. Since the deaths in year 2 have been separated into

(i) deaths among the infants born in the same year $(D^s{}_2)$ and

(ii) deaths among the infants born in the previous year $(D^p{}_2)$ with the help of the separation factor f; formula for calculating the *IMR* is called the *numerator separation formula.* Similarly we can adjust denominator of the conventional *IMR* to make it a probabilistic measure as follows:

$$6.\ IMR_2 = \frac{D_2}{(1-f)\,B_2 + f\,B_1} \times 1000$$

The estimation of '*f*' should be based on the experience of a population having similar level of infant mortality. When infant mortality is high, *f* may be taken as 1/3. The value of *IMR* is, however less sensitive to the value of separation factor unless change in infant mortality is drastic in one year, and births also fluctuate. Given a rough level of infant mortality, the separation factor '*f*' is estimated[2] to be as below:

IMR Level:	200	150	100	50	25	15
Separation factor *f* :	.40	.33	.25	.20	.15	.05

The study of separation factors indicates the fact that due to the congenital malformation and diseases of the new born, most deaths occur during the first few days after the birth and deaths are as such not distributed uniformly over the first year of life. The refinements of infant mortality so far suggested are based on division of either annual births or deaths.

An illustration of the computation of *IMR* using all possible precedures is given below in the Table 2.2:

TABLE 2.2

Data for the Calculation of Infant Mortality Rate for USA: 1975

Year	*Live births*	*Infant deaths to the*	
		Same year birth cohort D^s_i	*Previous year Birth cohort* D^s_i
1974 (1)	3,159,958 (B_1)	47,566 (D^s_1)	5,210 (D^p_1)
1975 (2)	3,144,198 (B_2)	45,321 (D^s_2)	5,204 (D^p_2)
1976 (3)	3.167,788 (B_3)	43,183 (D^s_3)	5,082 (D^p_3)

Source. U.S., NCHS, *Vital Statistics of the United States, 1974, 1975, 1976*, Vol. II. Mortality Part A, Tables 2—10.

Computations

$$\text{Conventional } IMR \text{ (1975)} = \frac{D^s{}_2 + D^p{}_2}{B_2} \times 1000$$

$$= \frac{50,525}{3,144,198} \times 1000 = 16.1$$

Adjusted Measures of IMR

(i) $$IMR \text{ (1975)} = \frac{D^s{}_2 + D^p{}_3}{B_2} \times 1000$$

$$= \frac{50,403}{3,144,198} \times 1000 = 16.0$$

(ii) $$IMR \text{ (1975)} = \left(1 - \frac{B_2 - D^s{}_2}{B_2} \times \frac{B_1 - D^s{}_1 - D^p{}_2}{B_1 - D^s{}_1}\right) \times 1000$$

$$= 1 - \frac{3,144,198 - 45,321}{3.144,198} \times$$

$$= \frac{3,159,958 - 47,566 - 5204}{3,159,958 - 47,566} \times 1000$$

$$= 16.1$$

(iii) $$IMR \text{ (1975)} = \left[\frac{D^p{}_2}{B_1} + \frac{D^s{}_2}{B_2}\right] \times 1000$$

$$= \left[\frac{5,204}{3,159,958} + \frac{45,321}{3,144,198}\right] \times 1000$$

$$= 16.0$$

(iv) $$IMR \text{ (1975)} = \left[\frac{fD_2}{B_1} + \frac{(1-f)D_2}{B_2}\right] \times 1000$$

$$= \left[\frac{.103 \times 50,525}{3,159,958} + \frac{.897 \times 50,525}{3,144,198}\right] \times 1000$$

$$= 16.0$$

where $f = D^x{}_2 / D_2 = \frac{5,204}{50,525} = = .1030$ and $1 - f = .8970$

(v) $$IMR \text{ (1975)} = \frac{D_2}{fB_1 + (1-f)B_2} \times 1000$$

$$=\frac{50,525}{325,476+2,820,346}\times 1000$$

$$=16.1$$

Since a high proportion of infant deaths occur during the first few days of life, and causes of death for infant deaths at earlier and later ages of infancy differ, the conventional infant mortality rate may be split into a rate covering the first month and the rate covering the remaining eleven months of the year. These rates are called neonatal mortality rate and post neonatal mortality rate respectively. They are computed as below.

(a) *Neonatal Mortality Rate*$=\frac{D<1 \text{ month}}{B}\times 1000$

Thus neonatal mortality is the number of deaths of infants under 4 weeks of age (exactly 28 days or approximately one month sometimes) during a year per 1,000 births during that year.

(b) Post-neonatal Mortality Rate $=\frac{D \gtrdot 1 \text{ month}}{B}\times 1000$

where $D \gtrdot 1$ denotes the infant deaths at the age of more than 1 month.

Pregnancy wastage due to foetal death can be measured by foetal death ratio and foetal death rate. The foetal death ratio is defined as the number of foetal deaths reported during a year per 1000 live births in the same year, *i.e.*, foetal death ratio$=\frac{F}{B}\times 1000.$

Where F is the number of foetal deaths in a year and B is the number of live-births during the same year. All the foetal losses occurring after 28 weeks of pregnancy are taken to be late foetal deaths or still births for this purpose. To ensure better comparability, foetal losses include abortion, miscarages and still births. The foetal deaths, some times, include only late foetal deaths.

Formula for computing the foetal death rate is:

$$\text{Foetal Death Rate} = \frac{F}{F+B} \times 1000.$$

Thus the foetal death rate is proportion of pregnancies which fail to result in live birth. The denominator $F+B$ is the estimate of actual number of pregnancies. This rate can be treated as indicator of the prenatal care facilities and their utilisation of health care facilities in the community. Since the foetal deaths and neonatal deaths occur almost mainly due to the biological reasons, the two deaths can be combined to make up perinatal mortality. Following are the two forms of perinatal mortality rate:

(a) $$\text{Perinatal Mortality Rate} = \frac{\text{Infant deaths under one week} + \text{late Foetal deaths}}{B} \times 1000$$

(b) $$\text{Perinatal Mortality Rate} = \frac{\text{Neonatal deaths} + \text{Foetal Deaths}}{B} \times 1000$$

2.2.1 Endogenous and Exogenous Infant Mortality

All the infant deaths can broadly be classified as endogenous infant deaths and exogenous infant deaths. Endogenous deaths arise from the congenital malformations and the circumstances related to confinement. Exogenous infant deaths are caused due to environmental conditions, such as diseases or accidents. Causes of death are, however not generally available. Bourgeois (1951, 1952), devised a biometric method to estimate the number of infant deaths due to endogenous causes in the absence of information on the causes of infant deaths. It is assumed that the deaths occurring in the last 11 months of the year of life are exogenous deaths. If $d_1, d_2, \ldots d_{11}$ denote the proportion of deaths occurring during the 2nd to 12th month to the total deaths occuring from 2nd to 12th month of the life, it is observed that these proportions are almost independent of the level of mortality. Since they relate to the exogenous deaths, it is assumed that the proportion d_o of exogenous deaths during the 1st month of life is also independent of the level of mortality. By trial and error, he has shown that d_n can be approximated as

$$d_o = \frac{\log^3_{10}[30.5(n+1)+1] - \log^3_{10}[30.5\,n+1]}{\log^3_{10}(366) - \log^3_{10}(31.5)}$$

Thus $d_0 = .25$. It means that the proportion of exogenous deaths during the 1st month of life is about one fourth of all the deaths in the last eleven months of the 1st year of the life. The endogenous deaths $D_o^{en} = D_o - (1+.25)\ D = D_o - 1.25D$. where D is the number of deaths from 2nd to 12th month of life and D_o is the number of infant deaths. Thus endogenous

$$\text{infant mortality rate} = \frac{D_o^{en}}{B} \times 1{,}000$$

$$\text{Exogenous infant mortality rate} = \frac{1.25\ D}{B} \times 1{,}000.$$

Maternal Mortality. The maternal morality ratio is defined as ratio of the number of mothers dying in a year due to puerperal causes to the total number of births within the same year multiplied by 10,000. When such deaths and the births are classified by age of the mother, even the age specific maternal mortality rates can be computed in the usual way.

2.3. ADJUSTED MEASURES OF MORTALITY

Age specific mortality rates are quite useful measures to study the variation in mortality by age of the persons. The differential mortality between males and females can be studied by the ratio of the male mortality rates to the female rates at the particular ages. To observe changes in the population over years it is expedient to compare age specific death rates according to sex, marital status, socio-economic class or occupation of persons or any other category. But for easy comparability one needs a single index of mortality which reflects an average of these death rates of the various segments of the population. Simplest index for this purpose is the crude death rate discussed earlier. But the *CDR* is not suitable for comparing the mortality of two populations which may differ in their age and sex structures. We must therefore, use such an index of mortality which uses some acceptable standard weights in averaging the death rates. The rate so found can be called adjusted or corrected or standardised rate. Often death rates are adjusted or standardised for both age and sex. There are four main methods to adjust the death rates namely, age standardised death rate calculated by direct method, age standardised death rate calculated by indirect method, the comparative mortality index and the life table death rate.

2.3.1 Direct Standardisation

For spatial or temporal purposes, the age specific death rates can be summarised by their arithmetic mean $\sum_{o}^{w} ASDR_x/n$ where n is the number of total rates involved, or their geometric mean $\left(\prod_x m_x\right)^{1/n}$ or simply by their sum. There are also direct standardised rates where the standard population comprises one person at each age. One may, however, choose an arbitrary population structure to enable the standardised rates to be comparable to the crude death rate in magnitude. Theoretically, it is irrelevant which population structure is chosen. Usually one takes a standard population structure similar to the study populations. It may be one of the populations under study or may be outside them. If mortality of the two areas is being compared, it is better to use the average of the age distributions of the populations under study as a standard. In a time series analysis, even the age distribution of the first year may be taken as the standard for calculating the standardised rates for the subsequent years for any area. Thus the choice of the standard population might differ and hence the different standards would yield different comparasions

(Kitagawa, 1964). The direct standardisation of crude death rate involves selection of a 'standard population' and computing of the weighted average of the age-specific death rates in a given area, using the age distribution of the standard population as weights. The formula for the direct standardised death rate (*SDR*(*D*)) for any population *A* is

$$SDR\,(D)^{A} = 1000 \sum m^{A}_{x}\left(\frac{P^{s}_{x}}{P^{s}}\right)$$

where m^{A}_{x} is the age specific mortality rate at age x for the populations A, P^{S}_{x} is the population aged x in the standard population, P^{s} is the total standard population. In fact $SDR(D)^{A}$ gives the expected death rate of the standard population if it experiences the age schedule of the morality as experienced by the Population *A*. For standardising a death rate for both age and sex, each age-sex specific death rate in the population under study (*A*) is multiplied by the proportion of the total population in that age-sex group.

The need of age adjusted death rate is more felt in studying the level of morality by causes in different countries because the observed level of death rate due to a particular disease, say, cancer is very much affected by the population at older ages. The standardised death rate for a specific cause is the weighted average of the age-cause specific death rates, weights being the age distribution of the standard population. In studies of occupational mortality an age adjusted death rate by direct method is weighted average of the age specific mortality rates by occupation in the productive period of life (say 20-60 years), the weights being the population by ages within the broad range of the standard population.

The adjusted death rate is easy to compute. If the mortality rates of a population *A* are uniformly double of the mortality rates of the population *B* this will be reflected in the difference of the adjusted rates or their ratios. The ratio of the age adjusted death rates by direct method is

$$\frac{\sum_x {}_nM_x^A \, {}_nP_x^S}{\sum_x {}_nM_x^B \, {}_nP_x^S}$$

This ratio is equal to 2 if ${}_nM_x^A = 2 . {}_nM_x^B$ for all ages x

The difference in the age adjusted rates by direct method is

$$\left\{ \sum_x \left({}_nM_x^A - {}_nM_x^B \right) {}_nP_x^S \right\} / \sum_x {}_nP_x^S$$

The above indicates that if ${}_nM_x^A \geqslant {}_nM_x^B$ for all x

the difference is greater or equal to zero.

The procedure of direct standardisation is illustrated in the Table 2.3.

2.3.2 *Indirect Standardisation*: A single summary index of mortality can also be obtained by indirect method, when age-specific mortality rates for the populations are not available. In case of indirect standardisation, the crude death rate of the standard population is multiplied by the ratio of actual deaths to the number of deaths expected on the basis of the age specific death rates of the standard population and the population distribution by age in the population under study. Symbolically

$$SDR(I)^A = \frac{D^A}{\sum_x {}_nM^s_x \, . \, {}_nP_x^A} * CDR^s$$

Where ${}_nM^s_x$ and CDR^s refer to the standard population. The above rate is, however, very much dependent on the age distribution of the population *A*. Unlike direct standardised rates, the indirectly standardised rates computed for a number of populations are not comparable as these populations vary in their age structures. The indirectly standardised death rate may, however, be expressed in terms of directly standardised rates :

TABLE 2.3

'Direct' Standardisation of Death Rates for the States of Kerala and Uttar Pradesh, India

Age Group	*Standard Population All India, 1971 (in 000)*	*Kerala*		*Uttar Pradesh*	
		Age specific death rate, (000) 1971	*Expected deaths =(2) × (3)*	*ASDR 1971 (in 000)*	*Expected deaths =(5) × (2)*
1	*2*	*3*	*4*	*5*	*6*
0—4	88,632	24.5	2,171,484	83.7	7,418,498
5—9	77,265	2.3	177,710	5 4	417,231
10—14	65,046	1.1	71,551	2.3	149,606
15—19	53,817	1·4	65,344	2.4	129,161
20—24	46,120	2.2	101,464	3.9	179,868
25—29	40,659	1.6	65,054	3.7	150,438
30—34	35,922	3.5	125,727	4.1	147,280
35—39	31,387	3.7	116,132	4.8	150,658
40—44	26,684	5.3	141,425	6.0	160,104
45—49	22,233	7.3	162,301	9.8	217,883

50—54	17,891	8.8	157,441	17.9	20,249
55—59	14,258	16.3	232,405	18.7	266,625
60—64	10,925	23.6	257,830	36.7	400,248
65—69	7,444	43.5	323,814	48.1	358,056
70+	9,877	103.8	1,025,233	94.1	929,426
Total	548,160		5,204,915		11,396,031
Standardized death rate			9.50		20.79
Crude death rate (for comparision)			9.00		20.10

Source: *Census of India, 1971*, Series I Paper 3 of 1977, Age Table and *R.G. of India*, *Reports on SRS* (1970-75).

We have

$$SDR(I) = \frac{D}{\sum_{x} {}_nM_x^s . {}_nP_x} \times DDR^s$$

$$= \frac{\sum_{x} {}_nM_x . {}_nP_x}{\sum_{x} {}_nM_x^s \, {}_nP_x} \times CDR^s$$

$$SDR(D) = \sum_{x} {}_nM_x \left[\frac{{}_nP_x^s}{P^s}\right] \times \frac{CDR^s}{CDR^s}$$

$$= \frac{\sum_{x} {}_nM_x . {}_nP_x^s}{\sum_{x} {}_nM_x^s . {}_nP_a^s} \times CDR^s$$

Formulae for $SDR(I)$ and $SDR(D)$ indicate that CDR^s is adjusted in both the cases. In case of the direct method, the adjustment factor is ratio of expected deaths to the observed deaths in the standard population if the age specific mortality rates of population under study is applied to the standard population. However, in case of indirect method, it is the ratio of observed deaths to the number of deaths expected in the population on the basis of age specific mortality rates of the standard population. Thus in case of indirect standardisation, the age distributions of the given populations vary and hence make the adjusted rates not comparable. This limitation does not apply to the direct method as the same age distribution (standard) is used as weight. Thus if required data are available, direct standardised death rate is preferable. The method of calculating indirect standardised death rate is illustrated in Table 2.4.

TABLE 2.4

Indirect Standardisation of Death Rate for Age

Age Group (1)	*Age Specific death rate of standard population All India 1971* (2)	*Kerala (1971)*		*Uttar Pradesh (1971)*	
		Population ('000) (3)	*Expected Deaths* (4) =(2)×(3)	*Population ('000)* (5)	*Expected Deaths* =(2)×(5)
0—4	51.9	3,151	163,537	14,315	742,948
5—9	4.7	2,836	13,329	12,389	58,228
10—14	2.0	2,648	5,296	10,349	20,698
15—19	2.4	2,345	5,628	8,317	19,961
20—24	3.6	1,930	6,948	7,167	25,801
25—29	3.7	1,608	5,950	6,311	23,351
30—34	4.6	1,352	6,219	5,615	25,829
35—39	5.7	1,148	6,544	5,005	28,528
40—44	6.7	997	6,680	4,333	29,031
45—49	9.5	866	8,227	3,706	35,207
50—54	16.8	697	11,710	3,038	51,038
55—59	21.2	558	11,830	2,483	52,640
60—64	34.0	438	14.892	1,981	67,354
65—70	48.4	318	15.391	1,408	68,147
70+	100.3	454	45,536	1,924	192,977
Total	15.0 (CDR)	21,346	327,717	88,341	1,441,738
Total deaths actually registered	:	192,126			1,775,657
Ratio $=\left[\frac{\text{Observed}}{\text{Expected}}\right]$	:	.586			1.232
Indirect Standarised death rates	:	8.79			18.48

Comparative Mortaiity Index (CMI): The comparative mortality index is a relative measure of mortality to indicate changes in the level of overall mortality or a population. It incorporates the effects of both age and sex composition of the current population as well as that of the standard of first year population. *CMI* is defined as the ratio of the weighted sum of the age specific death rates in each year to the similarly weighted sum of the age specific rates of the initial year. The weights are the average of (*a*) the proportion of the total population in the age group on the initial year and (*b*) the corresponding proportion in the given year. Symbolically,

$$CMI^t = \frac{\sum_a W_a M_a^t}{\sum_a W_a M_a^o}$$

Where

$$W_a = \frac{1}{2}\left[\frac{P_a^t}{P^t} + \frac{P_a^o}{P^o}\right]$$

m_r^t, P_a^t and P^t denote the age specific mortality rate at age of the population, population aged *a* and total population respectively in the year *t*.

The basic purpose of *CMI* is to compare the relative mortality of a place at two points of time. However, the ratios, or *CMI's* may be treated as satisfactory measures of relative mortality only over short periods. It is interesting to note that *CMI* was introduced in 1941 first in England and Wales and was also abandoned later on because it is very difficult to explain the *CMI* in general.

Life Table Death Rate: Life table death rate, is another adjusted rate, which is reciprocal of the expectation of life at birth. This requires, however, the construction of a life table (to be discussed subsequently) from the observed age specific death rates for each population under study. It is rarely used for comparing the mortality levels because of the labourious procedure involved in the construction of life table. Since the life table population is a stationary population where number of births equal the number of deaths in a year, the life table death rate is higher than the observed crude death rate because of the low birth rate of the stationary population. Since each set of observed age specific death rates generates a unique stationary population, the life table death rates would remain crude for the comparison because the two stationary populations would be different and hence, they are also not strictly comparable from area to area.

From the comparison of the methods discussed above to adjust the crude death rate it will be clear that there is no perfect method to remove the effects of age composition on it. In case of the direct standardisation, the choice of the standard population is quite crucial and the standard chosen may not be reasonable for various reasons for some areas and over a long period. Comparability of the indirect standardised death rates and comparative mortality index is affected because of changing weights. Though life table death rate avoids the arbitrary choice of a standard population it requires construction of a life table. It is however, possible to choose some standard weights based on the share of age specific deaths among all the total deaths for some ideal population and use the same to obtain the weighted average of the age specific death rates for different populations to compare their mortality.

2.4 LIFE TABLE

The measures of mortality discussed earlier describe the mortality conditions of particular group of a population or of total population in a summary form. Life table, however, combines mortality experience of a population at different ages in a single statistical model. It describes the life history of a hypothetical group, or cohort of people, as it is depleted gradually by death. The concept of the life table was developed to describe essentially the mortality conditions but later on it has found applications in several other areas, *e.g.*, fertility, nuptiality, migration, population projections. family planning evaluation, working life tables, schooling and so on. Life table in the context of mortality is a population model and hence can be used to answer many questions such as what proportion of the born children will live to celebrate their 20th birth day and how many of them will be able to cross 50 years of age and so on, if the cohort experiences the age specific death rates of the life table population. Life table shows both number of persons of a birth cohort dying between certain ages as well as the number of persons surviving.

The concept of life table goes back to 1663 when John Graunt published the rudimentary life table based on the Bills of mortality as such incorporating the mortality experiences alone. Halley (1693) was the first to develop a life table which contained most of the columns of the usual life tables and which was based on both birth and death statistics. However, the assumption in the preparation of his life table that the population of Breslan had remained stationary was wrong and his life table could not be regarded correct. The first scientifically correct life table was prepared by Milne in 1815 by using population and death data. A large number of life tables have been published since then. Credit for the systematic presentation of life tables for England and Wales however, goes to William Farr. Development of different techniques of constructing life tables in recent years is mostly due to the actuaries, who treat the life table as important tool in the analysis of mortality. Almost all the nations have now national and regional life tables. Quite reliable life tables are being prepared by the official statistical agencies in different countries by using data from censuses, vital statistics and sample surveys. In India, construction of life tables is based on the consecutive census age distributions. Some relevant methods of constructing life tables are discussed in the next chapter.

2.4.1 Typea of Life Table

There are different types of life table used in mortality

analysis depending on the nature of cohort studied, age details and the number of decrement factors considered in their construction. There are two main types of life tables in common use. They are the period (population) life table, and the cohort (or generation) life table. Period life table was historically first developed to analyse mortality conditions of the population. This life table is based on the mortality experience of population over a short period of time, such as, a year, three years, or one intercensal period. It incorporates the experience of mortality by different ages of the population during a given period of time. It assumes a hypothetical cohort of births subjected to the age specific death rates observed during a given period of time. Since it gives a vivid picture of the current mortality of the population, it is rightly called current life table. Cohort life table on the other hand, describes the actual survival experience of a group or cohort of individuals who were born at about the same time. This is also called a generation or longitudinal life table because the life history of a real cohort is followed till the last person dies. It requires the data over a long period of time to complete a life table of one cohort. It is, therefore, not possible to construct life tables for all the cohorts of population actually existing since they will be dying only in future. The generation life tables are, however, very useful to project mortality. Because of the data problems, they are the least used of all the life tables. Unless otherwise specified, life table will mean henceforth the current (period) life table.

According to the length of the age interval in which life table functions are presented, tables are classified as complete and abridged life tables. If the life table values are presented for every single year of the age from birth to the latest possible age, the life table is called a complete life table. In case of an abridged life table, the functions are presented by intervals of 5 or 10 years of age. Generally abridged life table is prepared because it is less cumbersome to prepare and often more convenient to use.

Life table in its more general usage, may be called a decrement table or attrition table where a cohort of birth is shown to decrease in number due to death as a factor of decrement as it ages over time. If the factor of decrement is death, the decrement table is most appropriately called a life table. We can prepare the decrement table (or survival table) for the patients admitted to a hospital where 'birth' may mean entry into the hospital and 'death' is discharge from the hospital. Discharge is only the factor for causing decrement to the group of entrants on a particular day or period. A number of other situations may be shown to conform to the above situation. A table describing the combined effects of several factors causing diminition in the size of the cohort is called multiple decrement table. It may describe mortality pattern by age due to several causes of death or mortality pattern along with changes in one or more socio-economic characteristics of the population (*e.g.*, nuptiality tables). Some times, we may have an increment—decrement table which describes the effect of accession to as well as withdrawal from a segment of the original cohort due to acquiring a given characteristics. A table of working life which combines mortality rates and labour force participation rates, and a table of school life, combining the mortality and enrolment rates are increment—decrement tables.

2.4.2 Assumptions in Life Table

A life table model traces the history of a cohort of babies newly born throughout their entire life according to a predetermined schedule of the age specific mortality rates and thus represents a situation which is artificial. No real cohort of babies will experience the rates of mortality as observed in the present population, in its entire life. This anomaly is reconciled by means of the following simplifying assumptions of the life table model:

1. The cohort under study is closed to migration. Its size can change only due to death of its members.
2. Each member of the cohort is exposed to the risk of death at each age according to the schedule which is fixed in advance and is unchanged. There is no varia-

tion in the risk of death over time and thus life table is a purely deterministic model.

3. The size of the cohort is always a fixed number of births of same sex, say, 1000, 10,000 or 100,000 which is called the radix of the life table in order to facilitate comparisions between different life tables.
4. The number of deaths during the year is assumed to be evenly spread over the age interval (except the first few years) especially when it is one year.

Life tables are generally constructed separately for males and females. It is possible to construct a life table for both sexes together but mortality experiences of males and females in the same population are found to be different. Assumptions (1), (2) and (3) together imply that all those born should die and no one should enter in the population at any age in between. Every year the entry into the population is at age 0 in the form of births equal to the radix and total number of deaths should also equal to the number of births. This makes the life table population a stationary population.

2.4.3 Life Table Functions and Columns

The basic life table functions describing the history of a cohort of persons are presented in a tabular form. Except the first column of a life table denoting age, each of the other six columns of a life table specify a life table function. The six basic life table functions calculated for each life table are $_nq_x$ l_x, $_nd_x$., $_nL_x$, T_x and e_x^o. Of these, three functions namely l_x, T_x and e_x^o are defined for exact age x and the rest for the age interval x to $x+n$ years. In general, the mortality rate ($_nq_x$) is the basic input of the life table or the initial function from which all other functions can be derived. For a cohort life table, information is available only on survivors (l_x) and hence it forms the basic input. The interpretation of different life table functions are as follows ;

Column 1; x to $x+n$: the period of life between two exact ages x and $x+n$. In case of abridged life table n is taken as 5 or 10, years. Age 'x' means exact age x in this column. In case of complete life table the column is designated by only age x where $x = 0, 1, \ldots w$

Column 2: ${}_nq_x$: The probability of dying before reaching age $x+n$ for a person who is of exact age x. In case of a complete life table, we use q_x instead of ${}_1q_x$. Then q_x implies the probability that a person who has reached age x would die during the interval $(x, x+1)$. Some times one can calculate another life table function p_x as complement of q_x. Thus

$$p_x = 1 - q_x$$

$${}_np_x = 1 - {}_nq_x$$

${}_np_x$ gives the probability of surviving of a person aged x during the interval x to $x+n$.

Column 3: l_x: The number of persons living at exact age 'x' (at the beginning of the interval (x to $x+n$) out of the total number of births given by the radix of the life table. This column starts with l_o, the size of the birth cohort, *i.e.*. the radix. l_x is a decreasing function of age. We can obtain this value from the value of ${}_nq_x$ as follows:

$$l_{x+n} = l_{xo}\ {}_np_x \qquad \text{(by definition)}$$

Thus $${}_np_x = \frac{l_{x+n}}{l_x}$$

Column 4: ${}_nd_x$: number of deaths out of l_x persons during the period of next n years. Thus

$${}_nd_x = l_x\,({}_nq_x).$$

Hence $l_{x+n} = l_x - {}_nd_x = l_x\,(l - {}_nq_x) = l_x\ {}_np_x$

In case of a complete life table $n = 1$ and hence

$$d_x = l_x\,(q_x)$$

and $$l_{x+1} = l_x \,.\, p_x$$

Column 5: ${}_nL_x$: The number of person years lived by the l_x persons during the interval $(x, x+n)$: In case the interval is of one year, this function is only denoted by L_x. This column gives the population of the life table by age. Thus ${}_nL_x$ gives the number of persons in the age interval $(x, x+n)$ in the life table population. Since the deaths at any age interval x (except first few years of life) are evenly distributed, the function l_x is linearly distributed over these ages and hence

$$L_x = \tfrac{1}{2}(l_x+l_{x+1})$$

$$\text{and } {}_nL_x = \frac{n}{2}\left[l_x+l_{x+n} \right] \quad \text{for } x>2$$

Since linear relationship is not valid for ages 0 and 1, the approximate values of L_o and L_1 are given as:

$$L_o = 0.3\, l_o + 0.7\, l_1$$

$$L_1 = 0.4\, l_1 + 0.6\, l_2$$

The above relations are obtained on the assumption that, on average, a person dying in the first year of the life lives for 0.3 year and one dying between the ages 1 and 2 lives, on average, for 0.4 years.

Column 6: T_x: Total life time after age x. This is total number of person years lived by the svrvivors l_x in the future. This is given by the cumulative sum of ${}_nL_x$ values after age x *i.e.*,

$$T_x = {}_nL_x + {}_nL_{x+n} + \ldots + L_y$$

Where L_y is the person years lived by the survivors at age y *i.e.*, l_y persons after the age y (for example $y=80$). It is obtained as

$$T_y = L_y = \frac{l_y}{m_y}$$

From the definition, it also implies that

$$T_x = L_x + T_{x+1}$$

Column 7: e°_x: The expectation of life at exact agc x, This is the average number of years to which the survivors l_x are expected to live. This is given by

$$e^{\circ}_x = T_x/l_x.$$

If $x = 0$, then

$$e^{\circ}_0 = T_o/l_o$$

e°_0 is of special importance and is commonly known as expectation of life at birth. This is a widely used measure of the level of mortality in a country. The interpretation of the functions in a complete life table is the same as in the abridged life table. The q_x, d_x and L_x are the values which relate to single age interval. We do not writc them as ${}_1q_x$, ${}_1d_x$ and ${}_1L_x$ in general.

The following Table 2.5 gives the portion of the complete life table of all India females (1961-70). Construction of Abridged life tables is studied in detail in a subsequent section of this chapter.

2.5 Some Relationships and Other Life Table Rates

It may be seen from the explanation of the different columns given in the preceding section that all the columns can be related to ${}_nq_x$ column. For example:

$$l_{x+n} = l_x\,(l - {}_nq_x) = l_x\;{}_np_x$$

where $\quad {}_np_x = P_x . P_{x+1} . P_{x+2} . P_{x+3} . P_{x+4} \ldots$

Since ${}_nL_x$ and other functions are related to l_x they can be related to ${}_nq_x$ without any problem. Some important relations are mentioned here:

TABLE 2.5

Complete Life Table for Females, India: 1961-70

Age	Probability of dying between ages x and x+1	Survivors at exact age x	Number of deaths between ages x and x+1	No. of Persons living between ages x and x+1	No. of Persons living beyond exact age x	Expectation of life at exact age x
1	2	3	4	5	6	7
x	q_x	l_x	d_x	L_x	T_x	e°_x
0	.12837	100000	12837	91014	4465447	44.7
1	.03406	87163	2969	85382	4374437	50.2
2	.01601	84194	1348	83520	4289051	50.9
3	.01446	82846	1198	82367	4205531	50.8
4	.01313	81648	1072	81326	4123164	50.5
5	.01205	80576	971	80091	4041838	50.2
6	.01122	79605	892	79159	3961747	49.8
7	.01057	78712	832	78296	3882588	49.3
8	.00935	77850	728	77516	3804292	48.8
9	.00852	77152	658	76823	3726776	48.3

Source: Office of Registrar General of India, *Life Tables*, Census of India 1971, Series I, Paper I, of 1977, p. 16.

We know that

$$T_x = \sum_{i=x}^{w-1} L_i$$

$$= \sum_{i=x}^{w-1} 0.5\,(l_i + l_{i+1})$$

In case of abridged life Table $T_x = \sum_{x} {}_nL_x$

$$T_x = \sum_{i=x}^{w-n} \frac{n}{2}\left[\; l_i + l_{i+n} \;\right] \qquad i = x,\ x+n,\ \ldots\ w-n$$

$$e^o_x = \frac{T_x}{l_x} = 0.5 + \frac{1}{l_x}(l_{x+1} + l_{x+2} + \ldots l_w)$$

for $x \geqslant 2$

if $x=0$, we can use separation factors for deaths between birth and age 1.

$$e^o_o = f + \frac{1}{l_o}\left[l_1(i - f + 0.5) + \sum_{2}^{w} l_x \right]$$

Where $f=2/3$ or $3/4$ (approximately). In case of an abridged life table,

$$e^o_x = \frac{n}{2} + \frac{n(l_{x+n} + l_{x+2n} + \ldots)}{l_x}$$

We can also prove that

$$e^o_x = \frac{{}_5L_x}{l_x} + \frac{l_{x+5}}{l_x} \cdot e^o_{x+5}$$

It can be shown that the mean length of life is also equal to the average age at death for the hypothetical cohort of births in the life table which is only subjected to mortality. Disregarding the problem of first age group.

We can write

$$\overset{o}{e}_o = \frac{1}{l_o}\left[\sum_{o}^{w}(x+0.5)\ (l_x - l_{x+1})\right]$$

$$= \frac{1}{l_o}\sum_{x}(x+0.5)d_x$$

However, in the actual population, average age at death is not equal to the mean length of life due to the effect of migration, differential mortality experiences and varying birth cohorts. For the stationary population, birth cohorts are of same size and there is no migration and hence the two measures are identical.

'Curtate' Expectation of Life (e_x)

The curtate expectation of Life e_x is defined as

$$e_x = \frac{l_{x+1} + \ldots + l_w}{l_x} = \sum_{i=x+1}^{w}\frac{l_i}{l_x}$$

Since,

$$\overset{o}{e}_x = \frac{L_x + L_{x+1} + \ldots L_{w-1}}{l_x}$$

$$= \frac{0.5(l_x + l_{x+1}) + .5(l_{x+1} + l_{x+2}) + \ldots + 0.5(l_{w-1} + l_w)}{l_x}$$

$$= 0.5 + \sum_{i=x+1}^{w}\frac{l_i}{l_x} = .5 + e_x$$

The concept of curtate expectation of life is not in use at present. It is also related to p_x as

$$p_x = \frac{e_x}{1 + e_{x+1}}$$

The Life Table Survival Rate

The life table survival rate of person aged x to $x+n$ for y years is given by

$$y \text{ years survival rate} = \frac{{}_nL_{x+y}}{{}_nL_x}$$

The survival rate gives the probability of a person aged x to $x+n$ to survive upto age group $x+y$ to $x+y+n$. Generally, 5 year survival rates are used in projecting the population in future. It is given by

$${}_5S_x = \frac{{}_5L_{x+5}}{{}_5L_x}$$

The probability of survival from birth to the age group x to $x+5$ is

$$S\left(B: x, x+5\right) = \frac{{}_5L_x}{5l_o}$$

Life Table Death Rate

In a complete life table, the death rate at age x can be defined as:

$$m_x = \frac{d_x}{L_x}$$

Where,

d_x is the number of deaths of persons aged x to $x+1$ in a year and L_x person years lived by the population betweem age x to $x+1$. m_x is called the central life table death rate. In a population we define the age specific mortality rate M_x as below.

$$M_x = \frac{D_x}{P_x}$$

Where,

D_x is the number of deaths at age x during a year, P_x is the mid-year population. Functions m_x and M_x have great resemblance. We also have a similar function q_x in the life table which is a probability measure of death rate at age x as the denominator of this function is the exact population exposed to death. However q_x and m_x can be shown to be related if d_x is assumed to be evenly distributed over the interval x to $x+1$.

Thus

$$m_x = \frac{d_x}{L_x} = \frac{d_x}{l_x - \frac{1}{2}\, d_x}$$

$$= \frac{(d_x/l_x)}{1-\frac{1}{2}(d_x/l_x)} = \frac{q_x}{1-\frac{1}{2}\, q_x}$$

or

$$m_x = \frac{2q_x}{2-q_x}$$

or

$$q_x = \frac{2m_x}{2+m_x}$$

In the case of an abridged life table, if deaths are assumed to be uniformly distributed over any interval, we have

$${}_nq_x = \frac{2n.\, {}_nm_x}{2+n.\,({}_nm_x)}$$

In general however,

$${}_nq_x = \frac{n.\, {}_nm_x}{1+(n-{}_na_x)\,({}_nm_x)}$$

Where

${}_na_x$ is the average length of year lived in the age group x to $x+n$ by a person dying in the age group per year,

Life Table Birth and Death Rates

We have seen that the life table population is a stationary population and the population by age group x is given by L_x in the complete life table and by ${}_nL_x$ in an abridged life table. The total population is given by

$T_o = \sum_{o}^{w} L_x$ and the total number of births every year is equal

to l_o and deaths $= \sum_{d}^{w} d_x$

$$\sum_{o}^{w} d_x = (l_0 - l_1) + (l_1 - l_2) + \ldots (l_{w-1} - l_w)$$

$$+ l_w = l_0$$

as $d_w = l_w$ (where w is the last age to which a person can survive).

Thus, both the number of births and number of deaths are equal to l_0, hence birth and death rates are same, *i.e.*, $\frac{l_0}{T}$ (per person) which is reciprocal of e^o_o the expectation of life at birth.

2.6 Continuous Life Table Functions

In case, age x is used as continuous variable, let us use the functional relations $l(x)$ for l_x and radix $l(o)$ in place of l_o. Thus the number of persons alive between ages x and $x+dx$ in the life table population is given by $l(x)\,dx$ and person years lived between ages x to $x+n$ is ${}_nL_x = \int_x^{x+n} l(x+t)dt$ and the number of persons in the population more than age x is

$$T_x = \int_o^{w-x} l(x+t)dt$$

Force of Mortality and its Applications

The instantaneous death rate is called the force of mortality in the continuous life table. If we denote it by $\mu(x)$, this is the limiting value of the age specific death rate when the interval becomes infinitesimally small,

Thus,

$$\mu_x = \lim_{\Delta x \to o} \frac{l(x) - l(x+\Delta x)}{l(x)\,\Delta(x)} = -\frac{1}{lx}\,\frac{dl(x)}{dx}$$

Thus,

$\frac{dl\,(x)}{dx} = -\mu(x)\,l(x)$ where $\mu(x)\ l(x)\ dx$ is called the curve of death,

Also we can write $\mu(x) = -\frac{d}{dx}\left[\ l_n\,1(x)\ \right]$

Where *ln* stands for the natural logarithm.

Hence by integrating over x and noting that $l(x)=l(o)$ for $x=o$,

we have

$$l(x) = l_o\ exp\left(-\int_o^x \mu(t)\,dt\right)$$

The probability that a person aged x will live for n years is given by

$$\frac{l(x+n)}{1(x)} = exp\left(-\int_x^n \mu(t)\,dt\right)$$

$L_x = \int_o^1 l(x+t)\,dt$. If L_x can be treated as mid year population and equal to $l_x + \frac{1}{2}$. We can easily see that

$$m_x = \frac{d_x}{L_x} = -\frac{1}{L_x}\,\frac{dL_x}{d_x} = -\frac{1}{l_x+\frac{1}{2}}\,\frac{d(l_x+\frac{1}{2})}{d_x}$$

$$= \mu(x+\tfrac{1}{2})$$

The number of persons dying between ages x and $x+dx$ is given by $l_{(x)}\ \mu_{(x)}\ dx$

Thus number of annual deaths at age x is

$$d_x=\int_0^1 l(x+t)\ \mu(x+t)dt$$

$$q_x=\frac{d_x}{l_x}=\frac{1}{l_x}\int_0^1 l(x+t)\ \mu(x+t)dt$$

$$=\int_0^1 {}_tp_x\ \mu(x+t)dt$$

Clearly

$$\int_0^w {}_tp_x\ \mu(x+t)dt=1$$

This means that death rate for population aged x after age x is one. This also gives the probability of its dying in future to be one.

$$\text{Again } l_0=\int_0^w l(t)\ \mu(t)dt$$

Hence,

$$e_0^\circ=\frac{T_0}{l_0}=\frac{\int_0^w l(t)dt}{\int_0^w l(t)\ \mu(t)dt}$$

Also,

$$e_x^\circ=\frac{T_x}{l_x}=\frac{\int_0^{w-x} l(x+t)dt}{\int_x^w l(t)\ \mu(t)dt}$$

$$e_x^{\circ} = \int_x^w l(t)dt \Big/ \int_x^w l(t)\, \mu(t)dt$$

e_x° is, in fact, the average prospective life time of an individual aged x and hence

$$e_x^{\circ} = \frac{\int_0^{w-x} t\, l(x+t)\, \mu(x+t)dt}{\int_0^{w-x} l(x+t)\, \mu(x+t)dt}$$

On comparing the two values of e_x°, we get

$$\int_0^{w-x} l(x+t)dt = \int_0^{w-x} t\, l(x+t)\, \mu(x+t)dt$$

or

$$T_x = \int_0^{w-x} t.\, l(x+t)\, \mu(x+t)dt$$

=total number of person years lived after age x by the cohort "l_0".

2.7 Mortality by Causes of Death

The attrition probabilities q_x can be calculated for any specific cause (c) in absence of all other causes of death ($\overline{C}$) at completed age x as

$$q_x^{(c)} = \frac{D_x^{(c)}}{(S_x - D_x^{(\overline{c})}/2)}$$

Where S_x is the population surviving at exact age x, $D_x^{(c)}$ represents the number of deaths due to cause (c) and $D_x^{(\overline{c})}$

the number of deaths due to all other causes. Thus using this $q_x^{(c)}$, a life table can be constructed as usual for the sole cause of death (*c*).

2.8 Life Table Functions for the Last Age Interval

Mortality rates at extreme old ages tend to be fluctuating because of small population figures and a lot of error of misreporting ages. Therefore, the probabilities of dying at older ages are generally obtained by using some graduation methods. It is, however, not necessary to construct a life table upto the end of the life. In practice, it is reasonable to terminate the life table with an open age interval 70+ or 80+. A question naturally arises about the life table functions at this age of 70 or 80. If we assume that last age interval considered in the life table is *y*, then q_{y+} implies the probability of persons aged y_+ to die. Since all the persons aged y_+ are to die, q_{y+} is unity and

$$l_y = d_{y+}$$

the value of l_y is obtained from the previous columns *i.e.*

$$l_{y-n} - {}_nd_{y-n} = l_y$$

and

$L_{y+} = \dfrac{d_{y+}}{m_{y+}}$ Where m_{y+} is the central death rate of population aged $y+$ and $L_{y+} = \dfrac{l_y}{M_{y+}}$

Where M_{y+} is the population death rate and is assumed to be equal to m_{y+}

Further $M_{y+} < 1$ and hence $L_{y+} > l_y$.

Obviously for the last age interval $y+$, we $T_y = L_{y+}$ and hence

$$T_y = l_y / M_{y+}$$

The value of life expectancy at age *y* is

$$e^\circ_y = T_y / l_y = \left(\frac{l_y}{M_{y+}} \right) \Big/ \; l_y = \frac{1}{M_{y+}}$$

Another method of estimating T_y is as below:

$$T_y/l_y = e^o_y$$

Hence, $$T_y = e^o_y . l_y$$

Assuming that the value of e^o_y at higher ages does not differ too much from one population to another, an estimate of e^o can be obtained from some model life table. It may, however, be noted that the above assumption is vaild only at very high ages (say after 80) and becomes less and less adequate as the terminal age y decreases.

2.9 Theories of Mortality

Study of several life tables suggests that the basic nature of the life table functions q_x, l_x, d_x and e_x remain almost unchanged irrespective of the levels of mortality. This suggests for some underlying law of mortality which can be described by a mathematical model. Model of mortality would help in understanding the past trends of mortality and thus provide an insight to project the mortality into future. The methods of projecting mortality, however, are altogether different than the model of mortality and they are discussed in the chapter on projections. Mostly the mathematical models of mortality are deterministic and they do not take into account the statistical variabitity in the observations on the mortality phenomenon. The first mathematical formula describing the adult mortality rates was proposed by Benjamin Gompertz in 1825 (see Beard, 1971). The mathematical model of Gompertz expressed in terms of the force of mortality is

$$\mu_x = Bc^x$$

The above model implies a geometric progression of mortality with increase in age x. This model is not suitable to describe the early childhood mortality and also at the older ages. In case of cohort mortality, however, this model is found to fit better. On solving the Gompertz curve in μ_x we have

$$l_x = AG^{C^x}$$

Where A and G are constants. From the knoweldge of l_x, we can get

$$ {}_nq_x = \frac{l_x - l_{x+n}}{l_x} = l - {}_np_x = l - G^{C^x(C^n-1)} $$

The method of obtaining the constants are discussed later on. Makeham modified the Gompertz law of mortality asserting that change in an extraneous factor independent of age contributes to mortality in addition to decreasing capacity of human being to resist destruction due to injury or infection. Makehan's law is

$$ \mu_x = A + BC^x $$

On solving the above curve we get

$$ l_x = K\, b^x \,.\, G^{c^x} $$

This curve has been also found fitting the mortality rates beyond age 20. Fitting of this curve can be done by taking second order difference of log (l_x), log (l_{x+n}), log (l_{x+2n}), log (l_{x+3n}) to get first the value of c as

$$ \frac{\Delta^{(2)} \log l_x}{\Delta^{(2)} \log l_{x+n}} = c_n $$

Since $\Delta^{(2)} \log (l_x) = c^x\,(c^n - 1) \log G$,

By putting the value of c in the above function G can be ascertained and values of c and G can be used to estimate b K from the Δ log (l_x).

Since Makeham's modification did not provide satisfactory results, he suggested another model:

$$ \mu_x = A + Hx + BC^x $$

Which is a mixture of polynomial and Gompertz curves. However even this modification failed to describe the mortality pattern over all the ages. Although Makehan's modifications improved the fit for the young adult ages, both Gompertz and

Makeham's curves yield excessively high mortality rates at the extreme ages. To overcome this difficulty, Perks proposed the following law :

$$\mu_x = \frac{A+BC^x}{1+DC^x}$$

Which is a logistic curve. The effect of the denominator is to reduce the rate of increase of mortality at the very high ages to conform to the actual observations. The observed feature that a wide range of adult human mortality tables could be generated by the logistic curve of the above form prompted Beard to advance the genetic theory of mortality.

His model is also deterministic and again assumes Makeham law of mortality for the different strata. It assumes that each individual is destined to some unique 'longevity'. But the studies of heredity donot support it. Beard, however, deviced a stock model. If l_x are the number of persons alive at age x with α units remaining and that the chance of losing a unit in the next interval is pdt times the number of units remaining then,

$$\frac{dl_x^{\alpha}}{dx} = -p\alpha l_x^{\gamma} + p(\alpha+1)\, l_x^{\alpha+1}$$

The solution to the above equation leads to

$$l_x^{\alpha} = (\alpha^r) \,.\, \exp(-p \,.\, \alpha \,.\, x)\ [1-\exp(-px)]^{r-\alpha}$$

Where r is the initial stock. If the initial population is so distributed that proportion with stock r is $\frac{D}{(1+D)(r+1-\alpha)}$, then the overall mortality is given by

$$\mu_x = \frac{p\alpha De^{px}}{1+De^{px}}$$

This is a logistic form given by (Beard, 1964).

In literature there are two distinct models which lead to the logistic forms of μ_x. The first is the stratified population with strata subject to Makeham mortality and the second is a different stratification but with mortality dependent on the state of deterioration reached at age x by a purely random process. The thesis of the models advanced by Beard is that each normal organ continues to function effectively so long as its biochemical structure is undisturbed.

Further attempt to model making in mortality analysis was to group the various causes of death according to their observed distribution and examine each group if their mortality patterns lead to different stochastic models. Beard selected mortality from cancer of the lung in Great Britain because of the increase in cancer incidence probably due to smoking etc. He first assumed that the mortality at any age x during year t may be expressed by

$$\mu_{x,t} = K \cdot H_{t-x} \, \phi'_t \cdot F_x$$

in which H_{t-x} is a function of the year of birth only, ϕ_t is a function dependent on the year of experience, and F_x is a function of attaind age only. The function H_{t-x} is assumed to be almost constant since the genetic composition of the population changes slowly with time. However, ϕ_t, may change rapidly due to strong effect of epidemics and environments. The function F_x is pure mortality function. In other words, deaths at age x were the function of age and a deterioration process acting on a purely random basis. The above model implies that the individual starts with a stock of resistance which is reduced overtime on a probability basis according to the quantity of cigaretes smoked if death is due to cancer of lung. The justification came from the agreement of expected frequencies with observed ones and a common model for both male and female lives. This model provides a good method to project mortality by causes on the knowledge of H, ϕ and F overtime.

By and large, the laws of mortality so far discussed in the liturature underline either the Gompertz relation or the logistic curve to describe age pattern of mortality. It may however, be mentioned that no single curve or distribution has been found suitable to describe the variation in mortality, over the entire life span of the human being. No doubt some stochastic models describing pure death processes, or birth and death processes, simple illness—death process have been developed in the literature. A stochastic model of the illness–death process seems to have been suggested first by Fix and Neyman (1951) in their study of the probabilities of relapse, recovery and death for cancer patients. In such models, an individual is treated to be in a particular state of illness if he contracts the corresponding disease and he is considered to be in a particular death state if he dies of the corresponding cause. The subject of topic is outside the scope of this book and hence readers are suggested to read the book of Chiang (1968).

3

Construction of Life Tables

Construction of any life table basically requires the knowledge of ${}_nq_x$ values and some assumptions to ascertain ${}_nL_x$ values from the l_x values. From the actual data pertaining to mortality, it is easy to obtain a measure of mortality rate but not ${}_nq_x$ which is a probability measure. Neither the deaths nor the population by age are available on a cohort basis for most of the populations. For example, the infant deaths registered in a particular calender year belong to the birth cohorts of that year as well as of the previous year. Similarly the infants counted at the time of censuses come from the survivors of the birth cohorts of the same year as well as previous year. Another anomaly in construction of a life table is that the life table population is a stationary population but it is used to represent the mortality conditions of the actual population which is seldom stationary. Infact, the linkage between the life table and the actual population is established by the basic assumption that

$$m_x = M_x$$

That is, the observed age specific (central) death rate M_x in the population is a good approximation to the central death rate of the life table, m_x.

Again the problem arises to convert the m_x values into the q_x values which form the basic input of any life table. The problem is completely solved in case of a complete life table by assuming uniform (or linear) distribution of deaths within the interval of one year of age and as such q_x can be obtained by using the relation

$$q_x = \frac{m_x}{1+\frac{1}{2}m_x} = \frac{M_x}{1+\frac{1}{2}M_x} = \frac{2(M_x)}{2+M_x} \qquad (1)$$

This relation between M_x and q_x is only approximate. The registered deaths and the mid-year population are never matched at any age and hence they do not belong to the same universe. This approximation, as such, involves unknown errors in the q_x values when calculated by the single years of age. That is why, the single year values of q_x show a lot of fluctuations. In construction of a complete life table, either the data on deaths or the q_x values should therefore be smoothed to avoid fluctuations in the q_x values.

The assumption of the uniform distri bution of deaths over an age interval is not valid when the interval is broader than the one year. While ${}_nm_x$ value can still be approximated by ${}_nM_x$ the age specific death rate in the population between ages x and $x+n$, ${}_nq_x$, can be approximated in several ways from the ${}_nm_x$ value. As such, there are several ways of constructing an abridged life table depending on the approximation used to estimate the ${}_nq_x$ values.

The life tables are also varying depending on the way ${}_nL_x$ column is derived from the l_x column. Calculation of ${}_nL_x$ is based on the behaviour of l_x in the age interval $(x, x+n)$. In case of the adult ages, assumption of the linear decline in l_x values is quite appropriate to derive ${}_nL_x$ if $n=1$. However, there is no single l_x function to describe the survivorship function for the entire life time. If the interval is greater than one year, some functional form of $l_{(x)}$ is, however, needed to approximate ${}_nL_{(x)}$ (in continuous sense) because we know that

$${}_nL_{(x)} = \int_0^n l(x+t)dt \qquad (2)$$

which requires a functional form of $l_{(x)}$ for the evaluation of the integral. The assumption regarding the from of $l(x)$ also stands in the way of equivalence between the ${}_nq_x$ and ${}_nm_x$ since

$${}_nq_x = \frac{l(x) - l(x+n)}{l(x)} \text{ and } {}_nm_x = \frac{l(x) - l(x+n)}{\int_x^{x+n} l(z)dz} \quad (3)$$

Thus an assumption has to be made regarding the functional form of the $l(x)$ curve over the age interval $(x, x+n)$. This constitutes the main problem in constructing an abridged life table from a set of age specific mortality rates. If $l(x)=a+bx$ (linear) in the interval $(x, x+n)$, one can easily get the relation

$${}_nq_x = \frac{2n\ ({}_nm_x)}{2+n\ ({}_nm_x)}$$

and

$${}_nL_x = \frac{n}{2}(l_x + l_{x+n})$$

In fact, a more general relation can be obtained in terms of the average number of years lived by an individual of age x who dies in the interval $(x, x+n)$. Let us define this number by ${}_na_x$ so that (4)

$${}_nf_x = \frac{1}{n}({}_na_x)$$

Which is the expected fraction of this last n years lived interval. The expected total number of years lived by l_x individuals, now aged x, over the years x to $x+n$, will be ${}_nL_x$ which is made up of (1) full n years for each of thc l_{x+n} survivors out of l_x and (2) ${}_na_x$ years for each of the individuals who die. Hence (5)

$${}_nL_x = n(l_{x+n}) + {}_na_x.\ {}_nd_x = n\ (l_x - {}_nd_x) + n.\ {}_nf_x\ .\ {}_nd_x.$$
$$= n[l_x - (1 - {}_nf_x)\ {}_nd_x]$$

or $$l_x = \frac{l}{n}[{}_nL_x + n(1 - {}_nf_x)\ {}_nd_x]$$

We know that

$${}_nd_x = l_x.\ {}_nq_x.$$

$${}_nm_x = \frac{{}_nd_x}{{}_nL_x} = \frac{{}_nd_x}{n[l_x - (l - {}_nf_x)\ {}_nd_x]}$$

$$= \frac{{}_nq_x}{n\ [1 - (l - {}_nf_x).\ {}_nq_x]}$$

Similarly ${}_nd_x=({}_nL_x)\ {}_nm_x)$

hence $${}_nq_x=\frac{{}_nd_x}{l_x}=\frac{{}_nd_x}{\frac{l}{n}\quad[{}_nL_x+n(1-{}_nf_x)\ {}_nd_x]}$$

$$=\frac{{}_nm_x}{\frac{l}{n}\quad[l+n\ (l-{}_nf_x).\ {}_nm_x]} \qquad (6)$$

Under the assumption of uniform distribution of death over the interval (*x*, *x*+n) (*i.e.* $l(x)=a+bx$) we have

${}_na_x=\frac{n}{2}$ or ${}_nf_x=\frac{1}{2}$ and this leads to

$${}_nq_x=\frac{{}_nm_x}{\frac{1}{n}\left(l+\frac{n}{2}\,{}_nm_x\right)}=\frac{2n\ {}_nm_x}{2+n\ ({}_nm_x)} \qquad (7)$$

(same as derived earlier)

The above formula leads to values of ${}_nq_x$ greater than one if ${}_nm_x>.4$ and $n=5$. Slightly different results are attained if we assume exponential distribution of age at death over $(x, x+n)$ with constant force of morality. In this case

$${}_nm_x=\mu_x \text{ and } {}_nq_x=1-e^{-n}({}_nm_x) \qquad (8)$$

$$\text{and } L_{x+n}=l_xe^{-n}({}_nm_x)$$

Below we shall discuss some special methods of constructing abridged life tables showing specific relations between ${}_nq_x$, ${}_nm_x$, ${}_nL_x$ and l_x values. Of course, an abridged life table can be prepared on the basis of complete life table functions. But in many situations, it is more desirable to construct an abridged life table first to avoid the effects of the errors in mortality data, especially, due to misreporting of age of the deceased and the under-reporting of the events of deaths more pronounced in the single year data and hence q_x values of the complete life table. The abridged life table can then be used to construct a complete life table by using asuitable interpolation formula. Further, the risk of deaths changes very slowly over most of the ages and as such there is no need for more elaborate and cumbersome construction of a complete life table. Some important and commonly used methods of constructing life tables are discussed below.

3.1 REED AND MERRELL METHOD OF CONSTRUCTING AN ABRIDGED LIFE TABLE

As noted earlier, some times, the assumption of the linear decline in l_x values lead to discrepant results for $_nq_x$ in terms of $_nm_x$. Reed and Merrell (1939) suggested the following direct relationship between $_nq_x$ and $_nm_x$ without assuming functional form of $l(x)$, (based on their empirical calculation on the life tables of U.S.A. over the years 1901-1930).

$$_nq_x = 1 - e^{-n(_nm_x) - an^3(_nm_x^2)} \tag{9}$$

Where a is a constant. They found that $a=.008$ would produce good results for $n=1, 2, \ldots 10$.

Read and Merrell's method is one of the most common and simple methods being used for the preparation of an abridged life table. To facilitate calculations, standard tables giving conversion of $_nm_x$ values to $_nq_n$ values are also given by them. Once $_nq_x$ values are calculated, the l_x values are calculated by using the relation.

$$l_{x+n} = (1 - {_nq_x})l_x$$

$$_nd_x = l_x - l_{x+n}$$

Reed and Merrell then suggest to calculate T_x values from the l_x for ages 10 and over or 5 and over by the use of the following relations:

1. $$T_x = -.20833\, l_{x-5} + 2.5 l_x + .20833\, l_{x+5} + 5 \sum_{\alpha=1}^{\infty} l_{x+5\alpha} \tag{10}$$

   (If the age intervals are of 5 years); and

$$2.\ T_x = 4.16667\, l_x + .83333\, l_{x+10} + 10 \sum_{\alpha=1}^{\infty} l_{x+10\alpha} \qquad (11)$$

(If the table is prepared for 10 years intervals)

These equations are based on the assumption that the area under l_x curve between any two ordinates is approximated by the area under a parabola through these ordinates and preceding and following ordinates (in case of 5 year intervals) or the following ordinate only (in case of 10 years intervals).

For the ages under 10, Reed and Merrell assumed the relation

$$_nL_x = a\, l_c + b l_x + c l_{x+n} \qquad (12)$$

Where $a+b+c=n$.

They derived putting by $x=0$ and $n=1$, $L_o = 0.276\, l_o + .724\, l_1$, by putting $x=1$ and $n=4$; $_4L_1 = .034\, l_o + 1.184\, l_1 + 2.782\, l_5$ and putting $x=5$ and $n=5$,

$$_5L_5 = .003\, l_0 + 2.242\, l_5 + 2.761 l_{10} \qquad (13)$$

Calculation of L_o should be, however, done by using separation factors appropriate to the level of infant mortality of the population under study to get the weighted sum of l_0 and l_1. Thus after determining $_nq_x$ values from $_nm_x$ by using the conversion Table and subsequently l_x and T_x values as mentioned above, $_nL_x$ values for ages 10 and above are obtained by using the relation $_nL_x = T_x - T_{x+n}$. Other remaining columns of life table can easily be ascertained by following the general procedure.

It has been observed that upto very high ages, the Reed and Merrell formulae do not yield better evaluations of the $_nq_x$ than the formula based on the linear assumption of l_x (See Peron, 1971). It is only after very high ages 75 and 80 that the Reed and Merrell's formula is preferable but even then the rates are very erratic at those ages and hence not reliable. Also the scheme of calculating $_nL_y$ values from the T_x values seems to be cumbersome and has no logical basis for doing so. It has also been observed that the $_nL_x$ values are not correctly obtained

TABLE 3.1

Calculation of Abridged Life Table for Females in Rural Kerala by the Reed-Merrell Method (Based on Mean Age Specific Death Rates for 1975, 1976, 1977).

Age (x)	$_{m}m_{x}$	$_{n}q_{x}$	$_{n}d_{x}$	l_x	$_{n}L_{x}$	T_x	e_x^{o}
0	.05544	.049902	4990	100000	96507[a]	6500089	65.00
1	.00959	.036177	3437	95010	370648[a]	6403582	67.40
5	.00209	.010399	952	91573	455485	6032934	65.88
10	.00105	.005237	474	90621	451920	5577449	61.55
15	.00129	.006429	580	90147	449285	5125529	56.86
20	.00166	.008266	740	89567	445985	4676244	52.21
25	.00231	.011486	1020	88827	441585	4230259	47.62
30	.00173	.008613	756	87807	437145	3788674	43.15
35	.00220	.010943	952	87051	432875	3351529	38.50
40	.00340	.016865	1452	86099	426865	2918654	33.90
45	.00459	.022706	1922	84647	418430	2491789	29.44
50	.00744	.036567	3025	82725	406062	2073359	25.06

55	.01217	.059173	4716	79700	386710	1667297	20.92
60	.02160	·102788	7707	74984	355652	1280587	17.08
65	.03125	.145487	9788	67277	321915	924935	13.75
70	.09378	1.000000	57489	57489	613020[b]	613020	10.66

(a) Calculated directly from l_o, l_1 and l_5 by use of the formulas $L_0 = .3\, l_o + .70\, l_1$ and ${}_4L_1 = .034\, l_o + 1.184\, l_1 + 2.782\, l_5$. All other values are calculated by using ${}_5L_x = (5/2)\,(l_x + l_{x+5})$.

(b) Calculated from $l_x \div {}_\infty m_x$.

Source: Observed death rates (${}_nm_x$) from *Sample Registration Kerala-Rural* (Directorate of Economics and Statistics, Trivandrum, 1980) Annual Report No. 15, 1977, Table XX, p. 39.

TABLE 3.2

Calculation of Abridged Life Table for Females in Rural Kerala by Greville's Method: (Based on Mean Age Specific Death Rate for 1975, 1976, 1977)

Age (x)	$_nm_x$	$1/2+\frac{n}{12}$ $x(1-.09)=$	$\frac{1}{n}+$ $(1)x(2)=$	$_nq_x$ $(1)\div(3)=$	$_nq_x$	l_x	$_nL_x$ $(5)\div(1)=$	T_x	e_x^o
	1	*2*	*3*	*4*	*5*	*6*	*7*	*8*	*9*
0	(x)	(x)	(x)	.046407@	4641	100000	96751[b]	6522070	65.22
1	.00959	.47320	.25454	.037676	3593	95359	374661	6425319	67.38
5	.00209	.46337	.20097	.010400	954	91766	456459	6050658	65.94
10	.00105	.46294	.20049	.005237	476	90812	453333	5594199	61.60
15	.00129	.46304	.20060	.006431	581	90336	450388	5140866	56.91
20	.00166	.46319	.20077	.008268	742	89755	446988	4690478	52.26
25	.00231	.46346	.20107	.011488	1022	89013	442424	4243490	47.67
30	.00173	.46322	.20080	.008616	758	87991	438150	3801066	43.20
35	.00220	.46342	.20102	.010944	955	87233	434091	3362916	38.65
40	.00340	.46392	.20158	.026867	1455	86278	427941	2928825	33.95
45	.00459	.46441	.20213	.022708	1926	84823	419608	2500884	29.48
50	.00744	.46560	.20346	.036567	3031	82897	407392	2081276	25.11
55	.01217	.46757	.20569	.059167	4725	79866	388250	1673884	20.96

60	.02160	.47150	.21018	.102769	7722	75141	357500	1285634	17.11
65	.03125	.47552	.21486	.145444	9806	67419	313792	928134	13.77
70	.09378	(x)	(x)	1.000000	57613	57613	614342[c]	614342	10.66

(x) Not applicable

@ Infant Mortality Rate

(b) Calculated from l_0 and l_1 by use of the formula $L_0 = .3\, l_0 + .7\, l_1$.

(c) Calculated from $l_x \div \infty m_x$.

Source: Same as Table 3.1

unless the l_x values are available beyond the age of 85 because of the approximation involved in the last term of the formula of

T_x. i.e. $5 \sum_{\alpha=1}^{\infty} l_{x+5\alpha}$ or $10 \sum_{\alpha=1}^{\infty} l_{x+10\alpha}$.

It is, therefore, suggested that one can calculate ${}_nq_x$ values as suggested by Reed and Merrell's formula but calculate ${}_nL_x$ values by using the simple linear function of $l(x)$.

$${}_nL_x = \frac{n}{2}(l_x + l_{x+n})$$

For the last age,

$${}_\infty L_x = \frac{l_x}{{}_\infty m_x}$$

4.2 GREVILLE'S METHOD OF CONSTRUCTING AN ABRIDGED LIFE TABLE

By considering the non-linearity of the l_x values over the age interval $[x, x+n]$, Greville (1943) arrived at the relation

$${}_nq_x = \frac{{}_nm_x}{\frac{1}{n} + {}_nm_x \left(\frac{1}{2} + \frac{n}{12} [{}_nm_x - \log_e c] \right)} \quad \ldots(14)$$

Where the constant c comes from the assumption that ${}_nm_x$ follows an exponential curve in accordance with Gompertz law

$${}_nm_x = Bc^x$$

It has been observed that at the older ages, the mortality rates conform to the Gompertz law in most of the situations and the ${}_nq_x$ values are quite insensitive to the value of c. Thus same value of c may be taken for the entire span of the life table. c may be approximated by taking an average of c values calculated for higher ages using

$$c = \left(\frac{{}_nm_{x+n}}{{}_nm_x} \right)^{\frac{1}{n}} \quad \ldots(15)$$

Empirically, the value of c is found to lie between .08 and .104. Log $_e c$ could be assumed to be .095 as an intermediate value.

To compute life table functions by Greville's method, the mortality rates for the first few ages are obtained by any of the procedures using births and deaths. ${}_nq_x$ can be calculated *for ages 5 and over*, by using Greville's relation between ${}_nq_x$ and ${}_nm_x$. Once ${}_nq_x$ values are obtained, the other functions are calculated in the usual way. Greville also suggested following approximate formula for calculating ${}_nL_x$, *i e.*

$$ {}_nL_x=\frac{n}{2}\left(l_x+l_{x+n}\right)+\frac{n}{24}({}_nd_{x+n}-{}_nd_{x-n}). \qquad \ldots(16)$$

Tables 3.1 and 3.2 illustrate the procedure of constructing the life tables by using Reed and Marrell Method and Greville's method.

3.3. Chiang's Method

Chiang's method (1968) is based on the derivation of a relation for ${}_nL_x$ in terms of ${}_na_x$, the average number of years lived by an individual of age x who dies in the interval $(x, x+n)$. As shown in the beginning of this section, we get the following relations :

$$ {}_nL_x=n(l_x-{}_nd_x)+{}_na_x\,.\,{}_nd_x \qquad \ldots(17)$$

$$ {}_nq_x=\frac{n\,.\,({}_nm_x)}{1+(n-{}_na_x){}_nm_x}. \qquad \ldots(18)$$

Once ${}_nq_x$ and ${}_nL_x$ are obtained, all other functions of the table are easily obtained in the usual manner. While ${}_nm_x$ can be replaced by ${}_nM_x$, the age specific death rate in the population which are readily available, ${}_na_x$ cannot be calculated from the published data. It has, however, been shown that ${}_na_x$ neither depends on ${}_nq_x$ nor on age specific death rate ${}_nM_x$ in the population, but rather on the trend of mortality within the age interval. Since the trend of mortality within an age group does not change very much from one population to another, ${}_na_x$ (except a_0) can be calculated from sample observations and may be applied for other groups of the population. In case deaths are linearly distributed within

TABLE 3.3

Illustration for the Construction of an Abridged Life Table by Chiang's Method for Females in Rural Kerala from Mortality Experience of Current Population (based on Mean Age Specific Death Rates for 1975, 1976, 1977)

Age (x)	${}_nm_x$	${}_nq_x$	${}_nd_x$	l_x	${}_nL_x$	T_x	e_x^0	${}_na_x^*$
0	.05544	.052900	5290	100000	95419	6475809	64.76	0.134
1	.00959	.037525	3554	94710	370595	6380390	67.37	1.680
5	.00209	.010438	951	91156	453212	6009795	65.93	2.300
10	.00105	.005238	472	90205	449954	5556583	61.60	2.730
15	.00129	.006430	577	89733	447315	5106629	56.91	2.660
20	.00166	.008266	737	89156	443956	4659314	52.26	2.525
25	.00231	.011486	1016	88419	439631	4215358	47.67	2.575
30	.00173	.008615	753	87403	435245	3775727	43.20	2.650

35	.00220	.010944	948	86650	431055	3340482	38.55	2.685
40	.00340	.016867	1446	85702	425155	2909427	35 95	2.680
45	.00459	.022706	1913	84256	416804	2484272	29.48	2.660
50	.20744	.036561	3010	82343	404642	2067468	25.11	2.640
55	.31217	.059151	4693	79333	385590	1662826	20.96	2.640
60	.02160	.102762	7670	74640	355099	1277236	17.11	2.640
65	.05125	.145582	9750	66970	311986	922137	13.77	2.655
70	.09378	1.000000	57220	57220	610151	610151	10.66	10.660

*Taken from Chiang's Study, White Females 1969-71.

Source : Same as Table 3.1.

the age group, ${}_na_x=\frac{n}{2}$. Following are the values of ${}_na_x$ found by Chiang for U.S. Life Table 1969-71 (Males).

Age Interval :	0-1	1-5	5-10	10-15	15-20	20-25	25-30	30-35	35-40	40-45
${}_na_x$	.13	1.72	2.35	2.99	2.75	2.51	2.44	2.59	2.68	2.69

Age Interval :	45-50	50-55	55-60	60-65	65-70	70-75	75-80	80-85	85+
${}_na_x$	2.68	2.68	2.65	2.61	2.58	2.54	2.48	2.40	4.93

Chiang's procedure of construction of life table is quite simple and quick if one has knowledge of ${}_na_x$ for the given population. The method of calculation is illustrated in Table 3.3.

3.4. Keyfitz Method of Constructing Life Table

In constructing life table usually the life table age specific death rates (${}_nm_x$) are assumed to be equal to the observed age specific death rates in the population (${}_nM_x$). Keyfitz (1966) tackled the difficulty that arises in assuming that the population in successive cohorts remains constant when in fact it is clear that in most countries in the world the population is increasing. The essential feature of Keyfitz method is its allowance for a supposed constant rate of growth. In this method, the growth rate specific for the age group x to $x+n$ is represented by ${}_nr_x$. The value of ${}_nr_x$ is estimated from mid year population age structure, and mortality data in two adjacent age groups $x-5$ to x and x to $x+5$, applying Greville's cubic approximation and using iterative procedure. The detail of the methodology is as follows :

The age specific death rate ${}_nm_x$ in a life table population can be written as

$$ {}_nm_x=\frac{\int_0^n l_{(x+t)}\ \mu_{x+t}\ dt}{\int_0^n l_{(x)}\ dt} $$

In the simplest case when population is stable and grows with the rate '*r*' then the age specific death rate is

$$ {}_nM'_x = \frac{\int_0^n e^{-rt} \,.\, l(x+t) \,.\, \mu_{x+t}\, dt}{\int_0^n e^{-rt}\, l(x+t)\, dt} \tag{19}$$

After simplifying the integrals in the numerator and denominator of (2) we have

$$ {}_nM'_x = {}_nm_x\,[1 - r\,({}_na_x - {}_nA_x)]$$

where ${}_na_x$=average number of years lived in the age interval x to $x+n$ by those dying between x to $x+n$.

${}_nA_x$=Average number of years already lived within the interval by the stationary population from age x to $x+n$

Numerically,

$$ {}_na_x = \frac{{}_nL_x - n\,.\,l_{x+n}}{{}_nd_x}$$

$$ {}_nA_x = \frac{\int_0^n t\, l_{x+t}\, dt}{{}_nL_x}$$

By using Greville's cubic fit to l_x function through l_{x-n}, l_x and l_x+2n, ${}_nL_x$ is approximate by

$$ {}_nL_x = \frac{n}{2}\,(l_x + l_{x+n}) + \frac{n}{24}\,[{}_nd_{x+n} - {}_nd_{x-n}]$$

Using this value of ${}_nL_x$ we get

$$ {}_na_x = \frac{n}{2} + \frac{n}{24}\;\frac{({}_nd_{x+n} - {}_nd_{x-n})}{{}_nd_x}$$

By similar process by fitting a cubic curve to Tx we have

$$ {}_nAx = \frac{n}{2} + \frac{n}{24}\;\frac{[{}_nLx_{+n} - {}_nLx_{-n}]}{{}_nLx}$$

Keyfitz remarks that the value of ${}_nA_x$ is around 2.5. It should be however, kept in mind that above formulae hold good for ages 15 and above. Also we know that

$$ {}_nq_x = \frac{n \cdot {}_nm_x}{1+(n-{}_na_x)\,{}_nm_x} $$

Keyfitx now suggests an iteractive scheme to construct a life table as below

(1) Calculate

$$ {}_nM_x = \frac{{}_nD_x}{{}_nK_x} $$

= Age specific death rate from data where ${}_nK_x$ is the observed population in age group and put ${}_nm_x = {}_nM_x$.

(2) Then calculate

$$ {}_nq_x = \frac{n \cdot {}_nM_x}{1+(n-{}_na_x)\,{}_nm_x} $$

$$ \left({}_na_x = \frac{n}{2} \text{ on first cycle}\right). $$

(3) Calculate

$$ l_x = l_{x-n}\,(1-{}_nq_x),\; {}_nd_x = l_x\,({}_nq_x) $$

(4) Calculate

$$ {}_na_x = \frac{n}{2} + \frac{n}{24}\,\frac{[{}_nd_{x+n} - {}_nd_{x-n}]}{{}_nd_x} \quad \text{and} $$

$$ {}_nL_x = \frac{n}{2}\,(l_x + 1_{x+n}) + \frac{n}{24}\,[{}_nd_{x+n} - {}_nd_{x-n}] $$

(5) Calculate

(1) $${}_nA_x = \frac{n}{2} + \frac{n}{24}\,\frac{[{}_nL_{x+n} - {}_nL_{x-n}]}{{}_nL_x}$$

(2) $${}_nm_x = \frac{{}_nd_x}{{}_nL_x}$$

(3) $${}_nr_x = \frac{1}{2n}\,l_x\,[{}_nK_{x-n}/{}_nL_{x-n})/({}_nK_{x+n}/{}_nL_{x+n})]$$

The above value of rate of growth is a sort of replacement index for the concerned age.

(6) Now we can get

$${}_nM'_x = {}_nm_x \, [1 - {}_nr_x \ ({}_na_x - {}_nA_x)]$$

(7) $${}_nm^*_x = {}_nm_x \, . \, \frac{{}_nM_x}{{}_nM'_x}$$

(8) Treating ${}_nm^*_x$ as ${}_nm_x$, we can repeat the process of calculation starting from step 2 to step 8 till the iterated value of ${}_nm_x$ is comparable to ${}_nM_x$ to atleast 5 decimals.

It may, however, be mentioned the above iteration would not yield the value ${}_nL_x$ below $x=10$. But after using Beer's interpolation formula, we have

$${}_5L_5 = 1.9012\, l_5 + 3.7676\, l_{10} - 0.4824\, l_{15} - .5704\, l_{20} + .5116\, l_{25} - 0.1276\, l_{30}$$

$${}_5L_{10} = -.1529\, l_5 + 2.5381\, l_{10} + 2.8766\, l_{15} - .2294\, l_{20} - .0589\, l_{25} + .0265\, l_{30}$$

For calculating ${}_1L_0$ and ${}_4L_1$ we can safely use Reed and Merrel formula discussed earlier with some change in the multipliers of l_0, l_1 and l_5 to suit the mortality conditions (childhood) of the population under study.

Some of the formulae were revised further by Keyfitz (1968) subsequently.

3.5. Construction of an Abridged Life Table by Reference to a Standard Table

Construction of an abridged life table by reference to standard table assumes that in each age interval the relation of ${}_nq_x$ to observed ${}_nm_x$ shown by the standard table applies to the table under study. In constructing abridged life table for U.S. from 1946 to 1953, the 1939-41 U.S. complete life table was used as a standard. This method is useful for calculating life table for regions of a country when a full national life table is available or for calculating annual tables for a country in years immediately following the calculation of complete life table. We use the relation,

$$_nq_x = \frac{n \,.\, _nm_x}{1+(n - {_na_x})\, _nm_x} = \frac{n \,.\, _nm_x}{1+ {_ng_x}\, _nm_x} \quad \ldots(20)$$

where $_ng_x = n - {_na_x}$

Solving the above for $_ng_x$ we have

$$_ng_x = \frac{n}{_nq_x} - \frac{1}{_nm_x}$$

Using the above relation, incase of a standard table gives $\{_ng_x\}$ which can be used subsequently to calculate $_nq_x$ values of the life table from $_nm_x$ values. For calculation of $_nL_x$ in the abridged table, we can calculate $_nG_x$ from the standard table as

$$_nG_x = \frac{n l_x^{(s)} - {_nL_x^{(s)}}}{_nd_x^{(s)}} \quad \ldots(21)$$

and then calculate for the new table

$$_nL_x = n l_x - {_nG_x} \,.\, {_nd_x}$$

For the last interval, $_\infty L_x$ is calculated as

$$_\infty L_x = \frac{l_x r_x}{_\infty m_x} \quad \text{where } r_x = \frac{_\infty m_x^{(s)} \,.\, L_x^{(s)}}{l_x^{(s)}} \quad (22)$$

Construction of a Complete Life Table from an Abridged Life Table

A complete life table should really be constructed from the single year data on mortality. When such data are not available in published form or have a lot of reporting error, the complete life table can be constructed from an abridged life table using some interpolation schemes (*i*) for very young (0 – 1) and young ages (1 – 9), (*ii*) for the broad class of ages (10 – 74) and (*iii*) for very old ages (75 and above). Different methods are however used. Use of six-point Lagrangian interpolation formulae over the age range 1–74 and smoothing l_x values by fitting a Gompertz curve for ages above 75 represent satisfactory results (See Johnson and Johnson (1980)) special methods are however, needed for the first year of life. In fact in most of the Abridged life tables we may have l_1 (and q_0).

3.6. Construction of Life Tables from Incomplete Data

Sometimes, complete and reliable information on mortality by age may not be available for a country. But data on age distribution of population corresponding to two consecutive censuses conducted in the country may be available. Life tables have been constructed by using only census age data in many countries including India (Sinha, 1987). In earlier days, use has been made of death records only. We will discuss some methods derived to use fragementary data in construction of life tables.

3.6.1. Life Tables Based on Death Records Only

It was Halley, the astronomer who first used the data from burial records for the city of Breslau to calculate a life table function and communicated his results to the Royal Society of England in 1863. He was aware that his technique was valid only if the population was stationary. Since age structure of the population was known, he examined the trends in baptisms and burials in the city for a period of years. If the population is stationary and ages at deaths are known, we can use life table relations.

$$l_x = \sum_{x}^{\infty} d_x$$

and thus l_x column can be constructed and from this q_x is estimated by using

$$q_x = (l_x - l_{x+1}) / l_x$$

Now a days, the above method should not be used because hardly any population is stationary. It is however being still used by archaelogists or zoologists who find skeletons of men or animals from which the age at death of individuals can be estimated and whei population can not be known, but can assumed to have been stationary.

3.6.2. Life Tables Based Upon a Single Census Record Only

If there are good reasons to believe that total number of annual births and annual deaths are constant over time and population is closed to migration, the situation is equivalent to that of the stationary population of a life table and we can get survival ship probability :

$$p_{x+1/2}=P^{z}_{x+1}/P^{z}_{x}$$

where z refers to the year of census.

If population is known to grow at a constant rate r, then

$$P^{z}_{x}=(1+r)\,P^{z-1}_{x} \qquad \ldots(23)$$

if all other conditions are same as in case of stationary population.

$$\text{Thus} \qquad p_{x+\frac{1}{2}}=\frac{P^{z}_{x+1}}{P^{z-1}_{x}}=\frac{P^{z}_{x+1}}{P^{z}_{x}\,(1+r)} \qquad \ldots(24)$$

Thus survival rates by single ages can be calculated if data on age by single years are available from single censns which is known to grow uniformly at a known rate r. The more general case was considered by Stolnitz (1956).

Now if S^{z}_{x} denotes the probability of surviving from birth to the census date for a person born x years ago, we have

$$P^{z}_{x}=B^{z-x}\,.\,S^{z}_{x}$$

$$\text{and} \qquad P^{z}_{x+1}=P^{z-1}_{x}\,.\,p_{x+\frac{1}{2}}=B^{z-1-x}\,S^{z-1}_{x}\,.\,p_{x+\frac{1}{2}}$$

Hence,

$$\frac{P^z_{x+1}}{P^z_x} = \frac{B^{z-1-x}}{B^{z-x}} \cdot \frac{S^{z-1}_x}{S^z_x} \cdot p_{x+\frac{1}{2}} \quad \ldots(25)$$

The three ratios in the above relation are known as the population ratio, the birth ratio and the survival ratio respectively. The solution for $p_{x+\frac{1}{2}}$ is therefore based on an observed population ratio and suitably chosen survival and birth ratios. The survival ratio's may be borrowed from some suitable life table comparable to the life table under consideration.

3.6.3. Life Tables Based on Two Consecutive Census Age Distributions

In the absence of reliable birth and death data, life tables have been computed on the basis of the age distributions of population at successive censuses (R. G., India, 1977). If population is closed to migration, the chance of survival of population aged x at the census date z to age $x+n$ at the census date $z+n$, is

$$p_x \, p_{x+1} \ldots\ldots p_{x+n-1} = \frac{P^{z+n}_{x+n}}{P^z_x}$$

But $\qquad {}_nq_x = 1 - p_x \, p_{x+1} \, p_{x+2} \ldots\ldots p_{x+n-1}$

Thus $\qquad {}_nq_x = 1 - \dfrac{P^{z+n}_{x+n}}{P^z_x} \qquad \ldots(26)$

From this it is possible to theoretically construct a life table. There are, however, serious difficulties due to heavy influence of in-accuracies and biases of age data. Migration will always be a serious problem in an area without vital registration system. However, for certain countries like India and Brazil, this approach has been used to calculate the life table functions.

3.7. Arriaga's Method of Constructing Life Tables Based on Age Data

Arriaga's method (Arriaga, 1968) is based on stable population theory. Readers are suggested to familiarise themselves with the stable population theory before reading this method. The principal characteristics of this method is that it does not use death statistics. The basic data used are the five-year age group distribution between ages 10 and 59, and the natural growth rate of the population. It assumes that the completeness of enumeration in the census is relatively the same in all the ten year age groups between ages 10 and 59. Some times misreporting of ages causes the completeness in these ten year groups to differ. But by smoothing the population, it may be ensured that the hypothesis of equal completeness holds good. Thus completeness of enumeration under age 10 and above 60 does not affect the results. Following conditions however, must hold good before the method is deemed applicable :

(*a*) almost constant fertility in the past years and (*b*) relatively insignificant international migration.

In a stable population the proportion of population in age group x to $x+5$ is given by

$$C(x, x+5) = b\, e^{-r(x+2.5)}\, {}_5L_x$$

(taking radix of the life table as one).

From which

$${}_5L_x = \frac{1}{b}\, C(x, x+5)\; e^{r(x+2.5)}$$

Thus ${}_5L_x$ can be found if $C(x, x+5)$, b and r are known; while proportion of total population in age group $(x, x+5)$, $C'(r, xx\ 5)$ can be obtained from census and estimate of r at the census date by considering intercensal geometric growth rates or the existing estimates, the problem is to estimate the intrinsic birth rate, b which will be different from the crude birth rate. To estimate the intrinsic birth rate consistent with the age distribution and rate of growth and also to get smoothed age distribution, the equation can be written as (after taking logarithm) ;

$$\frac{l_n C(x, x+5)}{{}_5L_x} = l_n b - r(x+2.5) \qquad \ldots(27)$$

This equation is a straight line whose slope is the growth rate of the population. One faces two problems here *(a)* it is difficult to obtain a straight line from the values given for C (x, x +5) in the census and *(b)* ${}_5L_x$ values are seldom available for the population. Concerning the first problem Arriaga suggests to initially adjust, the population in age groups between 10 and 59 years using the following equation (or any other formula) :

$$S^*_{x,\ x+10} = \tfrac{1}{4}[S_{x-10,\ x} + 2\ S_{x,\ x+10} + S_{x+10,\ x+20}]$$

where $S^*_{x,\ x+10}$ represents the adjusted population of the decennial age groups and the $S_{x,\ x+10}$ etc. (without austeriks) are the population of the decennial groups coming from the census.

The adjusted decennial group populations are then to be divided into quinquennial groups under the hypothesis that a second degree function would pass through each of the three central points of the decennial groups. By integrating this function between certain limits, we get following equations :

$$\ldots(28)$$

$$(1)\ Q_{x,\ x+5} = \frac{1}{24}\ [-S^*_{x-15,\ x-5} + 11\ S^*_{x-5,\ x+5} + 2\ S^*_{x+5,\ x+15}]$$

(2) When the decennial group corresponds to an extreme age (the youngest group)

$$\ldots(29)$$

$$Q_{x-15,\ x-5} = \frac{1}{24}\ [8S^*_{x-15,\ x-5} + 5\ S^*_{x-5,\ x+5}\quad S^*_{x+5,\ x+15}]$$

The quinquennial groups thus obtained for ages 10-59 are adjusted to the total population given by the census for the same ages. Next, the quinquennial groups are expressed in proportions with respect to the total population say $C\ (x, x+5)$ for ages 10-59.

In absence of any acceptable ${}_5L_x$ values available, some approximate level of mortality can be chosen and then ${}_5L_x$

values taken from some model life table (to be discussed later on). Thus $l_x\,[C\,(x, x+5)/_5L_x]$ are calculated between ages 10 and 59 and adjusted to a straight line determined by the least squares method. With this linear approximation, graduated values for the age groups between 10 and 59 are established. Then the extreme age groups are determined simply by extrapolation to include all ages from 0 to 84. Also by calculating the ordinate of origin, the birth rate is obtained. Then by using antilogarithms and multiplying the values by the same $_5L_x$ used previously, the smoothed values of $C\,(x, x+5)$ are obtained. Again the value of $_5L_x$ except for the open age group 85 and above, can be estimated by using $C'\,(x, x+5)$ and the estimates of r and b.

In order to estimate the l_x function, some values of l_x by using Beer's (1945) multipliers are obtained. We find values of l_1 and l_5 by interpolation with third degree function values of $_5L_x$: Thus

$$l_1 = .3125\,L_0 + .9375\,L_1 - .3125\,L_2 + .0625\,L_3$$

$$l_5 = .0625\,L_3 + .5625\,L_4 + .5625\,L_5 - .0625\,L_6$$

l_x values for ages 10–80 are obtained by interpolating with third degree functions values of $_5L_x$. Thus

$$l_{10} = .0625\,{}_5L_5 + .1875\,{}_5L_{10} - .0625\,{}_5L_{15} + .0125\,{}_5L_{20}$$

For ages 15–75,

$$l_x = -.0125\,{}_5L_{x-10} + .1125\,{}_5L_{x-5} + .1125\,{}_5L_x - .0125\,{}_5L_{x+5}$$

and

$$l_{80} = .0125\,({}_5L_{65}) - .0625\,({}_5L_{70}) + .1875\,({}_5L_{75}) + 0.625\,({}_5L_{80})$$

The probabilities of survivorship are calculated by

$$_5p_x = \frac{l_{x+5}}{l_x}$$

$_5p_{80}$ is however calculated by extrapolation.

$$l_{85} = l_{80}\;{}_5p_{80}.$$

where $\quad {}_5p_{80} = {}_5p_{55} - 5({}_5p_{65}) - 10({}_5p_{70}) + 5({}_5p_{75}).$

The value of L_{85+} is estimated as $L_{85+} = l_{85}\,(\log l_{85})$.

All other functions are then calculated in the usual manner.

It may, however, be noted that the life table so prepared will be affected by the model life table used in smoothing the age data. Further, life tables so constructed are very sensitive to high growth rates over 3.5 and to mortality when $e^\circ_\circ$ exceeds 60. The countries with $e^\circ_\circ$ of 60 and more are developed ones and they have already reliable data on mortality. The main use of the Arriaga's method is that one can use it where practically no mortality data or accurate mortality data exists.

3.8. Model Life Tables

The study of mortality trends have shown that changes in mortality are not unrelated. There is a typical age pattern of mortality irrespective of the level with some variations. Several authors have attempted to derive age patterns of mortality by condensing the experiences of actual population as evinced by their life tables. A typical life table giving set of probabilities of dying at different ages corresponding to a given level of mortality ($e^\circ_\circ$) has been called *model life table.* The use of 'model' is however confusing. In many statistically under developed countries, it is almost impossible to get an over all picture of mortality and to construct a life table. A set of model life tables ideally depicting the average age patterns of mortality for different levels may be of immense help to construct life tables for such countries if the level of mortality is indirectly estimated. The model life tables are also useful to visualize the change in mortality in future even in the case of developed countries.

There are four sets of Model Life tables which are in common use. The United Nations Model Life Tables; Coale and Demeny's Regional Model Life Tables, Lender man's system of Model Life Tables and the Logit System of Model Life Tables. Recently U.N. has published a new set of model life tables for the developing countries.

3.8.1. U.N. Model Life Tables

These tables were prepared on the basis of 158 life tables collected from a wide selection of countries and representing different periods of time. The fact that mortality in an age group depends on the mortality of the preceding age group led to derive model life tables by age and sex using chain parobolic regressions of probabilities of dying starting from q_0. By fitting through the method of least squares, a second degree parabola of the type $y=a+bx+cx^2$, a relationship was developed between the mortality rates of the successive age groups. Thus, the value of ${}_4q_1$ was estimated from a value of q_0 and the value of ${}_5q_5$ was estimated from the calculated value of ${}_4q_1$, which in turn serves as an estimator of ${}_5q_{10}$ and so on until the life table is completed. A system of model life tables were thus derived corresponding to the values of q_0=20, 25, ..., 100 and thereafter q_0=110, 120, ..., 330. The U.N. Model Life tables so prepared cover the range of expectation of life at birth from 20 to 73.9 years (for males and females combined). Upto age 55, the tables are spaced at intervals of 2.5 years in terms of e_0° . Intervals beyond e_0° =55 have been used to reflect a hypothetical typical course of mortality decline in mortality over time. The successive tables are representing the maximum expected decline of mortality over periods of 5 calendar years.

The U.N. Model life tables were extensively used for projections and for analysing the population data of countries where mortality tables were either lacking or unreliable. The construction of these tables has however, been criticised on several grounds, mainly for the use of infant mortality as the starting point of the construction of life table and the bias introduced by the use of chain parabolic regressions. Further the set of 158 life tables used to calculate regression equations are not representative of the whole range of reliably recorded human mortality experience. This included even the life tables of India, wherein the child mortality values were essentially extrapolations from a set of mortality values at the older ages and hence cannot be regarded as indicative of reliably recorded mortality experience. These tables are now not appropriate to represent mortality patterns of the populations,

3.8.2. Coale and Demeny's Model Life Tables

In order to meet the need for more elaborate and comprehensive model system of life tables, Coale and Demeny (1967) published their well known Regional Model Life Tables consisting of 4 sets of model life tables, labelled as 'West', 'East', 'North' and 'South'. These names were chosen because most of the life tables on which observations were based came from the relevant regions of Europe. Each set contains 24 tables calculated for males and females separately, with equal spacing of the values of the expectation of life at birth for females from $e_0^\circ = 20$ years (level 1) to $e_0^\circ = 77.5$ (level 24). The mortality level shown in the male tables differs from that of the female tables with which they are paired, indicating the typical relationship between mortality levels of male and females in a particular population. These model tables are based on the experience of 326 male and 326 female life tables, which are based on data originated from continuous registration and census returns and satisfied the criterion of selection laid down by the authors.

Among the four sets of model tables, the 'East', 'North' and 'South' models are based on relatively small collections of tables and they are typically of a regional character. The 'East' tables are based on Central European Experience, where as "North' and 'South' tables were developed from the life tables of Scandinavian and South European Countries. The 'West' tables are however representative of broad residual group based on 125 life tables from over 20 countries including Canada, United States, South Africa, Israel, Japan, Taiwan and a number of countries of West Europe. The 'West' model has a mortality pattern of an average world pattern and hence can be used as an overall one parameter average pattern of mortality. The 'North' set shows a relatively low old age mortality, and also low infant mortality as compared with rates at ages

1 to 4. The East' pattern shows high rates at infancy and old age. 'South' set shows higher rates at 1-4 and low rates in the late middle ages. The calculations of model life tables for each set were based on the double system of regression equations, namely linear and logarithmic regression equations between e°_{10} and the ${}_nq_x$ values, of the type ${}_nq_x = A_x + B_x e^{\circ}_{10}$ and $\log {}_nq_x = A_x^1 + B_x^1 e^{\circ}_{10}$. For one initial values of q_0 one finds therefore four different values of ${}_5q_x$ depending on the pattern (or family) of mortality by age.

The U.N. system of model life tables was developed before the wide spread use of computers in the demographic studies and consequently life tables could be generated for only 24 selected mortality levels. As compared to the U.N. System, regional model life tables published by Coale and Demeny are more extensive. Derived measures of several kinds are given for the use of model stable populations given thereby. The existence of several tabulated measures make the Coale and Demeny system easy to use. In general, 'East', 'North' and 'South' models should be used only after verifying that the age pattern of mortality has the peculiarities characterising these three models. Otherwise the 'West' model is recommended for the use. In case of India, whore e°_{0} for females is lower than that of males, usually west model was found suitable. However, it is found that childhood mortality show quite different pattern in case of India than observed in any of these sets of models.

3.8.3. Ledermann's Model Life Tables

Ledermann (1969) published 7 sets of model life tables (both one and two parameter life tables) based on 154 life tables that had greater geographical coverage. This basic method is again a regression model of the type

$$\log {}_nq_x = a_{x0} + a_{x1} \log {}_nq_j$$

and

$$\log {}_nq_x = b_{x0} + b_{x1} \log {}_nq_i + b_{x2} \log {}_nq_j$$

The seven tables are based on seven different measures of mortality such as e_o^3, q_o, ${}_5q_0$, ${}_{15}q_0$, ${}_{20}q_{30}$, ${}_{20}q_{35}$, and m_{50+}. Thus one has a choice of using the most easily available or most reliable piece of information about mortality as the basis of regression estimates of the rest of the life table.

Ledermann's tables are also empirically based. The historical series included are entirely from Europe but are given less weight than in the Coale and Demeny models. Observations fromLatin America, Asia and Eastern Europe are given greater representations in Ledermann's Model.

Ledermann's tables are no doubt the more refined sets of model life tables than the U.N. and Coale and Demmey's model life tables, but they are not easy to use as the choice of the life table becomes difficult when the input parameters cannot be reliably estimated.

3.8.4. The Logit System of Model Life Tables

An emirical study of the relationship between the logits of l_x values of different life tables showed this relationship to be linear. This prompted Brass to relate the logit of observed $l_{(x)}$ to the logit of same $l_{(x)}^s$ of a standard life table by the equation

where $$\text{logit } l_{(x)} = \alpha + \beta \text{ . logit } l_x^s$$

or $$y_{(x)} = \alpha + \beta \text{ . } y_{(x)}^s$$

where $$\text{logit } l_{(x)} = \frac{1}{2} \log_e \frac{l_{(x)}}{1 - l_{(x)}}$$

and $$-\text{logit } l_{(x)} = \text{logit } [1 - l_{(x)}]$$

and $y_{(x)} = \text{logit } l_{(x)}$ of population, $y_{(x)}^s$ is the logit of l_x^s the function of standard population. If α and β are known, the table of the study population can be derived with the help of standard life tables, Ideally, the standard life table should be chosen so as to match the typical characteristics of the age pattern of mortality of the population under study. If one is interested to find out changes in mortality of any population over time or the differences in the mortality rates of different regions within a country, one of the life tables under study will be 'ideal' standard. In case of developing societies, it is however, unlikely to get reasonably accurate life tables which can form the base.

As such, we should have a standard life table which is a kind of 'average'. Such a general standard has been constructed, using with adjustment, one of the U.N. average patterns of mortality (Brass, 1971). The original general standard has been slightly modified by Hobcroft to give smoother mortality patterns at the older ages. Extensive use has been made of the so called 'African' standard depicting high rate of mortality in the second and third years of life compared with infant mortality. The usefulness of the African standard base has been established by the publication of Stable Population Models (Carrier and Hobcraft, 1971) and derived measures of the subsystem based on them for the one parameter set with β equal to one and also selected features of the two parameter set. Advantage of the logit system is however on retaining the maximum amount of flexibility and on using any specific standard only when its applicability to the population under study is well established.

In the logit system, $y'_{(x)}$ is zero, when $l'_x = 0.5$ and then $y_{(x)} = \alpha$. A positive value of α in this situation will mean that in the study population $1_{(x)} = .5$ will be reached at an early age than the standard life table. Negative value of α implies that the population under study has experienced much higher level of mortality than the standard table. Thus α may be regarded as measure of the level of mortality. The other parameter β is the scale parameter. If $\beta = 1$ the difference $y_{(x)} - y'_{(x)} = \alpha$ implying that $l_{(x)} - l'_{(x)} =$ constant for any value of x. $\beta > 1$ implies rapid decline in the number of survivors in the study population with age. The opposite holds for $\beta < 1$. Thus β influences the slope of the life table and reflects the change in the underlying mortality pattern. Varying β changes the relationship between the mortality at older and younger ages. Theoretically α may have a positive or negative value but β must always be positive. Emirically it has been found that α ranging between 1.0 and -1.5 and β between 0.6 and 1.6 produce model tables which give reasonable fits to most of the observed mortality data. The parameters α and β may de estimated from the reliable estimates of childhood survival, $p(2)$ and an overall estimate of adult mortality in the form of $p(30)$ or $p(50)$ given the accepted value of $p(2)$. The values of α and β can then be estimated using

$$\text{logit } p(2) = \alpha + \beta \text{ logit } p^s(2)$$

$$\text{logit } p(50) = \alpha + \beta \text{ logit } p^s(50)$$

where suffix s denotes the values of the standard table. The transformation of the standard table with estimated values of α and β will generate a life table of the study population.

It has been, however, found that logit transformation keeps intact the mortality pattern of standard population chosen. The procedure suggested by Brass to construct the life table through the logit transformation is usually applied to the mortality data obtained from the surveys. If the reported adult mortality is not consistent, β may be taken as unity, otherwise model can be modified accordingly. Apparently the logit system of model life tables are better than the earlier existing models, but its use in the developing countries is quite limited because of unreliable estimates of $p(2)$ and $p(5)$. Only future researches in this direction can throw light on its prospective value.

3.8.5. U.N. Model Life Tables for Developing Countries

Coale and Demeny Model life tables published in 1966 have become the most commonly used sets of model life tables by the Demographers. Recent evidences, however, indicate that the age patterns of mortality in many developing countries differ systematically from those of the historical experience of European countries and hence the Coale and Demeny model tables are found not suitable for the demographic studies in the developing countries. United Nations (1982) has given some new sets of age–sex patterns of mortality which are based on reliably documented developing country data and hence are expected to describe better the age pattern of mortality in the developing world. The model life tables have been constructed after careful analysis and evaluation of available data on mortality. First, the different age patterns of mortality were stratified into clusters by graphical and statistical procedures, each cluster having a typical average age pattern of mortality. A principal component model was then fitted to the deviations of each age pattern of mortality from its own cluster average. The age pattern of mortality for each observed life table characterised by the vector of logit $({}_nq_x)$; the cluster average as the arithmetic average of logit $({}_nq_x)$ values within the cluster and the deviations of each pattern from its cluster average as the arithmetic differences for each age group. In all cases the age groups involved were 0 – 1, 1 – 4, 5—9, 10—14, ... 80 – 84. For clear pattern groups and a few life tables not clearly belonging to any other group were identified. The four patterns are labelled as the Latin American pattern and the Far Eastern pattern according to the geographical region which is predominent within each pattern group. The Life tables from Israel, Kuwait and for the female population of Hong Kong and the Republic of Korea did not conform to any pattern identified and hence were excluded from the principal component analysis and included only in construction of the general pattern of mortality forming the fifth pattern. The male and female Life tables are presented for each of the five patterns (the four regional patterns plus the general pattern) for life expectancies at birth between 35 years and 75 years at one year increments. The Life tables consist of 9 columns including age, central death rate $({}_nm_x)$, ${}_nq_x$, l_x, ${}_nD_n$, ${}_nL_n$, T_n, e°_n and ${}_na_n$. For ages 15 and over, the expression for ${}_na_x$ is derived using Greville's results.

$$_na_x = 2.5 - \frac{25}{12}\ (_nm_x - k)$$

where
$$k = \frac{1}{10}\ l_n\ (_nm_{x+5}/_nm_{x-5})$$

For ages 5 and 10, $_na_x = 2.5$ and for ages under 5, $_na_x$ values from the Coale and Demeny West Region relationships are used. With $_nq_x$ as input, the procedure is identical except that an iteractive procedure is used to find $_nm_x$ and $_nq_x$ consistent with the given $_nq_x$ in the Greville expression. To complete the life table the last six $_nq_x$ values are used to fit the Makeham type expression. $_nq_x/(l - {_nq_x}) = A + BC^x$. Using this curve $_nq_x$ values are extrapolated until there are no survivours remaining. These extrapolated $_nq_x$ values are converted to l_x and $_nL_x$ values with appropriate separation factors and $_nL_x$ added up to obtain the final T_x. The probabilities of dying by single years of age under 5 are also presented. They are calculated according to the 3 parameter interpolation equation.

$$l_n\ (_1q_x) = -t_1\ (x + t_2)t_3$$

The values of t_1, t_2 and t_3 were solved so as to reproduce tbe $_1q_0$, $_4q_1$ and $_5q_5$ values of the given model life table.

These life tables are quite useful in estimating childhood mortality through Brass type methods to be discussed later on. It is expected that these new life table models might describe better the age patterns of mortality in the developing countries. However, it has been found that the age pattern of mortality in case of India (1971) is not fully covered by the South Asian pattern even though Indian life table of 1971 was included in the construction of these life tables. There is, therefore, a need of preparing detailed regional model life tables, which can take into consideration more peculiarities of the pattern for their construction. Since data an mortality are becoming available, there may be no need to use model life lables in future.

3.9. Applications of Life Table in Demographic Studies

The life table model and life table technique as special tool for measuring mortality are also used in the study of fertility, reproductivity, migration and population structure. It is widely used in the estimation and projection of population size, structure and change at a future date. There are several ways in which life table technique may be utilised. Some of the uses are being given below :

1. *Analysis of Mortality.* The most common use of a life table is to measure the level of mortality in terms of a summary measure $e^\circ_\circ$; the life table death rate $\left(m=\frac{1}{e^\circ_\circ}\right)$ which is unaffected by the age composition of the population, whose age composition is described by ${}_nL_x$ column and age specific death rates are given by ${}_nm_x$ column. Sometimes, the value e°_1, the expectation of life at age, is used to represent overall level of mortality in conjuction with infant mortality q_0 because $e^\circ_\circ$ is highly affected by the level of infant mortality. In order to measure old age mortality, e°_{65} has also been commonly used. Model life tables may be used to evaluate the quality of mortality data of the developing countries. The measures based on the life table may also be used to study variations in the mortality over time, between population groups, by age, sex, marital status, residence or by any other demographic characteristics having effect on mortality.

2. *Measurement of Morbidity and Health.* Life table technique has been used to estimate the risks of contracting a disease or acquire specific inability. The technique may be used for analysing hospital stays after the patient is admitted where hospital admission can be regarded as birth and discharge from the hospital as death. Other functions of such a life table can be interpreted accordingly.

3. *Analysis of Mortality by Cause of Death.* Life tables have been prepared showing the number of deaths at various ages by cause and the probabilities of death by various causes at each age. Such a life table with two or more factors (causes of death) of decrement is called multiple decrement life table. It can be used to estimate the gain in life expectancy in case of elimination of a specific cause of death alongwith estimation of reduction in mortality risks by age. Multiple decrement life table can also be used to study variations in mortality due to different causes overtime or between different population groups.

4. *Life Table Survival Rates.* Survival rate give the probability of surviving of a person from an younger age to an older age group. The survival rate for a person in age group $(x, x+n)$ for further Z years is given by :

$$_zS_{(x,\ x+n)}=\frac{_nL_{x+z}}{_nL_x}$$

The commonly used survival rates in demographic studies are for 5 years age groups. It is given by

$$_5S_{(x),\ x+5)}=\frac{_5L_{x+5}}{_5L_x}$$

and the probability of survival from birth to age group $(x, x+5)$ can be expressed as

$$\frac{_5L_x}{5.l_0}$$

These survival rates are very useful in projecting the future population.

5. *Estimation of Migration.* Assuming that the population is closed to migration during the intercensal period, the population at the latter census can be obtained as

survivors of the population in different age groups existing at the previous census (except the child population). The difference of the estimate of survivors and the actually counted population in different age groups can be treated as an estimate of intercensal net migration by age in the population. The details of using life table survivorship rates for estiming net migration are discussed in the Chapter on Migration.

6. *Analysis of Fertility and Reproductivity and Age Structure.* Age-specific fertility rates multiplied by life table survival rates from birth to the particular age of the mother give net reproduction rate when summed up over the entire range of reproductive life. Life tables can be used to study relationship between age structure, mortality and fertility. One can know the effect of changing levels of mortality on age structure of the population. Life table is in itself a stationary population with a given level of mortality and zero growth rate. Life table techniques are also used to analyse data on open and closed birth intervals or delay in having conception by a mother.

7. *Evaluation of Family Planning Programme.* Life table technique has been found very useful for studying the continuation of IUD after insertions. The joint survivorship probabilities of couples have been utilised in calculating the users of a particular method of family planning at any future date.

8. *Analysis of Socio-economic Structure and Dynamics.* In addition to analysis of mortality by cause, multiple decrement life tables have been prepared for the analysis of the labour force, marital composition and educational status. Following tables have been commonly studied.

(*a*) *Nuptiality Tables.* A detailed discussion of nuptiality tables is given in the Chapter on Nuptiality. In a nuptiality table two factors of decrement by age operate on a population of singles. These tables provide information on the proportion of the single population who ever marry, the average age at marriage and the average years of single life. Life table can be constructed also for the married women to combine mortality of both the sexes so as to compute the probability of becoming a widow or widower and the average length of marital life.

(*b*) *Working Life Table.* By considering the factors of mortality and labour force participation rates working life tables can be prepared to provide information on expected number of working years to a person in the labour force at any age along with the age specific rates of accession to, and separation from the labour force. There are several ways of constructing a working life table. The procedure generally is to use the life table stationary population and then derive the distribution of population according to the observed work status.

(*c*) *School Life Table.* The School life table combines mortality rates and school enrollment rates to provide estimates of the average number of years of school life for the total population and the enrolled population. This table is also a type of combined increment-decrement table like the working life table.

The detailed discussion of the multiple decrement life tables is outside the scope of the present book.

4

Measures of Fertility and Reproduction

4.1. Definition, Concepts and Need

Fertility is defined as the child bearing performance of a woman or a group of women measured in terms of the actual number of children born. Age at which the woman starts child-bearing in most of the societies, begins with the onset of ovulatory menstruation cycle or the marriage date whichever is later and ends with the attainment of menopause or secondary sterility (natural or voluntary) whichever is earlier. On an average, the reproductive life span of a woman extends over the ages between 15 to 50 years. Again not all the women in their reproductive life can bear children as some of them are not fecund. Fecundity of the woman is her physiological capacity to reproduce or to conceive. Some of the women who do not have this physiological capacity from the beginning of their reproductive life are called as primarily sterile. Sterility is the opposite of fecundity. Sometimes, women may be fecund initially but subsequently may be rendered permanently infecund and become secondary sterile. Childlessness of a married woman may not be always due to her infecundity. This may be either due to sterility of either of the spouses or due to some incompatability in bearing the child by the couple or due to even voluntary control on child bearing by the couple. Actual number of children born to a woman is far below the maximum number of children implied by fecundity due to incidence of foetal losses and still births on the one hand and use of contraception, induced abortion and the practice of breast feeding on the other hand. Like mortality, process of human reproduction is also a biological process but it is more complex as within the limits set by the physiological factors, it is affected by a host of social, cultural economic and psychological factors. The number of births occuring in a population in a year is determined partly by the demographic factors such as age and sex composition of the population, number of married women and their distribution within the reproductive age span by age, duration of marriage and the number of children already born to them; and partly by many socio-economic, cultural and psychological factors of that time, such as, housing conditions, education, income, religion, occupation, their current attitude towards family size, practice of contraception and induced abortion etc.

Fertility is the most important factor in the study of population dynamics. The excess of births over the deaths occuring in any human population over a given period of time determines its natural growth. Thus fertility is responsible for the biological maintenance of population being continuously depleted by martality. It not only affects the size of a population but also affects its age and sex structure. The age composition of population closed to migration is determined by the prevailing fertility and mortality levels of the population in the past. Any change in the level of fertility immediately affects the young age population and hence the whole age distribution of the population. On the other hand, mortality affects the population of all the ages and therefore, any change in the level of mortality does not disrupt the age structure so significantly. With fertility level remaining constant and mortality declining, the more and more children survive longer and the population becomes younger and younger. On the other hand if the fertility declines, the population necessarily becomes older because of the decrease in the child population. Effects of decline in mortality is very little on the middle ages. Of course, decline in fertility coupled with decline in mortality would necessarily increase the proportion of older population.

Spurt in the growth of population of most of the developing countries caused mainly due to the spectacular decline in their mortality after 1950 till sixties necessitated the launching of the family planning programmes by most of the governments in the developing world to bring down the level of their fertility. Unlike reduction in mortality, to achieve decline in fertility beyond some limits is, however not so easy. In fact, fertility is a more complex phenomena than studied so far and this complexity has made the study of fertility all the more significant and challenging in the recent past. A number of studies including the World Fertility Survey of the mid seventies speak of its importance.

Sometimes a more gerneral term "natality" is used to represent the role of births in the population change and human reproduction. In a more restricted sense, fertility analysis refers to certain refined measures of natality. Further a distinction must be made between fertility and reproduction. While fertility analysis deals only with the child bearing activity of a population, reproduction deals with the ability of a population to replace itself and to grow. The terms natality, fertility and births generally refer to total live-births, henceforth called births. W.H.O. defines live birth as a complete expulsion or extraction from its mother of a product of conception, irrespective of the duration of pregnancy, which after such separation breathes, or shows any other evidence of life, such as beating of the heart etc. As such still births, miscarriages and abortions are types of foetal death and hence different from the live birth.

The basic data for fertility studies come from (1) the vital statistics registration system, (2) national censuses and (3) sample surveys or national registers. While the vital statistics registration system provides data on births registered in a given period of time, the censuses and surveys may provide both direct and indirect information on fertility. Census provides data on age distribution of the population from which recent level of fertility can be inferred, in addition to some direct information on the number of births in the last one year and children ever born to the women by their ages and other characteristics. Demographic surveys, however, provide more detailed data on fertility, such as, number of births in the most recent past, children ever born to women, age at marriage, intervals between the consecutive births, open birth intervals, attitude of women towards family planning, proportion of women using contraceptives, average family size of different socio-economic groups etc. While the latter two systems of the data collection stand on their own providing the estimates of the level of fertility in a population, the registration system alone cannot give the level of fertility unless population size is known from other sources.

Unlike mortality, a considerable number of problems arise while measuring fertility as the frequency of births in a given period of time. Some of these problems are :

1. *Choice of Interval* : For measuring child bearing performance of the women, one may consider either a short time period usually of one calender year or some period of the reproductive life.

2. *Two persons involved* : A birth involves two persons. Thus the measures of births can be defined either by mother's characteristics, or by father's characteristics or by the couple's characteristics. However, the data usually collected, refer to the mother so that it is more customary to define measures of fertility in relation to the mother. This also eliminates the problems in case of the unknown father. Also the reproductive life of

females is almost fixed and shorter. Nevertheless, the procedures adopted in measuring fertility of women can be extended to measure the fertility of males.

3. *Multiple Births* : Incidences of twins and multiple births raise the issue whether the unit of measurement of fertility should be the number of children born or the number of confinements leading to these births. Because of the emphasis in most of the countries on collecting data on number of births rather than on the confinements and also because of small proportion of multiple births among the total births, it is the total births which are considered for measuring fertility.

4. *The Denominator of the Birth Rate* : In case of measuring fertility as a frequency, to find out the population at risk is very difficult. Not all the women in the population are married and not all the married women are capable of bearing child in the given period of time for which fertility is being defined. Further, with increasing proportion of illegal births, the measurment of true level of fertility has become all the more problematic.

5. The distinction between a live birth and a still birth is hard to be made consistently in many cases. The customs of classifying such events vary among the countries.

6. Unlike death, parenthood is an event which can occur more than once. There is thus an element of choice of the parents involved in achieving the family size.

4.2. Approaches to Measure Fertility

There are two main approaches to measure fertility. One approach consists of ascertaining the children ever born to any group of women by some age. This is called cohort fertility. The number of children ever born to a group of women of same age cohort also denotes their cumulative fertility performance upto that age. The second approach refers to ascertaining the reproductive performance in a given period of time (for one year or so) for the women of different age groups (a cross section of women in the reproductive ages). The measures of fertility based on the latter approach are called the period measures. Measures of fertility ascertained for any cohort of women are called measures of cohort fertility. Below we discuss some basic measures of fertility which need data on the number of births and the size of population in that year.

4 3. Basic Measures of Period Fertility

Following are some basic measures of fertility from which a number of other measures can be defined :

1. *Crude Birth-Rate* (*CBR*) : This is the most simplest and commonest measure of the period fertility which requires minimum amount of details of the birth statistics. It is defined as a ratio of the total number of births during a given year to the average (or mid-year) population ever lived in the last year. Symbolically

$$CBR=\frac{B}{P}\times K$$

where B is the total number of live births during a year; P is the average population that lived in that year and is approximated by the total mid-year population in that year; K is a constant and usually taken as 1,000. Thus *CBR* is also defined as the number of births per 1000 mid-year total population. On the basis of the analysis of the birth rates of a number of populations where little or no fertility control was practised, Henry suggested 60 to be the highest birth rate ever possible. Further crude birth rates may be computed for any period, but typically they are computed for a calender year or the 12 month period. In computing the CBR for the geographic sub-divisions of a country, it is preferable to use births allocated by place of usual residence of the parents. Sometimes, an annual average crude birth rate covering data of two or three years is computed in order to cover longer period or to add stability to the rates. When the *CBR* is calculated by using the registered births; the births should be adjusted for their under-registration and the population should be adjusted for the underenumeration provided the satisfactory estimates of these errors are available.

No doubt, the crude birth rate is a valuable measure of fertility because it directly indicates the contribution of births to the natural growth rate of the population, its analytical utility is reduced as it is affected by several factors, particularly the age sex-structure of the population, distributions of married women in the reproductive period and other characteristics of the population. In its calculation, both the populations exposed and not exposed to the risk of births are included and hence it does not conform to the concept of probability and remains a crude measure of fertility. Thus *CBR* cannot be used to compare the levels of fertility for any two populations because they may differ widely in their age-sex compositions and some other characteristics which affect the births. Another major weakness of this measure is that it is not very sensitive to small changes in fertility. In fact, it may tend to minimise the changes occurring in fertility.

2. ***General Fertility Rate*** : General Fertility Rate (*GFR*) is the simplest overall measure of fertility. It is defined as the number of births per year per thousand mid-year women of the child bearing ages.

Symbolically,

$$GFR = \frac{B}{W_{15-44}} \times 1{,}000$$

where W_{15-44} is the total number of women of child bearing age 15 – 44 at the mid point of the year. For the sake of more precision and comparability, the age interval 15 – 44 should be adopted as standard with births under 15 and over 44 allocated to women of ages 15 – 19 and 40 – 44 respectively. Many times, women of 15 – 49 are also considered in the calculation of *GFR* or other related measures. We shall, however, define measures restricted to the age range of 15 – 44 years for the sake of uniformity in our treatment. The chief virtue of the *GFR* is that it includes the female population in their reproductive ages who are supposed to be exposed to the risk of birth and that is why it is much more acceptable measure of fertility than the *CBR*. It is also easy to compute and interpret. However, it also remains a crude measure of fertility because in the denominator, even the unmarried, divorced and widowed women of reproductive ages are included. Nevertheless, to make it more sensitive, it is perferable to relate the births in any year to the currently married women in the reproductive ages and not to all the women. In this way we obtain another refined measure known as general merital fertility rate GMFR which can be defined as number of births per year per 1,000 married women in the reproductive ages. Sympolically,

$$GMFR = \frac{B}{W^{m}_{15-44}} \times 1{,}000$$

where W^m_{15-44} denotes the number of married women in the reproductive ages of 15– 44 years at the middle point of the year.

But again the chance of giving birth for married women is not the same for all the ages within the reproductive ages, hence both the *GFR* and *GMFR* are affected by the distribution of women within the reproductive ages. If we wish to compare the *GFR* or *GMFR* of the two populations which have similar age pattern of fertility, it will be higher for the population which has more concentration of women (or married women) in the ages where fertility is highest. The peak ages of fertility are 20-29 years for most of the populations and hence the concentration of more women in this age group will increase the value of *GFR* and also *GMFR* if the age pattern of marriage is similar. Thus we can not compare directly the *GFR* or *GMFR* for two countries, unless we adjust them for the age distribution of women within the reproductive ages. Further refinement in measure of fertility can, however, be achieved if fertility rates are calculated for specific ages and marital durations.

3. *Age-Specific Fertility Rates* (*ASFR*) : The age pattern of child bearing in any population is best revealed by computing age specific fertility rates. The age specific fertility rate is the number of births per year per woman of a specified age, Symbolically,

$$_nf_x = \frac{_nB_x}{_nW_x}$$

where, $_nf_x$ is the age specific fertility rate of women aged x to $x+n$ years,

$_nW_x$ is the number of women aged x to $x+n$ years at mid-year $_nB_x$ is the number of births in a year to the women of ages x to $x+n$ years. n is usually taken as 5 years.

The age specific fertility rates can be calculated by single years of age or by age intervals of women, usually by five years age intervals. The single year rates may be too detailed and clumsy to comprehend. Further, the set of single yeai age specific rates are more affected by the misreporting of the ages of the women. As such, the *ASFR* are conventionally calculated by the quinquennial age groups 15 – 19, 20 – 24 and 40 – 44. Thus the age specific fertility rate for age group 20-24 may be calculated as

$$ {}_5f_{20} = \frac{{}_5B_{20}}{{}_5W_{20}} $$

There is a characteristic feature of the age pattern of fertility in a population. The curve of the *ASFR* rises (see Figure 1) sharply from zero at about age 15 to a peak in the early or mid 20's depending upon the marriage pattern in the population and thereafter it declines more gradually to reach again to zero at about the age 45 or 50. Age pattern of fertility can be measured also in terms of the median age of the child bearing (median age of the mother) or the mean age of the child bearing. The mean age of the child bearing ($\bar{m}$) can be easily calculated from the knowledge of *ASFRS* :

$$ \bar{m} = \sum_{15}^{40} (x+2.5)\,{}_5f_x \Big/ \sum_{x=15}^{40} {}_5f_x \qquad x = 15, 20, \ldots 40. $$

This is the weighted mean of the ages of child bearing, weights being the age specific fertility rates.

It is generally observed that in a population of high fertility, the mean age of fertility schedule is usually high and a large fraction of women continues to bear children in the latter years of childbearing. However, in case of the population with low fertility, child bearing (even if it starts late) stops earlier for most of the women and therefore the mean age of fertility is lower.

The age specific fertility rates as measure of fertility may be further improved by considering only the currently married women and we can define an anologous measure, that is age specific marital fertility rate (*ASMFR*), which would denote the number of births per year per currently married women, at the mid years as follows :

$$_ng_x = \frac{_nB_x}{_nW_x^M}$$

$$= \frac{_nB_x}{_nW_x} \times \frac{_nW_x}{_nW_x^M}$$

$$_ng_x = {_nf_x}/{_nM_x}$$

where $_nM_x$ is the proportion of married women at ages x to $x+n$.

The *ASMFR* does not suffer from the variations in to marriage patterns and hence can be directly used for the comparison of the child bearing performances of women in any two populations. No doubt, when these rates are calculated by 5 years age groups, age composition of the women within each age group might affect these rates. In practice, however, this effect will be quite small and can be ignored.

While the set of age specific fertility or age specific marital fertility rates do provide the detailed picture of the variation in fertility by age we need composite and summary measure of fertility to indicate the level of fertility which does not suffer from the effects of variation in either age-sex composition or in distribution of the women within the reproductive span or age pattern of marriage so that it can be used for comparing the fertility levels of two populations. Total fertility rate defined below is one such measure.

4. *Total Fertility Rate.* This is an over-all summary measure of fertility and is obtained by summing the age specific

fertility rate for each age of the child bearing span. Symbolically,

$$TFR = \sum_x f_x \qquad \text{for } x = 15, 16, \ldots\ldots, 44$$

$$= 5 * \sum_x {}_5f_x \qquad \text{for } x = 15, 20, \ldots\ldots, 40$$

Thus the total fertility rate is the number of children which a woman of hypothetical cohort would bear during her life time if she were to bear children through out her life at the rates specified by the schedule of age specific fertility rates for the particular year and if none of them dies before crossing the age of reproduction. This rate is not affected by the age structure of the women under study and at the same time it measures the level of current fertility as it is obtained only by summing the current age specific fertility rates by giving equal weight of unity for each age. It is thus standardized for age and can be regarded as a standardised (direct) measure of fertility. Being a summary measure it is also an alternative to *GFR*. It has, however, the advantage over the *GFR* since it is standardised for age. Thus *TFR*s of any number of populations can be used to compare their fertility levels because all the *TFR*s are based on the same age composition of the women. The *TFR* may also be viewed as representing the completed fertility of a synthetic cohort of women.

When only a count of total births is available, and tabulation of births by age of the mother is lacking, the indirect method of arriving the *TFR* may be used :

$$TFR = \frac{B}{\sum_x {}_5f_x' \, W_x} \times TFR'$$

where TFR' and ${}_5f_x'$ are the *TFR* and *ASFR* for the standard population.

Mostly the *TFR* is calculated for one woman but where it is calculated for 1000 women, it should be specifically mentioned. Some demographers calculate a similar measure known as the gross reproduction rate (*GRR*) by taking into consideration only the female births. In otherwords, the *GRR* is calculated by summing the age specific female birth rates. If we multiply *TFR* by the proportion of female births among all the births, we obtain a very close approximation to *GRR*. Symbolically

$$GRR = \sum_{x=15} \left[\frac{{}_5B^f_x}{{}_5W_x} \right]$$

$$= TFR \times \text{proportion of female births}$$

$$= \frac{TFR}{1+SRB}$$

where $5B^{\prime}_{2}$ denoted the number of female babies born to women of age x to $x + 5$ in a year and *SRB* is the number of male baby per female baby.

GRR indicates the number of daughters ever born to a woman by the end of the reproductive life if she bears the births according to a given schedule of age specific fertility rates without experiencing any mortality till the end of her reproductive life. It may be defined as the ratio of female births expected in two successive generations under the given fertility schedule assuming no mortality. This is an important measure of replacement which indicates the number of girls who will replace the existing cohort of born girls in one generation if there is no attrition in the size of cohort due to mortality and if they continue to experience the same age specific fertility rates as of the particular year. In otherwords, this measures the capacity of women to replace themselves as implied by the set of current fertility rates without taking into consideration the effect of mortality. Later on we will however, discuss, in details another measure known as net reproduction rate (*NRR*) which is a better index of the reproduction as it accounts for the effect of mortality as well.

5. *Age-Cumulative Fertility Rate* (*ACFR*). Utilising the concept of a hypothetical cohort of women bearing children throughout their lives at the rate specified by the *ASFRS* for a particular year, we can also calculate the cumulative child bearing performance of the cohort by some age by simply cumulating the *ASFR* for all ages upto the desired age. We can also find out some measures showing the timing of fertility by ascertaining the percentage of the total life time fertility that cohort will achieve by certain age; or by obtaining cumulative percentage of the total fertility achieved by the given age. The timing of fertility can also be ascertained by calculating the mean or median age of fertility as discussed earlier.

STANDARDISED RATES AND INDICES OF FERTILITY

As mentioned earlier, some measures of fertility such as crude birth rate, general fertility rate and general marital fertility rate cannot be used directly for comparing the levels of fertility of two populations as they may have different age and sex structures. The analysis of time trends and or the group fertility differences is facilitated by eliminating, as completely as possible, the effect of differences in the age sex composition of the population being compared. On the other hand, the measures like *TFR* and *GRR* (also *TMFR*) are quite useful measures for comparing the levels of fertility of different populations as they are already standardised for the age composition of the females in the population. Some times, some indices of fertility can however, be developed by relating the observed number of births to the expected number of births by assuming that the females experience age specific fertility rates as applicable to some standard population. Some of these standardised rates and indices are discussed below :

Age-sex Adjusted Birth Rate. Like standardised death rate we can standardize the birth rate as below :

(*a*) Direct age standardised birth rate

$$= \sum_{15} ASFR_x \cdot W_x^s \,/\, P^s$$

(*b*) Indirect age-standardised birth rate

$$= \frac{B \times CBR^s}{\sum\limits_{15} ASFR^s_x \cdot W_x} \times 1000$$

The notations have usual meaning and suffix's refers to a standard population. It may be noted that the directly standardised birth rate will be of the same order as the *CBR*. If the standardised birth rate is more than the *CBR*, it only shows that the age structure of the population under study is less favourable to fertility as compared to the age structure of the female population in the standard population. If b_1 and b_2 denote the standardised birth rates (direct) of the two populations; $b_1 - b_2$ easily gives the difference between the levels of fertility of the two populations if they were to have the age structure of the standard population (generally chosen). Birth rates standardised by the indirect method are useful when the age specific fertility rates for the population under study are lacking or defective.

The table 1 illustrates the procedure of computing standardised birth rates by direct and indirect methods. The general fertility rate can also be standardised as below :

(*i*) Directly age standardised *GFR*

$$= \left[\sum_{x=15}^{44} {}_5f_x \ W^s_x \Big/ \sum_{x=15}^{44} W^s_x \right] \times 1000$$

(*ii*) Indirectly age standardised *GFR*

$$= \frac{B}{\sum\limits_{x} {}^5f^s_x \ast W_x} \ast GFR^s$$

In the above formula f_x denotes the age specific fertility rate at age x (per woman). United Nations has devised another method of indirectly standardising the birth rate for the age and sex where only the total number of births and the age distribution of women in the quinquennial age groups of the reproductive span, 15 to 44 are available. The U.N. sex age adjusted birth rate (*SAABR*) can be expressed as :

$$SAABR = \frac{B}{\sum_{i} w_i \, W_i} \times 1000$$

where w_i is the standard weight for the age group i ($i=1, 2, \ldots 6$, starting with age group 15–19) in the reproductive span and W_i is the number of women in the *i*th age group. *SAABR* may thus be interpreted as the number of births per 1,000 of the weighted sum of the woman in the age group 15 to 44. The standard set of weights are selected on the basis of average percentage distribution of the age specific fertility rates of 52 countries representing both the low and high fertility countries so as to represent the relative fertility rates by age. These weights are 1, 7, 7, 6, 4, 1 for the age groups 15–19, 20–24, 25–29, 30–34, 35–39 and 40–44 respectively. The absolute values of these weights are selected in the manner such that the sum of their products with the corresponding numbers of women in the various age groups is of the order of the total population and *SAABR* is of the order of *CBR*. In calculation of the U.N. *SAABR*, one does not need to select a standard population. Further it is simple to compute. The method of calculation is illustrated in the table 1. The set of standard weight may vary overtime and place. The change in the *SAABR* is, however, not significant.

CBR for country $A = 17295000/439000000 \times 1000$

$= 39.396$ per thousand population

CBR for country $B = \dfrac{1239 \times 1000}{34700}$

$= 35.706$ births per thousand population.

TABLE 4.1

Calculation of ASPR, GRR, SAABR, Standardised Birth Rates and TFR for Countries A and B, 1971

Age Group	*Female Population (in ,000) of Country*		*Births in (,000) in 1971 for Country*		*ASFR of Country*			
	A	*B*	*A*	*B*	*A*	*B*		
	W_x^A	W_x^B	B_x^A	B_x^B	${}_5f_x^A \times 1000$	${}_5f_x^B \times 1000$	$f_x^B * W_x^A$	${}_5f_x^A * W_x^B$
(1)	*(2)*	*(3)*	*(4)*	*(5)*	*(6)*	*(7)*	*(8)*	*(9)*
15—19	17263	1271	1683	107	97.49	84.19	1453303	193912
20—24	16799	1312	4595	358	273.53	272.87	4583876	358869
25—29	16343	1337	4632	361	283.42	270.01	4412724	378938

30—34	14453	1170	3284	221	227.22	188.89	2730013	265845
35—39	12622	1055	1908	134	151.16	127.01	1603171	159478
40—44	10795	876	892	42	82.61	47.95	517566	72385
45—49	8584	721	281	16	32.74	22.19	190479	23602

Total Population of Country *A*=439 million and total Population of Country *B* =34.7 million in 1971.

$$GFR^{(A)} = \frac{17295 \times 1000}{96859}$$

= 178.558 births per thousand women in age group 15 − 49 years.

$$GFR^{(B)} = \frac{1239 \times 1000}{7742}$$

= 160.036 births per thousand women in age group 15 − 49 years.

$$SAABR\ (A) = \frac{\text{Births for country } A \times 1000}{\Sigma\, w_i \quad W_i^A}$$

where $\sum w_i \quad W_i^A = 1 \times 17263 + 7 \times 16799$

$+ 7 \times 16343 + 6 \times 14453 + 4 \times 12622 + 1 \times 10795 = 397258$

$$SAABR\ (A) = \frac{17295 \times 1000}{397258}$$

= 43.536 per thousand population

Similarly $SABBR\ (B)\ \dfrac{1239 \times 1000}{31930}$

= 38.3804 per thousand population

$TFR\ (A) = 5\ \Sigma ASFR$

$= 5 \times 1148.193$

= 5740.965 per 1000 women

= 5.74 per women

$TFR\ (B) = 5 \times 1013.097$

= 5065.485 per 1000 women

= 5.065 per women

Standardised Birth Rate for *B* (Direct) by treating Population of country *A* as standard

$$=\frac{\text{Sum of column (8)}}{\text{Population of } A}$$

$$=\frac{15521278}{439000000}\times 1000$$

$$=35.356$$

Standardised B.R. for *B* (Indirect)

$$=\frac{\left(\sum B_x^B\right).\,CBR^A}{\text{sum of col. 9}}$$

$$=\frac{1239000\times 39.396}{1383029.8}=35.293$$

Indices of fertility. A.J. Coale has devised certain indices for expressing the level of fertility in ways that show the contribution of Malthusian and neo-malthusian factors. Low fertility caused by the reduction in proportions married can be called Malthusian low fertility and if it is caused by the birth control, it can be called neo Malthusian low-fertility. Low levels of fertility are actually achieved in most of the instances by the mix of Malthusian and neo-Malthusian limitations modified by two complicating considerations :

(*a*) Non-married women do not usually have zero fertility;

(*b*) In the absence of birth control, marital fertility does not reach the same high level in every population due to variation in the social and cultural factors, in addition to the differences in biological components of fertility.

Coale chose the standard schedules of births per married woman in each age group (highest possible in case of the uncontrolled fertility prevailing among the Hutterite women during 1921-1930 and as reported by Henry) as below.

Age group :	15-19	20-24	25-29	30-34	35-39	40-44	45-49
ASMFR :	.300	0.550	.502	.447	.406	.222	.061

Coale defined the following four indices

Index of over all fertility (I_f)

$$=\frac{\Sigma f_i W_i}{\Sigma F_i W_i}$$

Index of marital fertility (I_g)

$$=\frac{\Sigma g_i m_i}{\Sigma F_i m_i}$$

Index of fertility of non-married women (I_h)

$$=\frac{\Sigma h_i U_i}{\Sigma F_i U_i}$$

Index of the proportion married (I_m)

$$=\frac{\Sigma F_i m_i}{\Sigma F_i W_i}$$

where

i =1, 2, ... 7

f_i =births per woman in the ith quinquennial age group of the reproductive span starting from 15−19,

F_i =births per woman in the ith age group in the standard population

g_i =births per married woman in the ith age group

h_i =births per non-married woman in the ith age group

W_i, m_i and U_i denote the number of women, married women and non-married women respectively in the ith age group.

The index of overall fertility is the ratio of the observed number of births in the given population to the number of births in the given population that would occur if the women in each age group experienced the age specific marital fertility rate of the standard population (which can be any population). The index of marital fertility is the ratio of the number of births occurring to married women to the number that would occur if married women experienced the standard fertility schedule. The index of fertility of the non-married woman has also similar meaning. The index of the proportion married (among the women of child bearing age) is the ratio of the number of children that married women would bear if subjected to the standard fertility schedule to the number that all womenwould bear with the same fertility schedule It is a weighted index of the proportion married with large weight being given to those married women who are in the peak fertility ages and small weight to the married women above the age 40. All the four indices are related to each other in the following form :

$$I_f = I_g \cdot I_m + (1 - I_m)\, I_h$$

I_g shows the extent to which marital fertility falls short of the maximum reflecting neo-Malthusian fertility reduction; I_m shows the extent to which marriage is less than the universal and thus reflects the effect of Malthusian fertility reduction. In societies, where fertility of the non-married women is negligible, we have $I_f = I_g \cdot I_m$, which factorises the index of fertility into Malthusian and neo-Malthusian components. We can see that the above indices can easily be utilised for ascertaining the mechanism of changes in fertility. It is observed that changes in fertility due to change in age at marriage generally occurs below the age of 30 and reduction in fertility beyond age 30 is mainly because of the contraception. Hence it will be more appropriate if the above indices are defined separately for below age 30 and above age 30 and so also the *TFR* and *TMFR*. Calculation of the Indices I_f, I_g and I_m are illustrated in Table 2. These indices are however found to retain the effect of age and marital distribution of women in the population. Hence they are to be used with caution for comparing fertility of two populations.

TABLE 4.2

Calculation of Different Indices of Fertility Given by Coale for India Rural 1972

Age Group	No. of Women (,000) (W_i)	No. of Married Women (,000) (m_i)	ASFR (f_i)	ASMER (g_i)	Actual Births $(W_i f_i)$	Expected Births $(W_i F_i)$	$m_i F_i$	$g_i m_i$
(1)	(2)	(3)	(4)	(5)	(6)	(7)	(8)	(9)
15—19	22236	12510	0.095	0.069	2112	6671	3753	2112
20—24	21520	19235	0.265	0.296	5703	11836	10579	5703
25—29	20473	19561	0.271	0.284	5548	10277	9820	5548
30—34	11889	16909	0.229	0.242	4096	7996	7558	4097
35—39	15629	14338	0.159	0.173	2485	6345	5821	2485
40—44	13261	11211	0.078	0.092	1034	2943	2489	1034
45—49	10379	8146	0.037	0.047	384	633	497	384
					21363	46703	40517	21393

$I_f = 0.457$ $I_g = 0.527$ $I_m = 0.868$

Rates adjusted for Marital Status. Birth and fertility rates may be adjusted for other population characteristics in addition to the age and sex, such as urban-rural residence, ethnic group, marital status and duration of marriage. An age-sex marital status adjusted birth rate, for example, is derived as ;

$$\frac{\sum_i g_i W^s{}_{im} + \sum_i h_i W^s{}_{iu}}{P^s} \times 1000$$

where

g_i = fertility rate of the married women in *i*th age group in the actual population

h_i = age specific fertility rate of unmarried women in the actual population.

$W^s{}_{im}$, $W^s{}_{iu}$ and P^s denote the number of married women, unmarried women and total population of the standard population. The adjusted *GFR* can also be similarly derived by replacing P^s in the denominator by $W^s{}_{15-44}$ or $W^s{}_{15-49}$.

The *TFR*, though already adjusted by the age and sex distribution, can further be adjusted for the marital status as below :

$$\text{Marital status adjusted } TFR = \sum_i (g_i R_{im} + h_i R_{iu})$$

where R_{im} and R_{iu} are the proportions of women married and unmarried at age *i* respectively. The *TFR* can also be adjusted jointly for marital status, parity and fecundity by using the age parity specific birth rate and age-specific proportions of women who are married and fecund.

4.5 Fertility Rates Specific for Order of Births

The child-bearing performance of the women can be further analysed by order of the birth. Order of the birth qualifies the birth and not the mother. This refers to the order of children born alive to the mother, including the present birth. Births of higher order say above 3 or more are quite restricted in a contracepting society. For studying changes in fertility of the given population due to contraception in recent years, distribution of births by their order might be a better indicator than the fertility rates based on all the births even in case of the deficient registration system. The simplest way of analysing the birth order statistics is to calculate the percentage distribution of births by order. If we assume the incompleteness of registration of births independent of the order of birth, the percentage of births of any order to the total births will be almost correct. It may, however, be mentioned that the percentage distribution of the births by their order cannot be used for comparing the levels of fertility of two populations because it is affected largely by the age, sex and marital composition of the population Percentage of births of order 3 and above and median (or mean) order of births are quite good indices of fertility to measure its changes over time. However, the measures like general and specific fertility rates can also be obtained for the births of each order. For example, the general order specific birth rate (*GOSBR*) can be defined as

$$GOSBR\ (i) = \frac{B^{(i)}}{W_{15-44\ or\ 49}} \times 1{,}000$$

where $B^{(i)}$ is the number of births of order i in a year and $W_{15-44\ or\ 49}$ is the average number of women in the reproductive ages in the year. It is quite obvious that the *GFR* will be the sum of the order specific birth rates over all orders *i.e.*

$$GFR = \sum_{i=1} GOSBR_{(i)}$$

The age order specific fertility rate (*AOSFR*) can be defined as

$$AOSFR\ (i) = {}_5B_x^{(i)} / {}_5W_x$$

where $B_x^{(i)}$ denotes the births of order i to the women at age x. The sum of age and order specific fertility rate over all the orders of births at a particular age gives the age specific fertility rate at the age The age order specific birth rates corresponding to any order i may be cumulated upto any age to ascertain the proportion of the women in the synthetic cohort having given to at least i births by any age x. Thus, if we add the first order age specific birth rates for all ages till the end of the reproductive life of women, we get a measure say $TFR^{(1)}$, very similar to TFR where $TFR^{(1)}$ gives the proportion of ever mothers at the end of the reproductive life. Its compliment helps in estimating the extent of primary sterility in the population. Similarly $TFR^{(2)}$ is obtained by summing over the second order age specific birth rates for all ages upto the end of reproduction which would give the proportion of women in the synthetic cohort who are to give at least 2 births. In the same fashion, one can define $TFR^{(3)}$, $TFR^{(4)}$ and so on. Clearly

$$TFR = \sum_{i=1}^{n} TFR^{(i)}$$

where n is the last order of birth.

Median ages of the childbearing may be computed for each order of birth from the age order specific birth rates. These median values indicate the typical ages at which the mothers of a synthetic cohort would have their first, second, etc. child if they experienced the current age order specific fertility rates. Differences between the median ages for the consecutive orders of births give an approximate idea of the implied spacing time between the consecutive births. The median age for the typical last child may, however, be ascertained as the median age for the ith birth corresponding to the completed fertility rate for the cohort.

Variation in order specific birth rates may be further analysed in terms of age parity order specific birth rates. Parity denotes the number of children over born to the woman at the time of survey. A rate of this type is represented by the relation :

$$APSFR\ (i) = f_{x^{,}\ (i-1)}^{(i)} = \frac{{}_5B_x^i}{{}_5W_x^{i-1}}$$

where W_x^{i-1} is the number of women with parity $i-1$ and of age x. We can also calculate the generally parity order specific fertility rate in the usual way as follows :

$$GPOFR\ (i) = \frac{B^{(i)}}{W_{15\ 44\ or\ 49}^{(i-1)}} \times 1000$$

4.6. Cohort Measures of Fertility

The objective of the cohort analysis of fertility is to observe how many children a particular birth and marriage cohort has borne during its life-time. The fertility of the real cohort may be expressed either in terms of its current fertility, that is, births in a particular year of age or in terms of its cumulative fertility, *i.e.*, births upto a specified age since the beginning of the child-bearing When all the members of the cohort have passed through the childbearing span, the cumulative fertility becomes completed generational fertility or completed family size. The need to study cohort fertility is due to the fact that each real cohort experiences age pattern of fertility which is not exactly duplicated by any other real cohort. The fertility experience of any real cohort at any time is solely determined by the conditions of that time, its cumulative fertility experience and its attitude towards future happenings to its family. Thus the factors determining fertility performances of the woman do not act uniformly for each cohort.

Though we can define the basic measures of cohort fertility similar to the period measures of fertility discussed earlier, it will not be easy task to trace the number of births to each woman in the past at its different ages starting from the child-bearing from the registration data on births. It is, however, possible to build up cohort measures of fertility by means of current or period fertility rates available for several past years. The age specific fertility rates for successive single ages from age 15 onwards in successive years may be combined to derive the cumulative fertility rates by any age for any age cohort in any age as below :

$$f_{15}^{y} + f_{16}^{y+1} + \ldots f_{15+x}^{y+x}$$

where y refers to the calander year when the cohort is 15 years of age. If $a=35$; we obtain the completed fertility rate of the cohort who has reached 50.

Timing of the childbearing for the cohorts. Each age cohort of women experiences different spacing pattern of their births. A more specific measure of spacing between the births to a cohort can be obtained from the analysis of order specific birth rates for the birth cohorts and taking differences in the median ages for the successive order of births.

The cumulative fertility rates by order of birth and by age of the mother of a birth cohort at any time may also be utilised to obtain the parity distribution of women of the cohort at that age. The proportions of women at individual parities one and over can be obtained by taking the difference between cumulative fertility rates for successive orders (yielding the number of n parity women per 1000 women) and dividing by 10 (to obtain percentage of n-parity women) :

Per cent at parity n

$$= \frac{\left(\begin{array}{ll} \text{Cumulative rate} - \text{Cumulative rate} \\ \text{order } n \qquad\qquad\quad \text{order } n+1 \end{array} \right)}{10}$$

The percentage of women in a terminal (open-ended) parity group is found by dividing the cumulative rate for the lowest parity (*i.e.*, 7 in case of 7+ group) included in the terminal group by 10. The per cent of zero parity women at ages 45-49 reflects approximately the extent of childlessness among the women. This may be different for each new cohort completing childbearing in the future. This will be maximum estimate of infecundity for a given cohort and if proportion of non-married women is substracted from it, we can obtain the estimate of childlessness among the married women, which may indirectly estimate primary sterility. This will be obviously an over-estimate.

Birth Probabilities

Fertility analysis by cohort method can be sometimes more refined by obtaining birth probabilities by ages of the woman. If $\bar{P}_x$ denotes the age specific probability of birth for age x, then

$$\bar{P}_x = \frac{B_x}{W_x + \frac{1}{2} D_x^f} \simeq \frac{B_x}{W_x} \simeq f_x$$

where D_x^f denotes the deaths among the females aged x within a year W_x refers to the women of age x at the mid-year. If births are analysed further by order, it is possible to obtain birth probabilities specific by parity which indicates the chance that a woman of a given parity at the beginning of the year will have a child during the year and attain the next parity. The general formula for calculation of an age parity specific birth probability is

$${}_n\bar{P}_x^{(i)} = \frac{{}_nf_x^{(i+1)}}{\sum\limits_{15}^{x} {}_nf_x^{(i)} - \sum\limits_{15}^{x} {}_nf_x^{(i+1)}}$$

where ${}_n\bar{P}_x^i$ represents the probability that a cohort of women aged x to $x+n$ and of parity i at the beginning of the year will have exactly an $(i+1)$th child during the calender year, and

${}_nf_x^{i+1} = (i+1)$th order birth rate for women of age group x to $x+n$ in the calendar year.

Calculation of the age-parity specific birth probabilities are specifically useful in explaining changes in fertility at particular ages. They are also quite useful in the projection of births, if parity progression method is the basis of the projection.

An elaborate measure of the chance of having a child is *the parity progression ratio* by Henry. The parity progression ratio a_i for a woman is defined as the probability that a woman of parity i will have atleast one more child. It is defined as

$$a_0 = m_{1+}$$

$$a_1 = \frac{m_{2+}}{m_{1+}}$$

$$\vdots \qquad \vdots$$

$$a_i = \frac{m_{i+1+}}{m_{i+}}$$

where m_{1+}, m_{2+} .... m_{i+1} are the proportion of married women in a given year who have had 1 or more, 2 or more, ..., $i+1$ or more children and $a_0, a_1, \ldots\ldots a_i$ denote the chance that a family will be enlarged by an additional child. Parity progression ratios can be directly calculated only for the cohorts of women who have completed the childbearing. They can, however, be calculated indirectly from the birth statistics and in such case they will refer to the cross-sectional experience of different cohorts. Thus they will characterise the pattern of childbearing in a population. For a population where fertility is not controlled, the parity progression ratios for higher parities will be remarkably higher than the corresponding ones for the populations with controlled fertility. From the knowledge of parity progression ratios, a number of other probabilities, such as, the probability that a married women will have in her life-time atleast n children etc., can be obtained. Thus, chance of having atleast one child for a women of particular birth cohort is a_0, atleast two children is $a_0\, a_1$, at least three children is $a_0\, a_1\, a_2$ and at least r children is $a_0\, a_1\, a_2 \ldots\ldots a_{r-1}$.

Following table gives an illustration for calçulation of *PPR*.

TABLE 4.3

Calculation of Parity Progression Ratios for Married Women Aged 45–49 of Hong Kong Enumerated in 1971 and 1981

Parity (i)	No. of Women		Women of parity i and above		Parity progression ratio (per 1000 women)	
	1971	1981	1971	1981	1971	1981
0	71,178	126,287	879.633	1,204.820	919	895
1	149,814	219,440	808,455	1,078,533	815	796
2	159,385	258,226	658,641	859,093	758	699
3	137,308	190,884	499,256	600,867	725	682
4	120,968	144,175	361,948	409,983	666	648
5	92,169	101,344	240,980	265,808	618	619
6 +	148,811	164,464	148,811	164,464	—	—

Also $a_0+a_0\,a_1+a_0\,a_1\,a_2+\ldots\ldots$ gives the mean number of children per marriage according to the current fertility conditions, which are measured by the sequence of a_i. Thus, if each one of the a_i diminishes by 10 per cent in a given year, relative to the preceding year

$$a_0 \text{ becomes } .90\, a_0$$
$$a_1 \text{ becomes } .90\, a_1$$
$$a_2 \text{ becomes } .90\, a_2$$

and $a_0\,a_1\,a_2$ becomes $(.90)^3\,.a_0\,a_1\,a_2=.729\;a_0\,a_1\,a_2$ which is about 27 per cent lower than that of the preceding year. Again

$1-a_0$ represents the proportion of married women having 0 child.

$a_0-a_0\,a_1$ represents the proportion of married women having exactly one child.

$a_0\,a_1-a_0\,a_1\,a_2$ represents the proportion of married women having exactly two children and so forth.

The parity progression ratios can be defined either for a birth cohort or for a marriage cohort. The parity progression ratios can also be calculated from the birth order statistics. Births of order $i+1$ are produced by women of i parity with different intervals since the last birth (ith birth). The period parity progression ratios in such a situation are calculated as

$$a_i=\frac{B^{i+1}}{\sum\limits_{j} O_{i+1,\,j}\;.\;B^i_j}$$

where B^i_j represents the women who gave ith order birth

years ago and this will be equivalent to the number of births of order i, which occured j years reduced by mortality. The weights $O_{i+1,\,j}$ is the proportion of births of order $i+1$ according to interval j since the birth of the previous order (i). For order 1, weights are proportions of births by interval since marriage. If the population is stationary and the size of cohorts is same, one can easily calculate the P.P.R. as ratio of births of adjacent orders in a current year as :

$$a_i = B^{i+1}/B^i \quad \text{(See Henry, 1953)}$$

It is worth mentioning that in case the calculation of period parity progression ratios is based on the birth order fertility rates, sometimes the values of a_1 come out to be greater than unity. In case of parity progression ratios of cohort, it is impossible to record more second order births than first order births but it may occur in case of the period parity progression ratios. Whelpton was first to point out this phenomena. A value of a_1 greater than 1 will be a certain index of a recovery of births due to war or so intervening the experience of several marriage cohorts.

Usually births of higher order are grouped together in an open class of order $n+$; this while calculating parity progression ratios we can only calculate upto a_{n-2} which is equal to ratio of $F^{(n-1)}/F^{(n-2)}$ where $F^{(i)}$ is the cumulation of ith order age specific fertility rates upto the last age of reproduction.

4.7 Measures of Reproduction

The measure of reproduction is slightly different than fertility measures. This is directly concerned with measuring an extent to which a group is replacing its own numbers by natural process. In this sense the measures of reproductivity or population replacement are the measures of natural increase expressed in terms of a generation rather than a year or other period of time. The analysis of reproductivity has led mathematical demographer, to stable population theory. Sometimes, however, the difference between birth and death rates is also considered a measure of reproductivity which is called the crude rate of annual natural increase. Another measure called vital ratio also comes under this measure.

$$VI = \frac{B}{D} * 1000$$

The conventional measure of reproductivity called gross reproduction (GRR) rate measures the replacement of the female population only. So GRR is defined as :

$$GRR=5\left[\left(\frac{1}{1+SRB}\right)^{*}\sum ASFR_i\right]$$

If the births are tabulated by sex and age of women, we do not need SRB (Sex ratio at birth). Like TFR, GRR is also :

(*a*) an age-standardized fertility rate with each age given a weight of one;

(*b*) the average number of daughters that a group of females starting life together would bear if all intial group of female survive the child-bearing period;

(*c*) the ratio between the number of females in one generation at say age 15 and the number of their daughters at the same age, if there were no mortality during the child-bearing period; and

(*d*) the ratio between female births in two successive generations assuming no deaths before the end of the child-bearing period.

Net Reproduction Rate

NRR : is a measure of the number of daughters that a cohort of new born girl babies will bear during their life time assuming a fixed schedule of $ASFR$ and $ASMR$ (age specific mortality rate).

So,

$$NRR=\frac{1}{1+SRB}\left\{\sum_{x=15} ASFR_x * \frac{L_x}{l_0}\right\}$$

$$=\frac{1}{1+SRB}\left\{\sum {}_5f_x\ {}_5L_x\right\} \text{ with } l_0=1$$

Where ${}_5L_x$ is person years lived by a women in x to $x+5$ age group

Now, $NRR=1$ implies exact replacement

>1 implies more than replacement

<1 implies not replaceing itself and negative growth rate in long run.

The ratio of NRR to GRR is known as Reproduction Survival Ratio. We also have the following relation :

$NRR=e^{rT}$ Where T is mean length of generation. This relation is established in the stable population.

$$NRR=GRR\ \frac{l_T}{l_0}$$

$$TFR=GRR\ (1+SRB)$$

Replacement Index : The replacement index (I) is defined as

$$I=\frac{P_{0-4}}{W_{15-44}} \Big/ \frac{L^T_{0-4}}{W^f_{15-44}}$$

$$L^T_{0-4}=\frac{1.05\ L^M_{0\cdot 4}+L^f_{0\cdot 4}}{2.05}$$

The I gives us indirect method for approximating NRR in the absence of $ASFR$.

$$I=R_0\left[\frac{\alpha_2-\alpha_1}{\mu}\right]$$

Where,

α_1=Mean or median age of 0—4 population

α_2=Mean age of women in 15—45 age gronp in life table

μ=Mean of Maternity function.

R_0= Net Reproduction Rate

When $\frac{\alpha_2-\alpha_1}{\mu}=1$ then $I=R_0$

4.8 Model Age Patterns of Fertility

The curve of Age-specific Fertility Rates (*ASFR*) has two dimensions; area and shape. In demographic terms, the area under the curve is represented by total fertility rate (*TFR*) whereas shape of the curve is designated as the age pattern of fertility. When the characteristics of the fertility pattern are approximated by a standard mathematical curve, the generated *ASFRS* denote a model age pattern of fertility. The model age patterns of fertility are the basic tools of the several indirect techniques fos estimating fertility. They may also be useful in population projections, and for setting targets for family planning programmes and their evaluation. The changes in *ASFR* and their parameters like mean age and variance of fertility over a period of time are definitely linked with the transition taking place in fertility of the population.

United Nations distinguished the different patterns of *ASFRS* namely early peak, late peak and broad peak type with respect to the peak age of fertility. In an early peak type, maximum fertility occurs in the age group 20 - 24 years whereas in a late peak and broad peak types, maximum fertility occurs in age group 25-29 and 20 - 24 and 25—29 respectively. It has been observed that low fertility countries reflect remarkable homogeniety in the age patterns of their fertility but the high fertility countries differ substantially in this respect.

There are a number of mathematical curves which are fitted to *ASFRS* for different purposes. Here we would discuss two fertility models generally being used in demographic analysis.

Brass Polynomial Model

The standard pattern of fertility described by Brass is a simple third degree polynomial given as below :

$$f(x)=K(x-s)\ (s+33-x)^2$$

where $f(x)$=fertility rate at age x

K=scale parameter

s=starting age of child bearing

The 33 years of reproductive period was taken to make the variance of the function about 43.6; close to the average for observed distribution (Brass 1968). Some of the characteristics of the above are :

$$TFR = \int_{s}^{s+33} f(x)\, d_x$$

$$= 98826.75\, K$$

$$\text{Mean Age of Childbearing } (MAC) = \frac{\int_{s}^{s+3} x f(d_x)}{\int_{s}^{s+33} f(x)\, d_x}$$

$$MAC = s + 13.2$$

$$\text{Median Age} = MAC - .471$$

$$\text{Maximum fertility} = f(s+11) \doteq 5324\, K$$

This curve has been used to develop the multipliers for the well known P/F Brass procedure. The multiplier may be calculated using the following equation :

$$K = 5\left[\frac{P(x, 5) - M(x)}{M(x+5) - M(x)}\right]$$

Where

$$P(x, 5) = \frac{1}{5}\int_{s}^{x+5} M(y)\, dy \text{ ; Children ever born in } x \text{ to } x+5 \text{ age group}$$

$$M(x) = \int_{s}^{x} f(y)\, dy \text{ ; Cumulative fertility rate by age } x$$

It may be noted that this curve is not fitted to the actual *ASFR* but multipliers are selected using parameters like $f1/f2$

(fertility in 15 – 19/fertility in 20 24 age group) and *MAC*. Nevertheless, it has been observed that the Brass polynomial does not fit the set of *ASFRS* at both the ends of the reproductive period. Brass also suggested the use of Relational Gompertz model which is discussed in Chapter 8.

Coale-Trussell Model

The model schedules of fertility described by Coale and Trussell (1974) are obtained by multiplying the two model schedules :

(1) Model representing proportion married at each age. This model is described in Chapter 5 and

(2) Model schedule of marital fertility.

In mathematical symbols, it can be represented as :

$$f(x)=G(x).\,r(x)$$

where $f(x)$, $G(x)$ and $r(x)$ are respectively the model *ASFR*, proportion married, and *ASMFR* at age x. The description of the model corresponding to the observed *ASFR* is achieved through the specification of three parameters where two parameters are required for marriage and one for the marital fertility.

The age pattern of marital fertility $r(x)$ is specified in terms of standard natural fertility $n(x)$ and level parameter (M) as

$$r(x)=M\,n(x).$$

For developing standard natural fertility schedule, they omitted three of the thirteen schedules used by Henry (1962) *viz*., those of Guinea, India and Iran. Further under the condition of controlled fertility, they added second parameter to describe the extent of deliberate fertility control (m),

so we have $$r(x)=M\ \ n(x)\ \ e^{m\nu(x)}$$

Where $\nu(x)$ gives the standard pattern of departure of controlled fertility from natural fertility. Value of $V_{(a)}$ was calculated using following equation for 43 countries (mostly developed)

$$V_i(x)=\mathrm{l}_n\left[\frac{r_i(x)}{M_i\ n(x)}\right] \qquad \text{if } m=1.00$$

M_i for i^{th} country is chosen so that $V_i(x)$ is zero in 20-24 age group. Simple average of $V_i(x)$ is taken to represent $V(x)$. The value of $n(x)$ and $v(x)$ are given below :

Age	15-19	20-24	25-29	30-34	35-39	40-44	45-49
$n(x)$	.4110	.4597	.4309	.3946	.3223	.1671	.0237
$V(x)$	.0000	.0000	-.279	-.677	-1.042	-1.414	-1.671

The value of M and m can be estimated if $r(x)$ is available for any population :

$$M = \frac{r(20\text{-}24)}{n(20\text{-}24)}.$$

This is done on the assumption that there is no deliberate control of fertility in the 20-24 age group *i.e.*, M provides the level of natural fertility. After estimating M, m can be estimated for each age group from 25-29 as

$$m_n = \frac{1}{v(x)} \ln \left\{ \frac{r(x)}{M\, n(x)} \right\} \qquad x = 25\text{-}29 \text{ to } 45\text{-}49$$

If the natural marital fertility model fits, the estimate of m would be almost same for each age group. The mean value of m for 25-29, 30-34, 35-39 and 40-44 may be taken as single estimate of m. The value of M and m may also be estimated using the least square procedure. We have

$$r(x) = M\, n(x) \quad e^{m \cdot v(x)}$$

$$\ln \left[\frac{r(x)}{n(x)} \right] = \ln M + m\, V(x)$$

The estimate of M and m from the above procedure may be different than what can be obtained from using the first procedure. However, many researchers question the utility of Coale-Trussell model as well as the generalization of the pattern of natural fertility observed by Henry. It may be difficult to estimate the level of natural fertility (M) from this simple model especially in the presence of deliberate control of fertility in the population.

It is also to be noted that much depends an pattern of V(x) which are empirically derived. If most of the women get married at early ages, the pattern of natural fertility is bound to differ from the one are postulated. Nevertheless M and m can be said so characterise a pattern and help in accruing changes in "m" over-time by assuming "M" to be contact.

4.9 Trends in Fertility

Different measures of fertility so far discussed may be used to study the changes in fertility of a country over-time. However, the potential use of CBR and CFR as measures of fertility gets impaired because of their dependence on the age-sex and marital composition of the population. For a better appraisal of changes in the level of fertility, one may either use standardised rates of fertility or isolate the contribution of the different components through a well defined standardisation procedure. One may also use the indices of marital fertility, proportion married and over all fertility discussed earlier in this note, to understand the changes in fertility. One can in fact analyses the trends in cohort fertility measure, children ever born for each age cohort over-time and ascertain the change. In some cases, data on order of births can be utilised to understand the changes. Notwithstanding the underregistration of births, the percentage distribution of births by their order can be treated to represent the true distribution and decline in percentage of births of order 3 and more (say) over-time can be treated as a measure of decline in fertility of older women. In fact, this index can be separately worked out for the women below age 30 and above age 30 (say) it can be easily inferred whether decline is occurring due to spacing between the births of higher order births or due to the limitation of the higher order births. Even the study of trends in mean age of briths or mean order of births or average parity of the women can be used to indicate change in fertility. Of course, from the above discussion it is clearly seen that in study of trends, estimation of the levels of fertility over-time is a pre-requisite. We have already discussed in details various methods to be used for estimating the levels of fertility. Below we shall discuss the standardisation method to decompose the changes in fertility level into its various components.

1. *Decomposition of Change in CBR:* Whatever be its defects, CBR is a widely used and easily available measure to ascertain the changes in fertility over-time. The change in CBR is due to its four major components: (1) proportion of women of reproductive age in the total population, (2) age structure of

women of reproductive ages, (3) proportion of married women of reproductive ages, and (4) marital age specific fertility rates. One can adopt suitable standardisation approach to determine the contribution of these four demographic components to change in the magnitute of the observed crude birth rate. We shall discuss here a classical approach. As we know the relationship between the CBR and these components is multiplicative we have

$$CBR = \frac{B}{P}$$

$$= \frac{B}{W} \cdot \frac{W}{F} \cdot \frac{F}{P}$$

Where,

W = number of women of reproductive ages

F = number of females in the total population

Thus, CBR = GFR W/P where GFR = B/W

The point is then to decompose GFR into its three components. For this

$$B = \sum_i B_i,$$

Where, B_i = number of births to women a age group i

$$W = \sum_i W_i,$$

Where, W_i = number of women in age group i

Thus,

$f_i = B_i / W_i$

= age specific fertility rate in age group i

Hence,

$B_i = W_i f_i$

and $B = \sum_i W_i f_i$

Assuming that number of illegal births is neglible,

$f_i^m = B_i / W_i^m$, where, W_i^m = number of women married in i age group

Hence, $B = \Sigma W_i^m . f_i^m$

Again $W_i^m / M_c\ M_i$ = proportion of married women in age group i.

Hence $B = \sum_i W_i = M_c M_i f_i^m$

$$\text{Thus CBR} \quad \frac{\sum_i W_i M_i f_i^m}{W} \frac{W}{P}$$

$$= \sum_i A_i M_i f_i^m \frac{W}{P}$$

Where, $A_i = W_i / W$

The above relationship helps in decomposing the crude birth rate.

Because two points in time constitute the reference for measuring changes in fertility, the notations are given additional suffixes 1 and 2 to denote time t_1 and t_2. Thus,

$CBR_1 = (\Sigma_i A_{1i} M_{1i} f_{1i}^M) W_1 / P_1$

$CBR_2 = (\Sigma_i A_{2i} M_{2i} f_{2i}^m) W_2 / P_2$

Hence, change in CBR is given by,

$D\ CBR_1 = CBR_2 - CBR_1$

If we ignore the interaction terms, the rate of each component is assessed according to the formalae shown in the table given below, with population P_1 as the standard.

If population P_2 had been chosen as the standard, the formulae would have remained the same except for an appropriate interchange of the subscripts in the factors kept constant. Theoretically the sum of the contribution of each component should equal the total change as resulting from $CBR_2 - CBR_1$.

TABLE 4.4: FORMULAE FOR DECOMPOSITION INTO FACTORS

Change in CBR due to Change in	*Procedure*
1. Proportion of women of reproductive ages in the total population	$GFR_1 \frac{W_2 W_1}{P_2 P_1}$
2. Age structure of women of reproductive ages	$\frac{W_1}{P_1} \Sigma_i (A_{2i} - A_{1z}) M_{1i} f_{1z}^m$
3. Marital status distribution	$\frac{W_1}{P_i} \Sigma_{li} M_{1i} (f_{2z}^m - f_{li}^M)$
4. Marital fertility	$\frac{W_i}{Pi} \Sigma_i Aiz\ Miz\ (f^m_{2i} - f^m_{1i})$

This may not be the case because joint effects are not taken into accounts. For more details one may red UN Manual IX. Before we interpret the results we should however keep in mind the following basic assumptions which have been made in the above standardisation procedure:

(i) It is assumed that the four components of the crude birth rate for which standardisation is taken can be added in order to assess the individual effects of each component during the period under study. This is a strong assumption. It is assumed that components of the crude birth rate are functionally independent. It is, however, not valid always. For example, while one assumes independence between the proportion of women married and age-specific marital fertility, these may be the cases where particular changes in age at marriage with a five year age group affect marital fertility through the women's fecundity rather than family planning. Further, interaction effects of two or more components may not be negligible.

(ii) It is assumed that there are no illegitimate births.

(iii) Any component of the crude birth rate that is not standardised has no role in the observed change. For example, effect of changes in socio-economic and cultural factors are being totally ignored in this type of standardisation.

(2) Decomposition of TFR: Bongarts (1978, 82)*has demonstrated that nearly all variance in the fertility levels of a population is due to difference in only four factors:

(1) The proportions married among females; (2) The prevalence of contraceptive use; (3) The incidence of induced abortion, and (4) The fertility inhibiting effect of breast-feeding. In his formulation TFR is expressed as the product of four indices measuring the fertility inhibiting effect of these four factors and the Total Fecundity (TF). The total fecundity rate is the average number of live births expected among women who, during their entire reproductive period, remain married, do not use contraception, do not have any induce abortion, and do not breastfeed their children.

---

* Bongaarts, John, 1978: "A Framework for Analysing the Proximate Determinants of Fertility", *Population and Development Review 4,* No. 1 (March) 105-132.

—1982 The Fertility-inhibiting Effects of the Intermediate Fertility Variables, *Studies in Family Planning,* Vol. 13, No. 617, pp. 179-189.

According to Bongaarts's model:

$TFR = C_m \times C_c \times C_a \times C_i \times TF$

Where,

C_m is an index of proportions married

C_c is an index of non-contraception

C_a is an index of induced abortion

C_i is an index of lactational infecundity.

The estimates of TFR in any given year for any population derived by using equation (1) are not accurate because the value of TF varies substantially between 13 and 17 births among the populations. The total fecundity rate in a population is a function of mostly biological proximate determinants frequency of intercourse, natural sterility, and spontaneous intrauterine mortality. Although minor fluctuations can be expected in these biological determinants, for the same population, one can reasonably assume no change for studying change in fertility over short span of 10 to 15 years. Thus, if one assumes TF to be constant for the period understudy, the change in fertility can be expressed in terms of changes in the indices of proximate determinants i.e.,

$$\frac{TFR\,(2)}{TFR\,(1)} = \frac{C_m\,(2)}{C_m\,(1)} \cdot \frac{C_c\,(2)}{C_c\,(1)} \cdot \frac{C_a\,(2)}{C_a\,(1)} \cdot \frac{C_i\,(2)}{C_i\,(1)} \qquad \text{(A)}$$

Where, TFR (1) etc., refer to period 1 and TFR (2) etc. refer to period 2.

The index proportions married, C_m is defined as the weighted average of the age specific proportion married. The age specific marital fertility rates are used as weights. Thus,

$$C_m = \frac{\Sigma\, m(a)\, g(a)}{.\ \Sigma\, g(a)}$$

Where, m(a) is the proportion married, g(a) is the marital fertility rate, 'a' refers to the age category and the summation is taken over seven age categories. For studying change in C_m overtime the same g(a) is to be taken for both the periods. It may also be taken average of g(a).

Index of non-contraception C_c is calculated as

$C_c = (1 - 1.08\ u\ e)$

where 'u' is the prevalence of current contraceptive use (including small method and sterilisation operations) among married women of the reproductive age (15-49); 'e' is the average use-effectiveness of contraception, and 1.08 is a sterility contraception factor. Since estimates of contraceptive effectiveness are difficult to obtain, following standard method specific values may be used for the developing countries.

Method	*Estimated Use-effectiveness*
Sterilisation	1.0
IUD	0.95
Pill	0.90
Condoms, Nirodh and other methods	0.70

The average use-effectiveness, e, is estimated as the weighted average of the method specific use-effectiveness levels, e(m), with the weights equal to the proportion of women using a given methods, u(m) : Thus,

$$e \sum_{m} e(m) \left\{ \frac{u(m)}{u} \right\}$$

Index of Induced Abortion, C_a can be calculated as

$$C_a = \frac{TFR}{TFR + 0.4 \times (1 + u) \times TA}$$

Where, TA equals the total induced abortion rare including only abortions among married women). Thus, if induced abortion rate is zero; $C_a = 1$.

Index of postpartum infecundability, C_i is calculated as

$$C_i = \frac{20}{18.5 + i}$$

Where, i is the mean duration of postpartum infecundability. In case data on i is not available it can be estimated using the following relations suggested by Bongaarts,

$$i = 1.753 \quad e0.1396B - 0.001872\ B^2$$

Where, B is the average period of breastfeeding.

In order to decompose the change in TFR between year 1 and 2, we define the proportional changes in all the indices in equation (A) as:

Proportional change in TFR (P_f) = 1 - TFR (2) / TFR (1) ... (b)

Proportional change in Marriage Index (P_f) = 1 - C (2) / C (1) ... (c)

Proportional change in Contraception (P_c) = 1 - C (2) / C (1) ... (d)

Proportional change in Induced Abortion (P_a) = 1 - C (2) / C (1) ... (e)

Proportional change in Postpartum Infecundability (p_i) = 1 - C (2) / C (1) ... (f)

Proportional change in TF (P_r) = 1 - TF_2 / TF_1 ... (g)

= 0 if TF is constant.

The equation (A) with above definition can be rewritten as —

$$1 + P_f = (1 + P_m)(1 + P_c)(1 + P_a)(1 + P_i)(1 + P_x)$$

By rearranging this equation we get:-

$$P_f = P_m + P_c + P_a + P_i + P_r + I$$

where I measures the interaction we get:

The above equation can be interpreted as the proportional change in TFR equivalent to the changes due to marriage (P_m), due to contraception (P_c), due to Induced abortion (P_a) and due to changes in postpartum infecundability (P_i) and due to TF (P_r). In other words it gives the contribution of each of four proximate determinants in the reduction of TFR. We can present the results of decomposition in the tabular form as shown below:

TABLE 4.5 : DECOMPOSTION OF THE CHANGE IN TFR BETWEEN YEAR 1 AND 2

Change due to Proximate Determinants	*% of Change in TFR (1)*	*Distribution of Change in TFR (2)*	*Absolute Change in TFR*
(1) Marriage	P_m	P_m/P_f	Cal2 * Δ
(2) Contraception	P_c	P_c/P_f	Cal_2 * Δ
(3) Induced Abortion	P_a	P_a/P_f	Cal_2 * Δ
(4) Postpartum Infecundability	P_i	P_i/P_f	Cal2 * Δ
(5) Due to Change in TF	P_r	P_r/P_f	Cal2 * Δ
(6) Interaction	I	I/P_f	Cal2 * Δ
Total	P_f	1.00	$\Delta = TFR_2 - TFR_1$

Bongaarts model has also been used for Target setting and for evaluating fertility impact of contraceptive use which known as prevalence method.

5

Nuptiality

The study of nuptiality deals with the frequency of marriage *i.e.* union between persons of opposite sexes, which involves rights and obligations fixed by law or custom; with the characteristics of persons united in marriage and with the dissolution of such unions. By extension, it also includes the study of other conjugal unions where their frequency makes their inclusion necessary. The nuptiality relates to marriage and dissolution in the same way as fertility and mortality does to births and deaths respectively. Marriage and its dissolution play very important role in the study of population dynamics. Malthus considered postponement of marriage as positive check on population growth to keep it below the sustenance level. The formation of the marital union with acceptable social norms infact, affects all the three components of the population growth.

Marriage means the legal union of persons of opposite sex constituted by an act, ceremony or process. The legality of this union may be established by civil, religious or other means recognised by the laws of each country. Marriage provides for the biological continuity of the society through procreations and also for its cultural continuity by providing a suitable atmosphere for socialisation. The age at which the female marries also marks the beginning of reproductive life if she is biologically mature to bear child. It is through the intervening variables of marriage that replacement indices become sociologically meaningful. In the more developed societies, recent changes in the level and trend of fertility owe much to the changes in the amount of, and age at marriage.

There are mainly three sources of data for analysing marriages and their dissolution. They are : (*i*) Census, (*ii*) Survey, and (*iii*) Registration system. Census and survey provide almost similar information on marital status which is static representation of the population characteristics. There are generally four categories of marital status : (*i*) Single or never married, (*ii*) married, (*iii*) widowed, (*iv*) divorced or separated. The registration system provides the dynamic aspect of the marriage. It is obvious that there would be different procedures and measures to analyse the two types of data.

5.1. Direct Measures from Registration Data

(i) Crude Marriage Rate (CMR) :

Like crude rates in fertility and mortality, we define as follows :

$$CMR = \frac{\text{Number of Marriages in a year}}{\text{Mid year population of Particular Sex}} \times 1000.$$

The mid year population has to be estimated from the census totals because registration system does not provide the population.

This measure is called crude because in the denominator, we take total population – not the eligible population. If we assume certain minimum and maximum age, say, 15 and 60 respectively, the population below age 15 and above age 60 years as well as already married persons are not eligible for marriage. From the demographic points of view, the maximum age can be taken as 50 for the females. In fact the *CMR* is affected by the age-sex distribution of the population in marriageable ages. The *CMR* is widely used due to its simplicity and less data requirement. However, the standardized *CMR* can be used for the comparison purpose.

(ii) Nubile and General Marriage Rate :

The nubile marriage rate like general fertility rate is defined as

$$NMR = \frac{\text{Number of Marriages in a year}}{\text{Mid year population of single widowed and divorced above age 15 (or minimum age) for particular sex.}} \times 1000$$

This rate should be calculated for each sex separately (or denominater should be divided by two). In this rate, we may also fix the upper age for marriage or include only prime age span say 15-50. In such case, *NMR* becomes the General Marriage rate (*GMR*). After age 50, very few marriages take place and below age 15 we have more unmarried women or men. *GMR* is more appropriate for women than men as number of marriages for men above age 50 is comparatively more. This is analogous to *GFR*. This measure is again affected by age-sex distribution of population in age range 15-50 but it is better than *CMR*. Since marriage rate changes rapidly with age, it would be more meaningful to calculate the rate by single year age. From the definition, it is clear that this rate is valid only for the populations in which monogamy is the only acceptable form of the marriage.

If the marital status data is not available for the country, this rate can not be calculated. Related to the *NMR*, we can define some rates as follows :

(*a*) First Marriage Rate

$$= \frac{\text{Number of first marriage}}{\text{Single population of particular sex above age 15 or minimum age of marriage.}} \times 1000,$$

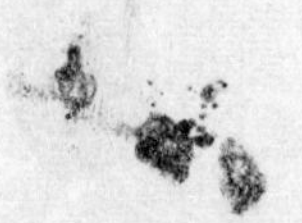

(*b*) Remarriage Rate

$$= \frac{\text{Number of marriages of persons previously married}}{\text{Population of widowed and divorced of particular sex above age 15}} \times 1000$$

We may also define the rates by order of marriage like first marriage rate, second marriage rate and etc.

(*iii*) Age-Sex Specific Marriage Rates

The age specific marriage rate (*ASMR*) is defined as –

$$ASMR_x = \frac{\text{No. of marriages at age } x \text{ of particular sex}}{\text{No. of unmarried persons of that age and sex}} \times 1000$$

This rate is similar to *NMR* calculated for each age. It is clear that the marriage rates are concentrated in very limited span and change rapidly with age. It is therefore more meaningful to calculate *ASMR* for single year of age than 5 year age intervals Like *TFR*, we can also calculate total marriage rate by summing the *ASMR*. These rates are used in the construction of nuptiality tables.

5.2. The Nuptiality Tables Based on Registration Data

Nuptiality table is the best tool to analyse the marriage patterns and changes therein for any population. This provides the life time implication of the present age pattern of marriages for the cohort of person passing through the marriageable ages. There are basically two types of nuptiality table namely : (*i*) Gross nuptiality table, (*ii*) Net nuptiality table. In gross nuptiality table, there is only one factor *i.e.* marriage through which the size of the cohort of single persons decreases whereas in the net nuptiality table we have two factors – marriage and mortality. These tables reflect the patterns of first marriage because remarriages are not taken into account. The measures based on such tables are conceptually similar to gross reproduction rate and net reproduction rate. In this case, gross nuptiality rate indicates the proportion of men and women of any cohort who would eventually marry if none dies before the end of the marriageable ages and experience the current age specific marriage rates. On the other hand, net nuptiality rate is the proportion of men and women who would ever marry and survive. For the comparison of the marriage patterns, gross nuptiality table is more appropriate than the net nuptiality table.

The data required for constructing two types of nuptiality tables are age specific marriage rates and age specific mortality rates. In the absence of such data, marriage frequency can be calculated from the census data on marital status as discussed section 5.4.

(*A*) Columns of Gross Nuptiality Table:

(*i*) n_x. The probability of marriage by age can be calculated from *ASMR* central marriage rate. For single year data, we have

$$n_x = \frac{2r_x}{2+r_x}$$

where r_x is *ASMR* and n_x is nuptial probability and for grouped data we have

$$nx = \frac{2h \times h_x}{2+nxh_x}$$

where h is width of the class and n_x is the probability that a person who is single at age x would marry before his/her next birth day *i.e.* $x+1$.

(*ii*) Never Married at Age X (NM_x) :

This is the number of persons who survive to the age x as single. This is similar to l_x column in the life table. It can be calculated as,

$$NM_{x+1} = NM_x(1-n_x)$$
$$= NM_x - NM_x(n_x).$$

(iii) Number Marrying at Age x :

This column gives the frequency of marriages between age x and $x+1$, *i.e.*,

$$M_x = NM_x \cdot n_x$$

There is similarity between M_x and d_x; a column of the life table.

(iv) Number Ever Marrying (EM_x) :

This is the number of persons who would ever marry after attaining x,

$$EM_x = \sum_{x}^{\omega} M_x$$

where w is maximum age for marriage.

(v) Number of Ever Married Persons (EVM_x) :

The number of total persons ever married upto age x

$$EVM_x = \sum_{A}^{x} M_x$$

where A is the lowest marriagable age.

This column provides the ever married persons. Since we are not considering mortality and divorced cases in this procedure, this would be similar to married persons. It can be easily seen that :

$$EVM_x + NM_x = 100{,}000 \text{ } i.e. \text{ radix.}$$

(vi) Person Years Lived in Never Married Status (S_x)

This is similar to the L_x column in the life table and is calculated as

$$S_x = \frac{NM_x + NM_{x+1}}{2}$$

From this column, one can calculate the singlehood probability from one age group to another (higher). For example :

$$_{y}P_x = \frac{S_{x+y}}{S_x}$$

i.e. probability of remaining as single from age x to $x+y$.

(*vii*) Cumulative Single Person Years Lived (CPY_x)

This column gives the total number of person years spent as single by a cohort after attaining age x, which is the number of persons who are not exposed to marriage at age x.

$$CPY_x = \sum_{X}^{\omega} S_x$$

(*viii*) Percentage Ever Marrying (PM_x)

This is the proportion or percentage of persons of the cohort at age x who would ever marry before attaining the maximum marriageable age.

$$PM_x = \frac{EM_x}{NM_x} \times 100$$

(*ix*) Average Years Before Marriage (e_x^n)

This column provides the expected number of years a person would spend as a bachelor or spinster before first marriage. This is calculated as follows :

$$e_x^n = \frac{CPY_x}{NM_x}$$

In a gross nuptially table, each column has some demographic and social relevance. The value of S_{50} indicates the proportion of persons who remained single and did not contribute in reproduction. The column 5 is quite useful because it shows the age distribution of women exposed to child bearing. In fact, column 2 and column 5 provide the marital status of the cohort at each age in terms of never married and ever married respectively. The estimate of e_x^n provides after age 15 the number of years woman's reproductive life will be spent in a state of non-exposure to childbearing.

For example : If $e^n_{15} = 10$, it means that 10 years of reproductive life would be spent as single by a cohort of women aged

15. In otherwords nearly 28 per cent of the reproductive period is lost (10/35).

B. Columns of Net Nuptiality Table

In net nuptiality table, mortality is also taken into consideration. Therefore first two columns of this table are n_x and q_x *i.e.* probability of marriage and probability of dying at age x for those who were single at that age. Since we may not know the mortality condition by marital status, we have to assume that there is no mortality differential by marital status. The remaining columns of the table are as follows.

(*iii*) l'_x : The number of persons alive and single at age x out of the original cohort. They are the survivors from both marriage and mortality and sometimes called as net nuptial survivors. In gross nuptiality table, we have NM_x which are survivors from marriage similar to this column :

(*iv*) d'_x *and* (*v*) V'_x : The column (*iv*) and (*v*) together arc analogous to d_x in the life table.

They are calculated as :

$$d'_x = q_x\left(1-\frac{n_x}{2}\right)l'_x$$

$$V'_x = n_x\left(1-\frac{q_x}{2}\right)l'_x$$

(*vi*) N'_x : The number of single persons expected to ever marry after age x. This is analogous to EM_x in the gross nuptiality table

$$N'_x = \sum_{x}^{\omega} V'_x$$

(*vii*) This column is just percentage of column (*vi*) and is calculated as

$$\frac{N'_x}{l'_x} \times 100$$

(*viii*) L'_x : Person years lived as single by the survivors of the original cohort during ages x and $x+1$.

$$L'_x=\frac{1}{2}(l'_x+l'_{x+1})+\frac{1}{24}(d'_{x+1}+V'_{x+1}-d'_{x-1}-V'_{x-1})$$

(*ix*) T'_x : Total person years lived after age x *i.e.*

$$T'_x=\sum_{x}^{\omega} L'_x$$

(*x*) $E^{\circ\prime}_x$: Average number of years spent as single before death or marriage :

$$E^{\circ\prime}_x=\frac{T'_x}{l'_x}$$

5.3. Analysis of Marital Status Data from Census

The measures and methods discussed in the last section are based on the data from registration system. It is well known fact that the registration of marriages in most of the developing countries is either very poor or non-existant. However, the data on marital status are generally available from censuses and surveys, which can be used to study marriage patterns, or frequency of marriages.

The system of classification of population by marital status varies from country to country due to different customs and marriage law. But U.N. has recommended the following classification to be adopted internationally.

(*a*) Single (Never Married)

(*b*) Married (Currently Married)

(*c*) Widowed

(*d*) Divorced

Each category has its own religious, legal, social and demographic significance. Though religious, legal and social importance may vary from country to country, their demographic consequences are well recognized in all the countries. The marital status (currently married) directly indicates the portion of the population that would be eligible for child-bearing, and hence the changes in marital status will directly affect fertility. The analysis of marital status data is more meaningful when these data are tabulated by different characteristics of the population.

5.3.1. Proportion Single and Singulate Mean Age at Marriage (SMAM)

The analysis of proportion single by age of men/women gives us partial idea about the patterns of marriages in a population. The proportion single at different points of time or for different countries can indirectly provide an idea about differences or changes in marriage pattern. However, the proportion single at one point of time or for single country may not be very useful. The pattern of proportion single by age can be seen from Figure 5.1. The proportion single beyond certain age say 50 is taken as to reflect the extent of celibacy *i.e.* proportion who never marry in their life time.

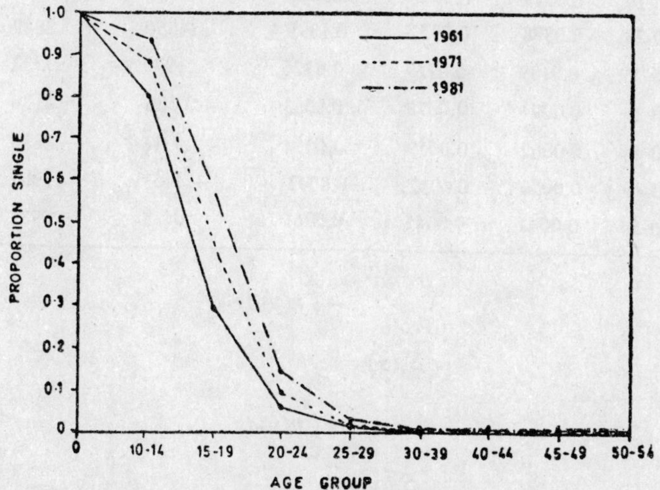

Fig. 5.1. Proportion Single for Females in India

Like mortality, if we have $n(x)$ as force of nuptiality then the proportion single $s(x)$ can be given as :

$$s(x)=e^{-\int_0^x n(y)dy}$$

If less number of persons remain single in one cohort than other cohort, it means that first cohort has experienced higher marriage rates. Let us assume that proportion single in one cohort is $S_1(x)$ and in the second cohort is $S_2(x)$, which experiences marriage rates k times that of the first cohort. Then

TABLE 5.1

Proportion Single for Females in India

Age	Proportion Single 1961	1971	1981	Value of K 1961-71	1971-81
0-9	1.0000	1.0000	1,0000	—	—
10-14	0 8045	0.8824	0.9339	0924	.0567
15-19	0.2919	0.4370	0.5585	.4035	.2453
20-24	0.0598	0.0952	0.1399	.4650	.3849
25-29	0.0189	0.0229	0 0326	.1920	.3532
30-39	0.0074	0.0078	0.0063	.0526	—.2136
40-44	0 0062	0.0059	0.0054	.9516	—.0886
45-49	0.0050	0.0032	0.0043	—.4463	.2955
50-54	0.0047	0.0045	0.0041	-.0435	—.0931

$$S_1(x)=e^{-\int_0^x n(y)dy}$$

$$S_2(x)=e^{-k\int_0^x n(y)dy}$$

$$=[S_1(x)]^k$$

$$\frac{\text{Log } S_2(x)}{\text{Log } S_1(x)}=k$$

If we are taking grouped data, formula would be slightly different, *i.e.*

$$K = \text{Log}_e \left[\frac{S_{2(x,\ n)}}{S_{1(x,\ n)}} \right]$$

Example

In India proportion female singles, aged 15 – 19 in 1971
$= 0.4370$

and Proportion female singles aged 15 - 19 in 1981
$= 0.5585$

Hence, $K = \text{Log}_e \left[\frac{.5585}{.4370} \right] = 0.2453$

It means that the latter cohort *i.e.* 15 – 19 in 1981 experienced marriage rates which is 0.25 times of that experienced by the cohort aged 15 – 19 in 1971, $K < 1$ indicates that marriage rates have declined. The value of K however, reflect the condition of last 10 – 15 years, not of single years. Index K can be used to study the differences in marriage patterns.

The frequency of marriages can also be calculated from the data on proportion singles by age. Once we have calculated frequencies, various measures of central tendency and dispersion can be calculated.

5.3.2 Method for Estimating SMAM

A method to estimate the mean age at marriage from proportion single was proposed by Hajnal (1953). If the proportion single for any population has remained constant in the past, it can be taken to represent the experiences of a single cohort passing through the marriageable ages. If so, we can calculate the marriage rate and frequency at each age from the rate at which the proportion single is reducing. This would come true only when the mortality and migration rates at each age are the same for the singles and for the total population. The mean age calculated under such assumption is called Singulate Mean Age at Marriage (*SMAM*). Its calculation is based on the following assumptions :

(*a*) no change in marriage pattern

(*b*) no mortality differentials by marital status

(*c*) no migration differentials by marital status.

Let $s(x)$ be the proportion single at age x, then

$$\frac{-d}{dx}[s(x)]=n(x)$$

or

$$-[S_{x+1}-S_x]=n(x)$$

where $n(x)$ is the number of first marriages. Now *SMAM* is given as

$$SMAM=\frac{\int_d^D x\,.\,n(x)dx}{\int_d^D n(x)dx}$$

where d and D are lower and upper ages of marriageable age span. It is clear that $S(d)=1$. The value for D is taken as 45 or 50 years.

$$SMAM=\frac{\int_d^D x\,.\,[-d\,s(x)]}{\int_d^D -d\,s(x)}$$

$$=\frac{d\,s(d)-D\;s(D)-\int_d^D s(x)dx}{s(d)-s(D)}$$

By adding and substracting $d\,s(D)$ in the numerator, we get :

$$SMAM=d+\frac{1}{S(d)-S(D)}\left[\int_d^D s(x)dx-(D-d)\;S(D)\right]$$

if $d=0$

$$SMAM = \frac{\int_0^D s(x)dx - D\,S(D)}{1 - S(D)}$$

In form of summation and proportion single in 5 years age interval, above equation can be written as

$$SMAM = \frac{5 \sum_{x=0}^{D-5} {}_5S_x - D\,S(D)}{1 - S(D)}$$

In this case $S(D)$ is calculated as follows :

$$S(D) = \frac{{}_5S_{D-5} + {}_5S_D}{2}$$

For example : if $D=45$ then

$$S_{(45)} = \frac{{}_5S_{40} + {}_5S_{45}}{2}$$

Example

TABLE 5.2

Estimation of SMAM for India 1981

Age	*Female Population* (*1*)	*Female never Married* (*2*)	*Proportion Single* (*2*)/(*1*) ${}_5S_x$
0-4	41282041	41282041	1.0000
5-9	45418306	45418306	1.0000
10-14	40646075	37962551	0.9339
15-19	30111819	16818760	0.5585
20-24	28337783	3966433	0.1399
25-29	24969871	813971	0.0326
30-34	20800401	244330	0.0117
35-39	18959698	118800	0.0063
40-44	16154363	87795	0.0054
45-49	13866000	59423	0.0043
50-54	11602684	47831	0.0041

Assume $D=45$ *i.e.* upper age limit of marriageable age.

$$_5S_x=\frac{\text{Female never married in } x \text{ to } x+5}{\text{Female Population in } x \text{ to } x+5}$$

$$_5S_{10}=\frac{37962551}{40646075}$$

$$=0.9337$$

$$5\sum_{x=0}^{40} {_5S_x}=5[S_0+{_5S_5}+{_5S_{10}}+\ldots\ldots+{_5S_{40}}]$$

$$=5[3.6883]=18.4415$$

$$S(45)=\frac{_5S_{40}+{_5S_{45}}}{2}=\frac{.0054+.0043}{2}=0.0049$$

$$1-S(45)=0.9951 \text{ and } 45^{*}\ S(45)=0.2183$$

$$SMAM=\frac{18.44-0.2183}{0.9951}$$

$$=18.31 \text{ years.}$$

The above procedure assumes the stability of the age patterns of marriage which is violated in the present situation. Agarwala (1962) proposed a method which does not assume constant marriage pattern. This method requires the proportion singles from the two consecutive censuses—five or 10 years apart. If censuses are not 5 or 10 years aprt suitable adjustment has to be made in the age groupings of the second census.

Now let us assume that there are two censuses 10 years apart and proportion single is denoted by $_5S_x$. The probability of remaining single for those who are aged x to $x+5$ in the first census and move to age group $x+10$ to $x+15$ by the second census can be given as

$$10^{*}\ ({_{(1)}k_{x:}})=\frac{_5S^2_{x+10}}{_5S^1_x}$$

where 1 and 2 on the top of S indicate first and second census respectively. This provides us the decadal probability for a cohort to obtain hypothetical proportion single by age. It means that synthetic cohort experienced the marriage rates prevailing during intercensal period. This method is therefore called decada synthetic cohort method. The procedure to obtain hypothetical proportion single is shown in Table 5.2 with the Indian data.

To obtain columns, it is clear that for first two age groups 10-14 and 15-19, the probability of remaining single is the same as proportion single in these two age groups in the recent census, because the cohort declines due to intercensal marriage rates. For other age groups probabilities are obtained as :

$$P_{20-24}=\frac{0.1399}{0.8824}=0.1585$$

$$P_{25-29}=\frac{0.0326}{0.4370}=0.0746$$

Now, the procedure for generating proportion singles for hypothetical cohort, which experiences the marriage probability of column 3 is as follows :

Under the assumption that there are no marriages below age 10, proportion single is one for 0-4 and 5-9 age groups. For 10-40 and 15-19, we would have the proportions single as of the 1981 (the recent census). If the census is 5 years apart, the proportion of 10-14 would be as of the recent census.

Now

$$S(20\text{-}24)=0.1585 * 0.9339=0.1480$$

$$S(25\text{-}29)=0.0746 * 0.5585=0.0417$$

$$S(30\text{-}34)=0.1229 * 0.1480=0.0182$$

and so on.

The *SMAM* for intercensal period can be calculated from the proportion single in the last column by using Hajnal formula:

We have

$$5 \cdot \sum_{0}^{40} {}_5S_x=18.63$$

TABLE 5.3

Estimation of Inter-Census SMAM, 1971-81, India

Age	*Proportion Single (Female)*		*Probability of Remaining Single during 1971-81*	*Proportion Single of decade Synthetic cohort*
	1971	*1981*		
	(1)	*(2)*	*(3)*	*(4)*
0–4	$1.0000 = S_0$	$1.0000 = S'_0$	—	$1.0000 = S_0^C = S'_0$
5–9	$1.0000 = S_1$	$1.0000 = S'_1$	—	$1.0000 = S_1^C = S'_1$
10–14	$0.8824 = S_2$	$0.9339 = S'_2$	$0.9339 = P_2 = S'_2$	$0.9339 = S_2^C = S'_2$
15–19	$0.4370 = S_3$	$0.5585 = S'_3$	$0.5585 = P_3 = S'_3$	$0.5585 = S_3^C = S'_3$

(Contd.)

	1	2	3	4
20 – 24	$0.0952 = S_4$	$0.1399 = S'_4$	$0.1585 = P_4 = S'_4/S_2$	$0.1480 = S^C_4 = P_4 * S^C_2$
25 – 29	$0.0229 = S_5$	$0.0326 = S'_5$	$0.0746 = P_5 = S'_5/S_3$	$0.0417 = S^C_5 = P_5 * S^C_3$
30 – 34	$0.0102 = S_6$	$0.0117 = S'_6$	$0.1229 = P_6 = S'_6/S_4$	$0.0182 = S^C_6 = P_6 * S^C_4$
35 – 39	$0.0078 = S_7$	$0.0063 = S'_7$	$0.2751 = P_7 = S'_7/S_5$	$0.0115 = S^C_7 = P_7 * S^C_5$
40—44	$0.0059 = S_8$	$0.0054 = S'_8$	$0.5294 = P_8 = S'_8/S_6$	$0.0096 = S^C_8 = P_8 . S^C_6$
45—49	$0\ 0045 = S_9$	$0.0043 = S'_9$	$0.5513 = P_9 = S'_9/S_7$	$0.0063 = S^C_9 = P_9 . S^C_7$
50—54	$0.0032 = S_{10}$	$0.0041 = S'_{10}$	$0.6949 = P_{10} = S'_{10}/S_8$	$0.0067 = S^C_{10} = P_{10} . S^C_8$

Note : If there are mrariage taking place below age 10, the actual proportion should be taken.

$$S(45)=\frac{{}_5S_{40}+{}_5S_{45}}{2}$$

$$=.0079$$

and

$$1-S(45)=.99205$$

$$SMAM=\frac{18.63-45 * .0079}{1-.0079}$$

$$=\frac{18.63-.3577}{.99205}$$

$$=18.42 \text{ years}$$

We obtained *SMAM* as 18.31 years for 1981 by using Hajnal method directly which is due to different assumptions in two methods, Agarwala method will always provide higher *SMAM* in case the proportion single is declining. When a cohort experiences higher marriage ratio *i.e.* proportion single is increasing during the intercensal period, Agarwala Method would provide lower age at marriage.

5.4. Net Nuptiality Table Based on Census Data

Nuptiality Tables discussed in the last section are based on statistics from vital registration. But it is well known fact that there is virtually no marriage registration system in most of the developing countries. In some countries of the third would, registration does exist but it is quite defective and incomplete. In such cases, census is the only source which provides data on the marital status. If data on marital status available from more than one census is conducted 5 years or 10 years apart we can indirectly infer the probability of marriages for the intercensal period.

The basic requirements for nuptiality table are probabilities of marriage by age (Gross Nuptiality Table) or probabilities of marriage and death (Net Nuptiality Table). For estimating the marriage probabilities in different age groups, we take never married population who are exposed to the risk of marriage and make the following assumptions :

(1) There are no mortality differentials among the single, married and widowed populations.

(2) All the marriages are the first marriage only.

(3) Population is closed to migration.

The first assumption is applicable only when there is no life table separately for each marital status. If no life table is applicable by marital status, under this assumption the mortality of general population can be taken to be true for the never married population. In the present methodology, we survive the cohort of earlier census to the next census and assume that there are only two competing risks for decreament in the cohort size – marriage and death – migration is not considered as a decreament factor. Further we are taking cohort of never married population who are exposed to the risk of first marriage only.

5.4.1 Estimation of Marriage Probability and Construction of Net Nuptiality Table for the Women

Let us consider the two consecutive censuses conducted at 0 and t with t years apart. We consider the following notations :

Z^0_x and Z^t_x : Number of singles (never married women) aged x at time 0 and t.

${}_tM_x$: Number of marriages occurring to Z^0_x during the intercensal period.

E^0_x and E_x^t : Ever married women aged x at time 0 and t.

${}_tM'_x$: Number of women married during intercensal period and survived upto second census.

${}_te_x$: Number of women married during intercensal period and died in that period.

${}_tM_x$: ${}_tM'_x + {}_te_x$.

${}_tg_x$: Probability of marrying in x to $x+t$.

$_tS_x$: Survival ratio for ages x to $x+t$ preferably census survival ratio.

$_tD_x$: Total deaths during intercensal period from $Z^0{}_x$.

$P^0{}_x$ and $P^t{}_x$: Total population at time 0 and t.

$C^0{}_x$ and $C^t{}_x$: Proportion of single at time 0 and t.

$P_x(g, s)$: Combined probability for remaining single and alive from age x to $x+t$.

Derivation :

By definition

$$_tg_x = \frac{_tM_x}{Z^0{}_x} \qquad ...(1)$$

or

$$_tg_x = \frac{_tM^s{}_x + {_te_x}}{Z^0{}_x} \qquad ...(2)$$

and

$$_tM^t{}_x = E^t{}_{x+t} - {_tS_x} \,.\, E^0{}_x \qquad ...(3)$$

$$= E^t{}_{x+t} - \frac{P^t{}_{x+t}}{P^0{}_x} E^0{}_x$$

We know that

$$\left.\begin{aligned} E^0{}_x &= P^0{}_x - Z^0{}_x \\ E^t{}_{x+t} &= P^t{}_{x+t} - Z_x{}^t \end{aligned}\right] \qquad ...(A)$$

If the events are evenly distributed,

$$t^e{}_x = \frac{_tD_x \times {_tg_x}}{2}$$

and

$$_tD_x = (1 - {_tS_x}) Z^0{}_x$$

so

$$\frac{_tD_x}{Z^0{}_x} = 1 - {_tS_x} \qquad ...(B)$$

so

$$_tl_x = \frac{(1 - {_tS_x}) Z^0{}_x \,.\, {_tg_x}}{2} \qquad ...(4)$$

Substituting the value of $_te_x$ in equation (2), we get :

$$_tg_x = \frac{_tM^s{}_x}{Z^0{}_x} + \frac{(1 - {_tS_x})\, {_tg_x}}{2} \qquad ...(5)$$

Further let us substitute ${}_tM^t_x$ from equation (3) in equation (5)

$${}_tg_x = \frac{E^t_{x+t} - {}_tS_x{}^0E_x}{Z_x{}^0} + \frac{(1 - {}_tS_x){}_tg_x}{2}$$

or $${}_tg_x\left[1 - \frac{1 - {}_tS_x}{2}\right] = \frac{E^t_{x+t} - {}_tS_xE^0_x}{Z^0_x}$$

$${}_tg_x\left[\frac{2 - 1 + {}_tS_x}{2}\right] = \frac{E_{x+t} - {}_tS_xE^0_x}{Z^0_x}$$

so $${}_tg_x = \frac{2(E^t_{x+t} - {}_tS_xE^0_x}{Z^0_x} \qquad \ldots(6)$$

Now let us substitute the equation (A) and value of ${}_tS_x$ in equation (6) and after simplification, we have.

$${}_tg_x = \frac{2{}_tS_x}{1 + {}_tS_x} \cdot \left[1 - \frac{C^t_{x+t}}{C_x{}^0}\right] \qquad \ldots(7)$$

where $$C^t_{x+t} = \frac{Z^t_{x+t}}{P^t_{x+t}}$$

$$E_x{}^0 = \frac{Z_x{}^0}{P_x{}^0}$$

So the equation (7) gives us the age-specific marriage probabilities for intercensal period. It is interesting to note that Agarwala had defined the intercensal marriage probability as

$${}_tg_x = 1 - \frac{C^t_{x+t}}{C^0_x} \qquad \ldots(8)$$

The equation (8) can be derived easily when we take

$${}_te_x = {}_tD_x \,.\, {}_tg_x$$

and proceed as discussed above.

Let us recall equation (5) again

$${}_tg_x = \frac{{}_tM^t_x}{Z^0_x} + \frac{(1 - {}_tS_x){}_tg_x}{2}$$

$$= {}_tg'_x + \frac{(1 - {}_tS_x){}_tg_x}{2}$$

where $\qquad {}_tg'_x = \dfrac{{}_tM^s{}_x}{Z^0{}_x}$

or $\qquad {}_tg'_x = {}_tg_x \dfrac{(1+{}_tS_x)}{2}$ ...(9)

We also know that

$$Z^s{}_{x+t} = Z^0{}_x - {}_tM^s{}_x - {}_tD_x$$

$$= Z^0{}_x\left[1 - \frac{{}^tM^s{}_x}{Z_x{}^0} - \frac{{}_tD_x}{Z^0{}_x}\right]$$

by equation (*B*)

$$Z^t{}_{x+t} = Z^0{}_x[1 - {}_tg^s{}_x - \{1 - {}_tS_x\}]$$

Now using eqn. (9) and simplifying

we get

$$Z^t{}_{x+t} = Z^0{}_x\left[{}_tS_x - {}_tg_x\frac{(1+{}_tS_x)}{2}\right]$$

$$Z^0{}_xP(g,\ s) \qquad \text{...(10)}$$

where $\qquad P(g,\ s) = {}_tS_x - {}_tg_x\dfrac{(1+{}_tS_x)}{2}$ ...(*C*)

is combined probability for remaining single and alive from age *x* to $x+1$.

5.4.2 Construction :

The census generally taken at 10 years interval provide marital status data in 5-years age interval. Using equation (7) we can derive the marriage probability for 10 years age interval of unconventional age group. For example from 12.5 to 22.5, 17.5 to 27.5 and so on. The 5-years marriage probability in conventional age group is obtained as follows :

We have

$$1 - {}_{10}g_{x+2\cdot5} = (1 - {}_5g_{x+2\cdot5})(1 - {}_5g_{x+7\cdot5})$$

$$X: 0,\ 5,\ 10\ldots\ldots$$

or $\qquad {}_5g_{x+7\cdot5} = \dfrac{{}_{10}g_{x+2\cdot5} - {}_5g_{x+2\cdot5}}{1 - {}_5g_{x+2\cdot5}}$ ...(11)

$$X: 0,\ 5\ldots\ldots$$

For example :

when $x=0$

$$ {}_5g_{7\cdot5}=\frac{{}_{10}g_{2\cdot5}-{}_5g_{2\cdot5}}{1-{}_5g_{2\cdot5}} $$

$$ ={}_{10}g_{2\cdot5} $$

when ${}_5g_{2\cdot5}=0$

i.e., no marriage in early age group

when $x=5$

$$ {}_5g_{12\cdot5}=\frac{{}_{10}g_{7\cdot5}-{}_5g_{7\cdot5}}{1-{}_5g_{7\cdot5}} $$

So using equation (9) we can estimate ${}_5g_{7\cdot5}$, ${}_5g_{12\cdot5}$, ${}_5g_{17\cdot5}$...... etc. 5 years marriage probabilities. To obtain these probabilities in conventional age groups.

We can use following approximation :

$$ 1-{}_5g_{10}=\sqrt{(1-{}_5g_{7\cdot5})(1-{}_5g_{12\cdot5})} $$

$$ 1-{}_5g_{15}=\sqrt{(1-{}_5g_{12\cdot5})(1-{}_5g_{17\cdot5})} $$

or in general :

$$ 1-{}_5g_x=\sqrt{(1-{}_5g_{x-2\cdot5})(1-{}_5g_{x+2\cdot5})} $$

$$ X: 10, 15\ldots\ldots 35 \qquad \ldots(12) $$

The methodology discussed above is illustrated in Table 5.4 and 5.5 which uses the $P(g, s)$ function defined in equation (C) to estimate the never married women at each age.

5.5. Marriage Dissolution and Duration of Fertile Union

Marriage dissolution and duration of fertile union are regarded under intercourse variables through which social change may affect fertility in Davis and Black framework. In Bongaarts model however, these variables do not find place but duration of fertile union does have relation with fertility. Earlier to the introduction of family planning programme, the fertility differentials by caste in India were assumed to be mostly due to ban on the widow remarriages in some castes. So

TABLE 5.4

Estimation of Marriage Probability for Female in India, 1971-81

Age	*Mid age*	*Female Population in* 1971 (P^0_x)	*Never Married female in* 1971 (Z^0_x)	*Female Population in* 1981 (P^t_x)	*Never Married female in* 1981 (Z^t_x)	*Ceasus Survival ratio* ($_tS_x$)
(*1*)	(2)	(*3*)	(*4*)	(*5*)	(*6*)	(*7*)
0— 5	2.5	42051160	42051160			0.90952
5—10	7.5	36236717	36236717			0.88434
10—15	12.5	30300538	26692125	38248464	36294688	0.90963
15—20	17.5	25337299	108005558	32045521	18041484	0.96197
20—25	22.9	24987931	1955690	27562269	4505385	0.84642
25—30	27.5	19473032	223582	24373748	503545	0.94712
30—35	32.5	17102301	123761	21150403	134921	0.93787
35—40	37.5			18443281	103280	
40—45	42.5			16039697	80955	

(Contd.)

Age	Mid Age	Population Single 1971 (C^0_x)	Population Single in 1981 (C^t_x)	$\frac{C^t_{x+t}}{C^0_x}$	$\frac{2\,{}_tS_x}{1+{}_tS_x}$	${}_{10}g_x$	${}_5g_{x+5}$
(8)	(9)	(10)	(11)	(12)	(13)	(14)	(15)
0—5	3.5	1.00000		0.948897	0.95262	0.04861	—
5—10	7.5	1.00000		0.56300	0.93862	2.41018	0.04861
10—15	12.5	0.88091	0.94897	0.18556	0.95268	0.77590	0.38004
15—20	17.5	0.42627	0.56300	0.01857	0.98062	0.93309	0.63852
20—25	22.5	0.07827	0.16346	0.08151	0.91682	0.84209	0.81490
25—30	27.5	0.01148	0.02066	0.48780	0.97284	0.49829	0.14690
30—35	32.5	0.00724	0.00638	0.69751	0.96794	0.29279	0.29279
35—40	37.5		0.00560				
40—45	42.5		0.00505				

TABLE 5.5

Net Nuptiality Table for Female, India, 1971-81

Age	*Probability of marriage* ($_5g_x$)	*Probability of survival life table* ($_5S_x$)	$P(_xg,s)$	*Number of singles alive at age* (sl_x)	*Person years lived as single* SL_x*	*Person years lived after age* $x(T_x)$	*Average number of years expected to live as single*
(1)	(2)	(3)	(4)	(5)	(6)	(7)	(8)
10—15	0.2320	0.9894	0.7586	100000	439650	870043	8.70
15—20	0.5266	0.9842	0.4618	75860	277230	430393	5.67
20—25	0.7413	0 9788	0.2453	35032	109063	153163	4.63
25—30	0.6026	0.9780	0.3820	8593	29690	44100	5.13
30—35	0.2233	0.9767	0.7560	3283	14410	14410	4.39

the high incidence of widowhood combined with social ban on the widow remarriage may be important factors in reducing fertility.

With the improvement in Mortality, there has been continuous decline in proportion of widows. This increases the average age at widowhood thereby duration of fertile union. The changes in the proportion of widows are exhibited in the Table 5.6.

The table 5.6 clearly shows the reduction in proportion widows by more than 50 per cent during 1961-71 decade.

TABLE 5.6

Percentage of Widows by Age in India

Age Group	*Percentage of widows by Age*		
	1961	*1971*	*1981*
10-14	0.13	0.05	0.03
15-19	0.53	0.33	0.21
20-24	1.30	0.88	0.69
25-29	2.89	1.94	1.50
30-34	6.42	4.09	3.12
35-39	11.15	7.03	5.42
40-44	20.66	14.38	10.86
45-49	28.84	20.65	15.96

Source : Census of India 1961, Vol. I Part II-(*i*), Census of India, 1971, Series-1 India, Part II-C (II), Census of India, 1981, Series-I, India Part II C (*ii*).

5.5.1 Estimation of Mean Age at Widowhood

Information about the frequency of widowhood by age is generally not available for India. There is no possibility therefore of directly calculating the mean age at widowhood. Nevertheless, Agarwala (1972) proposed a method under the following assumptions :

(*i*) population is closed to migration.

(*ii*) synthetic cohort of married and widowed over age do not decline by death

(*iii*) there is no remarriage of the widowed.

With the above assumptions, the mean age at the widowhood by age k can be estimated as :

$$\overline{X}_w = \frac{\sum_{x=0}^{k-n} n \cdot ({}_nW_x) - K \cdot W_k}{1 - W_k}$$

where

${}_nW_x$: proportion of currently married among the ever married and widowed between ages x and $x+n$

$$= \frac{\text{married women}}{\text{married} + \text{widowed}}$$

W_k : proportion of the currently married women among the married and widowed group at exact age k

$$= \frac{{}_nW_{k-n} + {}_nW_k}{2}$$

If the data on widow-remarriages is available by age, the above formula can be modified. The formula after incorporating information on widow remarriages becomes :

$$\overline{X}_{wr} = \frac{\sum_{x=0}^{k-n} n\left({}_nW_x - {}_nr_x\right) - k\,(w_k - r_k)}{1 - (W_k - r_k)}$$

where

${}_nr_x$: proportion of widow remarriage among the non-widowed group between ages x and $x+n$.

r_k : proportion of widow remarriage among the non-widowed group at exact age k.

5.5.2 Mean Duration of the Fertile Union

Generally in fertility analysis span between 15 and 50 years is considered as reproductive period. However, whole of the reproductive period is not utilised for the reproduction due to various reasons. Therefore, we consider the effective duration of fertile union which begins with the age at effective marriage (age at the consumption of marriage) and terminates with separation or divorce, or death of either or both of the married partners or after crossing of the age of 50 due to occurrence of the secondary sterility. In the case of India, the incidence of separation and divorce is almost negligible though increasing over period of time. Let us consider the following three situations :

(*i*) Those who marry below the age of 15 become widowed before reaching the age of 15 years but do not remarry will not spend even single year in the fertile union. However, we have to consider the extent of remarriage to estimate how many women from this group reach age 15 as married.

(*ii*) Some proportion of women married by the age of 15 may survive alongwith their husband till they reach the age of 50 years Under the assumption that there is no sterility, they spend the whole of 35 years in fertile union. However, the primary sterile women have to be excluded from the calculation whereas one has to estimate the average age of those women who attain secondary sterility before age of 50 years.

(*iii*) The third group of women are those whose union is broken either due to divorce, death of the partner duriug 15—50 years and so spend only part of their reproductive period in the fertile union. In this case also, we have to examine, how many of these women become secondary sterile before their marriage was broken.

It is therefore very difficult to estimate the average age of leaving the fertile union. However, the weighted average of the mean age under three situations discussed above would be the average age of leaving the fertile union. So the mean duration of fertile union can be estimated as the difference of the average age of leaving the fertile union and the mean age of the effective marriage.

It has been shown by Agarwala (1973) that the average age of leaving fertile union can be estimated as :

$$\bar{y} = \sum_{k=0}^{k-n} n \; {}_nC_x \; n\bar{C}_{x+m}$$

where

${}_nC_x$: proportion of currently married females among the ever married between aged x and $x+n$.

${}_n\bar{C}_x$: proportion of currently married males among the ever married between ages x and $x+n$.

m : average age difference of the husband and wife which is generally taken as 5 years for India.

Thus the duration of fertile union is given as ;

$$D = \bar{Y} - \bar{X}$$

where $\bar{X}$: effective age at marriage.

The mean duration of fertile union for the different decade synthetic cohorts of women for India is given below :

Decade	*Age at Entry*	*Age at Leaving*	*Duration (in years)*
1901-11	16.1	37.1	21.0
1911-21	16.1	34.4	18.3
1921-31	16.0	39.9	23.9
1931-41	17.0	33.8	16.8
1941-51	17.0	39.9	22.9
1951-61	17.0	42.0	25.0
1961-71	17.8	42.9	25.1

Source : Agarwala S.N. 1972 : *India's Population Problems* Tata Mc-Graw-Hill Publishing Company Limited Bombay.

The above table indicates the fact that there has been increase of about 4 years in duration of fertile union over the period 1901-1971. Further out of maximum 35 years of reproductive span Indian women on an average enjoy about 25 years of duration of fertile union as of 1971. But this estimate seems to be on higher side probably because sterility factors are ignored. If we consider average birth interval of 3 years, the married women in India must get about 8 children. However, the total number of children per married women never exceeded 7. It is to be mentioned therefore, that 25 years is not actually a fertile union but the duration for which husband and wife live together. The effective fertile union may be assessed indirectly by estimating average age at marriage for those women who marry after age 15 and average age of the women at the birth of the last child. The average of the women at the birth of the last child is around 35.6 years but there is no estimate available for age at marriage for those marrying after age 15. It can however be assessed from following equation :

Duration of fertile union = Age at last child − [Age at first child-waiting time - Gestation.]

$$D = LC - FC + W.T + GP$$

where

D : duration of fertile union.

LC : age of the women at the birth of last child.

FC : age of the women at the birth of first child.

$W.T$: Waiting time.

GP : Gestation Period (9 months).

The age at the birth of first child is estimated to about 21.6 years and waiting time from marriage to first birth may be taken as 3 months.

So $D = 35.6 - 21.6 + (3+9)/12$

$= (14 - 1)$ year

$= 13$ years

It should be noted that after the birth of the last child, couple may be in fertile union but the fecundity may be zero either naturally or through the use of contraception.

5.6. Age Pattern of Marriage

Regularities in the age patterns of fertility and mortality have led demographers to propose mathematical or empirical models. But very less attention is paid to model the age pattern of marriage probably due to the fact that marriage is more closely related to social and cultural factors than the biological. Coale (1971) showed that there is a regular pattern of marriage observed in various countries and it can be approximated by a simple mathematical curve. His analysis was based on European populations but model has been applied to various countries to examine the age patterns of marriage. The standard risk of marriage at age (x) which was calculated from the Swedish data for 1859-69 was fitted very closely by the double exponential curve :

$$g_s(x)=0.174 \text{ exp. } (-4.411 \text{ exp. } (-0.309\,x))$$

For a cohort of population in which marriage begins at age x_0 and time scale of marriage is compressed by a factor k, the risk of marriage $g(x)$ among those who ever marry will be given by :

$$g(x)=\frac{.174}{k} \text{ exp. } \left(-4.411 \text{ exp. } (-\frac{.309}{K}\,(x-a_0)\right)$$

Here k is the scale factor expressing the number of years of nuptiality in the given population equivalent to one year in the standard population. For example, if $k=0.50$, it means that marriage rates are double of that experienced by the standard Swedish population.

Coale and McNeil (1972) provided the following equation of age specific marriage rate for generating the model fertility schedules :

$$g(x)=\frac{.19465}{k} \text{ exp. } \left[-\frac{.1741}{K}(x-a_0-6.06k)-\text{exp.} \left(-\frac{.2881}{K}\,(x-a_0-6.06k)\right)\right]$$

For the above curve, if a_0 and K are known we have

Mean Age $= a_0 + 11.37k$

Median $= a_0 + 10.04k$

Variance $= 43.34\ K^2$

For estimating a_0 and K, we require to calculate R_1, R_2 and R_3 as :

$$R_1 = \frac{\text{Number of Ever Married (15-19)}}{\text{Number of Ever Married (20-24)}}$$

$$R_2 = \frac{\text{Number of Ever Married (20-24)}}{\text{Number of Ever Married (25-29)}}$$

$$R_3 = \frac{\text{Number of Ever Married (25-29)}}{\text{Number of Ever Married (30-34)}}$$

If significant number of marriages takes place in 10–14 age group, we can shift one age earlier, in order to calculate R_1. We take R_1 and R_2 combination if $R_1 > 1 - R_3$ otherwise R_2 and R_3 combination. Once we have fixed the combination, a_0 and k can be interpolated from the Table 5.1 in the Appendix. Now, if the estimated value of a_0 comes out to be, say, 0.56 and the first age group used in calculation of R_1 is 10–14, the final estimate of a_0 would be 10.56 years. The estimated parameters for the females of India 1971 are $a_0 = 11.80$, $k = .496$ and $c = .991$. Hence

Mean age at marriage for the females in 1971

$= 11.80 + .496 \times 11.37 = 17.4$ years

Median age for the females in 1971

$= 11.80 + .496 \times 10.04 = 16.8$ years.

One can even use logistic curve and a mixture of two exponential distribution to describes age pattern of marriage. Same authors have also proposed distribution to describe marriage events to a what as it ages.

6

Migration

Population of an area may be affected in size due to exodus of its members to another area or due to the influx of persons from other areas. Persons who make moves from one area to another area, in general, form a selected group of individuals having particular demographic, social and economic characteristics. As such, their moves not only affect the sizes of the populations of the areas of their origin and destinations but also their characteristics and compositions The type of the moves made by persons which are effective in changing the size and composition of the population of an area, are termed as migration. The concept of migration thus involves a change in the locality of usual residence – a taking up of life in a new or different place. Most of the vital processes like nuptiality, natality and mortality analysed so far move steadily and take considerably longer time in affecting the age-sex composition of the population. Process of migration on the other hand, usually disrupts the normal course of the other vital processes ; and can be very fast in its effects transferring millions of persons in a comparatively short duration and changing significantly the distribution of the population and their activities. Demographically speaking, migration is an uncertain event in an individual's life, in common with others, such as marriage, divorce, etc. The only certain events are births and deaths.

6.1. Definitions and Concepts

A migration is defined as a move from one area to another area during a given interval of time. Process of migration infact continues over time. In order to assess its volume (size) one has to specify the interval during which movements of persons in and out side of a locality or area is to be studied. The interval may be definite, *e.g.*, one year, five years, ten years, the intercensal period or it may be life time of the population alive at a given date. In case of fixed interval, the migration is called period migration to distinguish from the life-time migration. Thus a migrant is a person who has changed his usual place of residence/or country at least once during the migration interval. In the Indian context, the areas of migration are, generally, a village in rural and a town in urban place. Thus a person who moves out from one village to another village or town is termed as migrant provided the movement is not of purely temporary nature on account of casual leave, visits, etc.

For a given migration interval, the number of migrants is always less than or equal to the number of migrants with respect to an area because some persons are likely to move more than once during the given interval. Thus the amount of migration is likely to be understated. The magnitude of understatement is positively associated with the length of the interval.

Life Time Migrant and Life Time Migration

A person whose area of residence at the census or survey date differs from the area of his birth or natioanlity is a life time migrant. The number of such persons in a population is termed as life time migration.

Immobiles or non-migrants

People who are seen living throughout their entire life time and die in the same place where they were born are defined as non-migrants or immobiles.

International and Internal Migration

The usage of the term "migration" is generally restricted to rather permanent changes in residence between specifically designated political or statistical areas or between types of residence areas such as, between rural and urban localities. For demographic studies, two broad categories of migration, namely, *international migration* and *internal migration* are studied. International migration refers to the movement across the national boundaries. It is called emigration from the point of the nation from which the movement occurs and immigration from the point of receiving nation The term, internal migration refers to the migration within the boundaries of a given nation. The internal migration is operationally defined in terms of residential moves across civil divisions such as districts, states, communes, rural and urban areas like cities. The residential moves which do not result in crossing such a boundary are termed "mobility" rather than migration. Out-migration and in-migration refer to internal migration from or to a given area within a country.

Gross and Net Migration

Movement into a country may be called gross immigration while movement outside a country as gross emigration. The difference between gross emigration and gross immigration is termed as net emigration or net immigration depending on the fact whether emigration or immigration is larger. With respect to the given area within a country, the sum of in-migration and out-migration or of in-migrants and out-migrants is called as *turn over*. Difference between the numbers of in-migrants and out-migrants with respect to a specified area is called net-migration. If the in-migration exceeds out-migration, the net gain to the area is called as net in-migration and takes apositive sign. In case the in-migration is less than out-migration, we have net out-migra-tion, which takes the negative sign.

Migration Streams

A migration stream is the total number of moves made during a given migration interval that have common area of origin and a common area of destination (UN, 1970). If the migration stream from area i to area j is represented by the symbol M_{ij}, the opposing stream is represented by M_{ji}. The larger of the two is designated as *stream* or the *dominant stream* and the smaller as the *counter-stream* or *reverse-stream*. The sum, $M_{ij}+M_{ji}$, is called gross-*inter-change*. When differences are taken between streams, and counter streams for individual pairs of streams, the balances are *net streams*. The algebraic sum of all the net streams for a given area is equal to the net migration for that area.

Primary Migrants and Secondary Migrants

A person who moves from the place of his birth to another place and if it is his first move, he is called primary migrant with respect to place of his destination; but if he moves from his place of birth or usual residence several times, he is called secondary migrant with respect to place of destination.

Return Migration

A return migrant is a person who moves back to the area where he formerly resided. Not all return migration is identified in the usual sources of migration data. It is necessary to know the origin and destination of individual migrants for at least two migration periods.

Birth Place Migrant

If at the time of census enumeration, there is change in the usual place of residence of an individual with reference to his/her birth place, he/she is defined as a migrant in accordance with "birth place" concept.

Last Residence Migrant

If at the time of census enumeration a change in the usual place of residence of an individual is noted with reference to his/her previous usual residence, he/she is defined as a migrant in accordance with "last residence" concept.

Fixed Period Migrant

If at the time of census/survey enquiry, a change in the usual place of residence of an individual is noted with respect to his/her usual residence prior to a given fixed period of time, he/she is termed as migrant during the given period of time.

Intra-district Migrants

When a person moves out from his place of usual residence or birth to another politically defined area which is within the district of enumeration, he/she is termed as an intra district migrant.

Inter District Migrants

A person who in the course of migration crosses the boundry of the district of enumeration but remains within the state of enumeration is termed as an inter-district migrant.

Intra State and Inter State Migrants can be similarly defined as intra district and inter district migrants by substituting state in place of district and country in place of state. This concept can be extended to cover intra country and inter country migrants defined generally as internal migration and international migration.

In this Chapter study of internal migration and international migration is done separately because of (*i*) difference in the modes of collection of data needed for their analysis, (*ii*) difference in the treatment of such data and (*iii*) their specific importance in the study of population growth. Throughout most of the world, international migration plays now a very modest role as a component of population growth and there is comparatively very little redistribution of population between nations. (Bogue 1969). On the other hand, internal migration is the principal mechanism of affecting the growth of states and districts within the country.

6.2 Internal Migration

Study of internal migration is important to study the dynamics of growth of sub-national population, changes in their characteristics and redistribution of population 'perse'. It is also of direct interest because of its interaction with different aspects of social and economic change and differentiation taking place within the country.

Principal Sources of Data on Internal Migration

Censuses, population registers and sample surveys are the main sources of information on internal migration. Census data have been and will remain the major source of information on internal migration in most of the countries of the world. The census data on internal migration are obtained directly by including a question on migration, and indirectly through estimation procedures that use data presumably obtained for other purposes. The usual direct questions on internal migration have to do with place of birth; place of last residence; duration of residence in the place of enumeration; place of residence on a specific date before the census. On the basis of these questions, the total population in any area may be classified into two groups *migrants* and *non-migrants*. Since 1881 in India, information only on place of birth has been regularly collected. In 1961 census of India, data on migration was however, collected in more details with reference to the following questions on the individual slips :

(*a*) Birth place

(*b*) Whether born in village or town

(*c*) Duration of Residence

The scope of data on migration was further expanded in 1971 census and following questions were put to each individual.

(*i*) Birth place

(*a*) Place of birth

(*b*) Rural/Urban

(*c*) District

(*d*) State/Country

(*ii*) Last Residence

(a) Place of last residence

(b) Rural/Urban

(*c*) District

(*d*) State/Country

(*iii*) Duration of last residence at the village or town of enumeration.

In 1981 census of India, the scope of data on migration has been further expanded by asking the individuals to supply reasons of migration. In addition to direct questions on migration, indirect information on internal migration can be obtained by comparison of total population counts for component areas in two censuses. The difference between the population counts at two censuses gives a measure of population change in the area. If this change cannot be accounted by births and deaths alone in the area, the balance is attributable to migration. An estimate of net migration for the area is obtained by subtracting natural increase from the total change. Correspondingly, areal estimates of net intercensal migration can be obtained from the sex-age distribution of two sucessive censuses.

Periodic sample surveys have also become an important source of demographic information in many countries. The potential uses of the sample surveys for providing migration statistics are enormous. The specific questions on internal migration that are asked in sample surveys can be the same as those asked in censuses. Howeve, their scope is limited to the extent that they can provide only limited geographical details. Surveys, provide an opportunity to study process of migration in more depth by asking information on status of migrants at fixed prior date, reasons of migrating and social and economic characteristics of individual migrants. Both censuses and surveys represent a *retrospective* approach to the measurement of migration. The results therefore refer to the migration of the surviving person at the date of enquiry. When survey data on migration are collected more frequently and at regular intervals, better time series data on migration may be made available than are available from the censuses.

6.3 Measurement of Internal Migration

Indirect Estimates of Net Migration

Indirect estimates of internal migration can be obtained from the population counts by age and sex or even from the population totals. The methods of computing indirect estimates of net migration are :

(*i*) *The national growth rate method* and

(*ii*) The *residual method*, comprising of (*a*) the *Vital statistics* method and (*b*) the *survival rate* method.

6.3.1 National Growth Rate Method

This is very simple and commonly used method. Let P_T^0 and P_T^1 be the national population at the beginning and end of the intercensal period, respectively. Also let $P^0_1, P^0_2 \cdots P^0$ and $P^1_1, P^1_2, \cdots P^1_i$ be the populations of the geographic subdivisions at the beginning and end of the period. Then the estimated migration rate m_i, for area i is given by

$$m_i = \left[\frac{P^1_i - P^0_i}{P^0_i} - \frac{P_T^1 - P_T^0}{P_T^0}\right] K \quad \ldots(1)$$

where k is a constant, customarily taken to be equal to 100 or 1,000 The positive value of m_i denotes the net inmigration and the negative value denotes the net out migration rate. The above procedure can be adopted to obtain the migration rate by agesex groups. The underlying assumption under this method is that the rates of natural increase and of net inmigration from abroad are the same for all parts of the country. The most important advantage is that it does not require any vital statistics and as such, this provides an useful tool for estimating the internal migration for the subdivisions of any developing country where registration of vital events are not reliable.

A variant of the above method assumes that the rate of natural increase is the same throughout the country and accordingly

$$m_i = \left[\frac{P^1{}_i - P^0{}_i}{P^0{}_i} - \frac{B_T - D_T}{P^0{}_T}\right]K \qquad ...(2)$$

where the last term is the national rate of natural increase. This formula gives an estimate of the total rate of net migration including both international migration and net internal migration. As such the estimate given by formula (2) is algebraically higher than those obtained by using formula (1). This method can, however. be used for the countries where registration of births and deaths are quite reliable and good. In case net immigration is negligible, the both formulae should yield virtually same results. Therefore if net immigration is not negligible, it can be estimated by substracting the natural increase from the total population change,

$$\text{Net immigration} = \left[\frac{P^1{}_T - P^0{}_T}{P_T{}^0} - \frac{B_T - D_T}{P_T{}^0}\right] \qquad ...(3)$$

However, a risk involved in estimating net immigration by the above approach is that there may be considerable under registration of births and deaths or that there may by differential amount of completness of the two census counts.

6.3.2 Residual Methods

(a) Vital Statistics Method

Vital statistics approach is based on the simple use of the balancing equation

$$M = (P^1 - P^0) - (B - D) \qquad ...(4)$$

The above formula gives an estimate of net migration for the total population of an area for which population counts at the beginning and end of the intercensal period and births and deaths registered in that area during the intercensal period are available. This estimate of net migration reflects both the in-migrants and out-migrants who died before the second census. This estimate also includes the international migration. This method can be used for estimating net migration for a sex, race, or nativity group or by any other characteristics which do not change over time and provided that the population and the vital statistics are published by that characteristic.

One source of error in these estimates of net migration is a *change in the boundaries of the geographic* area or areas in question. If the territory transferred is an entire administrative unit such as village, or district transferred from one state to another state, requisite statistics can usually be made available. In case a part of such administrative units is transferred, vital statistics may be attributed to the new area, on the basis of proportional area, as measured on the the basis of old and new maps of the higher units like state. Further transfer occurs during the intercensal period hence Vital Statistics for the following years for the new geographic area donot require any adjustment. However, if the transfer occurs during the year, and vital statistics are available for total area for whole year, a special proration must be made for the year of transfer.

Exclusion of the International Migration

Any variant of the residual method of estimating net migration includes in its estimation, net immigration from abroad also. To get the estimate of net migration alone, vital statistics method should be confined only to the native population provided that the native population is available separately from the two censuses and that deaths are also tabulated by nativity. The formula for calculation is as follows :

$$M=(P^1_N-P^0_N)-(B-D_N)$$

where P^1_N and P^0_N are the native populations at the end and beginning of the intercensal periods respectively, D_N is the total number of deaths occurring to the native population and B denotes the total births in the intercensal period. Obviously all the births in the area are native by definition. The other approach will be to allow for net immigration from abroad by subtraction. For this purpose one must know not only the total immigration but also the area (state or province etc.) of intended residence of the immigrants and area of last residence of the emigrants. The assumption involved is that the migrants actually went to the place they had announced and stayed there until the next census and that emigrants were counted at the proceding census in the area given as that of last residence. For most of the developing countries, this information is not available.

Effects of Errors in Census Counts and Vital Statistics

Since the estimate of net migration represents a residual obtained by subtraction, even moderate errors in population counts or in vital statistics on births and deaths may produce much larger errors in the estimate of migration. However, these errors may be cancelling some times. In the developing countries, vital statistics are generally of poor quality and their errors will be reflected in the estimate. However, a part of the error may cancel since B and D have opposite signs in the equation.

This method can also be applied to particular segments of the population which do not change (sex) or for which the change over time is determinable (age). The balancing equation to estimate the amount of net migration among the population aged x at the time of first census is given by

$$M_{(x)} = P^1_{x+n} - P^0_x + D(x) \qquad \ldots(4)$$

where $M(x)$ is the migration among persons who were aged x at the earlier census, P^1_{x+n} is the population aged $x+n$ years at the latest census taken n years after, P^0_x is the population aged x at the earlier census, and $D(x)$ is deaths among persons who were aged x at the earlier census. Problem is that vital statistics are unlikely to be available in the kind of detail required for the cohort approach. The deaths are usually tabulated by age at death rather than by age at a fixed date, *e.g.*, the date of the last census. In order to find net migration among the persons not present at the earlier census and who were born during the year, the difference between total births and total deaths occuring to persons who were born during the period provides the estimate of net migration. It may be noted that in estimating net migration by age, the age data for both the censuses should be smoothed by using a graduation formula which involves short range of ages.

6.3.3 Survival Rate Method

The survival rate method is commonly used in the statistically under developed countries because it does not require accurate vital statistics. This method is also useful in estimating net international migration at the national level. The basic formula for estimating net migration by using forward survival ratio method is :

$$M^1_{x+t} = P^t_{x+t} - SP^0_x$$

where P^0_x and P^t_{x+t} denote the population aged x and $x+t$ at the first census and second census respectively, second census taken t years after the first. S is the survival rate of the population aged x at the first census. The last term on the right hand side of the expression is the expected population at the second census on the assumption of no migration. The difference between the expected and observed populations thus yields an estimate of net change due to migrations of persons who survived in the second census. Two main types of survival rates are used, those from the life tables and those from the censuses. An alternative to estimate the expected number of persons at the second census by applying "Forward survival ratios" to the numbers in the first census is to apply the "Reverse Survival Ratios" to estimate the number of persons that would have been x years of age at the earlier census from the number who are enumerated as $x+t$ years old in the second census. The resulting estimate of net migration thus includes deaths to the migrant cohorts and is equivalent to an assumption that all migrations occurred at the beginning of the interval. Symbolically

$$M^{11}_{(x)} = S^{-1} P^{t}_{x+t} - P^{0}_{x}$$

These two procedures always give different estimates of net migration but they are related by the relation :

$$M^{1} = SM^{11}$$

Thus M^1 and M^{11} are of the same sign as '*S*' is always positive and less than unity. M^1 is also greater than M^{11}. The assumption of timing of migration involved in the calculation of M^{11} is not realistic. A third procedure, the *Average Survival Ratio Method*, yields an average of M^1 and M^{11}. That is,

$$M = \frac{M^1 + M^{11}}{2}$$

This estimate, like M^{11} includes migrant deaths but on the assumption that deaths and migrations were evenly distributed over the decade or all the migrations occurred at the middle of the interval (Siegel and Hamilton, 1952).

The main types of survival rates used, are those from life tables and those from the censuses. Below we discuss the issues and implications of using these two type of rates.

Life Table Survival Rate (LTSR) Method

If we we express the survival rate *S* for a 5 year age group and 10 year period in the life table notation, we can get the estimate of net migration in age group say 20-24 as follows :

$$M^{1}_{20-24} = P^{1}_{20-24} - \frac{{}_5L_{20}}{{}_5L_{10}} X \, P^{0}_{10-14}$$

$$M^{11}_{20-24} = P^{1}_{20-24} \frac{{}_5L_{10}}{{}_5L_{20}} - P^{0}_{10-14}.$$

In general

$${}_{10}S_x = {}_5L_{x+10} \div {}_5L_x$$

If there is an open ended interval, say 70+, in the census age distribution,

$${}_{10}S_{70+} = \frac{T_{80}}{T_{70}}$$

It is important to note that the life table used should measure the average mortality conditions of the intercensal period and should be reasonably applicable to the area for which migration estimates are required. If a life table is not available for the area, but the average mortality level of the period is approximately known, model life tables can be used to calculate the survival rates. In case the life tables are available corresponding to the dates of the two censuses, survival rates can be computed from both life tables and the results can be averaged so as to give a better representation of the conditions during the intercensal period.

If the intercensal period is not 5 or 10 years, there are snme complications. The survival rates will have to be calculated for the number of years in the intercensal period and this calculation will require extra work if only an abridged life table is available. Further more, as the survival will appear in unconventional 5 year age groups, they should be redistributed into conventional 5 year age groups so that they may be compared with the age groups of the second census.

If au appropriate life table is available and if the census data are free from errors, the *LTRS* method should give fairly accurate estimate of the net migration for persons who were still alive at the time of the second census. But usually the age data suffer from errors of coverage and misreporting. As such, these defects are also be present in the migration estimates. However, it is possible to get an irregular pattern of migration estimates by age and the sum of net migration balances for all areal units may not add to zero which it must do in each age group. The discrepancy may be eliminated by forcing the sum of positive balances to equal the sum of the negative balances increasing the one and decreasing the other, and prorating the adjustment. The lack of smoothness in the migration estimates by age may be over come by smoothing either the census age data before applying the formula or the migration estimates themselves. The former procedure is preferable. However, the graduation formula should be preferably limited to narrow ranges of age, otherwise the graduation process may distort the estimates of net migration.

Application of the survival rate method do frequently omit the cohorts born during the intercensal period even when adequate data on registred births are available. Shryock and others however recommend that births in first quinquennium of 10 year intercensal period will be 5-9 years old and those born during the later quinquennium will be under 5 years old. Births can be represented in radix l_0 of the life table so that estimates of net migration is given by

$$M_{0-4}=P_{0-4}-S_{0-4}\,(B^{5-10})$$

$$M_{5-9}=P^{10}{}_{5-9}-S_{5-9}(B^{0-5})$$

where $B^{0\text{-}5}$ and $B^{5\text{-}10}$ denote total births registered in the area during first quinquennium and second quinquennium of the intercensal period respectively and

$$S_{0-4}=\frac{{}_5L_0}{5l_0}.$$

The life table functions should also correspond to the quinquenniums.

Census Survival Rate Method (CSR) :

A census survival rate at age x is the ratio of the popula tion aged $x+n$ at the second census to that aged x at the first census, where the censuses are taken n years apart.

Thus

$$S^n_x=\frac{P^{t+n}_{x+n}}{P^t_x}$$

Survival rate at the national level are only dependent on mortality and not on the internal migration. However, if there is substantial amount of external migration, for calculating the census survival rates we can take only native population at the national level. Having obtained the survival rates at the national level, they can be used in place of life table survival rates and like *LTSR* method estimates of net migration among the population aged 10+can be obtained. It may however be mentioned that this method has two underlying assumptions (1) that the mortality conditions of the local area are same as of the nation and (2) that the pattern of errors in the census age data at the national level is the same as the local area level. It is not surprising that some of the survival rates so obtained may exceed unity or substantially low because of coverage errors and age misreporting in the census or because of net immigration (or emigration) from abroad. The U.N. Manual VI gives the following formula to estimate the net migration among the children born during the intercensal period :

$$\text{Net } {}_5M_0 = \tfrac{1}{4}\, CWR_0 \text{ Net } {}_{30}M_{15}{}^{(f)} \qquad \ldots \quad \text{(A)}$$

$$\text{Net } {}_5M_5 = \tfrac{3}{4}\, CWR_5 \text{ Net } {}_{30}M_{20}{}^{(f)}$$

When net ${}_{50}M_{15}{}^{(f)}$ and net ${}_{30}M_{20}{}^{(f)}$ are the area estimates of net migration for females aged 15-44 and 20-49 respectively. Net ${}_5M_0$ and net ${}_5M_5$ are the net migration of children aged 0-4 and 5-9 respectively; CWK_0 and CWR_5 are the ratios of children aged 0-4 to women aged 15-44 and of children 5-9 to women aged 20-49 respectively at the second census date. By assuming that the flow of migration has been uniform and fertility ratios are constant. We can easily see that (*i*) the children below age of 5 years were on average born 2.5 years ago and only $\frac{1}{4}$ of their mother's migration occurred after that date, (*ii*) the children between 5 to 9 years of age at the last census were born on average 7.5 years earlier and $\frac{3}{4}$ of their mother's migration occurred after that date. This is why the multipliers on right hand side of (*A*) are $\frac{1}{4}$ and $\frac{3}{4}$ respectively.

We observe that for the country as a whole natural increase $(B_T - D_T)$ during the intercensal period is 2290118 whereas the difference between two census populations is 2107707. This indicates the emigration, subject to the assumption of natural increase being correct, or registration of births and deaths being 100% complete.

In the case of emmigration, $m_i^{(2)}$, which includes the effect of international migration along with the internal migration, will be lower than $m_i^{(1)}$, which considers only internal migration. Thus we observe that rates of national growth rate method based on natural increase are consistently lower than those by

TABLE 6.1

Estimation of Net Migration for Districts of Sri Lanka 1963-71 : National Growth Rate Method

District	Population		Population Change		National Growth Rate Based on	
	1963 P^0	1971 P^1	Amount $P^1 - P^0$	Rate*	Population	Natural Increase
1	2	3	4	5	6	7
Colombo	2207420	2672265	464845	21.058	1.141	0.583
Kalutara	631457	729514	98057	15.529	—4.389	—6.113
Kandy	1043632	1187925	144293	13.826	—6.092	—7.816
Matale	255630	314841	59211	23.163	3.245	1.521
Numara Eliya	397756	450278	52522	13.205	—5.713	—8.437

(*Contd.*)

1	2	3	4	5	6	7
Galle	641474	735173	93699	14.607	—5.311	—7.035
Matara	514969	586443	71474	13.879	—6.038	—7.762
Hambantola	274297	3402546	65957	24.046	4.128	2.404
Jaffna	612596	701603	89007	14.529	—5.389	—7.112
Mannar	60124	77780	17656	29.366	9.448	2.725
Vavuniya	68621	95243	26622	38.786	18.878	17.154
Batticaloa	194689	2 6595	60406	30,790	10.782	9.148
Amparai	211732	272605	60873	28.750	8.832	7.109
Trinomalee	135553	188245	49692	35.865	16.947	14,224
Kurunegala	852661	1025633	172972	20.286	10.368	— 1,355
Puttalam	302546	378430	75884	25.082	5.164	3,440
Anuradhapura	279738	38870	10898	38.952	19.034	17.310
Polonnaruwa	113971	163653	49682	45.597	23.674	21.950
Oadulla	521845	615405	93660	17.929	— 1.989	—3,713
Monaragala	133260	193026	60766	45.940	26.022	24.298
Ratnapura	546037	661344	115307	81.117	1.199	— 0.524
Ragulla	578306	634752	73246	13.180	— 6.738	— 8.462
Sri Lanka	10582064	12689771	2417707	19.916	—	—

*Rate=$(P^1 - P^0) \sqrt{P^1}$

(*Source* : U.N. ESCAP Country Monograph of Sri Lanka).

TABLE 6.2

Estimation of Intercensal Net Migration by Vital Statistics Method for Sri Lanka 1963-1971

District	*Intercensal Period 1963—1971*		*Vital Statistics Method*		
	Births	*Deaths*	*Natural Increase (S—D)*	*Net Migration Amount*	*Net Migration Rates*
1	2	3	4	5	6
Colombo	595068	169460	425608	39237	1.778
Kalutara	150803	43274	107529	— 9472	— 1.500
Kandy	604612	86264	218348	— 74055	— 7.096
Matale	84744	20184	64560	— 5349	— 2.093
Nuwara Eliya	112601	3748	75115	— 22593	— 5.680
Gale	158203	45001	113201	— 19502	— 2.040

(Contd.)

1	2	3	4	5	6
Matara	151009	33424	117585	— 46111	— 8.954
Hambantola	83951	15793	68158	— 2201	— 0.802
Jaffna	171145	45888	125257	— 35250	— 5.917
Mannar	20528	4718	15810	1846	3.070
Vavuniya	25347	4396	20951	5671	7.264
Satticaloa	77961	19555	58406	2000	1.019
Amparai	78163	15267	62896	— 2023	— 0.956
Trinomalee	51622	8360	43262	6430	4.641
Kurunegala	248131	52921	195210	— 22238	—12.608
Puttalam	94968	21653	74515	2569	0.849
Anuradhapura	101467	17605	83862	25120	8.978
Polonnaruwa	39709	5721	33988	15694	13.770
Jadulla	169587	4388	126039	— 32497	— 5.224
Monaragala	53585	9190	44393	16367	12.375
Ratnapura	160554	44185	116369	— 1062	— 0.195
Kegalla	134622	34366	100256	— 24010	— 4.150
Sri Lanka	3068180	778062	2290118	—182411	— 1,724

TABLE 6.3

Comparison of Net Migration by Three Methods

District	*National growth rate method based on*		*Vital statistics method*
	Population	*Natural increase*	
Colombo	25178	−12874	39237
Kalutara	−27715	−28900	− 9472
Kanoy	−63575	−81565	−74055
Matale	8295	3889	− 5349
Numara Eliya	−26702	−33558	−22953
Galle	−34068	−45126	−19502
Matara	−31096	−29973	−46111
Hambantola	11323	6595	− 2201
Jaffna	−33008	−43568	−36250
Mannar	5681	4644	1846
Vevuniya	12954	11771	5671
Batticaloa	21330	17948	2000
Amparai	18701	15051	− 2023
Trinomalee	22096	19708	6430
Kurunegala	3141	−11557	−22238
Puttalam	15624	10408	2569
Anuradhapura	53255	48438	25120
Polonnaruma	26982	25017	15694
Badulla	−10379	−19375	−32479
Monaraggala	34417	32137	16367
Ratnapura	6549	− 2863	− 1062
Kegalla	−38979	−48951	−24010
Sri Lanka	—	—	182411

the national growth rate method based on the population change.

Out of 22 districts, the sign of net migration is same by all the three methods for 18 districts. It is different from other two methods for natural increase-national growth rate-method in the case of only one district (Colombo). For Population change national growth rate-method, such is the situation in the case of two districts *viz.*, Kurunegala and Ratnapura. The maximum number of deviations in signs are by the vital statistics methods, for three districts Matale, Hambantola and Amparai. Wherever the signs of net migration agree for the three methods, the values of the rates by vital statistics method are lower in most of the cases. The maximum number of persons have out migrated from Kandy district. This is shown uniformly by all the three methods. Anuradhapura district gets the first rank in attracting more in-migrants by both the versions of natural growth rate method, whereas by vital statistics method. Colombo is the first one and Anuradhapura, the second. It may be noted here that Colombo and Kandy had the first and second largest populations in both the censuses.

Illustration of Census Survival Rate Method (CSR Method)

In 1963 there are some males and females whose ages are unspecified. We distribute them in proportion with the persons whose ages are known. The inflating factor for males (Sri Lanka)

$$= \frac{5502850}{5502850-36850}$$

$$=1.00674167581$$

The inflating factor for females (Sri Lanka)

$$= \frac{5087210}{5087210-33640}$$

$$=1.00665668033$$

Considering national populations in two censuses and assuming that total national population is closed for migration, we can find out census survival ratios.

Survival ratio for persons aged x at the first census, *i.e.*, 1953 will be

$$=\frac{\text{Population aged } x+n \text{ at the second census 1963}}{\text{Population aged } x \text{ at the first census 1953}}$$

After having got a set of survival ratios we apply them to populations of Matara district in 1953. The 1953 populations of Matara district are also adjusted by distributing persons of unspecified ages on prorata basis. The inflating factor for

$$\text{Males} \quad =\frac{257600}{257600-1430}$$

$$=1.00558223055$$

$$\text{Females} \quad =\frac{257420}{257420-1740}$$

$$=1.0068053813$$

To estimate the net migrants of ages 0—4 and 5—9, we use following relations

$$M_{0-4}=\tfrac{1}{4}\, CWR_0 \times M^{(f)}{}_{15-44} \text{ and}$$

$$M_{5-9}=\tfrac{3}{4}\, CWR_5 \times M^{(f)}{}_{20-49} \text{ where}$$

$$CWR_0=\frac{\text{Children (0-4) in 1963}}{\text{Women (15-44) in 1963}}=\frac{78499}{108875}$$

$$=0.721$$

$$CWR_5=\frac{\text{Children (5-9) in 1963}}{\text{Women (20-49) in 1963}}=\frac{72112}{93069}$$

$$=0.77482$$

$M^{(f)}{}_{15-44}$ denotes female net migrants of age 15-44

$M^{(f)}{}_{20-49}$ denotes female net migratns of age 20-49

$$M_{0-4}=\tfrac{1}{4}\,(6.721)\,(-6289)$$

$$=-1133.5922$$

$$M_{5-9}=\tfrac{3}{4}(0.77482)\,(-4837)$$

$$=-2810.8532$$

We break them up sex-wise by using proportions of males and females in respective age-groups in 1963.

TABLE 6.4

Computation of Net Migration by Quinquennial Age Groups fnr Males of Matara District of Sri Lanka in 1963 Using CSR Method

Males

Age Group	Population of Sri Lanka		Survival Ratio	Population of Matara District			Net Migrants (x to x+10)
	1953 aged x	1963 aged x+10		1953 aged x	1963 aged x+10	1963 aged x+10	
0—4	609020	616457	1.1272	297. 1	33568	34331	763
5—9	550022	524361	0.9534	33334	31779	25129	—6650
10—14	474739	443238	0.9336	26238	24497	16441	—8056
15—19	364438	378817	1.0395	18517	19248	15566	—3628
20—24	395165	356729	0.9027	17219	15598	15798	200
25—29	371205	341869	0.9210	14864	13689	13495	— 194

30—34	285303	260041	0.9115	11378	10371	10438	67
35—39	232138	248967	0.8522	11625	9907	10297	390
40—44	210585	193737	0.9201	9264	8524	8195	— 329
45—49	211357	157112	0.7433	8476	6320	7059	757
50—54	159664	141669	0.8873	7504	6658	7663	1005
55—59	108944	84697	0.7774	5158	3987	4666	679
60—64	83958	55552	0.6617	4825	3193	3449	256
65+	152218	67373	0.4426	10216	4522	4747	225
TOTAL					191843	177274	—14567

* Col. 4=(3) / (2)
Col. 6=(5) * (4)
Col. 8=(7) — (6)

TABLE 6.5

Computation of Net Migration of Females by Quinquennial Age Groups for Males of Matara District of Sri Lanka During 1953-63

Females

Age Group	Populations of Sri Lanka		Survival Ratio	Population of Matara District			Net Migrants (x to x+10)
	1953 aged x	1963 aged x+10		1953 aged x	1963 aged x+10	1963 aged x+10	
0—4	599809	654689	1.0915	30461	33248	33748	500
5—9	535892	505140	0.9426	28654	27010	26237	733
10—14	445447	447207	1.0040	22919	23010	20760	2250
15—19	399412	374003	1.1019	19999	22037	18153	3884
20—24	372307	318567	0.8557	20136	17230	16934	296
25—29	337666	311762	0.9233	16388	15131	15394	263

30—34	235482	213149	0.9052	11872	10746	11397	651
35—39	243452	198603	0.8158	11954	9752	10431	679
40—44	161475	154039	0.9539	8815	8409	8548	139
45—49	158959	114819	0.7223	8347	6029	6705	676
50—54	118490	103887	0.8768	6786	5950	6504	554
55—59	79681	66047	0.8289	4541	3764	4219	455
60—62	69490	48330	0.6955	4460	3102	3443	341
65+	131603	58869	0.4773	9668	4325	4662	337
Total					189743	187133	−3608

Col. 4=(3)/(2)

Col 6=(5)/(4)

Col. 8=(7)/(6)

TABLE 6.6

Computation of Net Migration for Males of Matara District of Sri Lanka During 1953-63 by Averaging the Estimates Obtained by Forward Survival Ratios Methods and Reverse Survival Method

Age Group X	*Population of Matara 1963*	*Survival Rato*	*Expected 1953 aged X*	*Enumerated 1953 aged X*	*Net Migrants*		*Average*
					by RSM	*by FSM*	
0—4	34331	1.1271	30458	29781	677	763	720
5—9	25129	0.9533	26359	33334	—6975	—6650	—6813
10—14	16441	0.9336	17609	26238	—8629	—8056	—8343
15—19	15566	1.0395	14975	18517	—3542	—3682	—3612
20—24	15798	0.9027	17500	17219	281	200	241
25—29	13495	0.9210	14653	14864	—211	—194	—202
29—34	10438	0.9115	11452	11378	74	67	70

35—39	10237	0.8522	12082	11625	457	390	423
40—44	8195	0.9901	8907	9274	—357	—329	—343
45—49	7059	0.7434	9496	8479	1018	757	888
50—54	7663	0.8873	8636	7504	1132	1005	1068
55—59	4666	0.7774	6002	5428	874	679	3106
60—64	3449	0.6617	5213	4825	388	256	322
65+	4747	0.4426	10725	10216	509	225	367

* Col. (4)=(2)/(3)
Col. (6)=(4)-(5)

Proportion (0-4) males

$$=\frac{42224}{78499}=0.5379,$$

Proportion (0-4) females=0.4621

Proportion (5-9) males

$$=\frac{38102}{72112}=0.5284,$$

Proportion (5-9) females=0.4716

$$\therefore \quad M_{0-4}=-1134=(-610 \text{ males})+(-524 \text{ females})$$

$$M_{5-9}=-2811=(-1485 \text{ males})+(-1326 \text{ females})$$

It may however he borne in mind that the estimates of the local areas obtained by using *CSR* method represent net internal migration plus net immigration rather than net internal migration alone. Further the estimates so obtained are also affected by changes in area boundaries and include international migration. The accuracy of the estimate also depends upon the applicability of the survival rates used to the area in question. It can be seen that the *CSR* estimates obtained by the forward method will generally be smaller than those obtained by the vital statistics method. In case, estimate of net immigration is known it is advised to remove it before calculating census survival rates.

The residual methods of estimating internal migration have their own limitations. At the most they can give estimate of net migration only. They can not ordinarily be used for social and economic groups because during the intercensal period, they are likely to change. These methods should be used with great cautions for estimating net migration for smaller areas because the life tables for larger populations will be in-appropriate in varying degrees in such situation.

6.4 Estimation of Internal Migration from Direct Questions on Migration in Censuses and Surveys

The most common questions on internal migration which are asked at the time of census taking are :

(1) Place of birth;

(2) Place of last residence;

(3) Duration of residence and

(4) Place of residence on a specific date before the census. On the basis of answers to these questions, the population in any area can be classified into migrants and non-migrants. Below we discuss the methods of estimating migration using different kinds of these data.

6.4.1 Place of Birth Data

The most simple and easily understood question having direct bearing on migration is that on place of birth. The life time migrants and non-migrants from place of birth data can be obtained by classifying the persons enumerated by place of birth and place of enumeration. All those who are enumerated in their place of birth are non-migrants and the rest are life time migrants. The main characteristics and problems of migration data obtained from place of birth data is that we get number of migrants but not the number of migrations. Further, not all the migrants are included in it. While return migrants are completely ignored, secondary migrants are treated having made only one move even if they have made more moves. Again the deceased migrants are excluded completely. Assume that there are three subregions, *A*, *B*, and *C* in a country and in any census a lay out for the distribution of enumerated population is given as below :

TABLE 6.A

Male Population Classified by Regions of Birth and Region of Enumeration on a Census Date

Region of Birth	*Region of Enumeration*			*Total*
	A	*B*	*C*	
A	N_{AA}	N_{AB}	N_{AC}	N_A
B	N_{BA}	N_{BB}	B_{BC}	N_B
C	N_{CA}	N_{CB}	N_{CC}	N_C
Total	$N.A$	$N.B$	$N.C$	N

The sum along the first row of all the entries except the first element (on the diagonal) gives the out migrants from the region A and it is equal to $N_{AB}+N_{AC}=O_A$. Similarly the out migrants from regions B and C are $N_{BA}+N_{BC}=O_B$. and $N_{CA}+N_{CB}=O_C$ respectively. Similarly the sum of entries in any column excluding the diagnoal element would give the in-migrants to the region. Thus $N_{BA}+N_{CA}=I_A$, $N_{AB}+N_{CB}=I_B$ and $N_{AC}+N_{BC}=I_C$ are the in-migrants to region A, B and C, respectively. The diagonal elements N_{AA}, N_{BB} and N_{CC} denote the non-migrants of the regions A, B and C respectively. The net life time migrants to any region can therefore be obtained as difference of out migrants and in-migrants, *e.g.*, Net migrants to region $A=NM_A=I_A-O_A$. For estimating the net migration for any area between two censuses taken n years apart from the place of birth data, we use the formula.

$$NM=(I_{t+n}-O_{t+n})-(S_I I_t-S_0 O_t)$$
$$=(I_{t+n}-S_I I_t)+(S_0 O_t-O_{t+n})$$
$$=M_1+M_2$$

where I_t and I_{t+n} are the numbers of life time migrants in a particular area at two censuses at time t and $t+n$ respectively and O_t and O_{t+n} are the corresponding life time out-migrants. M_1 and M_2 are the respective net migration among the persons born outside the area and among the persons born inside the area. S_I and S_0 are the inter censul survival ratios giving the proportions of I_t and O_t that will survive the intercensal period. In practice, calculations of S_I and S_0 pose considerable difficulties. It we do not consider the survivorships S_I and S_0 usually the estimated net migration to the place is under estimated. In general, S_I and S_0 are different as in-migrants and out-migrants differ in their age structure. But in practice, it is better to have a single survivorship rather than to ignore mortality. For estimating the single survivorship rate, we can use any of the following procedures :

Procedure I

In case the age distribution of the out-migrants are not available, both S_I and S_0 may be taken as equal to the over all census survival ratio (ratio of persons aged n years and over in the country at the second census to persons of all ages in the first census, *i.e.*, P^{t+n}_{n+}/P^{t}_{0}, or overall life table survival ratio (T_n/T_0) if the appropriate life table for the inter censal period is available (here n is the length of inter censal period). For example, if the census survival ratio for males in a country A during 1961-71 was .86; the number of male in-migrants and out migrants for a State B of the country were enumerated as 992 and 2927 in 1961 and 1200 and 3165 in 1971, then the estimate of intercensal net migration among the male persons born out side the state is

$$M_1 = I_{t+n} - S_i I_t$$
$$= 1200 - .86 \times 992$$
$$= 1200 - 853$$
$$= 347$$

and the estimate of the intercensal net migration among the persons born in the state is

$$M_2 = S_0 O_t - O_{t+n}$$
$$= .86 \times 2927 - 3165$$
$$= 2517 - 3165$$
$$= -648$$

Hence the net migration to the state A during 1961-71 is

$$NM = M_1 + M_2$$
$$= 347 - 648$$
$$= -301.$$

Procedure II

In case the cross classification of the population by place of birth and place of residence is available by age only for the latter of the two censuses, an overall survival ratio may be calculated separately for persons born in each of the areal units but enumerated any where in the country by getting the ratio of the population 10 years old and over at the second census to that of all ages at the first census. The suitable survival ratio may be applied to the resident population of a given area at the earlier census and the resultant expected numbers (at the later census) are then substracted from the enumerated population 10 years old and over (by assuming that censuses are taken 10 years apart) at the latter census to estimate the net changes due to migration of each segment of the resident population. It is, however, assumed that the population native to each area is closed to external migration. The table 6.7 (*a*) illustrates the procedure for obtaining the net change due to migration among population aged 10 and over for males of region *A* of a hypothetical country for the intercensal period 1960-1970.

Procedure III

If the tabulations of place of birth statistics by age for all the areal units are available for two consecutive censuses the computations can be done for each birth cohort separately on the lines of procedure II discussed above. The advantage of this procedure is that one can get an idea at which age there is more migration during the intercensal period. For more details the readers can see the U.N. Manual *V* (Page 9).

The question on place of birth of a person is supposed to be answered with accuracy and completeness. There are, however, possibilities of response error in these data because answers to census questions are provided generally by senior member of the household who may not know the correct places of births of all the members, especially in case of in-laws. There may be some times deliberate mis-statement of the place of birth due to political, religious or prestige reasons. Many migrants (in urban areas) may prefer to report their place of birth as urban rather than rural areas for the sake of convenience of prestige. Some times boundary changes of the geographical units may not be noticed by the respondent, and he may report wrongly the state or district of his birth. Again, place of birth data does not take into consideration the migrations of those persons who are dead. In India, it is noticed that women often return to the father's household for deliveries in early years of their marital life and hence place of birth statistics might give rise to superflous migration in such cases. Another major problem connected with the birth place data for migration analysis is that it only gives the measure of life time migrations and hence includes those who came to the place of enumeration few days back as well as those who migrated since long. Thus this data does not give any idea about the timing of migration unless information is collected and analysed for more than one census date. It cannot be also used directly for studying recent migration streams as a substantial number of out born persons enumerated in an area might have moved from places other than their places of birth. This also ignores the cases of return migrations. In fact, the estimates of migration by using place of birth data always gives underestimate of migration because it assumes a single movement directly from the place of bi th to the area of enumeration It thus ignores intervening moves between departure from the first residence and arrival at the last residence. The measures of life time migrations, therefore, need to be supplemented with the indirect measures of period migrations.

6.4.2 Place of Last Previous Residence and Duration of Residence

The data on place of last residence is useful in identifying a person as 'migrant' if the place of present residence and last residence differ. Here 'migrant' would include all life time migrants and return migrants. Non-migrants would include those who never lived out side the area of birth and migrant would include all those who have ever moved out side area of birth. From the cross tabulation of the persons by place of their last residence and present residence on any census date we can obtain the amount of in-migration to, out-migration from and hence net migration of any area. This would also help in identifying the different migration streams. If the information on place of birth and place of last residence are further augumented with the information on duration of residence, it would be possible to know the number of persons moving from areas other than the areas of birth (secondary migrants) persons returning to their areas of birth (return migrants) and persons moving from the areas of birth alone (primary migrants). These will also not give full information about all the moves of a person especially those between place of birth and place of last residence. Nevertheless the information on the duration of residence and place of last residence can be analysed to give idea about the patterns of migration and their time trend.

6.4.3 Place of Residence at a Fixed Prior Date

The information on place of residence at a fixed prior date about a person coupled with his place of birth may be useful in determining his migration status, such as primary, return and secondary migrant or non-migrant. This would, however, not give any information about those who are dead during the fixed period implied by the question. This approach leads to an under estimate of the migrants since those who migrate from an area during the interval but return back to it before the date of census count are ignored. Estimate of migrants who are born during the interval can be obtained only if the data on place of birth is also analysed. These data however differ from those obtained from the place of last residence and duration of residence as here the place of origin is the place of residence at the fixed prior date rather than place of residence before the move and the moves made before the fixed prior dates are entirely missed. Thus it ignores all the moves made before the fixed date plus those moves which intervene during the fixed date and the present date. This information however, may be treated as a subset of the information on place of last residence and duration of residence. People may have even difficulty in recalling where they were living at some fixed date in the past. On the other hand, it is easier for them to remember the place of last residence and duration of present residence. Further it would be better if the question on residence x years age is equated to the intercensal period so that estimate of intercensal migration may be obtained to determine the components of intercensal population growth. Even these data, however, are not able to overcome the multiple and circular moves during the specified period prior to the census.

Example

From the following data, estimate the life time in, out and net migration for the places *A*, *B* and *C* as on 1 April 1970. Also calculate total number of migrants during the 1 April 1960 and 1 April 1970.

TABLE 6.7 (*a*)

Distribution of Persons Enumerated in Area A on 1 April 1970 According to their Residence on 1 April 1960 and their Place of Earth

Place of Birth	*Place of residence on 1 April 1960*		
	A	*B*	*C*
A	68,103	3,894	712
B	354	1,263	62
C	102	60	332

TABLE 6.7 (*b*)

Distribution of Persons Enumerated in Area B on 1 April 1970 According to their Residence on 1 April 1960 and Place of Birth

Place of Birth	*Place of residence on 1 April 1960*		
	A	*B*	*C*
A	773	408	46
B	3,900	221,993	3,739
C	45	519	899

TABLE 6.7 (*c*)

Distribution of Persons Enumerated in Area C on 1 April 1970 According to their Residence on 1 April 1960 and Place of Birth

Place of Birth	*Place of Residence on 1 April 1960*		
	A	*B*	*C*
A	274	56	120
B	54	1,531	373
C	1,111	7,905	227,380

In order to find out life time migrants, we arrange the given data by place of birth and place of enumeration on 1 April 1970. This is achieved by collapsing the columns of the given tables into a single column each *i.e.*, by ignoring the information about the place of residence on 1 April 1960 as below :

TABLE 6.7 (*d*)

Distribution of Persons According to Region of Birth and Region of Enumeration on 1 April 1970

Place of Birth (Area)	*Place of Enumeration on 1 April 1970*			
	A	*B*	*C*	*Total*
A	72,709	1,227	450	74,386
B	1,679	229,631	1,958	233,268
C	494	1,463	236,396	238,353
Total	74,832	232,321	238,804	546,007

From the above it is easy to get details about life time migration in 1970. The results can be summarised as below :

Area	*Inmigrants*	*Outmigrants*	*Net Migrants*	*Non migrants*
A	2173	1677	496	72709
B	2690	3637	—947	229631
C	2408	1957	451	236396
All ages	7271	7271	0	538736

Let us consider the recent migration during 1 April 1960 to 1 April 1970 for area *A* of the country. The same procedure can be followed in case of areas *B* and *C*.

1. In-migrants to Area A during 1 April 1960 to 1 April 1970

=Persons enumerated on 1 April 1970 in Area *A* and who were residing elsewhere (*i.e.* in Area *B* or *C*) on 1 April 1960.

Now these inmigrants can be further categorised into :

(*a*) Primary migrants to Area *A*. =Those persons enumerated in *A* on 1 April 1970 but enumerated elsewhere on 1 April 1960 which was their birth place.

=Persons enumerated in *A* in 1970, enumerated in *B* in 1960 and Born in B+Persons enumerated in *A* in 1970 enumerated in *C* in 1960 and born in *C*.

=1263+332 (from table 3*a*).

=1595.

(*b*) Secondary migrants to Area *A* =(Persons enumerated in *A* in 1970, enumerated in *B* in 1960 and born in *C*)+(persons enumerated in *A* in 1970, enumerated in C in 1960 and born in B).

$=60+62$ (from Table 3*a*)

$=122$.

(*c*) Return migrants to Area A = Persons enumerated in 1970, enumerated elsewhere in 1960, born in Area A.

=(Persons enumerated in A in 1970, enumerated in B in 1960 born in A) + Persons enumerated in A in 1970, enumerated in C in 1960, born in A.

$=3{,}894+712$ (from Table 3*a*).

$=4606$.

2. Outmigrants from A during 1 April 1960 to 1 April 1970

= Persons enumerated in A in 1960 and enumerated elsewhere (*i.e.* area B or C) in 1970.

These outmigrants include following categories of migrants :

(*a*) Primary out migrants from A = Born in A, enumerated in A in in 1960, enumerated in B or C in 1970.

$=773+274$ (Tables 3*b* and 3*c*)

$=1047$.

(*b*) Secondary out migrants from A = Born in B, enumerated in A in 1960 and enumerated in C in 1970 + Born in C, enumerated in A in 1960 and enumerated in B in 1970.

$=45+54$ (Tables 3*b* and 3*c*)

$=99$.

(*c*) Return out migrants from A = Born in B, enumerated in A in 1960 and enumerated in B in 1970 + Born in C enumerated in

A in 1960 and enumerated in C in 1970.

$=3{,}900+1{,}111$ (Tables 3b and 3e)

$=5{,}011$.

Following the similar procedure, it is easy to obtain in and out migrants and net migrants for each area A, B and C of the hypothetical country. The details of migration are given in the table 6.8.

6.5. Migration Rates and Ratios

It is known fact that migration involves two distinct areas namely place of origin and place of destination. Due to this, it is difficult to provide migration rates and ratio. The main problem is the selection of base population, *i.e.*, denominator of the rates and ratios. Nevertheless, we discuss some measures which are generally used in migration analysis, like *CEB* and *CBR*, we may define migration rate (*MR*) as :

$$MR = \frac{\text{Number of migrants or Migration in Specified interval } (M)}{\text{Total Persons who could have Migrated } (P)}$$

$$= \frac{M}{P}$$

It should be made clear that in above definition if M refers to migration, MR gives the incidence of moves by persons (P). In this case, a person is likely to appear more than once in the numerator. On the other hand, if M refers to migrants, MR gives the probability of move, *i.e.*, the proportion of persons moving at least once during a given migration interval. If we have distribution of migrants by number of migration, we can calculate the probability of moving once only, twice and so on. Since census data generally provides migrants therefore rates and ratios discussed here should be interpreted as probability or proportion, not the incidence.

TABLE 6.8

Estimates of In and Out Migrants—Primary, Secondary and Return for Areas A, B and C

	In-Migrants				*Out-Migrants*				*Net-Migrants*			
	Primary	*Secondary*	*Return*	*Total*	*Primary*	*Secondary*	*Return*	*Total*	*Primary*	*Secondary*	*Return*	*Total*
A	1595	122	4606	6323	1047	99	5011	6157	548	23	—405	166
B	1672	91	7639	9402	2794	116	11799	14709	—1122	—25	—4160	—5307
C	1805	110	9016	10931	1231	108	4451	5790	574	2	4565	5141
All	5072	323	21261	26656	5072	323	21261	26656	—	—	—	—

TABLE 6.9

Net Migration to Region A by Region of Birth for Native Male Population : 1960—1970

Region of Birth	*Native Males in the Country*				*Native Males in Region A*		*Net changr due to Migration 1960—1970*
	Total Males Enumerated in 1960	*10 Years old and above Enumerated in* 1970	*10 ears Survival Ratio* 1960-70 (2) / (1)	*Total in* 1970 *Enumerated in* 1960	*10 Years old and above in 1970*		
					Expected (4) * (3)	*Enumerared*	(6) — (5)
	(1)	(2)	(3)	(4)	(5)	(6)	(7)
Region A	$N^0_{A.}$	$N^1_{A(10+).}$	S_A	N^0_{AA}	$N^0_{AA} * S_A$	$N^1_{AA(10+)}$	$N^1_{AA(10+)} - N^0_{AA} * S_A$
Region B	$N^0_{B.}$	$N^1_{B(10+).}$	S_B	N^0_{BA}	$N^0_{BA} * S_B$	$N^1_{BA(10+)}$	$N^1_{BA(10+)} - N^0_{BA} * S_B$

(Contd.)

1	2	3	4	5	6	7	8	9
Region C	$N^0_{C.}$	$N^1_{C(10+).}$	s_C	N^0_{CA}	$N^0_{CA} * s_C$	$N^1_{CA(10+)}$	$N^1_{CA(10+)}$	$- N^0_{CA} * s_C$
	N^0_{0+}	N^1_{10+}	s_{0+}	$N^0_{.A}$	$N^0_{.A.} * s_{0+}$	$N^1_{.A(10+)}$	$N^1_{.A(10+)}$	$- N^0_{A} * s_{0+}$

Where $N^0_{i.}$ denotes the total male population in 1960 born in region i and counted in any region, $N^1_{i.}$ has similar interpretation for 1970. N_{ij} denotes the male population born in region i and counted in region j. Further 10+ inside the bracket indicates the population aged 10 and over.

Let M_{ij} be the number of migrants from ith area to jth area in given time interval and P_i and P_j are the population of ith and jth area in same time interval. Following theconcept out lined in above equation we may define ratio for each migration streams as :

$$MR_{ij}=\frac{M_{ij}}{P_i}$$

This gives the probability of moving from ith area to jth area. The selection of P_i would depend on the characteristics of M_{ij}. For example if M_{ij} is obtained from the question on residence at a fixed prior date the expected population would be :

where $$P_i=P_i^{t+n}-M_{.i}+M_{i.}$$

P_i^{t+n} : the population in second census

$M_{.i}$: in migrants to i

$M_{i.}$: out migrants from i

The above procedure to estimate P_i for life time migrants is also appropriate. We may even take the population at time t of ith area to calculate MR_{ij} In certain analysis the population of jth area at second census may be taken. This will indicate the pressure of migration upon the receiving area. For the net streams $(M_{ij}-M_{ji})$ or gross interchange $(M_{ij}+M_{ji})$, the population of both areas may be taken into consideration while calculating the rate. We may take the average of population in two areas. So, we have

$$MR'_{ij}=\frac{2(M_{ij}-M_{ji})}{(P_i^{t+n}-M_{.i}+M_{i.})+(P_j^{t+n}-M_{.j}+M_{.j})}$$

Similar to migration streams, we may calculate rates for in-migration, out-migration and net migration as follows ;

$$INMR_i=\frac{M_{.i}}{P_i} \qquad ...(a)$$

$$\text{Out } MR_t = \frac{M_{t.}}{P_t} \quad \ldots(b)$$

$$\text{Net } MR_t = \frac{M_{.t} - M_{t.}}{P_t} \quad (c)$$

There is no concensus about the value of P_t but its selection may depend on the objectives of the analysis and data availability Sometimes, same base may be used in all the three rates. However, we may take following estimates of P_t

For (*a*) $\quad P_t = P_t^{t+n}$

the population in second census.

For (*b*) $\quad P_t = P_t^{t+n} - M_{.t} + M_{t.}$

For (*c*) $\quad P_t = P_t^{t+n} - \frac{1}{2}(M_{.t} - M_{t.})$

The rates discussed above can be calculated for specific characteristics like age-sex etc. of the population.

6.6 International Migration

Population movements which cross national boundaries merit separate study because such movements are usually regulated by legal provisions and policies of the countries involved. Moreover, a country's net migration balance, being one of the components of its population growth, must be assessed in any analysis of population growth trends. Migration statistics are prepared primarily for national purposes, and international comparability is often difficult to achieve. Migration statistics are needed to appraise the size of the problems involved in these movements, and to design the policies intended to meet them. A knowledge of the number of immigrants entering a country is required together with census data and vital statistics in order to make a complete analysis of the changes observed in the course of time in the size and structure of the population of that country. Information on the numbers of immigrants in the occupations or industries is necessary to estimate the influence of foreign manpower on the labour market of the country. Data on the sex, age, citizenship, mothertongue of the inmigrants greatly facilitate an understanding of the nature and size of social and cultural assimilation problems existing at a given time and place (U.N. 1983). Further the international movements of men, women and children in varying proportions may have profound effects on the crude death rates of the receiving and sending countries since there are direct biological relations between mortality and sex and age. Immigration and emigration may also have important effects on the birth rates. Consequently, the statistical data on the sex and age composition of migratory currents are of paramount importance in understanding and appraising the phenomenon of change in birth and death processes.

Status of Data on International Migration

Statistics of international migration are now available for a fair number of countries. For the most part, those collecting such data normally collect only the data needed for their own administrative purposes. For most of the countries detailed statistics on migration are scattered through the publications of several national collecting and processing agencies. Several official publications present statistics on international migration for a particular country International compilations of migration data appeared most recently in the United Nations *Demographic Yearbook*, especially for 1962, 1966 and 1977. Corresponding data for earlier years back to 1948 are shown in earlier issues of the Yearbook. Statistics for the period 1918-1947 are available in one of the United Nations publications (U.N. 1953 *b*). The 'master' tables in the 1977 Yearbook setforth the number of international travellers by major categories of arrivals and departures for the years 1967 to 1976. Information on age and sex of both the short-term and long-term international migrants from 1967-1976; on foreign born population be country of birth, age, sex and residence, for latest census 1970-76; and an economically active foreign born population occupation and sex, according to the latest available censuses are also given in other tables.

International migration statistics are obtainable from border collection, registrations and field enquiries, *Border collection* encompasses the collection of information at points of entry into a country and at points of departure, regardless of whether they are actually located at the border or airports or other sites at which persons formally enter or leave the national territory. The information can be collected by the use of documents prepared for administrative purposes or through the use of *ad hoc* statistical slips. *Registration* encompasses the collection of information through the medium of permanent population registers, employment registers and other administrative records in addition to those completed at border collection. *Field enquiry* encompasses the collection of information through population censuses and sample surveys. The latter may range from surveys that include a simple question on place of birth or residence at a prior date to specialised surveys designed for the study of migration.

Border Collection

Border collection is widely suited to the gathering of data on continuous basis and on a seasonal basis. The method is amenable easily to sampling. In practice, the method has some shortcomings for the collection of information on arrivals and departures. It is unsuitable where there is little or no border survilliance and where borders are not clearly demarcated. An additional drawback of border collection for identifying migrants is that it depends to a considerable extent, on declarations of intent. Despite these defects, border collections provide useful information on the flow of migrants, especially on immigrants on annual basis see Table 6.10). Only current transit records provide the current information on migrants. Furthermore, they show movements in both directions, which is not shown by census data. They provide the only statistical description of the composition of the migrants at the time of migration.

Transit records are, however, not well kept except at international borders. Even they are incomplete. Some countries, include, and some exclude their own nationals from their statistics of external migration. Naturally clandestine migra-

TABLE 6.10

Migration to and from Hong-Kong : 1970-76

Year (1)	*Departures* (2)	*Arrivals* (3)	*Net migration* (4)=(3)−(2)
1970	2,881,856	2,908,606	+26,750
1971	3,110,870	3,112,927	+ 2,057
1972	4,010,107	3,977,116	−32,991
1973	4 808,495	4,844,255	+35,760
1974	4.809 066	4,855 413	+46,347
1975	4,630,853	4,633 576	+ 2,723
1976	5,259,152	5,292,264	+42.112
Total (1970-76)	29,501,399	29,624,157	122,758

Source : United Nations, *Demographic Yearbook* 1977, New York.

tion is not included in transit records, which are associated with border controls. This information can better he indirectly assessed. Owing to these problems, transit data are not always dependable. For Philippines, estimate of net immigration in 1970 by taking difference between number of emigrants (22,778) and immigrants (27,913) comes out to be 5,135 and by taking difference between number of departure (258,726) and arrivals (400,296) comes out to be 142,570. This is so because neither all arrivals are immigration nor all departures are emigration.

Registration

The identification of migrants and of some of their characteristics can be made from entries in permanent population registers, social insurance registers, labour or employment registers or any other set of administrative records maintained on a regular basis. Some of these sources have been designed specifically for control of migrantion, for example, registers of aliens or passport and visa-records. Others, such as permanent population registers and social insurance registers have usually been designed primarily for other purposes, but are often adoptable to the extraction of information on migrants. In some countries, the population registers are able to furnish data on immigrants with negligible time lag and hence serve the same purpose as border collection. However, the registration data is more likely to be based on facts but they may not contain all the facts needed for analytical purposes, and more seriously. they are likely to be less complete in recording of departures than of arrivals. On the other hand, permanent registers can be most useful source of information on the numbers and many of the characteristics of the immigrant stock of a country. Stock information extracted from special registers and other administrative sources is not likely to be as useful as that from permanent population registers because its coverage will be restricted to some particular groups and because of the overlapping that may occur, with some persons appearing in more than one register.

Field Inquiry

Field inquiry can be used by itself or as a supplement to border collection and registration for the investigation of international migration during a given time interval. It offers the opportunity of obtaining extensive detail that is not ordinarily available in registers and that cannot be investigated at border crossings. The information collected may make it possible to calculate net arrivals from various countries during the period under consideration but the calculation of net immigration requires further information to make possible the elimination of visitors, particularly if the inquiry is taken completely on de-facto basis. Population censuses and household surveys, however, offer better opportunities of collecting information on immigrant stock than on migrant flow because they are designed for obtaining data on the composition of the population at a given moment. Comparison of characteristics of the stock of immigrants with the characteristics of the native population can be accomplished as part of the regular census processing. Where both birth place and residence at some prior data are obtained, it is also possible to obtain some indication of return migration of earlier emigrants. One of the drawbacks of the use of field inquiry, however, is that at best it does not permit assessment of the flow of migration on a continuous basis because immigration coverage is restricted solely to net residual immigrants in the population at the time of the inquiry and information on emigrants collected in the country of emigration is dependent on proxy response, which is often inadequate for household members who have emigrated abroad and even more so when entire household has emigrated. Moreover because censuses are usually held decennially, or at the most quinquennially, they can provide information only infrequently. Household surveys on the other hand require large samples, and their repetitions become prohibitively costly unless it is possible to design a very efficient small sample survey.

A review of the concepts of international migrant used by different countries, while collecting and compiling immigrant statistics, gives the impression that immigration statistics are collected more frequently than those of emigration and that immigrants are generally more broadly defined than emigrants. An indication of the lack of comparability of available national statistics on international migration is provided by a comparison of the data on migratory flows among the countries of the Economic Commission for Europe (*ECE*) in 1972. Within Asia, immigrant implies persons entering and intending to find employment, for Burma, Aliens residing in the country, for Iran; nationals and alienes who enter the country from foreign countries in case of Japan; persons arriving in country and submitting disemberkation card for Sri Lanka; Aliens other than a returning resident admitted for permanent residence in case of Thailand. For Malaysia persons arriving in the country are immigrants but for Pakistan non-residents intending to remain for a period exceeding one year or to work for one year or less are immigrants, Emigrants, on the other hand, are residents who leave intending to find employment in another country for Burma; are nationals and aliens leaving the country for foreign countries, for Japan; are persons leaving the country for Malaysia; are residents intending to remain abroad for a period exceeding one year (permanent emigrants) and those intending to remain abroad for one year or less (temporary immigrants) for Pakistan; are the persons leaving the country for Sri Lanka and are resident aliens departing with the stated intention of residing abroad for 12 months or more for Thailand. A glossary of such concepts for different countries can be found in Tables A & B of U.N. *Demographic Year Book*, 1977.

6.7 Evaluation and Estimation of International Migration

Adequate data on immigration, emigration, or net migration are often not available for a country even though a number of direct sources of data bearing on international migration for that country may exist. One method of expanding the quantity of information on migration for a given country is to refer to the migration statistics for other countries furnishing or receiving migrants from the country under study (Shryock et. at. 1980). This may also serve as a basis for the evaluation of migration data. If immigration and emigration were completely and consistently reported for all the countries of the world, the total emigration reported for a given country would coincide with the immigration received by all other countries from the country under consideration.

As discussed earlier, the types of movement counted as migration and the categories of persons classed as migrant differ from country to country due to different concepts of migrants and different modes of collecting the information. The bi-national reporting of international migration however provides useful though not always adequate basis for evaluating the accuracy of migration data for a country. With available data, however, only the balance of migration can be satisfactorily estimated. There are several methods for estimating the net migration depending upon the availability of data and they may also be used alternatively to evaluate the available migration statistics.

6.7.1 Intercensal component Method for estimating the total volume of Net Immigration

The general formula for estimating the total volume of net immigration in an intercensal period involves a re-arrangement of the elements of the standard intercensal component equation (also called the balancing equation);

$$I-E=(P_1-P_0)-(B-D). \quad \ldots(5)$$

The method simply involves subtracting an estimate of natural increase ($B-D$) during the period from the net change in population during the period (P_1-P_0). Net immigration ($I-E$) is thus derived as residual. Since the census counts and statistics on births (B) and deaths (D) as recorded are subject to unknown degrees of error, the residual estimates of net immigration may be in substantial error. The relative error in estimate of net immigration may be considerable when the amount of international migration is small. This method has been applied below to estimate net immigration for Hong Kong.

TABLE 6.1

Calculation of the Estimated Intercensal Net Migration by Residual Method, for Hong Kong

Item	
1. Population, first Census 1961	3,129,648
2. Population, Second Census 1971	3,936,630
3. Net change (2)—(1)	806,982
4. Births	1,050,807
5. Deaths	213,648
6. Natural Increase (4)—(5)	837,159
Estimated net Immigration	
7. Residual Estimate, (3)—(6)	—30,177
8. Recorded Arrivals	19,554,312
9. Recorded Departures	19,399,116
10. (8)—(9)	155,196

Source: United Nations, *Populaion of Hong Kong*, Country Monographs, Series, No. 1, 1974, ESCAP, Thailand.

United Nations, *Demographic Year Books*, 1976 and 1974, New York.

The estimates obtained in (7) and (10) differ because of the use of two separate methods for a variety of reasons.

Theoretically, better estimates of net immigration should be derived from the census figures on the foreign born than from the total population since this is a more restricted universe of which the immigrants normally are the part. This method, however, assumes that all the migrants are foreign born and that mortality and fertility of the foreign born can be accurately measured. It is advisable to use total or native population for the calculation of the net immigration where the natives predominate among the immigrants.

6.7.2 Intercensal Cohort Component Method

This method is applicable for estimation of net migration, by age, for the total population and for segments of the population. In preparing estimates by age, the compilation of death statistics by age cohorts to allow for the mortality component is very laborious. It is in general, advisable to use, the survival rates, either, life table survival rates or so-called national census survival rates. *One formula for this purpose covering age cohort other than those born during the intercensal period is* :

$$I_a - E_a = P_a^1 - S(P_{a-t}^0) \qquad \ldots (6)$$

where I_a and E_a represent immigrants and emigrants in a cohort defined by age 'a' at the end of the period, P_a^1, the population at this age in the second census, P_{a-t}^0 the population t years younger at the first census, and S is the survivorship rate for the age a during the intercensal period of t years.

For the new born cohorts, during the intercensal period the formula is :

$$I_a - E_a = P_a^1 - S(B) \qquad \ldots (7)$$

where B represents the births which occurred in the intercensal period and which will give rise to P_a^1 at the time of the second census.

Age distribution of population at census points are generally reported in quinquenial age-groups. Further the age data suffer from the mis-reporting of ages of the persons of both the sexes. Under these conditions, one can use an appropriate smoothing technique to adjust the age data. However, too much smoothing of the data may affect the age specific estimates of net immigration, without affecting the estimate of total net immigration.

Defect of the conventional survival rate procedure is that it has a tendency to understate or overstate the number of (implied) deaths during the intercensal period. In "emigration" country, the initial population in an age cohort overstates the average population exposed to the risk of death during the intercensal period, and the terminal population understates the average population exposed to risk, because some persons emigrate. A more satisfactory estimate of deaths and net migration may be therefore made by ( ) 'aging' the initial population to the date of the second census; (2) calculating the corresponding 'forward' estimate of net migration (3) "younging" the terminal population to the cate of first census by dividing the terminal population by the survival rate and (4) calculating the corresponding "reverse" estimate of net migration by substracting the initial population from the 'younged' population and (5) averaging the two estimates of net migration. The formulae are :

Forward Estimate : $M_1=(I_a-E_a)=P_a^1 - S\,P_{a-t}^0$ ... (8)

Reverse Estimate : $M_2=(I_a-E_a)_2=S^{-1}\,P_a^1 - P_{a-t}^0$ ... (9)

Average Estimate : $M_3=(I_a-E_a)_3=\dfrac{M_1+M_2}{2}$ ... (10)

Calculation of deaths to the age cohorts born during the period requires special treatment. The survival rate for the cohort under 5 years of age at the end of the decade is

$$\frac{L_{0\text{-}4}}{5\,l_0}$$

and the survival rate for the cohort 5 to 9 is

$$\frac{L_{5-9}}{L_{0-4}}.$$

The forward and reverse survival procedures are then applied in the same way as for the older cohorts. the births in the two 5 year period being taken as the initial population for the first two age groups. The procedure of calculating the net migration is illustrated in last section.

6.7.3 Inter-Censal Component Method for the Foreign Born Population

The inter-censal change in the foreign born population under-states the net immigration of foreign born persons during an inter-censal period by the number of their deaths during the period. Thus applying the balancing equation for foreign born population in a country we have :

$$P^1_F = P^0_F + I_F - E_F - D_F \qquad ...(11)$$

$$I_F - E_F = P^1_F - P^0_F + D_F \qquad ...(12)$$

where suffix '*F*' refers to the foreign born person and $I_F - E_F$ thus refers to the net immigration of the foreign born persons in the country and D_F refers to number of deaths among the foreign born persons during the intercensal period. This method would give an estimate of only the net numbers of foreign born persons arriving. If large number of foreign born persons happen to have arrived in the country in the preced'ng decades, who would now be of advanced ages, the number of deaths in the intercensal period may be quite large and would therefore have a considerable effect on the estimate of net immigration. The difference in the number of foreign born persons may even suggest net emigration when net immigration actually occurred.

In developing countries, statistics of death of foreign born is very much lacking. The number of deaths can be estimated by applying appropriate central death rates to the mid period foreign born population to give average annual deaths during the intercensal period. Hence by multiplying the estimated annual deaths by the length of the intercensal period, total number of deaths can be estimated for intercensal period. Thus the balancing equation can be used to estimate the net Immigration in a country during the intercensal period.

Estimates of net immigration of the foreign born by age cohorts can be obtained by using a survival rate procedure as discussed earlier for the total population. Either life-table survival rates or census survival rates may be employed The forward survival method, however, does not provide an estimate of net immigration for the new born children. A reverse survival rate procedure on the other hand provides an alternate estimate for ages 10 and over and makes possible the calculation of estimates of net immigration of children born during the intercensal period. The two sets of net immigration so obtained may be combined.

The survival rates for the populations born abroad under 5 and 5 to 9 years respectively, in exact ages, are as follows :

$$\frac{L_{0-5}}{1.25\ 1, + L_{0-3.75}} \text{ and } \frac{L_{5-10}}{L_{1.25-6.25}}$$

Because the population under 5 years old at the time of a census has been at risk of death for only 1.25 years on the average (2½ × ½ years) and the population 5 to 9 years old has been at risk only for 3.75 years on average (7½ × ½ years). The first factors (*i.e.*, 2½ and 7½) represent the average period oftime between birth and the census date, and the second factor (*i.e.* ½) reflects the fact that the migrants entered the country or departed at various times during the period between birth and the census, uniformly and thus with their average residence in the area equal to one half of the period.

In place of life table survival rates, we can also use census survival rates often computed for the native population so as to exclude the effects of inter-national migration from the rates. Their advantage is that the estimates of net migration resulting from their use may be more accurate than when life table survival rates are used, since errors in census enumeration are incorporated in the census survival rates rather than in the estimates of net migration, as in the case when life-table survival rates are used. The procedure described earlier to estimate the net immigration of foreign born persons by age and sex, can be extended to derive the estimates of net immigration by age and sex, according to race, country of birth, mother tongue, or other stable ethnic characteristics.

Estimation of Net Immigration of Alien Populations

If the census counts of aliens are available for the country, the procedure discussed to estimate the net immigration of the foreign born persons during the intercensal period can be applied to estimate the net immigration (or change) in the alien population. The change in the number of aliens between two dates is affected by (1) naturalization (2) net Immigration and (2) deaths. The formula for estimating the net immigration of the aliens is

$$I_A - E_A = (P^1{}_A - P^0{}_A) + D_A + N \quad \ldots(13)$$

Where A refers to aliens and N refers to the number of naturalisations. For almost all the developing countries, data on aliens and their naturalisations are scanty and are not made available in their reports.

Estimation of Nationals Abroad

Estimates of the net migration of nationals of a particular segment (*e.g.*, employees of the national government and their dependent and armed (forces) during some period, may also be obtained from statistics or estimates of these groups living outside the country at the beginning and end of the period. The formula to estimate the net migration of this group is :

$$M_0 = (O_1 - O_0) - (B_0 - D_0) \quad \ldots(14)$$

where O_1 and O_0 represent the overseas population of the country at the initial and terminal date in the period, respectively, B_0 and D_0 refer to births and deaths respectively to the overseas populattion and M_0 net movement overseas. Net movement into the country of its nationals from overseas equals - M_0. In case information on B_0 and D_0 are not available they can be estimated by keeping in view the characteristics of nationals overseas.

Techniques of Analysis of International Migration Data

Unlike mortality and fertility analysis, analysis of international migration presents considerable amount of difficulties because of the variety of definitions in a given country and between countries and of a variety of collection systems. For both administrative and demographic issues, it is useful to collect the data on citizenship, type of migration (*e.g.*, permanent, temporary, and commuters' or border crossers and recently of refugee's) and the legal basis of country aliens. Most of the analysis is done in respect of social, economic and demographic characteristics of the migrants. Sometimes, various non-demographic factors, such as, changes in legislation regarding immigration and emigration, programmes to assist immigrants, modes and cost of travel, economic conditions of origion and destination, wars, persecutions of minority communities and similar factors are also taken into account for the analysis purposes.

If comparable international migration were available for every country for the same period the sum of the net immigration or emigration figures for the various countries would be zero. A net figure of zero may represent the balance of two equally large migration currents or the absence of all movements. Thus inspite of the fact that net movement is known it would be worthwhile to analyse immigration and emigration. In this context, the concept of *gross migration* or *migration turn over* defined as sum of immigration and emigration may serve a useful purpose. Various types of ratios may be computed to indicate this relative magnitude of immigration (I), emigration (E), net immigration ($I-E=M$) and Gross migration ($I+E=G$) to or from a country (Kuznets and Rubin 1954).

(i) $\frac{E}{I}$, (ii) $\frac{I-E}{I}$

(iii) $\frac{E-I}{E}$ Where $E>I$; (iv) $\frac{I}{I+E}$,

(v) $\frac{E}{I+E}$ (vi) $\frac{I-E}{I+E}$

The ratio to the selected depends upon the type of analysis being made and the migration characteristics of the country under study.

The negative sings in the ratios may be disregarded. Extremely small ratios resulting from very small numerators simply indicate that the effective addition or loss is small as compared to very small denominators and they should be interpreted with care.

Sevvral crude rates may also be constructed on the basis of international migration data. These rates represent the amount of annual immigration, emigration, net migration or gross migration, per 1,000 of the mid year population symbolically is as :

Crude migration rate $= \frac{I}{E} \times 1{,}000$

Crude Emigration rate $= \frac{E}{P} \times 1{,}000$

Crude net migration rate $= \frac{I-E}{P} \times 1{,}000$

Crude Gross migration rate $= \frac{I+E}{P} \times 1{,}000$

Where P symbolises the mid year population of a country.

TABLE 6.12

Volume and Ratios of Net and Gross Migration, for Some Selected Countries of the Asia Region, 1970

Country and Year	*Immigration*	*Emigration*	*Net Migration*	*Gross Migration*	*Ratio/net migration to immigration or emigration*	*Ratio/net migration to Gross migration*
(1970)						
Cypr'is	—	2318	—2318	2318	—1.0000	1.0000
Japan	46998	45234	—1764	92232	0.0200	0.0190
Keroa/Republic of	208208	220645	—12437	428855	—0.0600	0 0290
Malayasia	538290	538059	231	1076349	0.0063	0.0002
Philippines	27778	27913	—5135	50691	—0.1800	—0.1010
Thailand	2093	—	2093	2093	1.0000	1.0000
Yemen Republic of	2932	3331	—281	6153	0.0003	0.0470

Source : U.N. Demographic Year Book. 1977, Table 29.

TABLE 6.13

Various Rates of Migration, for the Selected Countries of the Asia, Circa 1970

Country and Year	*Immigration*	*Population*	*Immigration Rate*	*Emigrations*	*Emigration Rate*	*Net Migration Rate*	*Gross Migration Rate*
Iarael (1975)	20,028	3,493,200	5.73	—	—	5.73	5.73
Japan (1970)	46,998	103,355,900	0.45	1,764	0.02	0.43	0.47
Malayasia (1970)	538,290	8,780,728	61.30	538,059	61.28	0.02	122.58
Phillippines (1970)	22,778	36,684,486	0.62	27,913	0.76	0.14	1.38
Thailand (1970)	2,093	34,397,374	0.06	—	—	0 06	0.06

Source : (1) *U.N. Demographic Years Book* 1972, Table 79.
(2) *Ibid Table No. 6.*

The migration rates specific to age, sex, race, or other characteristics may be also calculated as usual. The most appropriate denominator for the calculation of ratio for a country during a period is the population of that area at the middle of the period. When the migration data are derived from a census or survey, they give only life time migrants if place of birth data is used. For finding out migration rates, because of census population being readily available, it is common to use the census population as the base, which is normally the terminal population.

6.8 Migration Models

Modelling of a any process may involve two stages namely (*i*) theoretical statement about the process and (*ii*) translation of a statement into mathematical model. The theories of migration attempt to explain the reasons for migration. At this stage, an attempt is made to list out infact the factors responsible for a person's movement. In the second stage, researchers try to parameterize the process so that it can have wider applicability and help in planning. Following are the theories which have emerged from various studies on migration ;

(*i*) Ravenstein's Law of Migration

(*ii*) Zipf's Gravity Model

(*iii*) Lee's Theory of Migration

(*iv*) Todaro's Model

(*v*) Stouffer's Model

(*vi*) L-F-R Model of Development theory

(*vii*) Sjaastad' Human Investment theory

(*viii*) Cost---Benefit Model

(*ix*) Mover—Stayer Model of Migration

In addition to the above theories, which explain the flow from one area to another one, attemps have been made to develop mathematical model for the age distribution of migrants or special type of migration; for example models showing the relation of marriage migration with distance. It has been observed that age profile of the migrants exhibit a regular pattern. Rogers et. al. (1978) therefore adopted the notion of model migration schedules in mathematical form. This has also been illustrated by Roger and Castro (1981). In this case age pattern may be given as :

$$M(x)=a_1 \exp(-\alpha_1 x)+a_2 \exp[-\alpha_2(x-\mu_2) - \exp(-\lambda_2(x-\mu_2))]+a_3 \exp[-\alpha_3(x-\mu_3) - \exp(-\lambda_3(x-\mu_3))]+C \qquad x:0\ 1\ 2\ldots\ldots z$$

It seems there are four curves representing different age segments of migration. They are :

(*i*) Pre-labor force ages (negative exponential with α_1 rate of descent).

(*ii*) Labor force (double exponential, with mean age μ_2, rate of ascent α_2 and descent λ_2).

(*iii*) Post labor force (double exponential with mean age μ rate of ascent α_3 and descent, λ_3.

(*iv*) A constant curve C.

For detail of this model and its utility one can see the given reference.

A Model for Marriage and distance was proposed by Morill and Pitts (1967) on the line of Zipf's Gravity model. The model is given by

$$M=\frac{a}{D}$$

Where M is migrants at distance D and a is a constant.

It was observed that like Gravity model, above model tends to over estimate close in frequencies (short distance). So they proposed the following modified model.

$$M=a\ e^{-b\ D}$$

$$M=a\ e^{-(b \operatorname{Log}_e D)^2}$$

Recently Sharma (1984) and Yadav (1989) have proposed a number of modifications over the above model. These

These models are not given here because the quoted research work is not widely available to the researchers.

We briefly discuss the theories of migration which are widely used in migration analysis :

(i) Ravenstein's Law of Migration

Revenstein made the following propositions :

(*i*) Migrants move from the areas of low apportunity to areas of high apportunity (economic motive);

(*ii*) The choice of destination is regulated by distance;

(*iii*) Migration takes place in steps, for example, migrants move from rural to nearby towns and then towards large cities;

(*iv*) Each rural–urban stream produces urban—rural counterstream but former one dominates the latter one.

Zipf's Gravity Model

According to this model, volume of migration of particular stream is inversely related to the distance. In other words people are drawn towards the place of destination by gravitational force which reduces with distance. So the volume of migration at particular place of destination from particular place of origin is directly proportional to the product of the two population and inversely proportional to the distance between them. So

$$V \frac{P_o P_d}{D}$$

Where

V : Volume of migration.

P_o : Population at place of origin.

P_d : Population at place of destination.

This is simple model but fails to explain all type of movements. This does not take into account the characteristics of both the places that could explain volume as well as direction.

(iii) Lee's Theory of Migration

Lee's theory is the general form of Ravenstein law of migration. From this model variety of forces exerting influence can be explained. He terms forces exerting influence on perception of migrants into 'pluses' and 'minuses' which may be similar to 'pull' and 'push' factors. In other words, factors which attract individuals towards particular place are pluses or pull factors and those which drive them away are minues or push factors. There are 'zeros' also, in which, these forces are, more or less evenly balanced. Lee classified the main factors in the following four groups :

(*a*) Factors associated with the area of origin

(*b*) Factors associated with the area of destination

(*c*) Intervening obstacles

(*d*) Personal factors.

(iv) Todaro's Model of Rural – Urban Migration

This model has following four major features :

(*i*) Migration is stimulated by rational economic considerations of relative benefits and costs, mostly financial, but also psychological.

(*ii*) The decision to migrate depends on 'expected' rather than real Urban – rural wage differentials and the chance of obtaining employment in the Urban modern sector.

(*iii*) The chance of obtaining an urban job is inversely related to the urban unemployment rate.

(*iv*) Migration rates in excess of urban job opportunity growth rates are not only possible but also rational. This may be the outcome of continued positive urban—rural expected income differentials.

The assumptions in Todaro as well as other income differential models are :

(*a*) All potential migrants have equal information about the urban labourmarket and equal access to urban job.

(*b*) Migrants often look for modern sector job.

(*c*) Wages are lower in traditional sectors compared to modern sectors.

(*d*) Decision to move is a 'once for all' decision.

(*e*) Potential migrants are homogeneous in respect of skill and attitudes.

(v) Stouffer's Model of Migration

Stouffer (1940) stated that the distance is a surrogate for the effect of intervening opportunities. The migration stream from origin *i* to destination *j* is assumed to be inversely related to the number of intervening opportunities between *i* and *j*. The relevent opportunities may be within a circle centered at *i* with a radius that equals the distance between *i* and *j*. Stouffer (1960) redefined opportunities and included the concept of competing migrants. In this case intervening opportunities fall within a circle centered at mid point of the distance between *i* and *j* with a diameter that equals the distance between *i* and *j*. The mathematical form of the intervening opportunities competing migrant model for inter—state migration is given as

$$Y = \frac{K\ X_m^A}{(X_B^B\ X_C^C)}$$

Where

Y : Gross interstate migration

X_m^A: Scale factor measures as the product of total number of in-migrants to *j* and total number of out-migrants from *i* during specified period.

X_B : Total intervening opportunities measured as total in-migration within a circle whose dia meter is X_o (distance as highway mileage between principal cities of states *i* and *j*).

X_O : Total competing migrants measured as total out migration within a circle centered at *j* whose radius is X_D.

K, *A*, *B* and *C* are unknown parameters to be estimated.

The thrust of this model is to provide more meaningful interpretation to the role of distance in the opportunities which is more important than the mere distance. To compare his work with gravity type models following model can also be estimated for comparasion :

$$Y = \frac{X^{A'}_{K',m}}{X^{D}_{D}}$$

Here *K*", *A*" and *D* are new parameters to be estimated. The various analysis have shown that this model is superior to the traditional distance model.

(vi) L-F-R Model of Development

This model was proposed by Lewis (1954) and extented by Rains and Fei (1961). The combined theory is known as L-F-R model. The model is based on a concept of dual economy comprising a subsistances agriculture sector characterized by full employment where "Capitalist" reinvest full amount of their profit. A such migration is equilibrating mechanism which through transfer of labour from the labour-surplus sector to the labour-deficit sector brings about the equality between two sectors. This model also considers the wage differentials in two sectors as one of the important factors. Their assumption that marginal productivity of labour is zero in subsistance sector however has not been confirmed empirically. Further, migration is not induced solely by unemployment or underemployment.

(vii) Sjaastad's Human Investment Theory

This theory treats the decision to migrate as investment decision involving costs and returns distributed over time (Sjaastad 1962). Costs (Money and non-money) includes the following components.

(*i*) Cost of transport

(*ii*) Disposal of movable and inmovable proparty

(*iii*) Wages foregone while in transity

(*iv*) Retraining for new job (if necessary),

(*v*) Leaving familiar surroundings,

(*vi*) Leaving languages and culture (sometime),

(*vii*) Exposure to new dietary habits and social customs.

On the other hand returns may include :

(*i*) Psychic benefits as change of location (non-money)

(*ii*) More net life span incomes.

Sjaastad model does not cosider the unemployment rate at the place of destination. Further it would be difficult to estimate non-money returns and costs in real situation.

(viii) Cost-Benefit Model

Sjaastad model presented earlier is based on the concept of cost benefit being used by economist in evaluation of family planning programme and other development plans. Speare (19:1) proposed a mathematical form of Sjaastad's model. Cost-benefit model is expressed as :

$$\sum_{J=1}^{n}\left[\frac{Y_{dj}-Y_{oj}}{(1+r)^{j}}-T\right]>0$$

Where

Y_{dj} : Earning in the j th year at the destination.

Y_{oj} : Earning in the j th year at the origin

T : Cost of movement

n : Total number of years in which returns are expected

r : Rate of interest used to discount future earnings.

If it is assumed that the difference in income at the two places is constant in the future, then the equation reduces to

$$h(Y_d - Y_o) - T > 0$$

Where

$$h = \sum_{j=1}^{n} \frac{1}{(1+r)^j}$$

Above equation overcome the problem of deciding the value of r and n. The value of h may be determined empirically. This model again is based on the assumptions stated in Todaro's model. However above equation may be put in following form to over come some of the assumptions :

$$IPCh\,(Y_d - Y_o) - T > 0$$

I : Extent of information about job opportunities.

P : Chance of getting employment at the destination.

C : Ratio of cost of living at origin to that at destination.

It may be mentioned that the non-monetary factor are not included in this model. If one can put value for each non-monetary factors then model can be modified as

$$IPCh\,(Y_d - Y_o) - T + h\sum Vi > 0$$

Where

Vi : difference in the annual monetary value of the ith non-monetary factor between the destination and the origin.

(ix) Mover—Stayer Model of Migration

The mover-stayer model, a generalization of the Markov-Chain model, assumes that there are two types of individuals in the population under study :

(*a*) The 'Stayer' who remains in the same category with probability one during the study period.

(*b*) The 'Mover' whose changes in category over time can be described by a Markov chain with constant transition probability matrix.

This model was first introduced by Blumen, Kogan and McCarthy (referred as *BKM*, quoted from Goodman 1961) in their study of the movement of workers among various industrial aggregates in the U.S.

The Markov model requires population homogeniety but transition from an origin state rarely conform to this assumption. If the population is hetrogeneous in its transition behavior, even if each individual were to satisfy the central assumption of a first order Markov process namely, that his probabilities of making particular transitions are determined solely by his present state and are independent of past history-the population level process would not be Markovian. To achive the homogeniety in the population one may fallow various ways. This may be done by dividing total population into sub-groups considered to be homogeneous. It may also be overcome by assuming that all individuals move according to an identical transition matrix when they move but differ in their rates of mobility. This is the crux of the Mover-Stayer model. It seems that the two categories considered in this model is out of necessity for keeping the process mathematically tractable not because of population heterogeniety can generally be attributed to two types of persons (Spilerman 1977).

Due to obvious reason we are not giving the details of this model but interested researchers are advised to read given references. In addition to these references one may also refer some articles of a book edited by Land and Rogers (1982).

7

Demographic Models

In the evaluation of any scientific thinking (discipline) there comes a period in which attempts are made to develop mathematical theories or models in order to account for and to explain the observations generated by the phenomena with which they are concerned. Any abstraction of an object may be considered as model but when any mathematical relation is used to describe the phenomena, it is called a mathematical model. In the social sciences, as well as in others, models are often constructed as deliberate oversimplification of complex situations, either to reduce the complexity to a level which the mind can grasp, or to make a rough approximation to the actual state of affairs. The economists were first to have used the expression model to describe the basic economic interrelationships. In demography, however, the term came into use only of late although some of the earliest results arrived at in theoretical demography might well deserve to be called the models. The ordinary life table discussed in earlier chapter may be considered as a simple demographic model.

A model systematises comparisons across time as well as over space (Sheldon and Moore 1968). Models may, infact, be algebraic, arithmetical, computer simulation or verbal (logical). Mathematical models have the advantage of applying a longer and tighter argument. On the otherhand, the verbal models often grasp most effectively the essentials of an action but fail to give quantified statements of the relationships.

We may select one of the two approaches while postulating a mathematical model to study the phenomena concerned. These two approaches are : (i) deterministic and (ii) stochastic (probabilistic). The difference in the two approaches lies in the nature of questions they pose and try to answer and in the interpretation of the results therefrom. The deterministic models describe the average relationship relating to the process under consideration. The statement that the sex of a born child is female is less than half the number of times deliveries take place to a woman is a description of the expected or average behaviour of the sex of born children. However if we make a detailed study, it would lead to a statement which is probabilistic in nature. If a woman is exposed to the risk of a conception for a period of T years, what is the probability of her having one son, two sons, etc. would require defining of a random variable over the sample space of the number of children born to a woman in T years. A sequence of events occurring over time in a probabilistic manner is known as a stochastic process and defining relations over such processes would lead to the formulation of stochastic models.

While mean or expected values obtained by probabilistic models might agree with those of the deterministic models on sufficiently similar assumptions, stochastic models offer better insight into the effects of chance and into the variation mechanisms which occur in the population system. Therefore, the stochastic models of population dynamics are more powerful and potential tools in its analysis. A suitable model of population provides insight into the importance of various factors like biological, social, cultural, economic and psychological factors and their modes of action and their quantitative effects on the demographic process. Models may be static or dynamic with respect to time to which they refer. However, this classification is not very important and they may ba easily interchanged.

Models in mortality studies seem to be the most ancient among the various branches of demography. During the middle ages in Europe, some kind of merchantile insurance paved the way for life insurance and other acturial studies. Life table constructions and stochastic models to describe the mortality phenomena under competing risks to the life are the illustrations of such models. The models have also been formulated to express migration by persons from one area to another area in terms of distance, availability of job opportunity or some demographic factors like marriage and births. However, a promising approach to model building in migration is Mark ov chain technique. Major difficulty in this type of approach is in relation to the assumption of stationarity of the transitional probabilities over different periods of observations. This difficulty may be overcome to some extent by defining the transitional probabilities in terms of duration of stay rather than in terms of place of birth. We however, discuss below mainly the models of population growth, stationary and stable populations and some special family building models.

7.1 Models of Population Growth

Deterministic models of population growth have been discussed in chapter 1 and they have been used in Chapter 9 for population projection. In the deterministic models for given 'r' and the initial and/or ultimate size of population, the population at any time is well determined. The problem of predicting the size of population of a country at any time t can be viewed stochastically if we assume that each individual in the population is independently exposed to the risk of giving birth, exposed to the risks of death and migration with some rates. A simple birth process where population grows due to birth alone is derived under the following assumptions :

(*a*) The probability that each of the n individuals of a population present at time t gives a single birth in the time element $(t, t+dt)$ is $\lambda dt + o\,(dt)$ and of giving more than one birth is zero, where λ is independent of size and age-structure of the population.

(*b*) The population is closed to migration.

(*c*) The chance of death for any individual is zero.

Let $P_n(t)$ denote the probability that population is of size n at time t, then under the above assumptions, it can be shown that $P_n(t+dt)$ is the sum of the probabilities of two mutually exclusive contingencies : (a) that the population numbers n by time t and there is no birth in time t to $t+dt$, and (b) that it numbers n-1 by time t and there is one birth in time t to $t+dt$.

In symbols :

$$P_n(t+dt)=P_n(t)\,[1-n\lambda dt]+P_{n-1}(t)\,[(n-1)\,\lambda\,dt] \qquad ...(1)$$

Transposing $P_n(t)$ to the left and dividing by dt

$$\frac{P_n(t+dt)-P_n(t)}{dt}=-P_n(t)\,n\lambda+P_{n-1}(t)\,(n-1)\,\lambda \qquad ...(2)$$

and proceeding to the limit as dt becomes small,

$$P'_n(t)=-P_n(t)n\lambda+P_{n-1}(t)(n-1)\lambda,\ n=1,2,\ ... \qquad ...(3)$$

In particular for $n=1$

$$P'_1(t)=-P_1(t)\lambda \qquad ...(4)$$

[we define $P_n(t)$ as 0 for $n\leqslant 0$ and $P_1(0)=1$]

Though (8) is an infinite set, the equation can be solved for any finite value of n. The solution (Yule, 1924) is

$$P_n(t)=e^{-\lambda t}\,(1-e^{-\lambda t})^{n-1} \qquad n=1,2,\ ...... \qquad ...(5)$$

Since sum of $P_n(t)$ for all n is unity, $P_n(t)$ is a proper probability distribution of the discrete variable n. The expected value of n at time t must be

$$E(n)=e^{\lambda t} \qquad ...(6)$$

This is also the solution starting with one individual for the continuous deterministic model of population growth, where increase is $n\lambda$ with certainty, expressed by the condition ;

$$\frac{dn}{dt}=n\lambda$$

Thus the deterministic model often mimics the probability model, at least in coming up with the correct expected value.

Starting with one individual, the generating function for the pure birth process is

$$\phi(Z, t)=P_0(t)+P_1(t)Z+P_2(t)Z^2+\ldots\ldots+P_n(t)Z^n+\ldots\ldots$$

$$=Ze^{-\lambda t}+Z^2 e^{-\lambda t}(1-e^{-\lambda t})+Z^3 e^{-\lambda t}(1-e^{-\lambda t})^2+\ldots\ldots$$

$$=\frac{Ze^{-\lambda t}}{1-Z(1-e^{-\lambda t})} \quad \ldots(7)$$

By differentiating the above generating function with respect to z and then putting $Z=1$, the number of individuals expected at time t is $e^{\lambda t}$. By differentiating it twice and putting $z=1$, we get second factorial moment, $E[(n)(n-1)]$ from which we can show that

$$V(n)=e^{\lambda t}(e^{\lambda t}-1).$$

To study the distribution $\phi_n(t)$ starting with n_0 individuals, we need examining the properties of its generating function

$$\left\{\frac{Z e^{-\lambda t}}{1-z(1-e^{-\lambda t})}\right\}^{n_0} \quad \ldots(8)$$

The above model of population growth can be applied though crudely to answer few questions relating to the size of population. Suppose India had in 1990 a female net reproduction rate of 1.50. This can be treated as growth of .50 female in a generation of say *length t* Then the result $E(n)=e^{\lambda t}$ gives $1.50=e^{\lambda t}$. Hence $\lambda=l_n(1.50)$ (by taking t as unit of measurement). Hence the chance of 5 girl children just born to have 10 grand, grand female children in India with female net reproduction rate=1.50 can be obtained by using the equation (13) taking $t=3$, $n_0=5$ and $\lambda=l_n(1.50)$ from the coefficient of Z^{10}, which is

$$e^{-5\lambda t}\left(\frac{5\times6\times7\times8}{(1)\ (2)\ (3)\ (4)}\right)\ (1-e^{-\lambda t})^5=.02759$$

It may be remembered that this result is obtained under the assumption of population being closed to migration and no mortality. A closer approximation to the demographic reality can be achieved by considering births and deaths, though still without recognising sex or age (Kendall, 1949, p. 241).

7.2 A Simple Birth and Death Process

Let us assume that

(*a*) The probability that an individual present at time t gives birth to an individual between time t and $t+dt$ is $\lambda dt+o(dt)$. λ is constant at all times t.

(*b*) The probability that a person present at time t dies between t and $t+dt$ is $\mu dt+o(dt)$. The force of mortality μ is the same for all individuals at all times t.

(*c*) The population is closed to migration.

Again we start by considering the period $(0,\ t+dt)$ divided into $(0,\ t)$ and $(t,\ t+dt)$. The chance that there are n individuals in the population by time $t+dt$ is equal to chance

(*i*) that there are n individuals in the population by time t and nothing happens between t and $t+dt$,

(*ii*) that there are $n-1$ individuals by time t and 1 is added by birth in $(t,\ t+dt)$,

(*iii*) that there are $n+1$ individuals by time t and l dies in $(t,\ t+dt)$.

These three contingencies are mutually exclusive and exhaustive. Since dt is sufficiently small, it cannot accomodate two events. Hence,

$$P'_o(t)=\mu P_1(t)$$

$$P'_n(t)=(n-1)\lambda P_{n-1}(t)+(n+1)\,\mu P_{n+1}(t)-n(\lambda+\mu)P_n(t) \quad \ldots (9)$$

It is rather difficult to obtain an explicit solution to this stochastic process. The expectation and variance of the population size $N(t)$ at time t may be derived in a simple manner, however. Consider the equation in $P'_n(t)$ multiplied throughout by n and summed for non-negative values of n. Then this equation simplifies to (See, Pollard, 1973, p. 62)

$$\frac{d}{dt} M_1(t) = (\lambda - \mu) M_1(t)$$

where $M_1(t)$ is the expected value of $N(t)$. It is clear that the expected population will follow the Malthusian growth pattern :

$$M_1(t) = e^{(\lambda - \mu)t} \quad \ldots (10)$$

(assuming a single initial ancestor).

Similarly it can be shown that

$$\text{Var }(N(t)) = \frac{\lambda + \mu}{\lambda - \mu} e^{-(\lambda - \mu)t} \left\{ e^{(\lambda - \mu)t} - 1 \right\} \quad \text{if } \lambda \neq \mu \quad \ldots (11)$$

When $\lambda = \mu$ the birth and death process reduces to the deterministic model denoted as stationary population. Clearly if $\mu > \lambda$, the population will become extinct ultimately.

7.3 The Stationary Population Model

A hypothetical model of a population, based on unchanging conditions of fertility, mortality and the total size, is called a stationary population. The life table is also a model, covering the simplest case when a cohort of people born at the same moment and closed to migration is followed through successive ages until they all die. Thus any population which is closed to migration and exposed to the same age specific death rates and whose birth rate is equal to its death rate will ultimately become stationary population whose rate of growth will be obviously zero. Not only its total size but also the size of the population in any of its age group will be constant.

This model has, however, limited descriptive value because in actual world, fertility and mortality of any population are not so closely related. A population generated by any given life table is essentially a stationary population. In fact, the ${}_nL_x$ column of a life table may be regarded as a hypothetical population, classified by age. It may be regarded as an entire population existing at one time, rather than one cohort observed successively at each age. Thus the stationary population is determined at each age only by the fixed rates of mortality of the life table and not by the structure of any actual population. It is assumed that these rates have remained fixed for every cohort represented in the population. Likewise the number of births must have remained fixed at the radix of the life table every year. Because of the balance between births and deaths being zero, the size of the population in the stationary population is stationary (constant). The age composition is also stationary. The crude birth and death rates of the stationary population are equal. In case of a life table, annual number of births equals l_0 and total population equals T_0 and therefore, birth rate is l_0/T_0. Since the population is stationary, the death rate is also equal to l_0/T_0, the reciprocal of e°_{0} .

To sum up, a stationary population is characterised by the following properties :

1. The total size of the population is constant.
2. The annual number of births (and also of deaths) is constant.
3. The age composition is invariable.
4. Crude birth rate is equal to crude death rate.

Thus in case of a stationary model, all the imaginable characteristics of the populations are fixed in time.

Continuous version of stationary population requires defining of the life table functions as continuous functions of age and is of great help in the analytical demography and in derivation of several functions. Several uses of stationary population (life tables) are already discussed earlier along with the uses of life tables in Chapter on Mortality Analysis. It is clear that there is never a real population strictiy conforming to the stationary population model but one can think that some human aggregates have developed, at certain periods in their history, in an obviously stationary manner. For example, before the demographic transition, when the total human population lived in a primitive demographic regime caused by high mortality and high fertility, the natural growth was virtually nil, as witnessed by the small total reached by the world population at the beginning of the nineteenth century, the various human populations must never have deviated from the stationary state. Again at the present time, in some of the highly developed countries, fertility is almost approaching the level of mortality rate. We thus find the establishment of a condition that might lead these populations progressively to a stationary state.

7.4 Stable Population Model

In 1911, Sharpe and Lotka (1941) and later on Lotka in the two Central Chapters of his "Theoriec Analytique des Association Biologiques" dealt in details with the concept of stable population. The theory of stable population provides an analytical frame-work to understand the exact relationships between regimes of fertility and mortality on the one hand, and the age distribution of a population, on the other hand. According to it if a population closed to migration experiences constant age specific fertility and mortality will, no matter what its initial age distribution, eventually develop into a constant age distribution and will eventually increase in size at a constant rate. Any population with a constant age distribution and which is increasing at a constant rate is called a stable population. A stationary population is thus a special case of a stable population in which the rate of growth is zero and the age distribution is same as the life table age distribution. The main assumptions of the stable model are :

1. The human population under study is closed to migration.
2. Since the formal analysis is identical for both the sexes it is enough to deal with female population, which has a better defined interval of fertile ages. In any case, only one sex is considered.
3. There is a probability $p(a)$, fixed through time, that a female child just born will survive to age a. The

function $p(a)$ is a continuous function of age and is sufficient to characterize the mortality conditions.

4. There is probability $m(a)$ that a female who is alive at age a, will bear a female child between ages a and $a+da$. The density function $m(a)$ is independent of time and is continuous.

5 There exist an age W, such that $p(a)=0$ for $a>W$, and ages u and v such that $0<v<u<W$, the $m(a)$ vanishing at all points outside the interval (v, u). u is the maximum age of reproduction.

Given these assumptions, the aim of the stable model is. to trace the dynamic characteristics of a population which starts off with an arbitrary age structure and is submitted from that moment to the specified demographic regime.

According to Lotka given the fertility and mortality condiditions and the absence of migratory movements, the birth function is all we need to calculate the population of any moment in time, the age distribution, the birth and death rates etc. The unifying feature of the model explains the importance attributed by Lotka to the discussion of integral equation for the birth function. If the expected number of birth at moment t is $B(t)$, then it has two components : the first one, $G(t)$, accounts for the expected number of births from mothers who were not born during the specified demographic regime, that is, $G(t)$ accounts for the daughters of the survivors of the initial population and the second part accounts for the expected number of daughters coming from the mothers who were born at some time between the initial moment and time t. Initial size of the latter component is given by the integral

$$\int_0^t B(t-a)p(a)m(a)da \qquad \ldots(12)$$

hence $$B(t)=G(t)+\int_0^t B(t-a)p(a)m(a)da \qquad \ldots(13)$$

Since the size and the age composition of the initial population is assumed to be given, $G(t)$ will also be a known function. If $N_0(a)$ is the initial number of women at age a, then expected value of $G(t)$ is

$$G(t)=\int_0^W N_0(a)\frac{p(a+t)}{p(a)}\, m(a+t)da \quad \ldots(15)$$

Since $m(a)=0$ for $a>u$, $G(t)=0$ for $t>u$. We assume $N_0(a)$ to be continuous so that $G(t)$ is also continuous.

The equation (16) according to Lopez (1961) has always a unique solution. Moreover, under our assumptions, the solution of $B(t)$ is a continuous function.

Now for $t>u$, $G(t)$ vanishes and hence the family of functions referred to is the set of solutions to the integral equation

$$B(t)=\int_v^u B(t-a)p(a)m(a)da \quad \ldots(16)$$

The above integral equation is homogeneous. It means that the solution remains a solution when it is multiplied by a constant, *i.e.*, if $B(t)$ is a solution, so also is $CB(t)$. More-, over, solutions are additive; if $B_1(t)$ and $B_2(t)$ are solutions, so is $B_1(t)+B_2(t)$ These two properties of the equation are referred together as linearity. Lotka anticipated a solution e^{rt} to the equation (17) for $r=r_1, r_2$ ..... The general solution is of the form

$$B(t)=Q_1e^{r_1t}+Q_2e^{r_2t}+\ldots$$

for all values of the arbitrary constants Q_1, Q_2, ..., Substituting function e^{rt} for $B(t)$, we can easily obtain

$$\int_0^t e^{-ra}p(a)m(a)da=1 \qquad t\geqslant u \quad \ldots(17)$$

This equation is called the characteristic equation of stable population in 'r'. The function $p(a)m(a)$ is called the net maternity function which may be denoted by $\phi(a)$. A number of procedures exist to solve for 'r' in the above equation. Before discussing these we will discuss two more relations obtained by Lotka which connect 'r' to birth rate and age distribution of the stable population. Birth rate (b), death rate (d) and growth rate (r) of the stable population are called intrinsic birth rate, intrinsic death rate and intrinsic growth rate as these rates are obtained from the fertility and mortality schedules of a population and are independent of the age structure of the population and prevail in the population in limiting case, if the same schedules of fertility and mortality continue to persist over a long period of time. Let $c(a, t)$ be the proportion of population at time t, then

$$c(a, t) = \frac{B(t-a)p(a)}{\int_0^\infty B(t-a)p(a)da}$$

putting again $B(t) = e^{rt}$, we have

$$c(a, t) = \frac{e^{-ra}p(a)}{\int_0^\infty e^{-ra}p(a)da} = c(a) \qquad \text{... (18)}$$

$c(a)$ is independent of time t. In otherwords, the age structure of the stable population is in variant of time t. Again $c(o)$ gives the birth rate where

$p(o) = 1$ and hence

$$b = \frac{1}{\int_0^\infty e^{-ra}p(a)da} \qquad \text{... (19)}$$

hence $\qquad c(a) = be^{-ra}p(a) \qquad$ ...(20)

Equations (18), (20) and (21) are the three salient equations of the stable population model linking intrinsic rates of birth, and growth with the age structure of the population.

Existence of Real Root of the Characteristic Equation

The solution to the characteristic equation

$$\psi(r) = \int_0^\infty e^{-ra}p(a)m(a)da = 1$$

can be obtained in several ways. It can be easily seen that this equation has only one real root. The integrand in the above equation consists of non-negative factors : If the integral is equal to unity for r, it cannot be equal to unity for $r'>r$, since $e^{-r'a}$ is less than e^{-ra} for every a. In the same way, a real number less than r cannot be a root. Since $\phi(a)=m(a)p(a)$ is positive or zero for all a, and, for any given a, e^{-ra} is a monotonic decreasing function of r, the integral $\psi(r)$ must be therefore a decreasing function of r. To prove that $\psi(r)$ is monotonically decreasing function, we observe that

$$\psi'(r)=-\int_v^u ae^{-ra}\phi(a)da$$

is always negative, since all the three factors of the integrand are non-negative, and over some range are positive. A monotonic decreasing function can cross the line $\psi(r)=1$ only once at the real root r_1. Since $\psi''(r)=\int_v^u a^r e^{-ra}\phi(a)da$ is positive, $\psi(r)$ must be concave upward throughout.

It can easily be seen that $-\psi'(r)/\psi(r)$ evaluated at $r=0$ is μ, the mean age of the childbearing in the stationary population and that $-\psi'(r)$ evaluated at a point r where $\psi(r)=1$ is Ar, the mean age of the childbearing in the stable population. The quantity $\psi\,0)=R_o$, the net reproduction ratio. If R_0 $\int_v^u \phi(a)da>1$ then the real root r_1 of the characteristic equation must be positive. For only a positive r makes e^{-ra} less than unity. Similarly if $R_o<1$, then r_1 must be negative. The converse also holds good. When $R_0=1$, clearly this implies that $r_1=0$ Since, $\psi(r)$ is a polynomial (infinite series in r), and it has only one real root, other roots must be complex which come always in conjugate pairs. Supposing that $u+iv$ is a complex root of the characteristic equation, then from De Moivre's theorem

$$e^{ra} = e^{ua+iva}$$

$$= e^{ua}[\cos (va + i\sin(va)] \quad \text{...(21)}$$

hence
$$\psi(r) = \int_v^u e^{-ua}[\cos (va) - i\sin(va)]\phi(a)da = 1 \quad \text{... (22)}$$

Since there is no imaginary portion on the right hand side,

$$\int_v^u e^{-ua} \sin (va)\phi(a)da = 0$$

and hence $u - iv$ must also be a root. Moreover, the value of u in the complex root must be less than r_1, the real root. By equating the real parts in the $\psi(r)$ above, we get

$$\int_v^u e^{-ua} \cos (va)\phi(a)da = 1 \quad \text{...(23)}$$

In case of real root r_1 we also have

$$\int_v^u e^{-r_1 a}\phi(a)da = 1 \quad \text{... (24)}$$

comparing the (24) and (25), $e^{-u\,a}$ must be greater than $e^{-r_1 a}$, because cosine of any angle is less than unity except for multiples of 2π. Hence u must be less than r_1 for a positive values of a. If $R_0 < 1$, then the real root is negative and all the complex roots have negative real elements. When $R_o > 1$, and therefore $r_1 < 0$, they could have positive elements as far as argument goes, though in practice, this does not always occur Keyfitz (1968).

Methods of Calculating Intrinsic Rate of Growth of the Stable Population

(1) Lotka computed the rate of increase of the stable population by solving the equation

$$\int_0^\infty e^{-ra}p(a)m(a)da = 1$$

Now, by expanding e^{-ra} within the integrand gives

$$\int_0^{\infty}\left(1-ra+\frac{r^2a^2}{2}-\ldots\ldots\right)p(a)m(a)da=1 \qquad \ldots(25)$$

Again neglecting higher orders of r more than two, we have

$$\int_0^{\infty}\left(1-ra+\frac{r^2a^2}{2}\right)p(a)m(a)da=1 \qquad \ldots(26)$$

or

$$\int_0^{\infty}\phi(a)da-r\int_0^{\infty}a\phi(a)da+\frac{r^2}{2}\int_0^{\infty}a^2\phi(a)da=1 \qquad \ldots(27)$$

or

$$R_o\left(1-r\frac{R_1}{R_0}+\frac{1}{2}r^2\frac{R_2}{R_0}\right)=1 \qquad \ldots(28)$$

where $R_r=\int_0^{\infty}a^r\phi(a)da$ is the rth moment of the net maternity function $\phi(a)$. Taking logarithm on both the sides,

$$\log_e R_0+\log_e\left(1-\frac{r.R_1}{R_0}+\frac{1}{2}\frac{r^2.R_2}{R_0}\right)=0 \qquad \ldots(29)$$

Again neglecting the terms containing higher powers of r than two, we have

$$\log_e R_0-r\frac{R_1}{R_2}+\frac{1}{2}\left[\frac{R_2}{R_0}-\left(\frac{R_1}{R_0}\right)^2\right]r^2=0 \qquad \ldots(30)$$

or

$$\tfrac{1}{2}\beta r^2+\alpha r-\log_e R_o=0 \qquad \ldots(31)$$

where

$$\alpha=\frac{R_2}{R_0}$$

$$\beta=\alpha^2-\frac{R_2}{R_0}$$

R_0 is the net reproduction rate and R_1 and R_2 are the first and second moments of the net maternity function. Solving the

$$r=\frac{1}{\beta}\left(-\alpha+\sqrt{\alpha^2+2\beta\log_e R_0}\right) \qquad \ldots(32)$$

This is the intrinsic rate of growth of the population. A first order approximation of r is

$$r=\frac{1}{\alpha}\log_e R_0 \qquad \text{... (33)}$$

or

$$R_0= e^{\alpha r} \qquad \text{...(34)}$$

Since the stable population is growing at the annual rate r, compounded continuously, and the net reproduction rate R_0 is rate of growth in one generation of length T years, we may also write

$$R_0=e^{rT} \qquad \text{... (35)}$$

Comparing the two equivalents of R_0, we get

$$T=\alpha=\frac{1}{r}\log_e R_0 \qquad \text{... (36)}$$

$$\text{Since } \log_e R_0=\frac{1}{2}\beta r^2+\alpha r$$

$$T=\alpha+\frac{1}{2}\beta r \qquad \text{...(37)}$$

Since every year the stable population is $(1+r)$ times larger than the year before, at the end of a generation, it will be larger by a factor equal to the net reproduction rate. Of course, if r is negative, R_0 will be less than one.

Coale (1955, 1957) has given however, some short-cut methods of calculating value of r. We know that

$$NRR=e^{rT}$$

$$\frac{NRR}{GRR}=l_T/1.$$

Where l_T is the number of persons surviving at exact age T, which is the mean length of generation.

Thus we can determine from the knowledge of NRR, GRR and the life table functions, the value of T. This value of T can be used to obtain

$$r = \frac{\log_e R_o}{T}$$

However, if r is very small, we can use the approximation

$$T = \alpha + \frac{1}{2}\beta\, r \text{ and write } T = \alpha$$

Hence we can get value of r equal to R_o $\log_e$ (R_o/R_1). Coale again in his another article has used 29 years as an estimate of T and got $r_1 = \log_e R_o/29$ as first approximation to the value of r which is then to be adjusted according to the difference.

$$\delta = \int_0^\infty e^{-r_1 a}\, p(a)\, m(a) da - 1$$

where the adjusted value of r becomes

$$r_1 + \frac{\delta}{29 - \delta/r_1}$$

(3) Functional Iteration Method

To ascertain the roots of the characteristic equation of the stable population from observations that provide a life table and age specific female birth rate, it is usual to approximate

$$1_o \psi(r) = \sum_{v}^{u-5} e^{-r(x+2.5)}\, {}_5L_x . F_x \qquad \ldots(38)$$

F_x being the birth rate to women aged x to $x+5$.

Since $\qquad \psi(r) = \int e^{-ra}\, p(a)\, m(a)\, da = 1$

We have

$$1_o = e^{-12.5\,r}\, {}_5L_{10}\ {}_5F_{10} + e^{-17.5r}\, {}_5L_{15}\, F_{15} + \ldots + e^{-47.5r}\, {}_5L_{45} F_{45} \qquad \ldots(39)$$

(if we assume that $v = 10$, $u = 50$).

Now, by multiplying the above equation by $e^{27.5r}$ on both sides, we have

$$e^{27.5r^*}=e^{15r}\frac{({}_5L_{10})}{l_o}F_{10}+e^{10r}\frac{({}_5L_{15})}{l_o}F_{15}+e^{5r}\frac{({}_5L_{20})}{l_o}F_{20}$$

$$+\frac{({}_5L_{25})}{l_o}F_{25}+e^{-5r}\quad\frac{({}_5L_{30})}{l_o}F_{30}+\ldots+$$

$$e^{-20r}\frac{({}_5L_{45})}{l_o}F_{45} \qquad \ldots(40)$$

We start choosing some arbitrary value for r, evaluating the expression on the righthand side of the above equation, then taking $\frac{1}{27.5}$ of the logarithm to obtain the improved r^*, Substitute r^* for r and continue till the difference between two consecutive values of r^* becomes very small.

Computation of Stable Age Distribution Corresponding to Given Level of Fertility and Mortality

After calculating intrinsic rate of growth 'r' corresponding to the prevalent level of fertility and mortality, we select the life table corresponding to the level of mortality. The ${}_5L^f_x$ column of this life table gives the age structure of a stationary female population per 100,000 (equivalent to radix l_o) female births. We then calculate $e^{-r(x+2.5)}$ for each five year age group where x=15, 20,...... , 45. The product $e^{-r(x+2.5)}\,{}_5L^f_x$ gives the female stable population. Corresponding to this female stable population, we can obtain the male stable population, where male births are equal to 100,000 x (sex ratio at birth). The *SRB* may in general be taken as 1.05. This is possible by multiplying ${}_5L^m_x$ with 1.05 $e^{-r(x+2.5)}$. Summing the male and female populations for all the ages, we obtain the total stable population and as such we can now obtain birth rate of the total population and all other characteristics of the stable population. The following illustration will demonstrate the procedure of calculating intrinsic rate of growth and then the stable population.

From the above table we obtain easily

$$GRR=5\Sigma \text{ Col. (1)}=5x\ .53240=2.662$$

$$NRR=R_o=\Sigma \text{ Col. (4)}=1.80988$$

TABLE 7.1

Calculation of Intrinsic Rate of Growth of the Female Population of India from the ASFR available for 1971-72

Age of the mother (x to $x+5$)	Annual births* of daughters ${}_5F_x$ (1)	Pivotal central age ($x+2.5$) (2)	$\frac{{}_5L_x^{f**}}{l_0}$ (3)	Products		
				R_0 (4)=(3)×(1)	R_1 (5)=(4)×2	R_2 (6)=(5)×(2)
15—19	.04261	17.5	3.68127	.15686	2.74505	48.03838
20—24	.12775	22 5	3.60203	.46016	10.35360	232.95600
25—29	.13469	27.5	3.50220	.47172	12.97230	356.73825
30—34	.10582	32.5	3.34718	.35420	11.51150	374.12375
35—39	.07045	37.5	3.14970	.22190	8.32125	312.04688

40—44	.03681	42.5	2.91244	.10721	4.55643	193.64828
45—49	.01427	47.5	2.65090	.03783	1.79693	85.35418
Total	.53240	—	—	1.80988	52.25706	1,602.90572

Source : * Office of the Registrar General, Indian, *Fertility Differentials in India, 1972,* Ministry of Home Affairs, New Delhi.

** Registrar General of India, *Life Tables, Series I —India,* Part I of India. Government of India, New Delhi (1977), Appendix A, pages 16 and 17.

$$\alpha = \frac{R_1}{R_o} = 28.87322$$

$$\beta = \alpha^2 - \frac{R_2}{R_o} = -51.97915$$

$$\text{Log}_e\ R_o = 0.59326$$

$$r = .02095$$

$$T = (\text{mean length of generation})$$

$$= \frac{1}{r} \log_e R_o$$

Taking $r = 0.21$, and e_o^o (female) = 47.00 and assuming the West Model Life Table pattern of mortality, calculation of the ultimate age distribution of the stable population is illustrated in example 2.

When registration data on births and deaths are lacking value of '*r*' may be indirectly estimated. If two census populations are known, and pupulation is assumed to be stable, the intercensal rate of growth can also be treated as a good estimate of '*r*'. In case only one census data on age distribution is available and the population is closed to migration, we can choose any two ages *x* and *y* and relate the counted population to the theoretical population of below.

$$P_y = B(t-y)L_y$$

$$P_x = B(t-x)L_x$$

Let us assume that the birth function is an exponential, say,

$$B(t) = Bo\ e^{rt}$$

Then we get

$$r = \frac{1}{y-x} l_n\ (P_x/L_x)/(P_y/L_y) \qquad \ldots(41)$$

Thus we get the simplest way to provide an estimate of *r* using current age distribution. Since the value of '*r*' is obtained for each pair of ages, potentially thousands of estimates can be obtained. Moreover, in case of real population, age data is generally distorted and use of single years may create some problems. We can, therefore, use group of ages to avoid the problem and then average out these estimates to get a single best estimate.

Calculation of Mean Length of Generation in a Stable Population

The mean length of generation is defined as the mean age of mothers at the birth of their daughters. Let us denote this length by A. If the risk of death is assumed to be zero, the mean age of the set of girls born throughout their lives would be A years less than the mean age of their mothers. But death does exercise its effect and the difference between the two mean ages declines as the generation of girls grows older. In a stable population as earlier mentioned, the mean length of generation $A(r)$ is given by

$$A(r)=\frac{\int_0^\infty ae^{-ra}\, p(a)\; m(a)\, da}{\int_0^\infty e^{-ra}\, p(a)\; m(a)\, da} \quad \text{...(42)}$$

In case $r=0$,

$$A(o)=\frac{\int_0^\infty a\; p(a)\; m(a)}{\int_0^\infty p\;(a)\; m(a)} \quad \text{...(43)}$$

It may be noted that in case of stable population we have proved that the mean length of generation T [which is same as $A(r)$] is given by

$$T=\frac{1}{r}\; \log_e\; R_o$$

$$=\alpha+\frac{1}{2}\beta r \quad \text{...(44)}$$

From example 1, we obtain $T=28.87322+\frac{1}{2}\;(-51.97915)$ $(.02095)=28.3$

When $r=0$, $T=\alpha=28.9$

Mean length of generation may be taken as average of 28.9 and 28.3 *i.e.* 28.6.

TABLE 7.2

Calculation of Age Distribution of the State Population

Age interval (x, x+5) Years	Mid-point (x+2.5) (1)	r=0.021 r(x+2.5) (2)	$e^{-r(x+2.5)}$ (3)	$e^{\circ}_{o}=47$ $\frac{_5L^f_x}{l^f_o}$ (4)*	Female stable Population (5)=(3)×(4)	$e^{\circ}_{o}=49$ $\frac{_5L^m_x}{l^m_o}$ S.R.B. (1.05) (6)*	Male stable population (7)=(6)×(3)	Stable population both sexes (5)+(7)=(8)	%age Distri. of St. P. (both sexes)
0—4	2.5	0.0525	0.94885	4.18045	3.96662	4.47097	4.24228	8.20890	15.235
5—9	7.5	0.1575	0.85427	3.91101	3.34106	4.25199	3.63235	6.97341	12 942
10—14	12.5	0.2625	0.76912	3.82470	2.94165	4.18339	3.21753	6.15918	11.431
15—19	17.5	0.3675	0.69246	3.73822	2.58857	4.11291	2.84803	5.43660	10.090
20—24	22.5	0.4725	0.62344	3.62819	2.26196	4.01273	2 50169	4.76365	8.841
25—29	27.5	0.5775	0.56130	3.50092	1.96507	3 89259	2.18491	4.14998	7.702
30—34	32.5	0.6825	0.50535	3.36204	1.69901	3.76223	1.90124	3.60025	6.682

35—39	37.5	0.7875	0.45498	3.21225	1.46151	3.61483	1.64468	3.10619	5.765
40—44	42.5	0.8925	0.40963	3.05321	1.25069	3.44186	1.40989	2.66058	4.938
45—49	47.5	0.9975	0.36888	2.88319	1.06332	3.23594	1.19341	2.25673	4.188
50—54	52.5	1.1025	0.33204	2 68492	0.89150	2.98440	0.99094	1.88244	3.494
55—59	57.5	1.2075	0.29894	2.44166	0.72991	2.67463	0.79955	1.52946	2.839
60—64	62.5	1.3125	0.26914	2.13366	0.57425	2.29348	0.61727	1.19152	2.211
65—69	67.5	1.4175	0.24231	1 75242	.042463	1.83886	0.44557	0.87020	1.615
70—74	72.5	1.5225	0.21816	1.30846	0.28545	1.33361	0.29094	0.57639	1.069
75—79	77.5	1.6275	0.19642	0.83935	0.16487	0.82739	0.16252	0.32739	0.607
80+		1.7325	0.17684	0.54532	0.09643	0.51541	0.09115	0.18758	0.351
					25.71370		28.16675	53.88045	100.000

**Source* : *Coale and Demny Model Life Tables*, pages, 12—15.

Stable male birth rate $bm = \frac{SR.\ B.}{\Sigma Col.\ (7)} = \frac{1.05}{28.16675} = 0.037277$ or 37.277 per 1000 males

Stable male death rate $dm = bm - r = 0.016277$ or 16.277 per 1000 males

Stable female birth rate $bf = 1/\Sigma Col.\ (5) = 0.038889$ or 38.889 per 1000 females

Stable female death rate $df = bf - r = 0.017889$ or 17.889 per 1000 females

Combined birth rate $b = \frac{1+SRB}{\Sigma Col.\ (5) + \Sigma Col.\ (7)} = \frac{2.05}{53,88045} = 0.038047$ or 38.047 per 1000 population.

Mean age of the Stable Population

It is easy to show that a stable population with $r>0$ is on average younger than a stationary population. If the current birth rate is b, then proportion of children under age 15 is

$$_{15}C_0=\int_0^{15} e^{-ra}\,p(a)\,da\Big/\int_0^{\infty} e^{-ra}\,p(a)\,da \qquad \ldots(45)$$

Differentiating both the sides w.r.t. r we obtain

$$\frac{d(_{15}C_0)}{dr}={}_{15}C_0\,(m-m_1) \qquad \ldots(46)$$

where m is the mean age of the entire stationary population and m_1 the mean age of the part of it less than 15 years old. Hence expanding $_{15}C_0$ as a function of r about $r=0$ gives

$$_{15}C_0=\frac{_{15}L_0}{e^\circ_0}[1+r(m-m_1)] \qquad \ldots(47)$$

where $_{15}L_0/e^\circ_0$ is the proportion of population under 15 in a stationary population.

The mean age of the stable population is given by

$$\bar{A}=\int_0^{\infty} a\,e^{-ra}\,p(a)\,da\Big/\int_0^{\infty} e^{-ra}\,p(a)\,da \qquad \ldots(48)$$

Now by expanding and integrating the separate terms both in the numerater and denominator, we obtain

$\bar{A}=\frac{\bar{L}_1}{\bar{L}_0}-r\,\sigma^2$, where $\bar{L}_1/\bar{L}_0$ is the mean and σ^2 is the variance of the age distribution of the stationary population.

Where $\bar{L}_i=\int_0^{w} x^i l(x)dx$ is the numerator of the ith moment about zero of the stationary population of the life table.

$$\sigma^2=\frac{\bar{L}_2}{L_1}-\left(\frac{L_1}{L_0}\right)^2$$

It can easily be proved that a growing population tends to be younger than the corresponding stationary population also within any particular age interval. Knowledge of the mean age of the stable population in terms of stationary population helps us in estimating the rate of growth of the population by knowing mean age of the life table population and the mean age of the actual population.

Some Applications of Stable Population Theory

The stable population theory as such has been found very useful to study the limiting behaviour of the age structure and its vital rates if the population is closed to migration and is submitted to the constant schedules of fertility and mortality. Again for some populations whose age structure is known on only one date or two, rate of their natural increase can be determined and hence we can venture to estimate other vital rates under some more convenient and stringent assumptions. We can also use the stable population to know what would happen to the age structure if fertility and mortality change in a particular way. For a detailed study of such experimentation, the reader can read books by Keyfitz (1968, 1977) and Coale (1972). We will however, give main applications in Chapter 8.

7.5 Generalized Population Model

Age distribution of population at any point of time is outcome of fertility and mortality in the past. Infact, age distribution reflects the history of population dynamics. The age-composition of population varies according to the history of fertility and mortality. If in a population same number of births takes place every year and mortality schedule is constant, this generate a stationary population. So in this population, number of persons at each age does not change with time. In such a population :

$$\frac{1}{N(a)} \quad \frac{d\,N(a)}{da} = -\mu(a)$$

Where $\mu(a)$ is force of mortality

$$\frac{d}{da}[\log N(a)] = -\mu(a)$$

By integrating both side we get

$$\log\left|\frac{N(a)}{c}\right| = -\int_0^a \mu(y)\, dy$$

Where c is constant of integration

$$\frac{N(a)}{c} = e^{-\int_0^a (y)\, dy}$$

When $a=0$, $c=N(o)$

$$\text{So } \operatorname{Log}\left(\frac{N(a)}{N(o)}\right) = -\int_0^a \mu(y)\, dy$$

$$N(a) = N(o)\, e^{-\int_0^a \mu(y)\, dy} \qquad \ldots(49)$$

Above equation is similar to a relationship established in life table as :

$$l(a) = e^{-\int_0^a \mu(y) dy} \qquad \ldots\ldots \quad l(o)=1$$

If fertility and mortality have been constant in the past for sufficient longtime, we get stable population in which age distribution is constant and thereby growth rate is also constant. In such case, each successive younger cohort is larger (or smaller if growth rate is negative) at every age than its older cohort by constant pultiple. In this population;

$$\frac{1}{N(a)} \frac{d}{da} N(a) = -\mu(a) - r$$

$$\frac{d}{da} \{\log N(a)\} = -\mu(a) - r$$

By integrating both side we get

$$\log\left\{\frac{N(a)}{C}\right\}=-\int_o^a \mu(y)dy-ra$$

$$\frac{N(a)}{C}=e^{-ra}\,e^{-\int_o^a \mu(y)dy}$$

When $a=o$, $C=N(o)$

So, $$N(a)=N(o)\,e^{-ra}\,e^{-\int_o^a \mu(y)dy}$$

or $$N(a)=N(o)\,e^{-ra}\,l(a)$$

$$\frac{N(a)}{N}=\frac{N(o)}{N}\;e^{-ra}\,l(a)$$

Where N : total population

$$C(a)=b\,e^{-ra}\,l(a) \;\ldots\qquad \ldots(50)$$

This equation has been derived differently by Lotka (1939).

In a stable population, r is same for each age but for general population it may not be true. If growth rate is changing, with age then

$$\frac{1}{N(a)}\;\frac{d\,N(a)}{da}=-\mu(a)-r(a)$$

Where $r(a)$ is annual growth rate of persons aged a,

$$\frac{d}{da}\left\{\log\frac{N(a)}{C}\right\}=-\int_o^a\left[\mu(y)\,dy-r(y)\,dy\right]$$

$$\frac{N(a)}{C}=e^{-\int_o^a r(y)\,dy}\;e^{-\int_o^a \mu(y)\,dy}$$

$$=e^{-\int_o^a r(y)\,dy}\;*\;l(a)$$

When $a=o$, $C=N(o)$

$$N(a)=N(o)\,e^{-\int_o^a r(y)\,dy}\;*\;l(a)\ldots\qquad \ldots(51)$$

Again by dividing both sides by total population, we get

$$C(a) = b\, e^{-\int_0^a r(y)\,dy} * l(a) \ldots \qquad \ldots(52)$$

The equation (53) is known as generalized population model and stable and stationary population are the special case of this population. The age-specific growth rate which can be easily calculated when country has two censuses, contain all the pertinent demographic history. The application of equation (53) is illustrated in Chapter 8.

7.6 Micro-Models of Fertility

Fertility is a complex phenomenon and is affected by a number of socio-economic and biological factors. Thus in order to study the effect of socio-economic factors on fertility, it is most interesting as well as most difficult task to estimate the natural fertility which is the fertility of a human population that makes no deliberate effort to limit the births. Natural fertility depends essentially on the biological factors. But the socio-cultural and psychological variables also affect fertility through these biological variables. The difficulties, however, encountered in the study of natural fertility stem from its very definition. No doubt, one can find populations living under the conditions of quasinatural fertility, but for the most part, little is known about such populations. Thus, it becomes rather necessary to adopt some indirect approach through the development of suitable mathematical models of the human reproduction. The development of the models of human fertility have been based on the considerations of mainly three factors :

(*i*) Fecundability (probability of conception to a woman per unit of time).

(*ii*) Outcome of pregnancy.

(*iii*) Duration of the non-susceptible periods that follow a conception *i e*., the period of 'lost time' (or rest period) from the beginning of pregnancy until the resumption of ovulation and cohabitation.

When the woman is married she is deemed to be susceptible to conception and the time to conception is a random variable determined by fecundability, which may depend on age, frequency of coitus, use of contraceptive etc. A pregnancy may end into the birth of a child who survives infancy, a live birth followed by an infant death, a spontaneous or induced abortion or still birth. The probabilities of the different outcomes may vary with maternal age or the rank order of the pregnancy. The duration of pregnancy is associated with its outcome, as is that of the post-partum amenorrhea period, which dependes also on lactation as it affects the ovulation.

7.6.2 Birth Intervals

Birth interval in human population are important not only because they reflect the reproductive behaviour of a population but also due to their influence on health status of mother as well as children. Birth interval are also related with the population growth. Two populations which have the same family size (*NRR*) but with different pattern of birth intervals can be expected to have different intrinsic growth of population Population having higher birth interval *i.e.* higher mean length of generation may be growing at a smaller rate than the other population. They can also be used in the estimation of certain bio-social parameters of the fertility, such as, the fecundability, incidence of foetal wastage, etc.

Birth intervals can be categorized into two broad types

(*i*) Closed interval which is the interval between the successive live births of a woman,

(*ii*) Open interval which is the interval from the date of the last livebirth to the date of enquiry.

Above two types of interval for a women of parity i can be represented as fallows :

Marriage		First Child		Second Child		(*i*—1)th Child		*i*th Child		Date of Survey
	T_0		T_1				T_{i-1}		U_i	

Where, T_i : Interval between ith and $(i - 1)$th birth

U_i : Open interval for women of parity i.

Thus a women of parity 'i' contributes i—closed intervals and one open interval.

Birth interval between two live births have four main components :

(*i*) The period of post-partum amenorhea following the birth of the earlier child [except T_0 *i.e.* from marriage to first birth].

(*ii*) Total waiting times between two live births.

(*iii*) The period of pregnancy and post termination amenorrhea (if any) of abortion or still births intervening the live births.

(*iv*) Gestation period though variable but generally taken as nine months.

These four components in a interval can be shown as below :

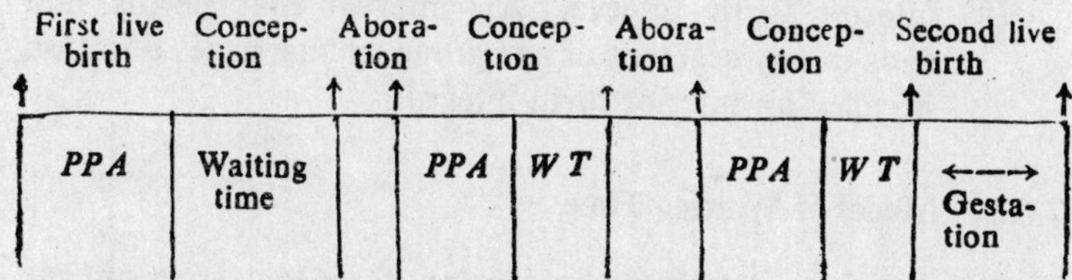

Analytical model has been developed for the probability distribution of the closed birth interval by considering the interval as the sum of the four components mentioned above assuming known functional forms for each of the component distribution and their statistical independence (Srinivasan 1967). In section Micro model we would discuss the modeling of some of these components. Here we only discuss the types of birth interval and problem associated with these analysis.

Types of Closed Birth Interval

(*i*) All closed Birth Interval : In this case all the birth intervals obtained from survey are taken together and analysis is carried out by birth order, age and marital duration.

(*ii*) Last Closed Birth Interval : This is the interval between the last and last but one live birth of each woman. A woman who has given birth to at least one child will contribute one interval of this type. In the analysis, we may put a condition that the last live birth has occured during a given period of time prior to the survey (one or two years). The interval without condition may be termed as last birth interval (births).

(*iii*) Straddling Birth Interval : An interval is considered to be straddling at a particular age or duration of marriage or at a particular point of time if one birth occurs before that age or point and the next birth occur later. If we consider the fact that one birth occur at a particular age or any duration of marriage and the next birth occurs after that age, the interval may be termed as prospective birth Interval.

(*iv*) Interior Birth Interval : An interval that begins and ends in any segment of age group or marriage duration is called an interior birth interval.

7.6.3 Model of Waiting Time

Treating fecundability to be constant for a long span of time within a woman's reproductive period, the probability distribution of waiting time of first or any order of conception can be obtained. It turns out to be a geometric distribution in its most simplistic form. Let the probability of conception for a non-pregnant woman in any month be p, and of not conceiving be $q=1-p$. Also let all the conceptions end into a live birth. Then the probability that the time to first conception will be one month is p, that it will be more than one month is q. The probability that it is 2 months is qp, that it is 3 months is q^2p and so on.

The mean of the time to conceive is

$$\bar{x}=1.p+2.qp+3q^2p+\ldots=\frac{1}{p};\ o<p<1$$

If p remains constant in any month of exposure of the woman who is not pregnant and is not in the amenorrhea period, it can easily be shown that the average interval between any two births (assuming that all conceptions end into live births) is given by

$C=\frac{1}{p}+h$ where h is the length of the gestation plus amenorrhea periods. Knowledge of the closed birth interval implies knowing the birth rate for the population. If all women on average produce a child every C months, the average monthly birth rate is $1/C$ and the annual birth rate is $12/C$. The purpose of contraception is to reduce fecundability and hence to increase the closed birth interval through increased conceptive delays. If a woman uses a contraceptive of e effectiveness then her fecundability is reduced from p to $p(1\ \ e)=p^*$. This may help us in ascertaining the value of e if we know the closed birth interval of the contracepting, women, because their closed birth interval becomes :

$$C^*=\frac{1}{p^*}+h=\frac{1}{p(1\ \ e)}+h.$$

Now, if we consider a heterogeneous group of women with varying fecundability (p), then the waithing time distribution becomes

$$P\,[X=x]=\int_0^1 pq^{x-1}f(p)\,dp$$

In literature $f(p)$ has been assumed to be the density of Beta Type I distribution because of its flexibility. As such

$$f(p)=\frac{p^{a-1}\,q^{b-1}}{\beta(a,b)}$$

where $$\beta(a,b)=\int_0^1 p^{a-1}\,q^{b-1}\,dp \quad a,\ b>o$$

From the above the mean, mode and variance of p are

$$\bar{p}=a/_{(a+b)}$$

$$P(\text{mode})=\frac{a-1}{a+b-2}$$

$$\sigma_p^2=\frac{ab}{(a+b)^2\,(a+b+1)}$$

Also the proportion of women conceiving in the jth month under the above assumptions is given by

$$P(j)=\int_0^1 p(1-p)^{j-1} f(p)\,dp$$

$$=\frac{\beta\,(a+1,\,b+j\quad 1)}{\beta\,(a,\,b)}$$

and the proportion of women conceiving up to the jth month is given by

$$1-\frac{\beta\,(a,b+j)}{\beta\,(a,\,b)}$$

If the time of exposure is infinite, the following results have been obtained by Potter and Parker (1964).

The mean conceptive delay $(\bar{w})=\int_0^1 f(p)\,.\,\frac{1}{p}\;dp$

$$=\frac{a+b-1}{a-1}(a>1)$$

The variance of the conceptive delay $\sigma^2(\bar{w})$

$$=\int_0^1 f(p)\sum_{J=1}^{\infty} pq^{j-1}\,(j-\bar{w})^2\,dp$$

$$=\frac{ab\,(a+b\quad 1)}{(a+1)^2\,(a-2)}\;,\;a>2$$

Without discretising the time parameter, some times we have to deal with the continuous random variables. The role of the geometric distribution for waiting time is then taken over by the negative exponential distribution. It is the only distribution having a Markovian character, that is, endowed with complete lack of memory. In other words, for a women who does not conceive upto the period x, the probability that she will conceive after the elapse of time t is given by $\lambda e^{-\lambda t}$. In case λ varies among the woman, Singh (1964) obtained an exponential type *III* distribution (assuming that λ varies as type *III* distribution) as below.

$$f(t)=\int_a^\infty \lambda e^{-\lambda t} g(\lambda)\, d\lambda$$

if,
$$g(\lambda)=\frac{h^a \lambda^{a-1} e^{-h\lambda}}{\sqrt{a}}$$

$$f(t)=\frac{ah^a}{(h+t)^{a+1}} \quad a,\ h>0$$

The above distribution may be applied to the actual data to obtain the estimate of a and h and hence the mean and variance of λ as

$$\bar{\lambda}=a/h$$

$$V(\lambda)=a/h^2$$

7.6.4 Distribution of the Number of Births

Singh (1963, 1964) derived a very simple model for describing the distribution of the number of children born to a women in first t years of her marriage under the following simple assumptions.

(*i*) That a woman conceives in a unit of time is constant and is given by p.

(*ii*) Either the woman is fecund during the period (o, t) or she is not fecund. The probabilities of such cases are a and $1-a$ respectively.

(*iii*) If there is a conception in a unit of time, there is no conception in subsequent $h-1$ units of time. Conveniently we can take the unit of time as equal to the menstrual cycle and hence equal to one month approximately.

(iv) The women is in the non-pregnant fecund state at the time of marriage (or $t=0$). Thus if x denotes the number of births, then we have

$$Pr\,[X=0]=1-a+aq^{t}$$

$$Pr\,[X=x]=ap^{x}q^{t-xh}\left[\binom{t-xh+x}{x}+\sum_{l=1}^{L-1}\binom{t-\overline{x-1}h+\overline{x-1}+1}{x+1}q^{h-l}\right]$$

$$Pr\,[x=n]=1-Pr[x\leqslant n-1] \quad x=1, 2, \ldots n-1$$

The model discussed above has treated time as discrete and have been invariably used to estimate fecundability, primary and secondary sterility of the women in any population based on the knowledge of the distribution of the women of same marital duration by the number of children. A continuous analogue can easily be obtained. We know that in case of continuous time model under the success rate or exposure rate λ, the time to first conception is exponentially distributed with density $f(t)=\lambda e^{-\lambda t}$ with mean time of $\frac{1}{\lambda}$ and a variance of $\frac{1}{\lambda^2}$ again on the assumption that there is infinite time available for conception. A number of modifications of the above distribution exist in the literature if time is not infinite and the women are not all in the fecund state at the beginning of their married life. Henry gave a model for births under some simple assumptions.

Let $F_0(t)$ be the probability that X_0, the time to the first conception, is not greater than t, and let $F(t)$ be the probability that $X_i(i\geqslant 1)$ is not greater than t. We assume that the density functions

$$f_0(t)=\frac{dF_0\,(t)}{dt}$$

and

$$f_r(t)=\frac{dF_r(t)}{dt} \text{ exist.}$$

Let

$$Fr(t)=pr\left[\sum_{i=0}^{r} X_i\leqslant t\right]$$

$$=\text{Prob}\,[N(t)>r]$$

where $N(t)$ denotes the number of recording of events in time t.

We can see that

$$fr(t)=\int_0^t F_{r-1}(t-x)f(x)dx \quad r\geqslant 1$$

Following Feller (1948)

$$F_0(t)=1-e^{-\lambda t}$$

$$F_r(t)=1-e^{-\lambda(X-h)}$$

where h is the non-fecund period associated with a pregnancy. In the poisson process we have

$$f_r(t)=\lambda e^{-\lambda t}\frac{(\lambda t)^r}{r\,!}$$

In our case t must be reduced by lost time, hence

$$f_r(t)=0, \qquad t<rh$$

$$=\lambda^{r+1}(t-rh)^r\frac{e^{-r(t-rh)}}{r\,!}, \qquad t\geqslant rh$$

The cumulative probability $R(r, t)$ is given by

$$R(r, t)=1, \qquad t\leqslant rh$$

$$=e^{-\lambda(t-rh)}\sum_{j=0}^{r}\left[\frac{\lambda^j(t-rh)^j}{j\,!}\right] \qquad t\geqslant rh$$

This result was obtained by Neyman (1949). Singh (1968) re-examined these models and reformulated the model obtained by Dandekar (1955), under the following assumptions :

1. (*a*) The number of coitious of a non-pregnant fecund married woman during any arbitrary time interval (t_1, t_2), $0\leqslant t_1\leqslant t_2\leqslant T$ is a random variable and follows a Poisson distribution with parameter $\lambda_1(t_2-t_1)$, $\lambda_1>0$.

   (*b*) The coitious are mutually independent and p_1, the probability that a coitious results in a conception at time t is constant when there is no conception (leading to a live birth) during $(t-h, t)$, h being the rest period associated with 0 live birth pregnancy. Otherwise the probability of conception is zero.

2. Either the woman is sterile during the period $(0, T)$ or fecund. Let $1-a$ and a be their respective probabilities.

3. There is one to one correspondence between a conception and a live-birth.

Now if X denotes the number of children born to a woman in the period $(0, T)$ then its probability function is

$$P[X=0]=1-\alpha+\alpha e^{-\lambda T}$$

$$P[X=x]=\alpha\left[e^{-\lambda(T-xh)}\sum_{i=0}^{x}\frac{\{\lambda(T-xh)\}^{i}}{i!}\right.$$

$$\left.-e^{-\lambda[T-(x-1)h]}\sum_{i=0}^{x-1}\frac{\{\lambda(T-(x-1)h)\}^{i}}{i!}\right]$$

$$x=1, 2, \ldots\ldots n-1$$

$$P[x=n]=1-P[x\leqslant n-1]$$

This distribution has been recently modified by several researchers. These are however, not being discussed here.

7.6.5. Models Dealing with Family Building Strategies

(*a*) Models with stopping rules :

Models for population may be obtained incorporating stopping rules. Sheps (1963) has shown that for parents who want to have a sons and b daughters, the probability that they will end up with k children $(k\geqslant a+b)$ is

$$\binom{k-1}{a-1}p^{a}q^{k-a}+\binom{k-1}{b-1}p^{k-b}q^{b}$$

where p is the proportion of male births and q is the proportion of female births such that $p+q=1$. It is presumed that the woman can have as many births as she wants to have *i.e.* the length of reproductive life is infinite.

The mean and variance of such families may be readily calculated. When couples stop with first son, the mean number of children is

$$E(X)=p+2qp+3q^2p+\ldots \quad =\frac{1}{p}$$

It can also be shown that

$$V(X)=\frac{1}{p^2}-\frac{1}{p}=\frac{q}{p^2}$$

By analogy it can be shown that the couples who stop after a boys will average a/p children with its variance equal to aq/p^2.

The probability generating function for the total number of children $X(X \geq a+b)$ to couples who stop after a sons and b daughters is given by

$$g(s)=\left(\frac{s\ q}{1-Ps}\right)^b+\left(\frac{Ps}{1-qs}\right)^a$$

In the above expression the terms of lower power than s^{a+b} are disregarded. This result can be used to show to what extent the inability of the parents to influence the sex of their unborn children will cause families to be larger in communities where the sex of the children is important. Assuming that $p=q=\frac{1}{2}$, the expected number of children to be born when couple wants a boy is $\frac{1}{p}=\frac{1}{.5}=2$. It is 3 when couple wants one boy and one girl, that is 50 per cent more than the size if they were satisfied with two children regardless of sex.

Sheps has also obtained the expression for the distribution of the size of the families when the couples stop at maximum number of children K. In case couple wants only one son but stops at K trials whichever is earlier, then

$$E(X)=\sum_{r=1}^{k} rq^{r-1}p+kq^{k}$$

$$=\frac{1-q^{k}}{p}<\frac{1}{p}$$

Mitra (1970) has derived expressions when the strategy is to have a sons and b daughters in not more than k trials. As such the couples may stop at birth of the $(K-l)^{th}$ child $(l>0,$ $a+b\leqslant K-l)$ when either the couple achieves the desired sex composition of the children or the sex of the $(K-1)^{th}$ child makes it impossible for the couple to achieve the goal. For example, in one son case. Krishnamoorthy (1974) extended the earlier results by considering the facts that the couples need a minimum number of children 'm' and then want to satisfy their desire for a sons and b daughters in not more than k trials. In case the couple wants one son and atleast m children then

$$\begin{aligned} Pr[X=r]&=0 && r<m \\ &=1-q^{m} && r=m \\ &=q^{K-1}p+q^{K} && r=K \\ &=0 \text{ otherwise} \end{aligned}$$

and the expected family size becomes

$$E_1(X)=m+\frac{q^{m}}{p}(1-q^{k-m})$$

which compares with $\frac{1}{P}$ when $m=0$ and $K=\infty$

Now the question arises whether a woman can conceive as many times as she desires. We know that

(1) the duration of her fertile life is limited;

(2) her conceptions are random events;

(3) a part of her reproductive life is wasted due to postpartum amenorrhoea periods; and

(4) due to the sex composition of the born children she may find impossible to achieve the desired composition and may deeide to stop abruptly at any size K.

Pathak (1973) obtained the composite result for the size of the family when couples stop either naturally or due to stopping rule in case they achieve either a sons and b daughters or $m(m>a+b)$ children.

Following distribution of the family size has been obtained :

$$P[X=x]=P_x,\ x=0,\ 1,\ 2,\ \ldots\ldots,\ a+b-1$$

$$=P_x\left[\sum_{i=0}^{a-1}\binom{x}{i}p^i q^{x-i}+\sum_{i=0}^{b-1}\binom{x}{i}q^i p^{x-i}\right]$$

$$+\sum_{i=x}^{n}P_x\left[\binom{x-1}{a-1}p^a q^{x-a}+\binom{x-1}{b-1}q^b p^{x-b}\right]$$

$$X: a+b,\ a+b+1,\ \ldots\ldots\ m-1 \qquad \ldots (53)$$

and

$$P(X=m)=1-P \qquad (X\leqslant m-1)$$

where $m=[T-G/h]+1$, G=Gestation period, h=infecundable period associated with a live birth, P_i is the probability of i live births in the period $(O,\ T)$ in the absence of any stopping rule, T is the total marital duration.

In the above expression P_i can be calculated from any fertility model. Because of the time factor involved in the above model, it is also possible to obtain the expected time when the couple will achieve its desired family size and also to ascertain what proportion of couples would remain unsatisfied as regards the unfulfilment of their desires with respect to the sex composition or size of their families. Recently Pathak and Saxena (1979) obtained the expressions for the mean and variances of the waiting times for achieving the desired family size in fixed period of the reproductive live.

7.6.6 Distribution of Family Size When Stopping Rules Depend on Surviving Children

Limitation of family size largely depends upon the number of living children and sex composition than on the number of children born. In developing countries, where infant and child mortality is considerably high, the couples will like to ensure the survival of their minimam desired number of sons and daughters before deciding to stop their reproductive process. Krishnamoorthy derived the distribution of the surviving children on the assumptions that (*i*) infant child mortality occurs in the first two years of life and later no death occurs among the children until the couples complete their fertility (*ii*) couples take decision in going for the next baby when the age of the previous baby born is two years. Now let δ be the probability of death among male babies in the first two years of life and p be the probability of death among female babies and

$$P_1=p(1-\delta),\ P_2=p\delta$$

$$q_1=(1-p),\quad q_2=q\rho$$

Then for parents who want to have a sons and b living daughter, the probability that they will end up with $(a+b+h)$ births is

$$P_b\,(a+b+h,\ a,\ b)=\binom{a+b+h-1}{a-1}\ P_1^a\sum_{i=b}^{h}\binom{b+h}{b+i}\ q_1^{b+i}\ (P_2+q_2)^{h-i}$$

$$+\binom{a+b+h-1}{b-1}\ q_1^b\sum_{i=0}\binom{a+h}{a+i}\ (P_2+q_2)^{h-i}\ P_1^{a+i}$$

and the probability that they will end up with $(a+b+K)$ living children, $\quad K\geqslant 0$

$$P_1(a+b+K,\ a,\ b)$$

$$=\frac{\binom{a+b+k-1}{b-1}\ q_1^b\ P_1^{a+k}+\binom{a+b+k-1}{a-1}\ p_1^a\ q^{b+K}}{\{1-(P_2+q_2)\}^{a+b+k}}$$

Again here it is assumed that woman can bear as many children as possible. Therefore if we impose the limitation of the reproduction process the probability function of the living children, X, when woman desires only a living sons and b living daughters or maximum m living children becomes

$$P\,[X=x]=\sum_{r=x}^{m} P_r \binom{r}{x} (P_2+q_2)^{r-x}\,(1-p_2-q_2)^{x}$$

$$x=0,\ 1,\ 2,\ \ldots\ldots,\ a+b-1$$

$$=\sum_{r=x}^{m} P_r \left[\binom{r-1}{x-1}\binom{x-1}{a-1}\ P_1^{a}\ q_1^{x-a}\ (P_2+q_2)^{r-x}\right.$$

$$\left.+\binom{r-1}{x-1}\binom{x-1}{b-1}\ q_1^{b}\ P_1^{x-b}\ (P_2+q_2)^{r-x}\right]$$

$$X: a+b,\ a+b+1,\ \ldots\ldots,\ m-1$$

$$P[x=m]=1-P[x\leq m-1] \qquad \ldots(54)$$

It is, however, desirable to relax the assumption regarding mortality and obtain the general results. At least, through simulation experiment the effect of mortality of children can be ascertained on the desire of the couples to stop. Undoubtedly the family size is considerably affected due to sex preference about the living children. In so far as parents wish to have atleast one boy or atleast one boy and one girl and keep having children until they attain their wish, the birth rate would be higher than it would otherwise be. A considerable literature (Goodman 1961, Mc Donald 1973, Pathak 1977) analyses the magnitude of this effect. If no limit is placed on the family size, the ratio of boy births to the total births in the population will be given by

$$\frac{np+nqp+nq^2p}{np+2nqp+3nq^2p}=P$$

where n denotes the number of couples who stop having children after the birth of first boy. Even under more realistic conditions of reproductive process, the sex ratio of born children is unaffected by any stopping as well as sex preference rules as long as having children meets the conditions of a fair gambling game and parents are homogeneous with respect to 'p' and do not have any control over the sex of their children. However, nothing prevents the parents from determining the probability of the last child being a boy. Thus on the rule of one boy, it would be certainty. In a case when each couple is supposed to stop with the first son, the proportion of boys in one child family is 1, in two child family is $\frac{1}{2}$, in a three child family is $\frac{1}{3}$ etc. The average proportion of boys is

$$p+\tfrac{1}{2}qp+\tfrac{1}{3}q^2p+\ldots=-p\log p/q \qquad \ldots(55)$$

If $p=q=\frac{1}{2}$, this turns out to be .693 which is greater than 0.50. This is true for one family case and not incase of a population.

Goodman (1961) analyses the consequences of preference for boys in a population using birth control in which couples have different probabilities of producing boys. Suppose p is distributed according to $f(p)$ so there are $Nf(p)\,dp$ couples who have probability of having a boy between p and $p+dp$ and total number of children contributed by such couples is

$$\left(Nf(p)\,dp\,\frac{1}{p} \right)$$

and through the distribution of p gives the grand total of children

$$N\int_0^1 \frac{1}{p}\,f(p)dp.$$

Since the total of boys is N, one to each couple in this case, the fraction of boys in the population is

$$\frac{N}{N\int_0^1 \frac{1}{p}\,f(p)dp} = \text{(Harmonic mean of } p\text{'s)}$$

Since the Harmonic Mean is less than A.M., it is proved that in case of heterogeneity, the fraction of boys is smaller than the fraction, if the couples are homogenous. Average number of children per couple, $\frac{1}{H}$, will be greater than $1/p$ that would occur with homogeneity in case couples stop at first boy. In otherwards, if couples want to increase the proportion of boys, they should stop at the birth of first girl.

It is shown by Smith (1974) that if couple want first a girl and then a boy then the expected number of children will be

$$A_g = g\left(1+\frac{1}{b}\right)+\left(1+\frac{1}{g}\right)b = g/b+1/g_{\,b=1-g} \qquad \ldots(56)$$

where g is the probability of getting a girl when couple wants to have a girl and b is the probability of having a boy when couple wants to have a boy. On the other hand if the strategy of the couple is to try first for a boy and then for a girl the expected number of children is

$$A_b = b\left(1+\frac{1}{g}\right)+(1-b)\left(1+\frac{1}{b}\right) = \frac{b}{g}+\frac{1}{b} \qquad \ldots(57)$$

For $b > g > \frac{1}{2}$, it can be shown that

$$(b-\tfrac{1}{2})^2 > (g-\tfrac{1}{2})^2 \quad \text{or} \quad b^2-b > g^2-g$$

$$\text{or} \quad b^2+g > g^2+b \quad \text{or} \quad \frac{b}{g}+\frac{1}{b} > \frac{g}{b}+\frac{1}{g} \qquad \ldots(58)$$

Thus the right strategy for couples in this situation will be to leave the more controllable contingency to the last if they seek equal number of boys and girls.

The policy implications of such partial and complete control of the sex of children is that the sex of the new generation may be biased in favour of one sex, say of boy. As a result of it, in the next generation there will be less marriages because of lack of partners and thereby unwed males would decrease the overall birth rate.

The other issue that comes up for consideration from population policy point of view is whether sex preferences and stopping rules will cause extinction of families faster than in the normal course. The common sense suggests that the more children one has the less likely is the extinction of one's line of descent. This is, however, only partially true. One can use theory of branching process to arrive at some conclusive results. It can however, easily be shown that the chance of extinction of the male line (x) is given by the equation,

$$x = P_0 + P_1 x + P_2 x^2 + \ldots\ldots \qquad \ldots (59)$$

where p_0, p_1, p_2 ..... are the probabilities of 0, 1 and 2 sons living upto maturity and x is the probability of extinction of the male line. It may be shown from this that extinction is more dependent on the variation in the number of children in later generations (not on the size of the family) and in particular on the chance of having zero child. In avoiding the extinction of the family lines, high birth rate does not necessarily provide an advantage over the low birth rate. But so long survivorship probability is less than unity, the stopping rules may affect the extinction probabilities adversely. It will, however, be interesting to study the extinction possibilities when existing marriage pattern changes and parity progression rates change due to sex preference and stopping rules.

These rules are bound to affect in different magnitudes the kinship relations. A more elaborate stochastic model needs to be developed to take into account variation in the components of population growth not only because of biological factors but also due to social. economic and psychological factors. A micro simulation model, may of course, be developed to answer various queries on the effects of different control strategies on various measures of fertility.

7.7 Human Reproduction Process as a Markov Renewal Process

It is clear that the reproductive history of a female is characterised completely by the knowledge of the sequence in which these states are visited and of the length of time spent in each state at each visit. Perrin and Sheps (1964) labelled the five states in which she is supposed to lie at any point of time as below :

S_0=non-pregnant, fecundable state

S_1=Pregnant state

S_2=Post partum sterile period associated with abortion

S_3=Post partum sterile period associated with stillbirth

S_4=Post partum sterile period associated with livebirth

Biological considerations make it natural to assume conceptive delays as random variables. We assume that a female has probability to enter the state S_1 from state S_0 in a unit of time (in a menstrual cycle). Under this assumption the total number of months spent in state S_0 during any single visit to S_1 can be seen to be a random variable with geometric distribution. In the same way, the lengths of stay of a woman in each of the other four states of the model may be viewed as random variables. Let f_i be the distribution function of the duration of time of staying in state S_1 given that next state visited is S_i, $i=2, 3, 4$ with the mean and variance of duration of stay as ν_i and ξ_i respectively. Similarly, the distribution function of the duration of time (in months) spent in the post partum state S_i is represented by g_i with mean and variance μ_{i0} and σ^2_{i0}, respectively. Finally let θ_i be the probability that a given pregnancy ends with a transition to state S_i $i=2, 3, 4$. Under these assumptions, the reproductive process may be treated as a stochastic process. In this process the length of stay in each state is, as mentioned earlier, a random variable whose distribution function can depend on the state being occupied as well as on the next state to which the process will move. If the parameters involved in the distributions are constant with respect to time, it can be shown thet the human reproductive process is indeed a Markov Renewal Process (M.R.P.) [Fyke R. (1961), Markov Renewal Process : Definition and Preliminary Properties. Annals Math. Stat. 32, 1231-42].

The three characteristics are important in the study of human fertility. (1) the distribution of the intervals between successive pregnancy terminations of the various types, (2) the distribution of the number of miscarriages, still-births or live-births per individual occurring in a given period of time, and (3) the monthly probability of the occurrence of a live-birth (*i.e.* the fertility rate).

(*i*) First Passage and Recurrence times :

Let T_{ij}, $i, j=0, 1, ..., 4$, represent the time (in months) required by a female for passage from state i to state j in our model, and let μ_{ij} and σ^2_{ij} represent the mean and variance, respectively, of that time. T_{ij} will then be the first passage time from i to j and T_{ii} the recurrence time as defined in classical renewal theory. Further, let T_{ij}^* be the time spent in state i given that j is the next state entered. It may be noted that T_{ij}^* is defined only if direct passage from state i to state j is possible. Hence T_{ij}^* need not equal T_{ij} since in the latter process any number of states may be visited before eventual passage to state j. From the assumptions $T_{01}=T_{01}^*$ and T_{01} has a geometric distribution with parameter ρ.

Hence

$$E[T_{01}]=\mu_{01}=(1-\rho)/\rho$$

$$V(T_{01})=\sigma^2_{01}=(1-\rho)/\rho^2....$$

Also

$$T_{00}=T_{01}+T_{12}^*+T_{20}, \text{ with probability } \theta_2$$

$$T_{01}+T_{13}^*+T_{30}, \text{ with probability } \theta_3$$

$$T_{01}+T_{14}^*+T_{40}, \text{ with probability } \theta_4.$$

Thus, the expected value of T_{00}, the recurrence time for the fecundable non-pregnant state, is a weighted mean of the expected time spent in each of the three paths leading to the recurrence. In particular, if we let $n_i = v_i + u_{io}$ $i=2, 3, 4$, we can write :

$$u_{oo} = E(T_{oo}) = E(T_{o1}) + \sum_{i=2}^{u} \theta_i \, (T^*_{1i} + T_{io})$$

$$= \frac{1-\rho}{\rho} + \sum_{i=2}^{u} \theta_i \, \eta_i$$

It can be seen easily after some simplification that

$$V(T_{oo}) = E(T_{oo}^2) - [E(T_{o}o)]^2$$

$$= V(T_{o1}) + \sum_{i=2}^{4} \theta_i \, V(T_{1i}^* + T_{io}) +$$

$$\sum_{i<j}^{4} \theta_i \theta_j \, [E(T_{1i}^* + T_{io}) - E(T_i^* + T_o)]^2$$

Thus if we let $\lambda_i^2 = \xi_i^2 + \sigma_{io}^2, \quad i=2, 3, 4$

we have

$$V(T_{oo}) = \frac{1-\rho}{\rho^2} + \sum_{i=2}^{4} \theta_i \, \lambda_i^2 + \sum_{i<j}^{4} \theta_i \theta_j \, [\eta_i - \eta_j]^2$$

A quantity of special interest is T_{44}, the waiting time between successive live-birth to a female. This time can be represented as below :

$$T_{44} = T_{40} + T_{01} + T^{(1)}_{11}, \bar{4} + T^{(2)}_{11}, \bar{4} + \ldots T^{(N)}_{11}, \bar{4} + T^*_{14} \quad \ldots (28)$$

where $T^{(k)}_{11}, \bar{4}$ represents the time spent in the kth consecutive recurrence of state l accomplished without passage through state 4. The total number of times, N, which the female cycles between pregnancies without the occurrence of a live-birth is a random variable and is easily seen in this model to have a geometric distribution with mean $(\theta_2+\theta_3)/\theta_4$ and variance $(\theta_2+\theta_3)/\theta_4^2$. We have

$$E(T_{44})=\mu_{40}+\frac{1-\rho}{\rho}+E(N)\,.\,E(T_{11,\bar{4}})+\nu_4$$

Now since

$$T_{11,\bar{4}}=\begin{cases}T_{12}^*+T_{20}+T_{01} \text{ with probability } \theta_2/(\theta_2+\theta_3)\\ T_{13}^*+T_{30}+T_{01} \text{ with probability } \theta_3/(\theta_2+\theta_3)\end{cases}$$

Hence

$$E(T_{11,\bar{4}})=\frac{\theta_2}{(\theta_2+\theta_3)}\eta_2+\frac{\theta_3}{(\theta_2+\theta_3)}.\eta_3+\frac{1-\rho}{\rho}$$

and
$$V(T_{11\bar{4}})=\frac{\theta_2}{(\theta_2+\theta_3)}\lambda_2^2+\frac{\theta_3}{(\theta_2+\theta_3)}\lambda_3^2+\frac{1-\rho}{\rho^2}+\frac{\theta_2\,\theta_3}{(\theta_2+\theta_3)^2}(\eta_2-\eta_3)^2$$

Hence

$$E(T_{44})=\mu_{44}=\frac{1}{\theta_4}\left(\frac{1-\rho}{\rho}+\sum_{i=2}^{4}\theta_i\,\eta_i\right)$$

Hence

$$\mu_{33}=\frac{1}{\theta_3}\left[\frac{1-\rho}{\rho}+\sum_{i=2}^{4}\theta_i\,\eta_i\right]$$

$$\mu_{22}=\frac{1}{\theta_2}\left[\frac{1-\rho}{\rho}+\sum^{4}\theta_i\,\eta_i\right]$$

Further one can get

$$\sigma_{44}^2+\lambda_4^2+\frac{1-\rho}{\rho^2}+\frac{\theta_2+\theta_3}{\theta_4}V(T_{11,\bar{4}})+\frac{\theta_2+\theta_3}{\theta_4^2}[E(T_{11,\bar{4}})]^2$$

It is also of interest to determine the expected length and variance of the waiting time, T_{04}, between the date of marriage and the first live-birth. This is easily done since $T_{44}=T_{40}+T_{04}$. Clearly

$$\mu_{04}=E(T_{04})=\mu_{44}-\mu_{40}$$

$$=\nu_4+\frac{1}{\theta_4}\left(\theta_2\eta_2+\theta_3\eta_3+\frac{1-\rho}{\rho}\right)$$

$$\sigma_{04}^2=\sigma_{44}^2-\sigma_{40}^2=\xi_4^2+\frac{\theta_2+\theta_3}{\theta_4}V(T_{11},\bar{_4})+\frac{1-\rho}{\rho}$$

$$+\frac{\theta_2+\theta_3}{\theta_4^2}E(T_{11},\bar{_4})$$

B. Expected Number of Variance of Live-births, Still-births, and Miscarriages in a Given Time Period

It is useful to consider the number of pregnancy terminations of the various kinds which can be expected to occur in a given period of time in a woman's reproductive history. If we let $N_i(t)$ be the (random) number of times a woman enters S_i, ($i=0, 1, \ldots 4$) in time t, the number of live-births in time t can be expected is given by $N_4(t)$. If we consider the sequence of recurrence times of states S_i, *i.e.*

$$\{T_{ii}^{(1)},\ T_{ii}^{(2)},\ \ldots\ldots\},$$

we note that these random variables from a renewal processes, and further. if we augment the sequence with first passage time from S_j to S_i ; *i.e.*

$$\{T_{ji}^{(1)},\ T_{ii}^{(2)}\}.$$

It is easy to show that we have a general renewal process From the cumulants for the general renewal process it follows directly that the mean and variance of $N_i(t)$ given that the process starts in S_j are given approximately by the following expressions ;

$$E[N_i(t)/J_0=j]=\frac{t}{\mu_{ii}}+\frac{\mu_{ii}^{(2)}}{2\mu_{ii}^2}-\frac{\mu_{ji}}{\mu_{ii}}$$

and

$$V\,[N_i(t)/J_0=j]=\frac{\sigma_{ii}^2}{\mu_{ii}^3}+\frac{5\,(\mu_{ii}^{(2)})^2}{4\,\mu_{ii}^4}-\frac{2\,\mu_{ii}^{(3)}}{3\,\mu_{ii}^{(2)}}-\frac{\mu_{ji}\mu_{ii}^{(2)}}{\mu_{ii}^{(3)}}+\frac{\sigma_{ji}^2}{\mu_{ii}^2}+\frac{\mu_{ji}}{\mu_{ii}}$$

where J_0 designates the initial stage of the process, and $\mu_{ji}(n)=$ n^{th} moment about the origin of T_{ji} and μ_{ii}, μ_{jj} denotes the first raw moments of T_{ii} and T_{jj} respectively. Thus, the expected number of live-births for a woman in time t months of marriage are

$$E[N_4(t)/J_0=0]=\frac{t}{\mu_{44}}+\frac{\mu_{44}^{(2)}}{2\,\mu_{44}^2}-\frac{\mu_{04}}{\mu_{44}}$$

likewise, the expected number of total pregnancies (in a sence, the total fertility) for a woman in t months of marriage is approximately

$$E[N_1(t)/J_0=0]=\frac{t}{\mu_{11}}+\frac{\mu_{11}^{(2)}}{2\mu_{11}^{(2)}}-\frac{\mu_{01}}{\mu_{11}}$$

C. Fertility Rate

Since each woman is assumed to enter marriage in a fecundable, non-pregnant state, she consequently has a greater probability, during the early months, of conceiving. The derivation of an exact expression for the monthly fertility rate as a function of the duration of marriage is exceedingly difficult. If we view again the model as a renewal process we see that Prob {Passage into S_4 at t}

$$=E[N_4(t)]-[N_4(t-1)]=\mu_{44}^{-1}$$

(due to Blackwell's Theorem *i.e.*, equal to the mean recurrence time for live birth). The above discussion of the model is based on the work of Perrin and Sheps. This model allows for more than one type of pregnancy. It also allows for a variable period of gestation and variable period of infecundability associated with each pregnancy, the length of these periods depending on the form of the pregnancy termination,

However, the model does not allow the probabilities of conception, still-birth or early foetal loss, or the lengths of the periods of gestation and infecundability to depend on such factors as age or birth order in the individual female. It is commonly held that the assumption of constant probability of conception in the absence of the use of contraceptives is reasonably valid over a large part, but not all, of a woman's child bearing life. Further, probabilities of foetal death are more opt to be a function of time than the probability of conception itself. Hence the period for which this model can be assumed to hold for each woman must necessarily be restricted to an interval of almost from 10 to 15 years in the middle of the child bearing age. Moreover, in this model there is a tacit assumption of independence between the distributions of durations of stay in each of the fertility states. This assumption may not always hold good. However, variations may be easily dealt with.

The above models can be viewed of generic nature. One could, even define the various states of the process as the successive stages of a disease, or as different disease entities, etc., through which an individual might pass in a given period of exposure. The stochastic relationships derived above would apply with equal validity to studies of this sort.

8

Estimation of Fertility and Mortality

Despite the existing laws for compulsory registration of births and deaths, there exists a very high degree of under registration of births and deaths in most of the developing countries. As such, levels of fertility and mortality can not be ascertained in these countries from registered births and deaths. However, for most of these countries, reasonably accurate census data are now available and they provide detailed tabulations of the population by age and sex.

There are several approaches to estimate vital rates under specified assumptions. One approach is to improve the data collection through surveys or repeated surveys or through combination of more than one ways to have control over omission and provide a cross checks on each other. A second approach is based on use of stable and quasi stable population model in conjuction with the population age data (See Chapter on Demographic Models for stable population theory). The third approach is to use retrospective questions in censuses or large scale surveys wherein questions are asked about number of children born and surviving to women in reproductive span. Fourth approach consists of deriving estimates of vital rates by using the age data from the successive censuses. We shall be discussing first few methods of estimating death rates from the two census age data and then also discuss the methods to estimate child and adult mortality.

8.1 Estimation of Mortality from Age Distribution

All the methods discussed below involve an identification of the level of mortality on the basis of some clues from the age distributions of the population and their intercensal rate of natural increase. A brief description of some methods is given below :

8.1.1 Differencing Method

Let us assume that two consecutive censuses are taken 10 years apart, say at times t and $t+10$. Obviously the persons aged 0 – 4 at time t will be aged 10 – 14 at time $t+10$. In the absence of migration $P^{t}_{0+} - P^{t+10}_{10+}$ is the total number of intercensal deaths occurred to the population attime t. These deaths may be assumed to have occurred on an average to the population aged x to $x+5$ at time t, then change in its size may be attributed to mortality in the absence of migration. Since the population under age 10, at the later census date $t+10$ is equal to the survivors of the births during the last 10 years, the difference in the population P^{t}_{0+} and P^{t+10}_{10+} can give an idea of mortality at ages 5 and above at the mid point of the intercensal period. The major hurdle is in respect of estimating deaths under age 5. The vital registration data on deaths by age and sex, though incomplete, do give the ratio of deaths above age 5 to total deaths. The reciprocal of this ratio, multiplied with the difference, $P^{t}_{0+} - P^{t+10}_{10+}$ gives the total deaths during theintercensal period. One tenth of these deaths divided by the intercensal mid point total population gives the crude death rate. Once crude death rate is obtained, the crude birth rate can easily be estimated from the knowledge of CDR and rate of natural increase. For estimating the level of mortality (e^0_0), we can select, through trial and error, an appropriate model life table whose age-specific death rates (${}_nm_x$) when applied to the mean decennial population by age, give one tenth of the total deaths estimated earlier for the entire intercensal period. This method needs two types of inputs. This method however suffers from the age mis reporting errors which transfer population under or across age 10. It also suffers from the difference by age in the degree of under-registration of deaths, in case total deaths are estimated by using the ratio of deaths over age 5 to the total deaths in the population. This ratio being over stated due to comparatively larger under-enumeration of deaths below age 5, leads to an under estimation of the death rate and over estimation of e_0^0. Again the determinations of e_0^0 depends not merely upon the age specific deaths rates (${}_nm_x$) of the life table but also on the age distribution of population. Because of misreporting error in the age data, estimate of e_0^0 is affected. On the other hand, there does not lie a unique method of smoothing the data and some amount of the subjectivity is involved in smoothing. We discuss below a procedure which does away with these problems.

8.1.2 Census Survival Rate Method

If censuses are taken 10 years apart, 10-year census survival rates can be calculated. However, due to the misreporting error in the age data, some of the survival rates may show erratic behaviour; some may even exceed unity. To overcome this problem either one should smooth the age data to remove the misreporting error prior to calculating the census survival rates or smooth the census survival rates. However to avoid the complexity and subjectivity involved in smoothing of age data (or of survival rates), one may calculate the cumulative survival rates S_{0+}, S_{5+}......S_{50+} which are likely to be quite smooth, where

$$S_{x+} = \frac{P^{t+10}_{(x+10)+}}{P^t_{x+}}$$

where P^t_{x+} and $P^{t+10}_{(x+10)+}$ denotes the population aged $x+$ and $(x+10)+$ at time t and $t+10$ respectively. After calculating the overall survival rates; the procedure involves the calculation of the model mortality levels corresponding to S_{0+} S_{5+}...... S_{50+} and then select the median level of mortality to correspond to the mid intercensal period. The procedure essentially assumes the existence of a set of model life tables and age pattern of mortality in the population. Once the mortality level is identified, the age specific mortality rates corresponding to the mortality level can be calculated from the model life table and applied to the mid period population by age to obtain the total deaths and hence the crude death rate for the intercensal period.

In practice, however, we need not calculate the overall survival rates S_{0+}, S_{5+}..... S_{50+} etc. The population given by 5 year age groups can be projected above age 10 at time $t+10$. The mortality levels are selected in such a manner that when the projected populations are cumulated to get expected values of P^{t+10}_{10+}, P^{t+10}_{15+}...... P^{t+10}_{50+} etc., the expected values so generated encompass the corresponding observed cumulated population figures of the last census. Each cumulated age population, P^{t+10}_{x+} ($x=10$, 15,......50......) will, therefore help to identify one level of mortality for the intercensal period. We may choose, however, the median level of mortality to avoid arbitrariness in the selection of the ultimate level of mortality. Tables 8.1 to 8.4 illustrate the procedure of calculating crude death rate and mortality level during 1961 and 1971 for India.

TABLE 8.1

Females of India by Age as Enumerated in 1961 and 1971

(in Thousands)

Age Interval (x to x+n)	*Population reported by Census*[1]		*Adjusted Population 1961 for age unknown*	*Adjusted Population 1971*		
	1-3-1961	*1-4-1971*		*For "age unknown*	*For "boundary changes"*	*For the length of the interceed Period*
(1)	*(2)*	*(3)*	*(4)=(2) × 1.0039*	*(5)=(3) × 1.00023*	*(6)=(5) × 99757*	*(7)=(6) × 99822*
1	2	3	4	5	6	7
0–4	32,877	39,356	32,890	39,365	39,269	39,199
5–9	31,558	39,796	31,570	39,805	39,708	39,637
10–14	22,994	32,275	23,003	32,282	32,204	32.147
15–19	17,256	22,246	17,263	22.251	22,197	22.157

(Contd.)

1	2	3	4	5	6	7
20—24	19,106	21,528	19,113	21,533	21,481	21,443
25—29	18,025	20,481	18,032	20,486	20,436	20,400
30—34	14,832	17,867	14,838	17,871	17,828	17,796
35—39	11,842	15,662	11,846	15,666	15,628	15,600
40—44	10,754	13,230	10,758	13,233	13,201	13,178
45—49	8,307	10,417	8,310	10,419	10,394	10,375
50—54	7,963	9,415	7,966	9,417	9,394	9,377
55—59	4,538	5,952	4,540	5,953	5,938	5,927
60—64	5,520	6,889	5,552	6,891	6,874	6,862
65—69	2,373	3,357	2,374	3,358	3,350	3,344
70 and over	4,432	5,579	4,434	5,580	5,566	5,556
Unknown	82	60	—	—	—	—
Total	212,459	264,110	212,459	264,110	263,468	262,998

[1]Census Age Tables 1961 and 1971 of India, Published by R.G. Office, New Delhi.

TABLE 8.2

Projection of Female Population ('000) of India from 1961 to 1971 Assuming Various Levels of Mortality

Age	Population	*10 year survival rates in "west" female model life table at various levels of mortality.*[1]					*Projected Population in 1971 assuming various levels of mortality*				
Age (*x to x+n*) *(1)*	*Population* 1961 *(2)*	*Level 7* (e°_0=35.0) *(3)*	*Level 9* (e°_0=40.0) *(4)*	*Level 11* (e°_0=45.0) *(5)*	*Level 13* (e°_0=50.0) *(6)*	*Level 15* (e°_0=55.0) *(7)*	*Level 7* *(8)*=*(7)* × *(3)*	*Level 9* (9)=(2) × *(4)*	*Level 11* *(10*=(2) × (5)	*Level 13* *(11)*=(2) × *(6)*	*Level 15* *(12)*=(2) × *(7)*
1	2	3	4	5	6	7	8	9	10	11	12
0—4	32,890	.8552	.8826	.9063	.9273	.9478					
5—9	31,570	.9271	.9401	.9516	.9618	.9715					
10—14	23,003	.9167	.9312	.9439	.9552	.9655	28,128	28,029	29,808	30,494	31,173

(Contd.)

1	2	3	4	5	6	7	8	9	10	11	12
15—19	17,263	.8986	.9157	.9309	.9444	.9562	29,268	29,679	30,042	30,364	30,670
20—24	19,113	.8838	.9031	.9203	.9355	.9488	21,087	21,420	21,712	21,972	22,209
25—29	18,032	.8704	.8917	.9106	.9273	.9419	15.512	15,808	16,070	16,303	19,507
30—34	14,838	.8578	.8805	.9007	.9186	.9340	16,892	17,261	17,590	17,880	18,134
35—39	11,846	.8459	.8692	.8899	.9083	.9239	15,695	16,079	16,420	16,721	16,984
40—44	10,758	.8251	.8496	.8713	.8986	.9067	12,728	13,065	13,364	13,630	13.859
45—49	8,310	.7853	.8130	.8377	.8597	.8777	10,020	10,296	10,542	10,760	10,944
50—54	7,966	.7212	.7541	.7836	.8101	.8315	8,876	9,140	9,373	9,667	9,754
55—59	4,540	.6308	.6696	.7045	.7361	.7614	6,526	6,556	6,961	7,144	7,294
60—64	5,522	.5185	.5605	.5987	.6335	.6609	5,745	6,007	6.242	6,453	6,624

65—69	2,374	.3852	.4264	.4644	.4992	.5265	2,864	3,040	3,198	3,342	3,457
70 and over	4,434	.1605[2]	.1779[2]	.1951[2]	.2128[2]	.2286[2]	4,489	4,896	5,274	5,627	5,913
Total	212,459						177,830	182,476	186,596	190,362	193,522

1. ${}_5L_{x+10}/{}_5L_x$
2. T_{80}/T_{70}

TABLE 8.3

Female Population of India at Age x and over in 1971 as Reported by the Census of 1971 and Projected from 1961 Assuming Various Levels of Mortality in "West" Female Model Life Tables*

Age x and Over	*Census Populations* ('000)	*Projected Population* ('000) *assuming various mortality levels*					*Levels of Mortality*	*Expectation of life birth*
		Level 7	*Level 9*	*Level 11*	*Level 13*	*Level 15*		
10 years and over	184,162	177,830	182,476	186,596	190,363	193,522	9.82	42.00
15 years and over	152,015	149,702	153,447	156,788	159,862	163,349	8.24	38.10
20 years and over	129,858	120,434	123,768	126,746	129,499	131,679	13.33	50.83
25 years and over	108,415	99,347	102,348	105,034	107,527	109,470	13.91	52.28
30 years and over	88,015	83,835	86,540	88,964	91,224	92,963	10.22	43.05
35 years and over	70,219	66,943	69,279	71,374	73,344	67,829	9.90	42.25
40 years and over	54,619	51,248	53,200	54,954	66,623	57,845	10.62	44.05

45 years and over	41,441	38,520	40,135	41,590	42,993	43,986	10.80	44.50
50 years and over	31,066	28,500	29,839	31,048	32,233	33,042	11.03	45.08
Median							10.62	44.05

• The last two columns of this table give the levels of mortality of females of India and corresponding expectations of life at age 'o' derived from the proportions surviving to age *x* and over in 1971 from age x—10 and over 10 years earlier.

TABLE 8.4

Calculation of the Crude Death Rate for the Female Population of India in the Period 1961-71 Corresponding to the Recorded Age Distribution and to a Mortality level Estimated from Cumulated Census Survival Rates.

Age (*1*)	*Mean Populaton 1961-1971* ('000) (*2*)	*Death rate* (*Level=10.62*) *"West" females*) (*3*)	*Mean Annual death* ('000) *1961-1971* (*4*)=(2)×(*3*)
0—4	36,044	.0578*	2,083
5—9	35,604	.0058	206
10—14	27,575	.0045	124
15—19	19,710	.0060	118
20—24	20,278	.0076	154
25—29	19,216	.0086	165
30—34	16,317	.0098	160
35—39	13,723	.0109	150
40—44	11,968	,0120	144
45—49	9,342	.0136	127
50—54	8,672	.0180	156
55—59	5,234	.0238	125
60—64	6,192	·0356	220
65—69	2,859	.0507	145
70 and over	4,995	.1180**	589
Total	237,729	.019631[1]	4,666

1 (3)=(4)/(2) : *Obtained from Coale and Demeny Model Life Tables as $\frac{(l_0-l_5)}{(L_{04}+L_1)}$

** Obtained from l_{70}/T_{70}

The Crude Death Rate for Female=19.63

Female Growth rate=.02134

Female birth rate=.01963+.02134=.04097 or 40.97

Total birth rate

$$=FBR\times\frac{1+\text{Sex Ratio at birth}}{1+\text{Sex Ratio of General Population}}$$

=0.4097 × (1+1.05)/(1+1.075)

=.04048 or 40.48

8.1.3 An Application of Generalized Population Model In Estimation of Adult Mortality

In the chapter on Demographic Models, it has been shown that in the generalized population model, age distribution of population can be given as :

$$C(a)=be^{-\int_0^a r(y)dy}\,p(a)$$

where notations have usual meaning.

The above equation can also be written as

$$N(a)=N(0)e^{-\int_0^a r(y)dy}\,p(a)$$

$$p(a)=\frac{N(a)}{N(0)e^{-\int_0^a r(y)dy}}$$

$$p(a)=\frac{N(a)e^{\int_0^a r(y)dy}}{N(0)} \quad \ldots(1)$$

Here $N(0)$ is analogous to l_0 and numerator of equation (1) is the number surviving to exact age a.

Now the L_a column can be estimated as follows :

$${}_nL_a=\int_a^{a+n} p(a)da=\int_a^{a+n} N(a)e^{\int_0^a r(y)dy}\,da$$

$$ {}_5L_a=\int_a^{a+5} N(a)e^{\int_0^a r(y)dy}\, da $$

The above integral can be approximated as

$$ {}_5L_a={}_5N_a\times\exp.\left[5\sum_{a}^{a-5}{}_5r_a+2.5\,{}_5r_a\right] \qquad ...(2) $$

${}_5N_a$ for the intercensal period may be calculated using the following equation :

$$ {}_5\overline{N}_a=\frac{{}_5N_a^{t+n}-{}_5N_a^{t}}{{}_5r_a{}^*n} $$

where n is the intercensal period.

Other columns of life table is calculated using equation (2)

so

$$ T_a=\sum_{x=a}^{\infty}{}_5L_x \qquad ...(3) $$

$$ l_a=\frac{{}_5L_a+{}_5L_{a-5}}{10} \qquad ...(4) $$

$$ e_a=\frac{T_a}{l_a} \qquad ..(5) $$

It can be seen that this life table would not have any l_0 and e_0^0 because they can be estimated only when $N(0)$ or birth of a population is known. Further there may be some problem in estimating life table values for open intervals. For estimating e_0^A (where A=60+, 70+ or any open interval) following methods may be used. In stable population, it may be shown that,

$$e_A = \frac{\int_0^{\infty} N(A+y)e^{yr(A+)}dy}{N(A)} \quad ..(6)$$

where $r(A+)$ is growth rate of the population aged A and above. By Mean value theorem the above equation becomes,

$$e_A = [yr(A+)]\frac{N(A+)}{N(A)} \quad ...(7)$$

where y is defined so that the equality of equation (7) and (8) holds. $N(A)$ can be estimated as

$$N(A) = \frac{{}_5\bar{N}_{A-5} \times e^{2.5\,{}_5r_{A-5}} + {}_5\bar{N}_{A-10}e^{-2.5\,{}_5r_{A-10}}}{10}$$

One may choose the value of y as 4 years or estimate it using following relation based on stable population assumptions :

$$y = e_A[0.802 - 0.0106e_A - 1.34r'A+)] \quad ..(9)$$

It is difficult to solve equation (9). Equations (8) and (9) are solved by iteration procedure. We can take the approximate values of e_A and estimate y from equation (9) and substitute y in equation (8) to estimate e_A. Again substitute estimated e_A in (9). We can continue this procedure until there is negligible difference in the two estimated values of e_A. Once e_A is estimated T_A can be estimated easily. This method is proposed by Preston and Bennett (1983).

In the above case, however the estimate of adult mortality may be effected by

1. the differential coverage and pattern of age misreporting in two censuses. This would affect age-specific growth rates (*ASGR*). If *ASGR* is high, the e_5^0 would be high. Error will be more at the younger ages.
2. intercensal migration may affect the *ASGR*. If there is net out-migration e_0^0 would be low and reverse is true when there is net in-migration.

Illustration

TABLE 8.5

Estimation of Adult Mortality in India, Female 1971-1981

Age group	ASGR ${}_5r_a$	$\overline{{}_5N_a}$	S_a	${}_5L_a$	l_a	T_a	e_a
	(1)	(2)	(3)	(4)	(5)	(6)	(7)
0– 4	0.00808	39658156	−0.02020	—	—	—	—
5– 9	0.01638	41885751	0.04095	41454142	8509078	427353942	50.22
10–14	0 02606	35785322	0.14705	34437249	7589139	385899800	50.85
15–19	0.03306	25643466	0.29485	38478647	7291590	351462551	48.20
20–24	0.03009	24468179	0.45273	40102722	7858137	312983904	39.83

	(1)	(2)	(3)	(4)	(5)	(6)	(7)
25—29	0.02252	22358224	0.58425	37817056	7791978	272381082	35.02
30—34	0.01756	19073696	0.68445	37294253	7511129	235064126	31.30
35—39	0.02153	17058672	0.78218	35332434	7262667	197769893	27.23
40—49	0.02215	14489458	0.89138	33229484	6856192	162437459	23.69
45—49	0.03061	11943146	1.02328	32974552	6620404	129207975	27.23
50—54	0.02294	10366569	1.15715	24815996	5779055	96233423	16.65
55—59	0.03047	6826475	1.29068	32361508	5717750	71417427	12.49
60—64	0.02609	7728306	1.43208	19393537	5175505	39055919	7.55
65—69	0.03584	3967118	1.58690	19662382	3905582	19662382	5.03
70+	0.03641	3357435	1.76753	—	—	—	—

8.2. Estimates of Mortality from Retrospective Enquiry

One can utilise the deaths occurred in the households in preceding years to obtain death rates. There does not exist any method to ascertain the extent of reference period error and hence to get reliable estimates. The assumption that the reference period error is of the same magnitude as the one estimated for data on births in the preceding years through Brass P/F ratio (see section on Fertility Analysis) is unacceptable, since the distortion in the perception of time elapsed is likely to be different in case of deaths.

However, an useful index of child mortality can be constructed from the data on children born and children surviving to the women past 15 years at the time of survey (Brass 1968). These data do not suffer from any reference error except that a minor bais occurs due to the possible correlation between child mortality and mortality of women in the child bearing age. If D_x is the proportion of children dead for women aged x, then

$$D_x = \frac{\int_{\alpha}^{x} f(y)\, q\,(x-y)\, dy}{\int_{\alpha}^{x} f(y)\, dy}$$

Where $f(y)$ is the density of child bearing at age y for a woman and $q\,(x)$ is the probability of dying between the date of birth and the present age of women and α is the age at which fertility begins. Thus numerator denotes the number of children dead for a woman of age x and the denominator denotes the number of children ever born to her.

The probability of dying for a child at age $(x-y)$, can be calculated and the first two terms of this series are (by using taylor's expansion).

$$q(x-y)=q(x-\bar{m})+(y-\bar{m})\,q'(x-\bar{m})+\ldots\ldots$$

where $\bar{m}$ is the mean value of the function $f(y)$. Since $\bar{m}$ is the mean value, $q'(x-\bar{m})=0$ and hence, if terms of an order higher than the first are negligible then

$$D_x=q(x-\bar{m}).$$

The proportion of children dead corresponding to mother aged 45-49 would be probability of dying between ages 0 and $47.5-\bar{m}$ or $q(47.5-\bar{m})$. Since $\bar{m}$ lies generally between 27 and 28, $q(47.5-\bar{m})=q(20)$. In most cases, however, data relating to the younger women are more reliable. For younger women only a segment of fertility curve is applicable and this segment is generally not symmetrical. Therefore, precise results of approximation as obtained for older ages do not apply in case of the younger ages. Hence when $x<\beta$, where β is the upper most age of reproduction, the proportion of children dead at given ages corresponds to the probability of dying in an interval from birth to T where $T\neq x-\bar{m}$ but is some function of age x and $\bar{m}$. This function is not so much dependent on the level as on the shape of the curve. Hence we can say that

$$D_x=q(T_x,\bar{m})$$

Generalising the formula for age interval x to $x+5$, the proportion

$$D_i=\frac{\int_x^{x+5}\int_\alpha^x f(y)\,q(x-y)\,dy\,dx}{\int_x^{x+5}\int_\alpha^x f(y)\,dy\,dx}$$

$$=q(T_i,\bar{m})$$

considering $f(y)=C(y-s)(s+33-y)^2$ as model fertility schedule and assuming different values of $\bar{m}$, the values of T corresponding to the age groups under consideration can be written as $T_i, \bar{m}$ where the subscript i refers to women in the ith age group :

Thus we have

$\bar{m}$	26.7	27.7	28.7
$T_1, \bar{m}$	1.21	1.06	0.90
T_2, m	2.13	1.93	1.75

These values indicate clustering of value of T_1 around 1 and those T_2 around 2, T_3 around 3; for T_4, the results are around 5 and for T_5, they are around 10 and increase by about 5 thereafter *i.e.* the average age of the *CEB* in each 5 year age group would be approximately equal to 1, 2, 3, 5 years and so on. The consistency of these results suggested for developing a set of K factors to give equivalence of

$q(i, \bar{m})$ to $q(T_i)$ dependent on m such that

$$q(T_i) = K_i D_i$$

Where D_i represents the proportion of children dead for women with ith five year age group starting from 15–19. Brass has given the table for multiplying factors K to be selected on the basis of the parameters P_1/P_2 or P_2/P_3 and $\bar{m}$, where P_i denotes the mean parity of women in ith age group (see Table 8.1 (a)). It is more important to take into account the changes in the slope of the fertility curve in the beginning of the child bearing; rather than $\bar{m}$ which is affected by the whole fertility curve. Subsequent work by Coale and Demeny suggests that P_2/P_3 might be more satisfactory parameter since P_1 is sensitive both to age reporting errors at the start of child bearing and to sampling fluctuations due to relatively small number of births. P_2/P_3 is particularly suitable for the estimates of $q(2)$, $q(3)$ and $q(5)$ which are comparatively the most reliable values.

Sullivan (1972) developed Brass type multipliers by using the empirical fertility schedule and regression technique combined with Coale-Demeny model life tables. In all, 65 fertility and 40 mortality schedules representing four mortality patterns, West North, South and East mortality schedules were used to generate the data. In case of mortality, e_0^0 varies from 30 to 52.5 years. Whereas in case of fertility, *ASFR* were selected such that P_1/P_2 varies from 0.045 to 0.175. Sullivan provided two types of multipliers. One relating to age group is (20-24, 25-29 and 30-34) and another by duration of marriage (0-4, 5-9 and 10-14). The multipliers for age model and duration model are given in Table 8.2 (*a*) and 8.3 (*a*) of the Apendix. The assumptions are same as in the Brass method.

Trussell (1975) generated a third set of multipliers using three parameter model fertility schedules given by Coale and Trussell (1974) and Coale-Demeny model life tables. He used the linear regression plane of the following type :

$$K_i = E_i + A_i \frac{P_1}{P_2} + B_i \frac{P_2}{P_3} + C_i ln \frac{P_1}{P_2} + D_i \, ln \frac{P_2}{P_3}$$

But the multipliers without logarithm terms are being used in general. These multipliers are given in Table 8.4 (*a*) of the Appendix. The basic concept and assumptions are same in all the three methods but Trussell method is said to be better than earlier two methods. Recently multipliers are also generated by Palloni and H. 'igman (1988), by using New Model life tables for developing countries which are given in Table 8.5 (*a*) of the Appendix.

It has been observed that the accuracy of the estimates obtained by using any procedure mentioned above depends on rate of mortality decline, onset of childbearing and the age of children. The error is more when childbearing starts early and higher is the age of children. Further, it is observed that the decline in mortality affects the estimate more than the decline in fertility. In addition to assumption, the quality of data also affects the estimates of infant and child mortality. Infact, the estimates based on data from 15-19 age group (q_1) seems to be unreliable. Generally, q_2, q_3 and q_5 are taken as reliable estimates of mortality and q_1 is extrapolated from these values.

In case of mortality decline, it is argued that the estimate of infant and child mortality may not pertain to census or survey year but to some time before census or survey date. The methods are given to estimate the reference period for estimated infant and child mortality. The reference period is regressed with $\frac{P_1}{P_2}$ or $\frac{P_2}{P_3}$. The regression co-efficients for estimating reference period are given in Tables 8.6 (*a*) and 8.7 (*a*). Feeney (1975, 1980) proposed a different method to estimate *IMR* by age of the mother and reference period. Using the children ever been and children surviving data and mean age at childbearing, one can easily estimates *IMR* and years prior to census (*i.e*: reference period for *IMR*). The mean age at childbearing can be estimated using either *ASFR* or average parity by age. If *ASFR* (${}_5f_x$) is available one can use following formula to estimate mean age of childbearing (*M*).

$$M = \frac{\sum_{15}^{45} (x+2.5)\,{}_5f_x}{\sum_{15}^{45} {}_5f_x}$$

In case, *ASFR* is not available we can use empirical relation to calculate *M* as follows :

$$M = 2.25\frac{P_3}{P_2} + 23.95$$

The proportion of deceased by age of mother can be calculated using *CEB* and *CS* data. For *i*th age group it is given as :

$$Q_i = \frac{CEB_i - CS_i}{CEB_i}$$

$$= 1 - \frac{CS_i}{CEB_i}$$

After estimating *M* and *Q*, the *IMR* and reference time are estimated using following table :

TABLE 8.6

Estimation of Infant Mortality Rates from Proportion of Deceased Children Among Children Born to Women in Five Year Age Groups and the Mean Age at Childbearing

Age group	*IMR*	*Years Prior to Census (YPC)*
20–24	$(-44.7+30.5M)Q_2-2.6$	$11.8-0.325M-0.17Q_2$
25–29	$(294+14.9M)Q_3-2.9$	$16.5-0.424M+0.16Q_3$
30–34	$(357+10.4M)Q_4-2.8$	$20.6-0.494M+0.77Q_4$
35–39	$(362+9.77M)Q_5-7.8$	$24.9-0.556M+0.80Q_5$
40–44	$(282+11.0M)Q_6-8.5$	$38.1-6.33M+0.87Q_6$
45–49	$(216+11.1M)Q_7-7.5$	$33.4-0.641M+1.58Q_7$

For more details reader should refer to Feeney (1980).

The methods discussed above are applicable when fertility and mortality for a population had remained constant. There are some other methods which overcome this problem but they require *CEB* and *CS* data at two points of time either 5 years apart or 10 years apart. Zlotnik and Hill (1981) provided one such method to estimate infant and child mortality under changing fertility and mortality. The assumptions in this method are :

(*i*) Female population is closed to Migration or there is no differentials in fertility and mortality between migration and non-migrants.

(*ii*) There is no relation between fertility of women and their mortality.

(*iii*) The pattern of age misreporting is similar in two census.

Since this method is based on *CEB* and *CS* data by age of women, there is always under estimation of mortality due to recall lapse at older ages. We require data at last census up to 35-39 age group (in case census is 5 years) or 40-44 age group (in case census is 10 years apart) which may have larger error. So one has to use this method vary cautiously. For details readers are advised to see above article or U.N. (1983).

Illustration of Trussell and Feeney Methods

1. Trussell Method

The required data on *CEB* and *CS* for Rural India (1981) are given below :

Age group	*CEB*	*CS*	*No. of Women*
15—19	4174604		22342448
20—24	24727240	2149455	20872334
25—29	45781828	39070496	18512287
30—34	56020151	46831921	15877576
35—39	63307655	51793819	14550775
40—44	60898286	48550665	12675367
45—49	55055695	42990221	10852040

Steps of Estimation

Step 1

Calculate Average Parity

$$P_i = \frac{CEB_i}{W_i}$$

$$P_1 = \frac{4174604}{22342448}$$

$$= 0.1868$$

The complete calculation is given in column (2) of Table 8.7

Step 2

Calculate Proportion of Children dead (D_i) as

$$D_i = \frac{CEB_i - CS_i}{CEB_i}$$

$$D_2 = \frac{24727240 - 21494555}{24727240}$$

$$= 0.1307$$

The results of this step are given in Col. (3) of Table 8.7

Step 3

Calculate Multipliers

For this we use Table 8.4(a) of Appendix. The selection of model life table is an important point in this step. We illustrate with West Model Life Table :

$$\frac{P_1}{P_2} = \frac{0.1868}{1.1847}$$

$$= 0.1577$$

$$\frac{P_2}{P_3} = \frac{1.1847}{2.4731}$$

$$= 0.4790$$

Now $$K_i = a_i + b_i \frac{P_1}{P_2} + c_i \frac{P_2}{P_3}$$

a_i, b_i and c_i are taken from the Table 8.4(a)

so, $$K_2 = 1.2563 - 0.5381*0.1577 - 0.2637*0.4790$$
$$= 1.0451$$

The whole calculation is shown in column (4) of Table 8.7

Step 4

Calculate q(x)

$$q(x) = D_i*K_i$$

where $x = 1, 2, 3, 5, 10, 15, 20$ Corresponding to $i = 1, 2, 3, 4, 5, 6, 7$ respectively.

For example, $q(2) = 0.1307*1.0451$
$$= 0.1366$$

$q(x)$ values so estimated are given in Column (5) of Table 8.7

Step 5

Calculate Time Reference

For this we use Table 8.6(a) given in Appendix

$$t(x) = a_i + b_i \frac{P_1}{P_2} + c_i \frac{P_2}{P_3}$$
$$= 1.3062 + 5.5677*0.1577 + 0.2962*0.4790$$
$$= 2.3261 \quad \text{for} \quad x = 2$$

The reference period for each age group is given in column (6) of Table 8.7

If we want to use multiplier from New Model life table, we can use Tables 8.5 (*a*) and 8.7 (*a*) given in Appendix.

Feeneys Method

We estimate mean age of fertility as

$$M = 2.15* \frac{P_3}{P_2} + 23.95$$
$$= 28.4381$$

The estimated values of *IMR* and *YPC* using Table 8.6 are given in Table 8.7

TABLE 8.7

Estimation of Infant and Child Mortality in India : 1981

Age group	Trussel Method				Feeney Method		
	P_i	D_i	K_i	$q(x)$	t_i	IMR	YPC
15—19	0.1868						
20—24	1,1847	0,1307	1.0451	0.1366	2.3261	104.9219	2.3799
25—29	2.4731	0,1466	0.9950	0.1459	0.2784	771.2391	4.2830
30—34	3.5283	0.1640	1.0043	0.1647	6.6116	652.7631	5.7783
35—39	4-3508	0.1819	1.0218	0.1859	6.8496	645.9888	8.2710
40—44	4.8045	0.2028	1.0095	0.2047	11.9336	591.9699	11.2204
45—49	5.0733	0.2192	1.0018	0.2196	14.8724	525.1199	13.5884

8.3 Estimation of Fertility from Age Distribution of a Population

It is noteworthy that the children enumerated in 0-4 age group in any census are the survivors of the births during the period of 5-years preceding the census provided there is no migration. Thus the current level of fertility can be estimated from the number of children enumerated in a census if we have the knowledge of mortality. There are several methods which provide fertility estimate by using age distribution of population and its size and all these procedures require not only the knowledge of mortality level but also the age pattern of mortality. Some of the important methods are :

1. Reverse Survival Method
2. Own Children Method
3. Rele's Method
4. Stable Population Method
5. Method using General Population Model

8.3.1 Reverse Survival Method (RSM)

In the *RSM* the number of children enumerated in 0-4 age group is reverse survived by the appropriate survival ratio in order to get the births which might have taken place during the past 5-years period before a census. This is very simple method to estimate vital rates but it suffers from three sources of error :

(*a*) Under enumeration of children.

(*b*) Age mis-reporting of children.

(*c*) The pattern of mortality selected to obtain survival ratio.

Requirements

(*i*) Population of age groups 0-4, 5-9 and 10-14 by sex,

(*ii*) Life table or some other mortality estimate say l_2, l_5, or e_0^0 at two points of time, (*iii*) Total population of the second census and age-sex distribution of population for calculation of *GFR*.

Assumptions

(*i*) Accurate age reporting,

(*ii*) No migration (not important),

(*iii*) Age Pattern of mortality, as in the model life table if life table for area under study is not available.

Method

Let P_{0-4} denote the population in the age group 0-4 according to 1981 census. Survival probability for both sexes combined from suitable life table can be calculated as

$$S_{B\to 0\ 4} = \frac{{}_5L_0}{5 * l_0}$$

$$= \frac{{}_5L_0}{5} \qquad \text{if } l_0 = 1$$

The average annual births during last 5 years

$$B_{0-5} = \frac{P_{0-4}}{S_{B\to 0-4}}$$

$$= \frac{P_{0-4}}{{}_5L_0}$$

For calculating birth rate we require the total population 2 5 years prior to the census, then

Mid period Population (P')

$$= P_{81} e^{-2.5r}$$

where, P_{81} = Total population in 1981; and r is the intercensal exponential growth rate during 1971-81

$$\text{Birth rate } (BR_{0-5}) = \frac{P_{0-4}}{P_{81}} * \frac{e^{2.5r}}{{}_5L_0} * 1000$$

$$= \frac{C_{0-4} e^{-2.5r}}{{}_5L_0} * 1000 \qquad \text{...}(a)$$

where C_{0-4} = Proportion of population in the age group 0-4.

Similar equation can be obtained when we want to use 0-9 and 0-14 age groups.

$$BR_{0-10}=\frac{C_{0-9}e^{5r}}{_{10}L_0} * 1000 \qquad ...(b)$$

$$BR_{0-15}=\frac{C_{0-14}e^{7.5r}}{_{15}L_0} * 1000 \qquad ...(c)$$

In the above equations the value of L_0's are for both sexes combined For example

$$_5L_0=\frac{1.05\,_5L^m{}_0+{}_5L^f{}_0}{2.05}$$

Sex ratio at birth is 1.05

If mortality is declining with faster pace, one has to use different life tables. We may overcome this problem if we use say l_2 for 0-4 age group l_3 for 0—9 and l_5 for 0-14 as obtained from *CEB* and children surviving data using a Brass type procedure in selecting the model life table.

Using similar concept, we can estimate *GFR* and *GMFR* also. For example

$$GFR_{0-4}=\frac{CWR_{0-4}e^{2.5r'}}{_5L_0}$$

$$GMFR_{0-4}=\frac{CWR'_{0-4}e^{2.5r''}}{_5L_0}$$

where $$CWR_{0-4}=\frac{P_{0-4}}{\text{Women (15-49)}}$$

r' is the growth rate of women aged 15-49

r'' is the growth rate of married women aged 15-49.

$$CWR_{0-4}'=\frac{P_{0-4}}{\text{Married Women (15-49)}}$$

Example

P_{0-4} in 1981 for India= 83750816

P_{5-9} in 1981 for India= 93638940

Total population=665287832
(Excluding Assam)

$_5L_0$ for female corresponding to e_0^0

of 54.7 years from South Asian Pattern=4.29394

$_5L_0$ for male corresponding to e_0^0

of 54.1 years =4.27689

$_5L_0$ for both sexes =4.2852

Exponential Growth Rate =0.0225

(per annum)

$$BR_{76-81}=\frac{C_{0-4}e^{2.5r}}{_5L_0}$$

=0.03108 *i.e.*, 31.08 per 1000 population.

where $C_{0-4}=\dfrac{P_{0-4}}{P_{81}}$

Similar calculations can be done with 5-9 age group.

8.3.2 Estimation of Fertility from 'Own' Children Data

Among the most useful fertility estimation techniques, is the own-children method, (Cho, 1973) which is applied to census or survey data to provide estimates of fertility levels and trends in years prior to enumeration. One of the advantages of this method is that it does not usually require any special data collection. Only simple tabulation of young children by age of the mother from the household schedules is needed. More importantly, such tabulation can be used in computing fertility rates by socio-economic characteristics included in the questionaire. Thus fertility estimates by the own-children method are extremely useful for the analysis of differential fertility.

The own children method of fertility estimation is virtually a reverse survival method. Enumerated children are computer-matched to mothers within the households by means of data on relation to the head of household, age, sex, marital status and number of living children. These matched own children by own age and mother's age are used in estimating, by reverse survival technique, births by mother's age in prior years. The technique is also applied to women by age in estimating the age-specific population at risk. Age specific birth rates and birth probabilities are obtained as suitably adjusted quotients of these two basic quantities. Following are the assumptions regarding data for getting reasonable estimate ;

(*a*) Children's ages are reasonably accurate.

(*b*) Most of the children live with their mothers.

(*c*) The relationship of each child to the head of the household is well defined.

(*d*) Mortality levels are relatively low during the estimation period prior to enumeration.

Further, the application of the method assumes that :

(*i*) Children aged x to $x+1$ are under enumerated to the same degree regardless of age and other characteristics of the mother.

(*ii*) Women aged a to $a+1$ are under-enumerated to the same extent regardless of their characteristics except age.

(*iii*) The proportion of non-own children is constant regardless of age and other characteristics of the mother.

(*iv*) Women are uniformly distributed by age within the age interval, and births to them are evenly distributed over a year.

(*v*) Age specific mortality rates remain unchanged.

Consider a birth cohort consisting of women aged a to $a+1$ at time 't' as shown in the lexis plane given in Fig. 8.1.

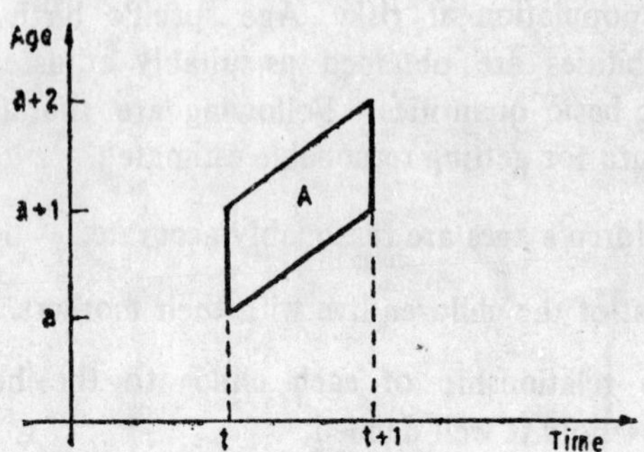

Fig. 8.1. Lexis diagram for net time-chorot age-specigc birth probability.

In the lexis plane, this cohert is exposed to the risk of births before reaching time $t+1$. The net time cohort age specific births probability is defined as the ratio of the number of births in area A to women aged a to $a+1$ at time t, to the number of women aged a to $a+1$ at time t. Following the notation developed by Rutherford and Cho, we can express the relationship's as below (assuming that census is taken in year t).

(i) $B^{T}_{a}\ (t\text{-}x\text{-}1)=C^{X}_{a+x+1}\ (t)U^{0}_{x}V_{a}r_{0\leftarrow x}$

(ii) $W^{T}_{a}\ (t\text{-}x\text{-}1)=W^{T}_{a+x+1}\ (t)U^{W}_{a+x+1}+R_{a\leftarrow a+x+1}$

(iii) $f^{T}_{a}\ (t\text{-}x\text{-}1)=B^{T}_{a}(t\text{-}x\text{-}1)/W^{T}_{a}(t\text{-}x\text{-}1)$

where $f^{T}_{a}(t)$=Single year net time cohort age specific birth probability for the calender year t to $t+1$.

$B^{T}_{a}(t)$=Births over the period t to $t+1$ to women aged a to $a+1$ at time t.

$W^{T}_{a}(t)$=Number of women aged a to $a+1$ at time t

$C_a^x(t)$ = Number of own children living in the household aged x to $x+1$ of the mothers aged a to $a+1$ at time t.

$U_x^c(t)$ = Adjustment factor for census or survey under-enumeration of children aged x to $x+1$.

$U^w(t)$ = Adjustment factor for under-enumeration of women aged a to $a+1$.

V = The inverse of the proportion of children aged x to $x+1$ living with their mother at the time of enumeration.

$R_{a \leftarrow b}$ – Reverse survival factor L_a/L_b.

$r_{0 \leftarrow x}$ = Reverse survival factor $\frac{L_0}{L_x}$.

Now these time cohort age specific probabilities can be used to estimate conventional central age specific birth rates. (see Fig. 8.2). Lexis diagram given below provides useful clue

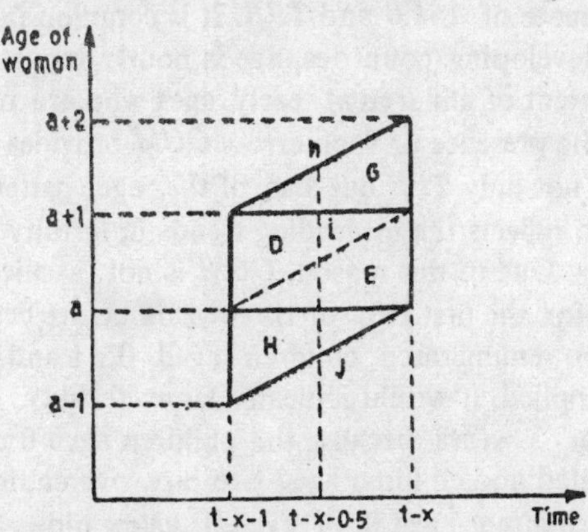

Fig. 8.2. Lexis diagram for computing central age-specific birth rate.

By definition, central rates refer to the ratio of the number of births in the square DE to women aged a to $a+1$ at time $t-x-5$

$$\text{(iv)} \quad B_a^c = (t-x-1) = 0.5\, B_{a-1}^{T}(t-x-1) + 0.5 B_a^{T}(t-x-1)$$

$$(v)\ W_a^c(t-x-1)=0.5W_{a-1}^{T}(t-x-0.5)+$$
$$0.5B_{a+0.5}^{T}(t-x-0.5)$$

$$(vi)\ f_a^c(t-x-1)=B_a^c(t-x-1)/W_a^c(t-x-1)$$

$f_a^c(t-x-1)$ is the single year central age specific fertility rate for the calender year t to $t+1$. The first term in the right hand side of equation (v) equals half the distance tj and the second term, half the distance t. Sum of these terms corresponds to mid-year population. Recently attempts are made to extend the own children method to obtain age parity specific fertility estimates with three types of rates namely time cohort, age cohort and central rates. These methods are, however, not given here. Readers can see the relevant literature cited in the reading list.

The own children method (*OCM*) requires accurate age reporting of mothers as well as of children in order to yield accurate estimate of *ASFR* and *TFR*. It is common fact that in most of the developing countries, age is poorly reported and there is larger extent of children at early ages who are not reported at all. In the presence of such errors *OCM* provides erroneous estimate of not only *TFR* but also of the age pattern of fertility. This also reflects the misleading trends in fertility over a period of time. Due to this reason, *OCM* is not applied to estimate fertility for the first two or three years before census or survey based on enumerated children aged 0, 1 and 2 years of age. If it is applied, it would indicate large fertility decline during last 2 or 3 years because the children aged 0 or 1 are underenumerated and children aged two are overenumerated at the cost of children aged 0, or even 3 years old. It is therefore suggested to compute *ASFR* and *TFR* for the 5 year periods preceding census or survey.

From the application of this procedure to several developing countries *i.e.* Pakistan, Srilanka, Thailand, Korea, it is found that the error in the age distribution of mothers introduces less error in fertility estimates than the error in the age distribution of children. In some cases overall level of fertility (*i.e. TFR*) is not affected significantly but the age pattern of fertility (*i.e. ASFR*) is distorted seriously due to age misreporting.

Age heaping of children on the other hand, has more serious consequences. Due to age heaping, *OCM* will directly provide higher (heaping) or lower (under enumeration) value of *TFR*. For example, heaping on age 5 inflates the estimate in 6th year prior to census date. To overcome this problem, births for different years based on different ages of children should be grouped properly to obtain smooth sequence of *TFR*.

It is likely that unmatched children may be more to younger women because older women are usually in more stable households than younger ones. Problems of unmatched children is also serious where adoption rate is high.

8.3.3 Rele's Method to Estimate GRR and Birth Rate

This procedure is based on the concept of stable population but procedure developed to estimate fertility indices is applicable to all the populations (Rele, 1967). For the given level of mortality, it was observed that the *GRR* is linearly related with *CWR* whereas birth rate has curvilinear relation with *CWR* (see Figs. 8.3 and 8.4). We have generally four *CWRS* but the *CWR* as defined in second and fourth row of table 8.8 provides better estimate. The estimate based on population in the age group 0-4 gives birth rate during the last 5 years from the census and that based on 5-9 age group gives birth rate during 5 to 10 years before census. Since population aged 0-4 is generally under-enumerated and 5-9 is over-enumerated, we get under and over estimation of birth rates. It is suggested that for intercensal period, we can take average of the two estimates to minimize the errors. If fertility is declining faster in recent years, it is not advisable to take the average.

Estimation of GRR

As mentioned above, *GRR* has almost linear relationship with *CWR*. Then for given e_0^0

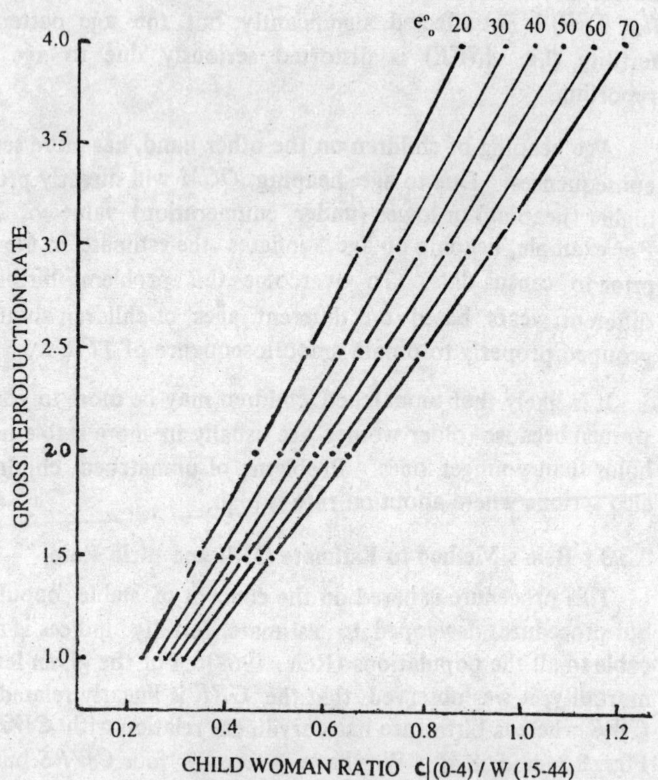

Fig. 8.3. Relationship between Child-Woman Ratio and Gross Reproduction Rate by Expectation of Life at Birth (e_0^0) for Stable Populations

$$GRR = a + bCWR_i \quad \text{...(10)}$$

$$i = 1, 2, 3 \text{ and } 4$$

where $CWR_1 = \frac{P_{0-4}}{W_{15-44}}$

$$CWR_2 = \frac{P_{0-4}}{W_{15-49}}$$

$$CWR_3 = \frac{P_{0-4}}{W_{20-49}}$$

$$CWR_4 = \frac{P_{0-4}}{W_{20-54}}$$

a and b are constants which are given in Table 8.8

It means that we have the approximate value of e_0^0.

Procedure for Estimating Birth Rate

Birth rate has curvilinear relation with CWR as shown in Fig. 8.4. This procedure has two steps :

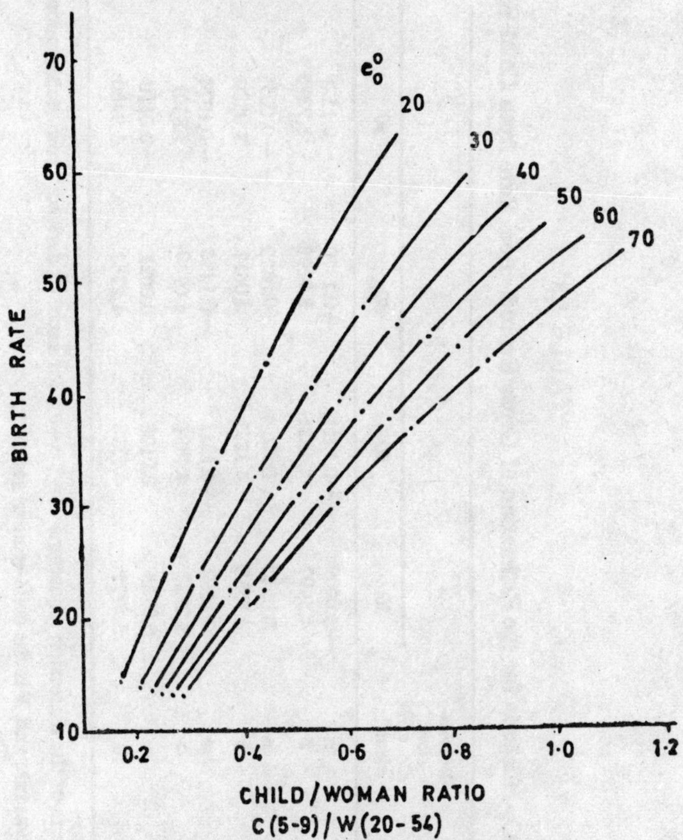

Fig. 8.4. Relationship between the Child-Woman Ratio and the Birth Rate by Expectation of Life at Birth (e_0^0) for Stable Populations.

TABLE 8.8

Co-efficients for the Estimation of Gross Reproduction Rate from Child-Woman Ratio

Type of Child-Woman Ratio	Regression Co-efficient*	e_0^0 20	30	40	50	60	70
$\frac{C(0\text{-}4)}{W(15\ 44)}$	*a*	—0.0909	—0.1211	—0.1370	—0.1529	—0.1645	—0.1754
	b	4.5907	4.1821	3.9298	3.7375	3.5556	3.3878
$\frac{C(0\text{-}4)}{W(15\text{-}49)}$	*a*	0.0547	0.02 4	0.0129	—0.0059	—0.0182	—0.0309
	b	4.7680	4.3293	4.0617	3.8589	3.6628	3.4829
$\frac{C(5\text{-}9)}{W(20\text{-}49)}$	*a*	—0.1162	—0.1311	—0.1436	—0.1574	—0.1675	—0.1779
	a	5.2927	4.4881	4.0940	3.8301	3.5967	3.3894
$\frac{C(5\text{-}9)}{W(20\text{-}54)}$	*a*	0.0245	0.0106	0.0021	—0.0110	—0.0226	— 0.0345
	b	5.4711	4.6398	4.2262	3,9480	3.7014	3.4821

* Co-efficients of the regression equations $Y =^{*} a+bX$ for each e_0^0 derived from stable population, where Y is the gross-reproduction rate and X is the child-woman ratio.

(*i*) estimating intrinsic birth rate (*IBR*) ; and

(*ii*) then converting *IBR* into *CBR*.

IBR may be estimated using the following relation

$$IBR = a + b\,CWR + c\,CWR^2 \qquad \ldots(11)$$

a, *b* and *c* are given in Table 8.9 for different levels of e_0^0 and *CWR*.

Once we estimate *IBR*, we can get *CBR* from the following equation :

$$CBR = K * IBR$$

$$\text{where} \quad K = \frac{\text{(Weighted sum/Total Population) for given population}}{\text{(Weighted sum/Total Population) for the corresponding stable population}}$$

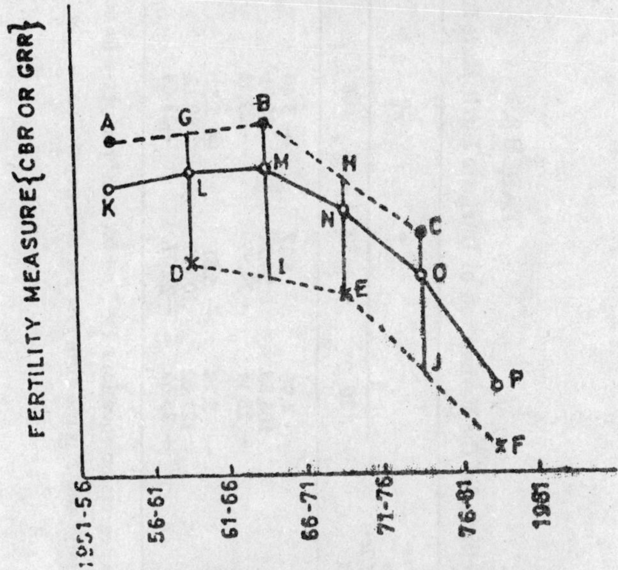

Fig. 8.5. Graphic Representation of Fertility Estimated by Rele Method.
Final Estimate : *K, L, M. N, O* and *P*.

The denominator of above equation is given in Table 8.10 for different values of *GRR* and e_0^0. This value can be inter-

TABLE 8.9

Co-efficients for the Estimation of Intrinsic Birrh Rate from the Child-Woman Ratio*

Type of Child-Woman Ratio	*Regression Co-efficient*	e_0^0					
		20	*30*	*40*	*50*	*60*	*70*
$\frac{C(0\text{-}4)}{W(15\text{-}49)}$	*a*	— 4.96	— 5.37	— 5.40	— 5.45	— 5.45	— 5.25
	b	106.85	94.21	85.91	79.93	75.02	69.92
	c	— 28.11	—24.92	—22.11	—19.96	—18.66	—16.94
$\frac{C(5\text{-}9)}{W(20\text{-}54)}$	*a*	— 5.28	— 5.61	— 5.52	— 5.52	— 5.52	— 5.32
	b	121.62	100.57	89.12	81.67	75.78	69,90
	c	— 35.57	—28.07	—23.64	—20.75	—19.00	—16.90

* Co-efficients of the regression equatiors $Y = a + bX + aX^2$ con ptted from stable populations for each e_0^0, where X is the Child-Woman ratio and Y is the birth rate per 1000 population.

TABLE 8.10

The Ratio of Weighted Sum of Women in the Reproduction Age Groups to Total Population for Stab' 'opulations by Gross Reproduction Rate (GRR) and ctation of Life at Birth (e_0^0)*

GRR	e_0^0					
	20	30	40	50	60	70
4.0	0..9667	0.9078	0.8758	0.8534	0.8299	0.8038
3.0	1.0255	0.9686	0.9396	0.9163	0.8966	0.8780
2.5	1.0470	0.9919	0.9652	0.9443	0.9270	0.9092
2.0	1.0535	1.0103	0.9782	0.9603	0.9443	0.9304
1.5	1.0338	0.9873	0.9617	0.9423	0.9354	0.9253
1.0	0.9413	0.8906	0.8697	0.8534	0.8449	0.8424

* The weighted sum is defined by $1.W(15\text{-}19)+7.W(20\text{-}25)+7.W(24\text{-}29)+6.W(30\text{-}34)+4.W(35\text{-}39)\times 1.W(40\text{-}44)$, where W denotes the number of women in the age group given in the parenthesis, and the weights 1, 7, 7, 6, 4, 1 correspond to the average pattern of relative age-specific fertility rates.

polated for given e_0^0 and estimated GRR as discussed earlier.

The numerator is calculated as :

$$\text{Numerator} = \frac{W_{15-19}+7W_{20-24}+7W_{25-29}+6W_{30-34}+4W_{35-39}+W_{40-44}}{\text{Total population}}$$

The weights, 1, 7, 7, 6, 4 and 1 are given by U.N. based on the age pattern of fertility.

The constants of equation (1) and (2) were estimated using 36 stable populations with GRR=4.0, 3.0, 2.5, 2.0, 1.5 and 1.0 and e_0^0=20, 30, 40, 50, 60 and 70 years.

Recently, Rele (1987) presented a revised verson of his earlier method which requires at least two censuses. This procedure not only provides level of fertility but also trends in the vital rates over time. It requires to obtain weighted average of the estimate based on 0-4 and 5-9 age groups in different censuses. Graphically it may be illustrated as in Figure 8.5.

The points A,B,C reflect the birth rate estimated by using 5-9 age group in 1961, 1971 and 1981 respectively. On the other hand, estimates representing D, E and F are based on 0-4 age group. With the observed trends, birth rate or GRR correspon-ding to points G,H,I and J can be estimated, For example :

$$G=\frac{A+B}{2}, \quad H=\frac{B+C}{2}$$

$$I=\frac{C+D}{2} \quad J=\frac{D+E}{2}$$

Now the adjusted fertility for all the periods except 1951-56 and 1976-81 can be obtained by taking the weighted average of points G and D for 1956-61, B and I for 1961-66, H and E for 1966-71 and C and J for 1971-76. The weights are 0.7 for estimates based on 5-9 age group and 0.3 for estimates based on 0-4 age group. These weights were estimated using smoothed and unsmoothed age distributions and were found almost constant for all the states of India. So the adujsted birth rate or GRR would be

$$L=0.7\,G+0.3\,D$$
$$M=0.7\,B+0.3\,I$$
$$N=0.7\,H+0.3\,E$$
$$O=0.7\,C+0.3\,J$$

Now trend line *LO* can be extended forward and backward to obtain the estimate for periods 1976-81 (*P*) and 1951-61 (*K*). There may be various ways to extrapolate the time series data but simplest way would be :

$$K=A * \frac{L}{G}$$

$$P=F * \frac{O}{J}$$

Instead of $\frac{L}{G}$ and $\frac{O}{J}$, one can also take $\frac{M}{B}$ and $\frac{N}{E}$ respectively.

8.3.4 Stable Population (Manual IV) Method

The sets of model stable populations given by Coale and Demeny include a range of age distributions bracketing all those likely to be found in the age distribution of actual population that (*a*) are themselves approximately stable and (*b*) have the age pattern of mortality conforming closely to that included in the set of model life tables. As such it is possible to locate a model stable population which resembles the actual population and hence to estimate its various demographic parameters by borrowing them from the model one. This resemblence can be by knowledge of either (r, $e^\circ_\circ$), (GRR, $e^\circ_\circ$), (r, GRR) or [r, $C(a)$]. The knowledge of (*i*) natural rate of increase of the population ascertained from two consecutive censuses after adjustment in the completeness of coverage or for any unknown rates of net gain or loss through migration and (*ii*) the proportion of population in any age group starting with age 5, 10 or 15 years of age would lead to the selection of same model stable papulation if there is no age misreporting. To avoid the problems of age misreporting, we can

Example (For Rele Method)

Karnataka

Period	e_0^0	CWR_1	CWR_2	*Estimated GRR*	*Proportion Census*	*Proportion Stable*	*Ratio*	*Preliminary IBR*	*Preliminary CBR*	*Final Estimate CBR*
1961—66	49.9	—	762	2.87	0.9073	0.9252	0.9807	44 94	44.07	42.00
1966—71	51.8	652		2.72	0.9073	0.9287	0.9770	37.70	36.83	40.43
1971—76	54.5		689	2.51	0.9460	0.9359	1.0108	39.45	39 88	38.00
1976—81	56.3	538		2.19	0.9460	0.9438	1.0023	30.35	30 42	33.39

Note :

(*i*) e_0^0 taken from Rele (1987).

(*ii*) $CWR_1 = \dfrac{P_{0-4}}{W_{15-49}}$ (from 1971 and 1981 censuses)

$CWR_2 = \dfrac{P_{5-9}}{W_{20-45}}$ (from 1971 and 1981 censuses)

(*iii*) $\text{Census (Proportion)} = \dfrac{W_{15-19} + 7W_{20-24} + 7W_{25-29} + 6W_{30-34} + 4W_{35-39} + W_{40-44}}{\text{Total Population}}$

take cumulated age proportions $C(x)$ (cumulatiue proportion of population upto age x), then the series of stable populations identified by $C(5)$, $C(10)$..... $C(40)$ and 'r' will exhibit little variation and encompass the ***Stable Population*** which would resemble the actual population.

Estimation of population parameters can be based on the age distribution of either sex. In the Latin American populations, the distortions of the females age distributions are found larger than in the male, but in the African and Southern Asian populations, the opposite is seen. In case of female Population being chosen, estimate of birth rate based on $C(35)$ and 'r' can be accepted and with more confidence if confirmed by the figure derived from r and $C(10)$. In case, male population forms the base of selecting the model stable population, the median value of the birth rates of stable population agreeing with C (5), C (10),..... C (45) is chosen. These estimates are expected to be at the right level except for the possible effects of recent mortality or fertility trends.

It may be mentioned that the information on age distribution and rate of growth which help in selecting a model stable population resembling with the actual population provide an estimate of the crude birth rate as a measure of fertility but do not provide an estimate of the total fertility (or gross reproduction rate in case of female stable population). It may be shown that for the same age composition of population, both low fertility but early child-bearing and high fertility but late child-bearing may produce the same birth rate. Each model stable population has been characterized by four sets of *GRR* values which are associated with different mean ages of fertility schedules. Thus while identifying the model stable population, one must have some idea of the, fertility schedule characterising the fertility behaviour of the females in the population. If the age specific fertility rates are known, mean age of the fertility schedules can easily be ascertained. However, in absence of knowledge of *ASFRS*, the mean age of the fertility schedule can be estimated by various indirect methods :

(*i*) One possibility is to estimate the age pattern of fertility by assuming that marital fertility follows the standard pattern given in Table 8.10.

TABLE 8.11

Standard Age Pattern of Female Marital Fertility Rates.

Age	*Index ϱ Marital Fertility Rate*
15—19	1.2—0.7 *M* (15—19)*
20—24	1.000
25—29	0.933
30—34	0.852
35—39	0.685
40—44	0.349
45—49	0.051

* *M* (15—19)—Proportion of married females at ages 15—19.

Source : They are adopted from Louis Henry, "Source Data on Natural Fertility" Euginicis Quarterly Vol. 8 (1961) pp. 81—91 and reported in *UN* Manual IV. p. 24.

This pattern is not applicable to population with high proportions of births outside marriage or in which there is a variety of sanctioned sexual unions, including, for example, widespread consensual unions. Multiplying the proportion married among women in each age group with the above standard fertility schedule; age pattern of fertility can be known and hence the mean age of fertility.

(*ii*) It is possible to estimate the mean age of the fertility schedule by using the relation

$$\bar{m} = 2.25 \frac{P_3}{P_2} + 23.95$$

Where P_2 and P_3 are the average parity of women at ages 20 24 and 25-29 respectively and $\bar{m}$ is the mean age of fertility schedule.

(*iii*) Another alternative may be to assign the population in question the mean age of fertility schedule of another population presumed to have similar factors affecting the age pattern of fertility.

(*iv*) The mean age of fertility schedule may also be obtained by using U.N. weights in absence of any knowledge of the age pattern of fertility.

8.3.4.1. Adjustment of Estimates for the Effect of Recent Declines in Mortality

The *UN* Manual IV includes a table of adjustments for decline in mortality to be applied to the birth rates and to gross reproduction rates derived from the stable populations. These adjustments correspond to a value of $k=0.01$ and for value of k other than 0.01 the tabulated adjustments are to be scaled up or down in the same proportion as the actual value of k differs from 0.01. For instance if $k=0.015$ the apropriate adjustment factors are to be increased by 50 per cent. Preferably k can be estimated as

$$k=17.8 * \frac{\Delta r}{t}$$

where Δr is the absolute change in the rate of growth as compared to the original stable rate, and t is the number of years that have elapsed since the change in mortality took place. After adjusting the birth rate and *GRR* for quasistability in the actual population, a quasi-stable estimate of the death rate is obtained simply by subtracting the intercensal annual growth rate from the adjusted birth rate. The estimate of e_0^o of the quasi-stable population is obtained from the stable population characterised by the adjusted death rate and one of the parameters *GRR*, *b* and *r*.

The procedure of estimating birth rate, death rate and *GRR* by using stable and quasi-stable population theory is illustrated by the following example :

Example

We illustrate below the estimation of birth and death rates for India from female age distribution, 1961. We know that the intercensal annual rate of growth (1951-61)= 0.0189. The mean age of fertility schedule can be estimated by using the standard marital fertility schedule of Henry and proportion married among the females 15-49 of 1961 which are given below :

15-19	20-24	25-29	30-34	35-39	40-44	45-49
0.696	0.918	0.942	0.915	0.871	0.777	0.698

The resulting $\overline{m}$ (the mean age of fertility) equals 28.8. The detailed calculations of birth rate and *GRR* are being given below in the table. The model of stable population is chosen from the set of the West Model of Coale and Demeny.

The estimates with regard to different $C(x)$ values indicate that the reported population is not strictly conforming to the age distribution of a stable population. This also indicates errors in the reporting of ages. In case the population is stable, all the $C(x)$ values should yield the same estimates of birth rate and *GRR*. If we accept the estimate corresponding to C (35), the estimate of birth rate is 0.0424, for female population and the *GRR* (28.8) corresponding to age 35 is 2.82.

The preliminary stable estimates of b and *GRR* are to be adjusted for the distorting effects of changing mortality using the adjustment listed in Table *III*.1 of *U.N. Manual IV*. For calculating we need $\frac{\Delta r}{\Delta t}$ which in this case is

$$\frac{0.0189 - 0.0043}{1956 - 1921} = \frac{0.0146}{35} = 0.000417$$

Here we assume that mortality started declining from 1921 when annual rate of growth of the population was 0.0043.

hence
$$k = 0.000417 * 17.8$$
$$= 0.0074$$

The adjusted birth rate is

$$bA = 0.0425\left(1 + \frac{0.0074}{0.01} * 0.092\right)$$
$$= .0454$$

TABLE 8.12

Procedure of Obtaining Birth Rate and Levels of Mortality Though Stable Population : India 1961.

Age	*% upto age x C(x) for India 1961*	*Vaules of C (x) and various parameters in Female model stable population with r=0.0189 and levels of mortality as indicated by*			*Interpolated value with r=0 0189 and observed C (x)*	
		Level 7	*Level 9*	*Level 11*	*Birth rate*	e°_{o}
5	0.154	0.16711	0.15877	0.15020	0.0400	42.8
10	0.303	0.30196	0.28856	0.27696	0.0476	34.7
15	0.412	0.41995	0.40376	0.38940	0.0447	37.5
20	0.493	0.52330	0.50529	0.48922	0.0391	43.8
25	0.583	0.61296	0.59407	0.57705	0.0396	43.2
30	0.668	0.68979	0.67104	0.65391	0.0415	40.9

35	0.738	0.75535	0.73421	0.72083	0.0425	39.8
40	0.794	0.81078	0.79424	0.77883	0.0421	40.1
Birth Rate ($\bar{b}$)		0.0472	0.0422	0.0383		
GRR ($\tilde{m}$=29) :		2.989	2.86	2.43		
GRR ($\bar{m}$=28.8) :		3.149	2.806	2.547		
GRR (m=29) :		3.168	2.820	2.56		

The value of adjusted *GRR* comes out to be 3.10

One of the drawbacks of the procedure for adjustment for the quasi-stability is that one must know since when the mortlaity started to decline in the particular population. For most of the developing countries, this information has to be generally guessed. The other problem that one faces in the application of the U.N. Mannual IV method, in general, is to ascertain the age pattern of mortality for the selection of the particular set of stable population generated by Coale and Demeny or any other set. Of course, recently Coale has suggested that selection of any set of stable population leads to almost same estimate of the birth rate if the selection is based on the estimated value of l_2 (probability of survivorship of a child from birth to exact age 2) and (l_5) (taking both male and female populations). This method is discussed below.

8.3.4.2. Robust Procedure to Estimate Fertility from Single Census

The procedure described by Coale (1981) provides rather a robust estimate of fertility even though census data is characterized by severe age-misreporting. Further it is robust against selection of any family of the Coale-Demeny model populations. Following are the steps involved in estimating the birth rate :

(*i*) Calculate l_5 from children ever born and children surviving data to women aged 30—34 or of marriage duration 10-14 using Brass or Trussell or Sullivan Procedure.

(*ii*) Calculate C (15) : proportion of population under age 15 for both sexes combined.

(*iii*) Interpolate the level of mortality in any family of Coale-Demeny model life-table for given l_5. We can use any other model set as well.

(*iv*) For the given level of mortality and C (15), one can easily interpolate the birth rate (*BRs*) and growth rate (r_s). The *BRs* is the average birth rate in the last 15 years before census or survey. *GRR* (29) can also be interpolated. Here, 29 year is assumed as the average age of fertility schedule.

(*v*) Estimate exponential population growth rate during the last 15 years of the population in question. This can be done using the intercensal rate of increase.

(*vi*) The adjusted Birth Rate can be given as :

$$BR = BR_s \, e^{7.5\,(r - r_s)}$$

where r is actual growth rate during the last 15 years. The similar steps can be carried out to estimate BR during 10 years and 5 years with the combination of l_3, C (10) and l_2 and C (5) respectively. But the population is severely affected by under-reporting, and therefore estimate may not be very reliable.

(*vii*) Estimate mean age of fertility schedule as

$$\bar{m} = 2.25 \frac{P_3}{P_2} + 23.95$$

(*viii*) The value of $\mu(\bar{m})$ can also be estimated from the selected female model life table earlier.

$$\mu(\bar{m}) = \frac{{}_5M_{25} + {}_5M_{30}}{2}$$

Where ${}_5M_x$ is the death rate between ages x and $x+5$

(*ix*) The *GRR* can be estimated as

$$GRR\,(\bar{m}) = GRR\,(29)\ \exp\{(\bar{m} - 29)\, r + \mu(\bar{m})\}$$

$$TFR = GRR(\bar{m}) * (1 + \text{Sex ratio at birth})$$

However the estimation of *GRR* and *TFR* may not be accurate.

The proportion under 15 is least affected by age misreporting than other cumulative values. The frequent upward transfer of the reported age of females across age 15 is countered by some downward transfer of male ages from over 15 to under 15. It is further observed that the estimate of birth rate is robust even populations are not stable. It may however be mentioned that the estimate of growth rate during last 15 years may not be available for a country where only one or two censuses are conducted so far. If growth rate of population has not been changing rapidly, intercensal growth rate may be substituted.

Example

From given information below estimate birth rate and *GRR*.

(*i*) Population for 0—4=93776900, 5−9=89181400 and 10—14=80366400 and total population as 802901300 in 1981.

(*ii*) Sex ratio at birth (SRB)=1.05

(*iii*) l_5=0.8153

(*iv*) Growth rate during last 15 years (female)=1 98

(*v*) Present growth rate of female population=2.149

(*vi*) $\bar{m}$=29 years.

Calculations

(*I*) $$C(15)=\frac{P_{0-4}+P_{5-9}+P_{10-14}}{Total\ Population}=0.3280$$

(*II*) For given l_5 estimate level of mortality in South model life table :

Level of mortality :	14	15
l_5 :	0.80278	0.82260

Given l_5=0.81530

Level of mortality=0.37 * 15+0.63+14=14.63.

(*III*) Estimate *BRs*, *GRR* and r_s as below : Where C (15) and r_s in stable population corresponding to level 14 and 15 encompass observed value of C (15)

	Level 14		*Level 15*	
	0.2986	0.3341	0.2932	0.3287
r_s	0.010	0 015	0.010	0.015
BRs	0.0265	0.0307	0.0254	0.0295
GRR (29)	1.809	2.083	1.744	2.008

So the interpolated rates corresponding to level 14.63 are

		Level	
	14	14.63	15
r_s	0.0142	0.0146	0.0149
BRs	0.0300	0.0296	0.294
GRR	2.036	2.015	2.003

$$BR\ (\text{female})=BR_s\ \exp\ [7.5\ (r-r_s)]$$

putting the value of BR_s, r and r_s in the equation we have

$$BR = 0.03078$$

and

$$GRR = 2.02$$

$$TFR = 2.02 * (1+SRB) = 2.02 * 2.05 = 4.14$$

If the mean age of child bearing is different than 29 years one can adjust *GRR* also.

8.3.5 Method using General Population Model

Using general population model, an integrated approach was developed by Preston (1983). As discussed in the last chapter, the age structure of generalized population model applicable to any closed population at any time t is given by

$$c(a) = b\, e^{-\int_0^a r(u)du}\, p(a) \qquad \ldots(12)$$

where notations have their usual meaning.

Hence

$$\frac{1}{p(a)} = \frac{b\, e^{-\int_0^a r(u)du}}{c(a)} \qquad \ldots(13)$$

where $c(a)$: Proportion of Population at age a,

b : birth rate

$p(a)$: proportion of survival from birth to age a,

Under the Brass's logit model of mortality

$$\text{Log}_e \frac{q(a)}{p(a)} = \alpha + \beta\, \text{Log}_e \frac{q_s(a)}{p_s(a)}$$

where suffix s refers to the standard life table.

$$\frac{q(a)}{p(a)} = e^{\alpha} \left[\frac{q_s(a)}{p_s(a)}\right]^{\beta}$$

$$\frac{1-p(a)}{p(a)} = e^{\alpha} \left[\frac{q_s(a)}{p_s(a)}\right]^{\beta}$$

$$\frac{1}{p(a)} = e^{\alpha} \left[\frac{q_s(a)}{{}_s(a)}\right]^{\beta} + 1 \qquad \ldots 13(a)$$

By substituting the value of

$$\frac{1}{p(a)}$$

in equation (2) we get

$$\frac{b\, e^{-\int_0^a r(u)du}}{c(a)} = 1 + e^{\alpha}\left[\frac{q_s(a)}{p_s(a)}\right]^{\beta}$$

$$\frac{e^{-\int_0^a r(u)du}}{c(a)} = \frac{1}{b} + \frac{e^{\alpha}}{b}\left[\frac{q_s(a)}{p_s(a)}\right]^{\beta} \quad \ldots (14)$$

$$= \frac{1}{b} + \frac{K}{b}\left[\frac{q_s(a)}{p_s(a)}\right]^{\beta} \quad \ldots (15)$$

where $K = e^{\alpha}$

In case $\beta \neq 1$, the equation (3) is a non-linear and it will be difficult to solve. Let us put $\beta = 1$

$$\frac{e^{-\int_0^a r(u)du}}{c(a)} = \frac{1}{b} + \frac{K}{b}\left[\frac{p_s(a)}{p_s(a)}\right] \quad \ldots (16)$$

It is known that the pattern of infant and childhood mortality may be substantially different in different populations. To overcome this problem, one introduces $p(5)$ estimated through Brass type procedures. Then

$$p(a) = p(5) * {}_5p(a)$$

for $a > 5$

where ${}_5p_{(a)}$= the probability of survival upto age a for a person who has survived upto exact age 5.

Substituting in equation (2) and rearranging the equation (5). We get

$$\frac{p(5)\, e^{-\int_0^a r(u)du}}{c(a)} = \frac{1}{b} + \frac{K}{b}\left[\frac{{}_5q_s(a)}{{}_5P_s(a)}\right] \quad \ldots (17)$$

for $a > 5$

With the help of this linear equation, one can easily estimate birth rate and K (index of adult mortality).

Steps for Calculations :

(*i*) Calculate Age Specific Growth rate ${}_5r_a$ as below.

$${}_5r_a = \frac{ln\ {}_5P_a\ (t+h) - ln\ {}_5P_a\ (t)}{h}$$

where h is intercensal period.

(*ii*) Estimate mid year population in age group $(a, a+5)$ as follows –

$${}_5\hat{P}_a = \frac{{}_5P_a\ (t+h) - {}_5P_a\ (t)}{{}_5r_a * h}$$

$$P = \text{Total Mid year population} = \sum_{a=0}^{\infty} {}_5\acute{P}_0$$

(*iii*) Estimate population at exact age a as follows

$$\dot{P}(a) = \frac{{}_5P_a + {}_5P_{a-5}}{10}$$

(iv) Now $c(a)$ can be calculated as

$$c(a) = \hat{p}(a)/p$$

(*v*) Get Estimated value of p (5) or l (5).

(*vi*) Calculate cumulative growth rate upto age a as

$$\sum_{x=0}^{a-5} {}_5r_0$$

(*vii*) Calculate

$$Y_a = \frac{p(5)e^{-5 \sum_{x=0}^{a-5} {}_5r_a}}{c(a)}$$

(*viii*) Calculate

$$\frac{{}_5p_s\,(a)}{{}_5p_s\,(a)}$$

for selected female life table on the basis of p (5)

$$\frac{{}_5q_s\,(a)}{{}_5p_s\,(a)}=\frac{l_5-l_a}{l_a}=X$$

(*ix*) Plot the points (X, Y) which would lie almost on line. So

$$Y=A+B\,X$$

where $A=1/b$

$B=K/b$

These parameters can be estimated using any two groups or two group average method.

Let

$$Y_1=\sum_{5}^{30} Y/N_1 \quad \text{and} \quad Y_2=\sum_{35}^{60} Y/N_2$$

where N_1 and N_2 denote the number of values involved in calculating the average value. Similarly

$$X_1=\sum_{5}^{30} X/N_1 \quad \text{and} \quad X_2/=\sum_{35}^{60} X/N_2$$

Clearly $Y_1=A+BX_1$ and $Y_2=A+BX_2$

These two equations would give

$$B=\frac{Y_1-Y_2}{X_1-X_2} \text{ and}$$

$$A=\frac{X_1Y_2-X_2Y_1}{X_1-X_2}$$

We can also use the least square method for obtaining the estimates of A and B and hence of $1/b$ and K/b.

TABLE 8.13

Estimation of Crude Birth Rate by Integrated Procedure : India 1971-81

	Female Population	Female Population	ASFR $[r(a)]$	$\sum_{x=0}^{a=5} Sx$	$C(a)$	Y_t	X_t
	(1)	(2)	(3)	(4)	(5)	(6)	(7)
0	42561634	43359366	−0.0019	—	—	—	—
5	46716129	37398031	0.0222	−0.0019	0.0285	28.8801	0
10	41678475	31241043	0.0288	0.0203	0.0265	27.7965	0.0172
15	31034665	26052046	0.0175	0.0491	0.0219	29.1242	0.0277
20	29177135	22591432	0.0256	0.0666	0.0184	31.7599	0.0431
25	25731827	20006884	0.0252	0.0922	0.0640	31.3519	0.0633

(Contd.)

1	2	3	4	5	6	7	8
30	21454528	17545045	0.0201	0.1174	0.0143	31.6994	0.0864
35	19526300	15001379	0.0264	0.1375	0.0124	33.0612	0.1116
40	16644305	12438319	0.0291	0.1639	0.0107	33.5760	0.1404
45	14252826	10196063	0.0335	0.1930	0.0090	34.5128	0.1741
50	11950023	8187710	0.0378	0.2265	0.0075	35.0282	0.2149
55	8156068	6626265	0.0208	0.2643	0.0059	36.8591	0.2738
60	21902693	13466793	0.0486	—	—	—	—
Total	230786808	264110376					

Clearly from the above table we have

$$Y_1=30.1020, \qquad Y_2=34.6075$$

and $$X_1=0.0396, \qquad X_2=0.1830$$

Using the relation we get

$$\bar{A}=18.8579, \qquad \bar{B}=31,4167.$$

Hence female birth rate$=Y_A=34.7$ birth per thousand women.

The birth rate for total population

$$=34.7^{*}\frac{1+SRB}{1+SRP}$$

$$=34.7\ \frac{1+1.05}{1+1.07}$$

$$=34.7^{*}\frac{2.05}{2.07}=34.4$$

The estimates of b through this procedure is less affected by changing coverage error in census and also by emigration. But the value of K; index of adult mortality will be affected substantially. The affect of omission in the age group 0—4 will be less but the errors in estimate $p^{*}(5)$ will directly effect the estimate. We can however use the integrated approach to study differential fertility by estimating birth rates of different socio-economic groups for which age distribution and estimates of $p^{*}(5)$ are available.

8.4 Assessment of Fertility from Retrospective Enquiry

In most of the countries, following retrospective questions are asked in censuses and surveys :

(*i*) For all ever married women

(*a*) Age at Marriage

(*b*) No of Children ever born (*CEB*) (*M*, *F*, *T*).

(*c*) No of Children surviving (*CS*) at present (*M*, *F*, *T*).

(*ii*) For currently married women an additional question "Whether any child born alive during the last one year" is also asked.

These data have various errors (under reporting, as well as over reporting, age mis-reporting). Several techniques are developed to evaluate and adjust them to get current estimate of vital rates.

Types of Errors in CEB Data

1. Mis-understanding the Question

1.1 The mortality error : It arises when the respondents report only the number of children who are still alive rather than those ever born.

1.2 Non-resident error : This is caused by over-looking the alive children who are not residing with the mother.

1.3 The marriage error : This occurs when the question is pertinent to all marriages and the women who have been married more than once do not include their children to previous marriages in their report.

2. Respondents' Lapse of Memory

2.1 The memory error which is caused by tendency on the part of some mothers, especially the elderly to forget to include some of their children who had died.

2.2 The baby error : caused by the common tendency to overlook reporting of the alive young children of particular sex.

3. Enumerators' Failure to Reach the Respondents

3.1 *The not at home error* occurs when after failing to find a knowledgeable adult, the enumerator finally may ask a neighbour or anybody in the household who does not know the women's parity and consequently she is tabulated as "not given". Bias arises in this case because "not at home" women usually have a smaller number of children.

3.2 *The coverage error* which arises when the enumerator does not ask the question on parity in the whole area or forget some households.

4. Zero Error

Sometimes, for women who have not got any child and 'investigator is instructed to put zero or some other specified mark indicating zero. Sometimes, instructions are not followed properly and the space is left blank or filled with a mark different from the one asked. In such cases, it may be difficult to find out the difference between "number of children not stated" and respondent of zero parity. This affects the average *CEB*. This may however be more pronounced at younger ages.

The following method is developed by El. Badry (1961) to correct for zero parity error.

Let C be the proportion tabulated in the "not given" parity category and L, be the corresponding proportion tabulated as childless, in ages below 40. The study of relationship between these two for large number of countries and communities, give a linear type relation

$$C_x = aL_x + b.$$

Suppose we have data on C and L for 20−24 and 25—29 age groups, then we can slove

$$C_1 = aL_1 + b$$

$$C_2 = aL_2 + b$$

and estimate a and b as

$$a = \frac{C_1 - C_2}{L_1 - L_2}, \quad b = \frac{C_1 L_1 - C_1 L_2}{L_1 - L_2}$$

For an adjustment of *CEB*, $(Ca - b)W_a$ where W_a is the number of women aged. a is deducted from the tabulated "not given" category and added to the tabulated number of childless women in that age group. It may be mentioned that some of the errors in *CEB* data mentioned above is also present in current fertility data (births duriug last one year or so).

Example

For Rural India, 1981

$$C_1 = 0.0589, \qquad C_2 = 0.0287$$

$$L_1 = 0.24666, \quad \text{and} \quad L_2 = 0.0929$$

Hence we have

$$0.0589 = 12466a + b$$
$$0.0287 = 0.0929a + b$$

By sloving the above equations

We get $\bar{a} = 0.2023$

$b = 0.0099$

$$= \frac{\bar{a}}{1+\bar{a}} = 0.1683$$

where Y is the degree of incidence of childlessness error.

$(Ca - b)W_4$ should be substracted from "Not Given" and should be added in the category of Zero Parity.

Type of Errors in Current Fertility Data

In addition to age mis-reporting, the current fertility data suffers from reference period error. The *CEB* data on the other hand does not involve time element in it and hence is free from such type of error. The reference period (say of one year) may be either underreported or over-reported. It means that instead of reporting the births of an average 12 months, they may relate to either more than 12 months or less than 12 months.

There is a considerable amount of uncertainty about the nature and extent of the reference period error. This type of error has very important and distorting role in the study of fertility trends from the maternity history data. Error of reference period is complicated and may be related with the reporting of time of earlier children. Unlike Brass, Potter (1977) says that relatively more births are reported in the middle of the marital duration and only fewer births are reported towards the two end points. The allocation of the time of birth of the *n*th child is affected by reported time of birth of the $(n-1)$th child. In such cases, it becomes difficult to visualize the pattern of reference period error, leave aside guessing the pattern and extent of reference period error.

8.4.1 P/F Ratio Method

The average number of children ever born to the women aged 50 years or to the women who have completed childbearing provides a measure of total fertility for such age cohort. If fertility has remained constant in the past, it is same as period measure of *TFR* provided there is no recall lapse in reporting of *CEB* by the women of the completed fertility.

Brass (1968) developed a technique generally known as *P/F* ratio to obtain the level of current fertility by comparing the average *CEB* and *CFR* based on births during last one year or so. This is based on the following propositions :

(*i*) The reference period error is independent of age. It means that the reported age pattern of fertility is correct but not the level. This pattern can be described by a simple polynomial

$$f(a)=k\ (a-s)\ (a+33-a)^2 \qquad s<a<33 \ldots (A)$$

(*ii*) The reporting of *CEB* by the younger women is accurate.

(*iii*) Fertility has remained constant in the past.

It is clear that children ever born and cumulated fertility are not directly comparable. Average parity of women belonging to any age group does not necessarily correspond to the cumulated fertility of the women of age at the mid point of the age group. If the age distribution of the women is uniform within the age group and fertility is constant at each age within that age group, then

$$P_i=F_{i-1}+2.5\ f_i \qquad \text{where} \qquad F_{i-1}=5(f_1+f_2 \ldots f_{i-1})$$

where F_i is the average parity and f_i is the age specific fertility rate fertility rate for the women of age group i, $i=1, 2 \ldots 7$ starting with 15 – 19 age group.

However if f_i is obtained from the civil registration system, then

$$P_i=F_{i-1}+3\ f_i$$

In general, however,

$$P_i = F_{i-1} + K_i f_i$$

where

$$K_i = \frac{P_i - F_{i-1}}{P_i - F_{i-1}} * 5$$

P_i and CF_i may be generated from any model age pattern of fertility. Brass multipliers obtained by using the model (*A*) are given in Appendix Table 8.8. It may be noted that Brass polynomial assumes the fixed shape but varying location of the onset of reproduction. From U.N. Mannual *X*, different sets are of multipliers using Coale and Trussell model fertility schedules are produced in Appendix Table 8.9(a) and 8.10(a). In this F_i is calculated as follows—

$$F_i = F_{i-1} + a_i f_i + b_i f_i + c_i F\ (7)$$

The values of a_i, b_i and c_i are given in Appendix Table 8.9(a). The estimates of *ASFRS* as mentioned earlier are for women 1/2 year younger than their present age. This can be adjusted using following equation.

$$f_i^+ = \{1 - W_{i-1}\} * f_i + W_i f_i$$

where

$$W_i = x_i + y_i \frac{f_i}{F(7)} + z_i \frac{f_{i+1}}{F(7)}$$

$$f_{(7)}^+ = \{1 - W_{(6)}\} * f_{(7)}$$

The value of x_i, y_i and z_i are estimated using Coale-Trussell model schedule of fertility and are given in Manual *X* (Here see Table 8.10(a) of Appendix).

The P_i and equivalent cumulated fertility *Fi* can be compared and when assumptions are valid, P_i/F_i would turn out to be unity provided there is no reference period error in current fertility data and recall lapse error in *CEB*. Under the assumption (*ii*), if P_i/F_i is greater than one in the age group 20–24 or 25–29, there seems to be reference period error. P_2/F_2 or P_3/F_3 may come more than one, even when there is rapid decline in fertility in the recent period. Therefore sometime, it would be difficult to decide whether P_i/F_i exceeds unity due to reference period error or due to fertility decline. Hobcraft and Chidambaram (1982) developed a new method to analyse the birth history data. The application of P/F procedure is shown taking data from 1981 census of Karnataka and U.P.

8.4.2 First Order Births

This method is very similar to P/F ratio method. Let us define $f_{i,1}$ as the age-specific first order birth rate of women in the age group i. The cumulative first order fertility $F_{i,1}$ is nothing but the proportion of ever mothers in particular age group and can be compared with the data obtained from any longitudinal surveys Let $P_{i,1+}$ be the proportion of women in age group i having at least one child. This information can be compared with $CF_{i,1}$ data. We need multipliers to make two information comparable. Hill and Blacker provided set of multipliers which are based on following equation—

$$f(a, 1) = k(a-s)^{\frac{1}{2}} (s+22-a)^{2}$$

This type of exercise can be carried out for higher order of births also but first order birth would be preferred because—

(*i*) This occurs mainly to younger women who are usually better educated;

(*ii*) Data on first births are free of the problem of omission compared to higher order;

(*iii*) Information as to whether a women has become a mother or not is likely to be better reported than the data on parity (*CEB*) for women who have had many children; and

Illustration of P/F Ratio Method :

Karnataka (1981)

Age	Pi	ASFR fi	Fi	Ki	Fi	Pi/Fi
15—19	.196	.052	.052	1.96593	.10223	1.91727
20—24	1.157	.155	.207	2.84302	.70067	1.65128
25—29	2.442	.148	.355	3.01097	1.48062	1.64931
30—34	3.465	.102	.457	3.64382	2.14667	1.61413
35—39	4.306	.063	.520	3.89082	2.53012	1.70189
40—44	4.713	.030	.550	4.70207	2.74106	1.71941
45—49	5.070	.013	.563	5.66514	2.82365	1.79555

$f1/f2 = .3471$ $TFR^{o} = 2.815$

$\bar{m} = 28.04$ $Ad\ TFR = 2.815 * P2/F2$

$= 4{,}65$

Illustration of P/F Ratio Method :

Uttar Pradesh (1980)

Age	*Fi*	*fi*	*CFi*	*Ki*	*Ei*	*Pi/Fi*
15—19	.185	.056	.056	1.82344	.10211	1.81172
20—24	1.206	.196	.252	2.81753	.83224	1.44911
25—29	2.552	.212	.464	3.00092	1.89619	1.34585
30—34	3.681	.197	.661	3.88551	3.08544	1.19302
35—39	4.569	.128	.789	4.14889	3.83606	1.19102
40—44	5.031	.074	.863	5.01395	4.31606	1.16565
45—49	5.276	.036	.899	6.0409	3.53247	1.16404

$f1/f2 = 2921$ $\qquad$ $TFR_o = 4.495$

$\bar{m} = 29.9$ $\qquad$ $AdTFR = 4.495 * 1.44911 = 6.51$

or $4.495 * 1.34585 = 6.05$

(*iv*) If the reference period is not reported correctly it can be easily detected in the case of first order births. Because proportion of women ever becoming mother would never exceed unity.

8.4.3 Birth Order Techniques for Defective Birth Registration Data

One can easily compute F_j for *j*th order birth by cumulating age specific *j*th order birth rates till the last age of reproduction and also the proportion of mothers having at least *j* children, (P_{J+}) at the end of reproduction. The completeness of civil registration is estimated generally from first or second order births on the assumption that the under reporting is same for all the orders of births. The estimate of completeness of birth registration using first order births may be estimated by ratio F_1/P_{1+}.

The adjusted *TFR* thus becomes :

$$F^* \frac{P_{1+}}{F_1}$$

where F is the *TFR* obtained from birth registration.

One may also use second order births instead of first order births for the adjustment of *TFR*.

As mentioned earlier, the first birth occurs mainly to younger women who may be comparatively more educated and therefore may be more aware of the importance of the registration. Hence such corrections may lead to under-estimation of the *TFR*.

For adjusting F_1 and F_2 so that the under registration for all births and for first and second order births comes to be the same, following two procedures are suggested.

(*i*) Fitting a linear line through 3rd and higher order births as

$$F_J = \alpha + \beta P_J \qquad j=3, 4......$$

From fitted regression line we can re-estimate F_1 and F_2.

Let it be $\hat{F}_1$ and $\hat{F}_2$.

(*ii*) Fitting a 2nd degree polynomial through the 3rd and higher order births when fertility is not constant—

$$F_J=\alpha+\beta_1 P_J+\beta_2 P_J^2 \qquad J=3, 4......$$

Here again we re-estimate F_1 and F_2.

Now the completeness of birth registration is given by

$$=\frac{\hat{F}_1}{P_{1+}} \text{ or } \frac{\hat{F}_2}{P_{2+}}$$

The adjusted *TFR* can be given as follows

$$\hat{F}=\frac{P_{1+}}{F_1}\left[F-F_1-F_2+\hat{F}_1+\hat{F}_2\right]$$

$$\hat{F}=\frac{P_{2+}}{F_2}\left[F-F_1-F_2+\hat{F}_1+\hat{F}_2\right]$$

It is observed that the *TFR* obtained by two methods (linear or polynomial) are probably lower and upper limits of level of fertility. But in case, fertility is declining rapidly, this procedure may not give reliable estimate of *TFR* and also of the completeness of birth registration.

Brass has developed different procedures to correct civil registration data which provide satisfactory estimates for moderate or high fertility countries. The equation is follows :

$$F_m=\frac{F}{F_1}=1.5\frac{B}{B_1}-1.25 \qquad ...(B)$$

This is extended to second order births as a check and it is possible that these will meet more closely the requirement of the assumption of same underreporting bias as that for all births. For the second order birth, the equation is as follows :

$$\frac{F-F_1}{F_2}=1.5\frac{B-B_1}{B_2}-1.25 \qquad ...(C)$$

Following equation links (C) with F_m

$$\frac{F_1-F_2}{F_1}\alpha/(\alpha+F_m-1)$$

The empirical comparisons with completed family size distributed over different orders give an average value for α of about 0.5. The substitution of the estimate of F_m in equation for $(F-F_1)/F_2$ gives

$$\frac{F}{F_1}=1.5\,\frac{B-B_1}{B_2}-0.75$$

$$\text{Adjusted } TFR=\frac{F}{F_1}\ {*}P_{1+}$$

8.4.4 P/F Ratio Method by Duration of Marriage

The assumption in this method are same as discussed in P/F ratio method for age. The main advantage of this procedure is said to be the better reporting of the duration of marriage. It is not however, clear how the duration of marriage is comparatively better reported. Generally in census, question asked to the respondent is age at marriage and present age. By substration we get the duration of marriage. If the data on age at marriage and present age are suffering from misreporting, the duration of marriage may be having confounded error and it would depend on the direction of misreporting on age at marriage and present age.

The calculation of average *CEB* and duration specific marital fertility $\{g(i)\}$ is usual. As mentioned in P/F ratio method, the cumulated fertility (Fi) is not directly comparable to average *CEB* by duration of marriage. The equivalent cumulated fertility $[G(i)]$ is calculated as follows (See Reference) :

For the first duration group 0 – 4

$$G(1)=3.137\ g(1)-0.324\ g(2)$$

For higher duration group, $i>1$ with marital duration starting with 0–4.

$$G(i)=F(i-1)+3.392\ g(i)-0.392\ g(i-1)$$

for $i=2, 3\ j-1$

and

$$G(j)=F(j-1)+0.392\ g(j-1)+2.608\ g(j)$$

where j is the last marriage duration group and $g(i)$ is the marital duration specific annual fertility rate of the ith age group.

The ratio P_i/G_i can be used to adjust current fertility data by duration provided the marital fertility has remained reasonably constant.

If the pattern of reference period error by duration of marriage and by age is assumed to be same, the same adjustment factor can be used to adjust $ASFR$.

If the data on current fertility is taken from birth registration, we have to use following equation to calculate equivalent cumulative fertility.

$$G(i)=F\ (i-1)+2.917\ g(i)-0.417\ g(i-1)$$

i : 1, 2......

for last or higher duration of marriage following equation may be more suitable—

$$G(j)=F(j-1)+0.417\ g(j-1)+2.082\ g(j)$$

Once we get $g_{(i)}$, we can calculate P/G for each duration of marriage. In this case also P_2/G_2 can be used as adjustment factors for the TFR or $TMFR$.

8.4.5 Estimation of Fertility from CEB Data Using Relational Gompertz Model

The cumulative fertility $F(x)$ is described by Gompertz's function as follows :

$$F(x)=F * A^{B^{x-x_0}}$$

$$0<A,\ B<1$$

$$F(x)>0$$

where x_0 is arbitrary origin and $F(x)$ is cumulative fertility rate by age x; F is the total fertility, A is the proportion of fertility attained by age x_0 and B is related with variance. Now transforming above equation as

$$Y(x)=-\text{Log}_e\left[-\text{Log}_e\frac{F(x)}{F}\right]$$

$$Y(x)=-\text{Log}_e\ (-\text{Log}_e\ A)+(-\text{Log}_e\ B)\ (x-x_0)$$

$$=a+b\ (x-x_0)$$

We see that double logarithm of $F(x)$ is linearly related to age. This is true over the middle range of childbearing, but is less valid at the tails of the distribution. To get better fit, age can be replaced by a standard function. In such case, the model becomes

$$Y(x)=\alpha+\beta Y_s(x)$$

where
$$-\infty<\alpha<\infty$$
$$<\beta<\infty$$

$$Y_s(x)=-\text{Log}_e\left[-\text{Log}_e\left(\frac{F(x)}{F_s}\right)\right]$$

Here $F_s=1.00$

The standard model can also be written as follows :

$$F(x)=F_s\, P^{Q^{Y_s(x)}}$$

where
$$0<P<1$$
$$0<Q<1$$
$$\alpha=-\log_e(-\text{Log}_e P)$$
$$\beta=-\text{Log}_e Q$$

The age at which $Y(x)=0$ can be regarded as the origin of the standard function ('x_{0s}). At the origin,

$$F_s(x_{0s})=\frac{1}{e} \quad \text{as :}$$

$$Y_s(x)=-\text{Log}_e[-\text{Log}_e\{F_s(x)\}]$$
$$0=-\text{Log}_e[-\text{Log}_e\{F_s(x_{0s})\}]$$
$$-\text{Log}_e\{F(x)\}=e^{-0}=1$$

So the comparison of P with $1/e$ indicates the relative proportions of *TFR* in observed and standard fertility achieved by x_{0s}. So we have three situations :

(*i*) $P=\frac{1}{e}$ for $\alpha=0$

indicates equal proportion and that the origins of two distributions are indentical.

(*ii*) $P=\frac{1}{e}$ for $\alpha=0$

indicates that a smaller proportion of observed than standard fertility is achieved by age x_{0s}, in other words observed fertility is generally later than standard.

(*iii*) The converse is true for

$$P > \frac{1}{e} \qquad \text{and} \qquad \alpha > 0$$

As α becomes more negative, child bearing distribution comes in the narrow range of reproduction.

Again with parameter Q we have

$$(i) \qquad Q = \frac{1}{e} \qquad\qquad \text{for} \quad \beta = 1$$

indicate that the patterns of $Y(x)$ and $Y_s(x)$ are the same, but it does not necessarily mean equal variance; this is true only when $\alpha = 0$. For given α,

$$Q < \frac{1}{e} \qquad\qquad \text{for} \quad \beta > 1$$

implies that $Y(x)$ is steeper than $Y_s(x)$ *i.e.*, $F(x)$, the observed distribution approaches its asymptotes more quickly than the standard indicating smaller variance than that for the standard. In practice, $Y_s(x)$ should be an average which minimizes the deviation from linearity for individual sets of values. Such standard has been derived from the selected standard schedules of fertility developed by Coale and Trussell which seem to be more appropriate for high fertility countries. For the application of above procedure, the knowledge of *TFR* is essential. Sometime P(7) is taken as an estimate of *TFR* but it may be affected by serious recall lapse of *CEB* in most of the developing countries and it also presumes that age schedules of fertility have not changed for the last 30 years.

Zaba (1981) has used this method taking

$$\frac{F(x)}{F(x+5)} \text{ ratio or } \frac{P_i}{P_{i+1}}$$

for estimating fertility from *CEB* data. This method does not assume constant fertility and age invariant reference error and therefore is said to be modification of P/*F* ratio method.

It may however be noted that this procedure invariably overestimates the fertility for areas where fertility has been declining. It is felt that any procedure which is based on actual experience of a cohort has implicit assumption about the constancy of the pattern of fertility in the past but not of the level. Further if the *CEB* is under-reported even by the younger women, this procedure may not give reliable estimate of fertility. It is also observed that when procedure is applied at subnational (may be rural-urban) or for sub-group of a population, this does not give consistant estimate of fertility.

Nevertheless, for better understanding about error and its pattern, graphic representation may be useful. In fact for estimating α and β, graph is very essential. From the graphs only those points are selected for using in the estimation of α and β which are on a line. This introduces however human biasedness and leads to arbitraryness in the estimates.

8.5.1 Hypothetical Cohort Method to Estimate Intercensal ASFR

This method can be applied whenever the information on *CEB* data is available from two censuses or surveys 5 years or 10 years apart. The main virtue of this procedure is that the data from two censuses are synthesized to generate third data set; representing the effects of intercensal vital rates on a hypothetical cohort. This third set of data can be used in *P/F* ratio method in order to obtain estimate that refer specifically to the intercensal period. Here we will discuss how the parity for hypothetical cohort is generated and how *ASFR* can be directly obtained from such parity. The assumptions in this method are :

(*i*) Population is closed to Migration or Migration does not affect average parity.

(*ii*) There is no relation between fertility and Mortality of women.

(*iii*) *CEB* is correctly reported at both the Censuses.

Method to Estimate Hypothetical CEB

Intercensal Period of 5 Years

Age	*1975*	*1980*	$\Delta P(i)$
15—19	$P(11)$	$P(12)$	$P(12) - P(01) = \Delta P(1)$
20—24	$P(21)$	$P(22)$	$P(22) - P(11) = \Delta P(2)$
25—29	$P(31)$	$P(32)$	$P(32) - P(21) = \Delta P(3)$
30—34	$P(41)$	$P(42)$	$P(42) - P(31) = \Delta P(4)$
35—39	$P(51)$	$P(52)$	$P(52) - P(41) = \Delta P(5)$
40—44	$P(61)$	$P(62)$	$P(62) - P(51) = \Delta P(6)$
45—49	$P(71)$	$P(72)$	$P(72) - P(61) = \Delta P(7)$

For first age $P(1\,h)$ will be same as $P(12)$ because these children are born during 5 years. It is however assumed that these children were evenly born during the last 5 years. In case fertility is declining very fast this does not reflect the experience of fertility during the last 5 years. Now

$$P(1\,h) = \Delta P(1)$$

$$\begin{aligned} P(2\,h) &= P(1\,h) + P(22) - P(11) \\ &= P(1\,h) + \Delta P(2) \\ &= \Delta P(1) + \Delta P(2) \\ &= \sum_{J=1}^{2} \Delta P(J) \end{aligned}$$

$$\begin{aligned} P(2\,h) &= P(2\,h) + P(32) - P(21) \\ &= \Delta P(1) + \Delta P(2) + \Delta P(3) \\ &= \sum_{j=1}^{3} \Delta P(j) \end{aligned}$$

In general $P(i\,h) = \sum_{J=1}^{i} \Delta P(j)$

This can also be given as

$$P(i\,h) = \sum_{J=1}^{i} [P(j, 2) - P(j-1, 1)]$$

Intercensal Period of 10 Years

Age	*1975*	*1980*	$\Delta P(i)$
15–19	$P(11)$	$P(12)$	$P(12) - 0 \quad = \Delta P(1)$
20–24	$P(21)$	$P(22)$	$P(22) - 0 \quad = \Delta P(2)$
25–29	$P(31)$	$P(32)$	$P(32) - P(11) = \Delta P(3)$
30–34	$P(41)$	$P(42)$	$P(42) - P(21) = \Delta P(4)$
35–39	$P(51)$	$P(52)$	$P(52) - P(31) = \Delta P(5)$
40–44	$P(61)$	$P(62)$	$P(62) - P(41) = \Delta P(6)$
45–49	$P(71)$	$P(72)$	$P(72) - P(51) = \Delta P(7)$

In this case $P(1, h)$ and $P(2, h)$ are same as $P(1\ 2)$ and $P(2\ 2)$ as these children are born during last 10 years. Here assumption of evenly distribution may not hold good.

Here $\quad \Delta P(i) = P(1, 2) - P(i-2, 1)$

and $\quad P(i\ h) = P(i-2, h) + \Delta P(i)$

Here it can be observed that the value of parity for Hypothetical cohort for even number of age group can be obtained by summing the differential parity (ΔP) for even age groups and for odd by summing differential for odd age groups; for example :

$$P(4, h) = \Delta P(2) + \Delta P(4)$$

$$P(5\ h) = \Delta P(1) + \Delta P(3) + \Delta P(5).$$

Once we get the parity for Hypothetical cohort, the cumulated fertility can be obtained as :

$$F(i) = 0.92834\ P(i\ h) + 0.45466\ P(i+1, h) + 0.0585\ P(i+2, h) - 0.3245\ F(i-1)$$

for $i<5$

$$F(6) = 0.02085\ P(4\ h) - 0.5574\ P(5\ h) + 1.0478\ P(6\ h) + 0.2869\ P(7\ h) + 0.20185\ F(4)$$

$$F(7) = 1.007\ P(7, h)$$

with this *ASFR* can be easily calculated. The above equation are obtained by fitting third order polynomial to successive average hypothetical parity. Using $P(i, h)$ and Intercensal *ASFR* from birth registration, we can use P/F ratio method also to estimate the completeness of the birth registration.

APPENDIX

TABLE 8.1(A)

A. Multiplying Factors for Estimating the Proportion of Children Born Alive who Die by Age a; q(a), From the Proportion Dead Among Children Ever Born to Women 15-20, 20-25, etc.

1	2	3	4	5	6	7	8	9	10
15—20	q(1)	0,859	0.890	0.928	0.977	1.041	1.129	1.254	1.425
20—25	q(2)	0.938	0.959	0.983	1.010	1.043	1.082	1.129	1.188
25—30	q(3)	0.948	0.962	0.978	0.994	1.012	1.033	1.055	1.081
30—35	q(5)	0.961	0.975	0.988	1.002	1.016	1.031	1.046	1.063
35—40	q(10)	0.966	0.982	0.996	1.011	1.026	1.040	1.054	1.069
40—45	q(15)	0.938	0.955	0.971	0.988	1 004	1.021	1.037	1.052
45—50	q(20)	0.937	0.953	0.969	0.986	1.003	1.021	1.039	1.057
50—55	q(25)	0.949	0.966	0.983	1.001	1.019	1.036	1.054	1.072
55—60	q(30)	0.951	0.968	0.985	1.002	1.020	1.039	1.058	1.076
60—65	q(35)	0.949	0.965	0.982	0.999	1.016	1.034	1.052	1.070

(Contd.)

1	2	3	4	5	6	7	8	9	10
Guide to selection of multiplier									
P_1/P_2		0.387	0.330	0.268	0.205	0.143	0.090	0.045	0.014
$\bar{m}$		24.7	25.7	26.7	27.7	28.7	29.7	30.7	31.7
$\bar{m}'$ (medium)		24.2	25.2	26.2	27.2	28.2	29.2	30.2	31.2
B. Ten-year Age Intervals of Women									
15—25	q(2)	0.982	1.000	1.021	1.045	1.072	1.105	1.144	1.193
25—35	q(5)	0.990	1.004	1.018	1.033	1.048	1.064	1.081	1.099
35—45	q(15)	0.977	0.993	1.009	1.024	1.040	1.056	1.071	1.086
45—55	q(25)	0.990	1.008	1.025	1.043	1.062	1.080	1.099	1.118
55—65	q(35)	0.990	1.007	1.025	1.043	1.061	1.080	1.099	1.119

Source : Brass (1968).

TABLE 8.2(A)

Results of Regression : Age Model

*Regression equation**	*Mortality pattern*	*Regression coefficients* *A*	*B*	*Standard error regression*	R^2
1	2	3	4	5	6
$q(2)/D_2 = A + B\,(P_2/P_3)$	West	1.30	—0.54	0.008	0.942
	North	1.30	—0.63	0.010	0.936
	East	1.26	—0.44	0.007	0.943
	South	1.33	—0.61	0.009	0.938
$q(3)/D_2 = A + B\,(P_2/P_3)$	West	1.17	—0.40	0.004	0.977
	North	1.17	—0.50	0.004	0.980
	East	1.14	—0.33	0.003	0.977
	South	1.20	—0.44	0.005	0.970

(Contd.)

1	2	3	4	5	6
$q(5)/D_4 = A + B\,(P_2/P_3)$	West	1.13	—0.33	0.009	0.846
	North	1.15	—0.42	0.011	0.851
	East	1.11	—0.26	0.007	0.839
	South	1.14	—0.32	0.009	0.845

* Each regression is based on 650 observations on the data.

Source : Sullivan (1972)

TABLE 8.3(A)

Results of Regression : Duration Model

Regression equation*	Mortality Pattern	Regression coefficients A	Regression coefficients B	Standard error regression	R^2
$q(2)/D_1 = A+B\ (P_1/P_2)$	West	1.34	—0.35	0.011	0.891
	North	1.34	—0.38	0.019	0.774
	East	1.29	—0.28	0.009	0.893
	South	1.40	—0.42	0.021	0.764
$q(3)/D_2 = A+B\ (P_1/P_2)$	West	1.18	—0.44	0.009	0.951
	North	1.18	—0.53	0.008	0.974
	East	1.16	—0.37	0.006	0.968
	South	1.22	—0.50	0.008	0.968
$q(5)/D_3 = A+B\ (P_1/P_2)$	West	1.17	—0.44	0.019	0.810
	North	1.20	—0.57	0.024	0.824
	East	1.14	—0.36	0.016	0.815
	South	1.19	—0.46	0.019	0.834

Source : Sullivan (19>2)

TABLE 8.4(A)

Coefficients for Estimation of Child Mortality Multipliers by Trussell Variant, When Data are Classified by Age of Mother

Mortality model	*Age group*	*Index* i	*Mortality ratio** $q(x) / D(i)$	*Coefficient* $a(i)$	$b(i)$	$c(i)$
North	15—19	1	q(1) / D(1)	1.1119	—2.9287	0.8507
	20—24	2	q(2) / D(2)	1.2390	—0.6865	—0.2745
	25—29	3	q(3) / D(3)	1.1884	0.0421	—0.5156
	30—34	4	q(5) / D(4)	1.2046	0.3037	—0.5656
	35—39	5	q(10)/ D(5)	1.2586	0.4236	—0.5898
	40—44	6	q(15)/ D(6)	1.2240	0.4222	—0.5456
	45—49	7	q(20)/ D(7)	1.1772	0.3486	—0.4624
South	15—19	1	q(1) / D(1)	1.0819	—3.0005	0 8689
	20—24	2	q(2) / D(2)	1.2846	—0 6181	—0.3024
	25—29	3	q(3) / D(3)	1.2223	0.0851	—0.4704
	30—34	4	q(5) / D(4)	1.1905	0.2631	—0.4487

	35—39	5	q(10)/ D(5)	1.1911	0.3152	—0.4291
	40—44	6	q(15)/ D(6)	1.1564	0.3017	—0.3958
	45—49	7	q(20)/ D(7)	1.1307	0.2596	—0.3538
East	15—19	1	q(1) / D(1)	1.1461	—2,2536	0.6259
	20—24	2	q(2) / D(2)	1.2231	—0.4301	—0.2245
	25—29	3	q(3) / D(3)	1.1593	0,0581	—0.3479
	30—34	4	q(5) / D(4)	1.1404	0.1991	—0.3487
	35—39	5	q(10)/ D(5)	1.1540	0.2511	—0.3506
	40—44	6	q(15)/ D(6)	1.1336	0.2556	—0.3428
	45—49	7	q(20)/ D(7)	1.1201	0.2362	—0.3268
West	15—19	1	q(1) / D(1)	1.1415	—2.7070	0.7663
	20—24	2	q(2) / D(2)	1.2563	—0.5381	—0.2637
	25—29	3	q(3) / D(3)	1.1851	0.0633	—0.4177
	30—34	4	q(5) / D(4)	1.1720	0.2341	—0.4272
	35—39	5	q(10)/ D(5)	1.1865	0.3080	—0.4452
	40—44	6	q(15)/ D(6)	1.1746	0.3314	—0.4537
	45—49	7	q(20)/ D(7)	1.1639	0.3190	—0.4435

Estimation equations

$k(i) = a(i) + b(i)\,[P(1)\,P(2)) + c(i)\,(P(2)\,P(3))]$

$q(x) = k(i)\,D(i)$

* Ratio of probability of dying to proportion of children dead. This ratio is set equal to the multiplier $k(i)$.

Source : Manual X, U.N. 1983.

TABLE 8.5 (*a*)

Estimates of Regression Coefficients for Specification M_{t-i+5}=a+bPAR 1+cPAR 2 for Conventional Age Groups

Age group	*a*	*b*	*c*	R^2	*RMSE*	*Mean*	*fx*
			Latin American Model				
15—19	1.0865	—1.4553	.3581	.912	.0166	1.0559	1
20—24	1.2102	— .4692	—.1787	.985	.0051	1.0388	2
25—29	1.1764	.0730	—.3629	.993	.0026	.9885	3
30—34	1.1806	.3115	—.4230	.884	.0089	.9969	5
35—39	1.2028	.4075	—.4491	.761	.0132	1.0198	10
40—44	1.1791	.4088	—.4428	.732	.0139	.9998	15
45—49	1.1636	.3838	—.4322	.758	.0129	.9861	20
			Chilean Model				
15—19	1.1906	—1.3677	.3316	.908	.0161	1.1592	1
20—24	1.1952	— .3163	—.1475	.984	.0038	1.0649	2
25—29	1.1410	.0662	—.2559	.990	.0020	1.0107	3

30—34	1.1275	.2115	—.2888	.879	.0063	1.0010	5
35—39	1.1379	.2756	—.3220	.782	.0092	1.0041	10
40—44	1.1397	.3162	—.3676	.769	.0109	.9872	15
45—49	1.1565	.3607	—.4242	.781	.0122	.9799	20

South Asian Model

15—19	1.0876	—1.5053	.3762	.909	.0173	1.0587	1
20—24	1.2186	— .4589	—.1838	.984	.0054	1.0474	2
25—29	1.1807	.0854	—.3556	.991	.0032	1.0005	3
30—34	1.1761	.3038	—.3932	.870	.0088	1.0093	5
35—39	1.1789	.3680	—.3855	.732	.0119	1.0264	10
40—44	1.1392	.3294	—.3345	.692	.0112	1.0084	15
45—49	1.1072	.2541	—.2731	.746	.0087	.9981	20

Far Eastern Model

15—19	1.0664	—1.1081	.2931	.901	.0131	1.0545	1
20—24	1.1573	— .3649	—.1314	.987	.0036	1.0278	2
25—29	1.1369	.0433	—.2929	.994	.0020	.9822	3
30—34	1.1492	.2480	—.3740	.903	.0076	.9819	5
35—39	1.1932	.3732	—.4646	.811	.0126	.9956	10
40—44	1.2115	.4767	—.5683	.785	.0163	.9730	15
45—49	1.2472	.5697	—.6646	.780	.0192	.9702	20

(Contd.)

General Model

15—19	1.0783	—1.2546	.3156	.910	.0144	1.0557	1
20—24	1.1822	— .4134	—.1537	.986	.0043	1.0332	2
25—29	1.1554	.0579	—.3265	.993	.0022	.9851	3
30—34	1.1631	.2805	—.3953	.892	.0082	.9898	5
35—39	1.1952	.3879	—.4445	.779	.0127	1.0117	10
40—44	1.1860	.4235	—.4724	.750	.0144	.9927	15
45—49	1.1853	.4319	—.4897	.762	.0145	.9838	20

Notes **: All numbers significant at less than .01 level,**

RMSE **is root of the mean square errors in** M_{i-i+5}.

Mean is the average of M_{i-i+5}.

l_i **is the corresponding age of child.**

Source **: Palloni and Heligman (1985).**

TABLE 8.6(A)

Coefficients for Estimation of the Reference Period t(x)* To which the Values of q(x) Estimated from Data Classified by Age Refer

Mortality model	*Age group*	*Index t*	*Age x*	*Parameter estimate*	*Coefficients*		
					a(t)	*b(t)*	*c(t)*
(1)	(2)	(3)	(4)	(5)	(6)	(7)	(8)
North	15—19	1	1	q(1)	1.0921	5.4732	−1.9672
	20—24	2	2	q(2)	1.3207	5.3751	0.2133
	25—29	3	3	q(3)	1.5996	2.6268	4.3701
	30—34	4	5	q(5)	2.0779	— 1.7908	9.4126
	35—39	5	10	q(10)	2.7705	— 7.3403	14.9352
	40—44	6	15	q(15)	4.1520	−12.2448	19.2349
	45—49	7	20	q(20)	6.9650	−13.9160	19.9542

(*Contd.*)

1	2	3	4	5	6	7	8
South	15—19	1	1	q(1)	1.0900	5.4443	—1.9721
	20—24	2	2	q(2)	1.3079	5.5568	0.2021
	25—29	3	3	q(3)	1.5173	2.6755	4.7471
	30—34	4	5	q(5)	1.9399	— 2.2739	10.3876
	35—39	5	10	q(10)	2.6157	— 8.4819	16.5153
	40—44	6	15	q(15)	4.0794	—13.8308	21.1866
	45—49	7	20	q(20)	7.1796	—15.3880	21.7892
East	15—19	1	1	q(1)	1.0959	5.5864	—1.9949
	20—24	2	2	q(2)	1.2921	5.5897	0.3631
	25—29	3	3	q(3)	1.5021	2.4692	5.0927
	30—34	4	5	q(5)	1.9347	— 2.6419	10.8533
	35—39	5	10	q(10)	2.6197	— 8.9693	17.0981
	40—44	6	15	q(15)	4.1317	—14.3550	21.8247
	45—49	7	20	q(20)	7.3657	—15.8083	22.3005
West	15—19	1	1	q(1)	1.0970	5.5628	—1.9956
	20—24	2	2	q(2)	1.3062	5.5677	0.2962
	25—29	3	3	q(3)	1.5305	2.5528	4.8962
	30—34	4	5	q(5)	1.9991	— 2.4261	10.4282

35—39	5	10	q(10)	2.7632	— 8.4065	16.1787
40—44	6	15	q(15)	4.3468	—13.2436	20.1990
45—49	7	20	q(20)	7.5242	—14.2013	20.0162

Estimation equation :

$$t(x)=a(i)+b(i)\ (P(1)\ P(2))+c(i)\ (P(2)\ P(3))$$

* Number of years prior to the survey.

Source: Manual X, U.N. (1983).

TABLE 8.7(A)

Estimated Coefficients of Time References for Specification $t_{(i,\ i+5)}$=a+bPAR 1+c PAR 2 for Conventional Age Groups

Age group	*a*	*b*	*c*	R^2	*RMSE*	*Mean*	t_i
			Latin American Model				
15—19	1.1703	0.5129	—0.3850	0.4637[a]	0.0179	0.5290	1
20—24	1.6955	4.1320	—0.1635	0.999	0.0079	1.7505	2
25—29	1.8296	2.9020	3.4707	0.999	0.0112	3.6886	3
30—34	2.1783	—2.5688	9.0883	0.975	0.1130	6.2683	5
35—39	2.8836	—10.3282	15.4301	0.887	0.3370	9.2451	10
40—44	4.4580	—17.1809	20.4296	0.7797	0.5641	12.4953	15
45—49	6.9351	—19.3871	23.4007	0.8789	0.6685	16.2597	20

			Chilean Model				
15—19	1.3092	1.9474	—0.7982	0.773[a]	0.0279	0.6748	1
20—24	1.6897	4.6176	—0.0173	0.922	0.0094	1.9195	2
25—29	1.8368	2.6370	4.0305	0.999	0.0105	3.9607	3
30—34	2.2036	—3.3520	9.9233	0.978	0.1337	6.6333	5
35—39	2.9955	—11.4013	16.3431	0.875	0.3702	9.6889	10
40—44	4.7734	—17.8850	20.8883	0.787	0.5881	12.9500	15
45—49	7.4495	—19.0513	23.0529	0.788	0.6607	16.6323	20
			South Asian Model				
15—19	1.1922	0.7940	—0.5425	0.477[a]	0.0240	0.5203	1
20—24	1.7173	4.3117	—0.1653	0.998	0.0097	1.7964	2
25—29	1.8631	2.8767	—3.5848	0.999	0.0241	3.7595	3
30—34	2.1808	—02.7219	9.3705	0.976	0.1267	6.3561	5
35—39	2.7654	—10.8808	16.2255	0.884	0.3619	9.4041	10
40—44	4.1378	—18.6219	22.2390	0.797	0.6162	12.8468	15
45—49	6.4885	—22.2001	26.4911	0.788	0.7633	16.9556	20
			Far Eastern Model				
15—19	1.2779	1.5714	—0.6994	0.707[a]	0.0274	0.6384	1
20—24	1.7471	4.2638	—0.0752	0.998	0.0099	1.8729	2

(Contd.)

25—29	1.9107	2.7285	3.5881	0.999	0.0119	3.8147	3
30—34	2.3172	—2.6259	9.0238	0.973	0.1185	6.3783	5
35—39	3.2087	—9.8891	14.7339	0.885	0.3260	9.2780	10
40—44	5.1141	—15.3263	18.2507	0.800	0.5097	12.2715	15
45—49	7.6383	—15.5739	19.7669	0.804	0.5557	15.5924	20
			General Model				
15—19	1.2136	0.9740	—0.5247	0.574[a]	0.0216	0.5775	1
20—24	1.7025	4.1569	—0.1232	0.999	0.0086	1.7842	2
25—29	1.8360	2.8632	3.5220	1.0000	0.0105	3.7180	3
30—34	2.1882	—02.6521	9.1619	0.974	0.1162	6.3107	5
35—39	2.9682	—10.3053	15.3161	0.885	0.3371	9.2719	10
40—44	4.6526	—16.6920	19.8534	0.796	0.5500	12.4518	15
45—49	7.1425	—18.3021	22.4168	0.793	0.6371	16.0975	20

Notes : All numbers significant at less than .01 level.

RMSE is root of the mean square errors in $t_{(i,\ i+5)}$.

Mean is the average of l_{t-t+5}.

$t_{(i)}$ is the corresponding age of child.

[a]Low R^2 for first age groups is explained by the lack of variance of the calculated values of l_{t-t+5}.

Source : Palloni and Heligman (1985).

TABLE 8.8(A)

Value of Multipliers (k_i) Given by Brass (with ½ Year Shift)

Age								
15–19	3.169	2.925	2.638	2.305	1.951	1.614	1.309	1.119
20–24	2.986	2.958	1.927	2.889	2.811	2.779	2.690	2.553
25–29	3.097	3.076	3.055	3.033	3.010	2.986	2.958	2.917
30–34	3.216	3.188	3.163	3.140	3.118	3.097	3.076	3.055
35–39	3.434	3.374	3.324	3.283	3.747	3.216	3.188	3.163
40–44	4.150	3.917	3.739	3.608	3.510	3.434	3.374	3.324
45–49	5.000	4.984	4.830	4.629	4.396	4.150	3.896	3.640
f_1/f_2	0.939	0.764	0.605	0.460	0.330	0.213	0.113	0.036
m	24.7	25.7	26.7	27.7	28.7	29.7	30.7	31.7

Source : Brass et al. (1968).

TABLE 8.9(A)

Values of Constants to be used in P/F Ratio Method

Age group	Shift a_i	Shift b_i	Shift c_i	No shift a_i	No shift b_i	No shift c_i
15—19	2.531	−0.188	0.0024	2.147	−0.244	0.0034
20—24	3.321	−0.754	0.0161	2.838	−0.758	0.0162
25—29	2.265	−0.627	0.0145	2.760	−0.594	0.0133
30—39	3.518	−0.763	0.0006	3.029	−0.823	0.0006
40—44	3.862	−2.481	−0.0001	3.419	−2.966	−0.0001
45—49	3.828	−0.016[a]	−0.0002	3.535	−0.007[a]	−0.0002

Source: Manual *X*, U.N. (1983).

a : This co-efficient should be applied to $f(i-1)$ not $f(i+1)$ *i.e.* to $f(6)$ instead of $f(8)$.

TABLE 8.10(A)

Coefficients for Calculation of Weighting Factors to Estimate Age-Specific Fertility Rates for Conventional Age Groups from Age Groups Shifted by Six Months

Age group	*Index i*	*Co-efficients* $x(i)$	$y(i)$	$z(i)$
15–19	1	0.031	2.287	0.114
20–24	2	0.068	0.999	– 0.233
25–29	3	0.094	1.219	– 0.977
30–34	4	0.120	1.139	– 1.531
35–39	5	0.162	1.739	– 3.592
40–44	6	0.270	3.454	–21.497

Source: Manual *X*, U.N. (1983).

9

Population Estimation and Projection

In demography, population estimation and projection methods are so intertwined that together they form one separate field of scientific endeavour. Population estimation provides quantification of population facts not obtained by other methods like census and surveys. A population projection may be defined as the numerical outcome of a specific set of assumptions regarding future trends in fertility, mortality and migration. On the other hand, a forecast indicates the specific projection that is believed to be most likely to happen. Following are three types of estimates which differ from each other only with reference to the time period that they cover :

(1) Inter Censal estimates.

(2) Post-Censal estimates.

(3) Future estimates or Projections.

First one may be regarded some kind of interpolation where as the next two as extrapolations.

Need and Uses of Population Estimates

In ancient days the population estimates were needed for the purpose of ascertaining the supply for the military forces, for assessing number of persons who could be slave and the number of persons who could be taxed etc. The functions of the present day governments have become increasingly complex but more plan-oriented. For the planning of socio-economic and welfare activities, we need a fairly accurate knowledge of the size of the country's population, its rate of growth, its spatial distribution, its age sex composition, educational groups and various other characteristics. The population estimates and projections are equally important for the governments as well as private agencies. The researchers too require the population projection as an analytical tool to experiment with demographic process for better understanding of the population dynamics. They (population projections) "Permit experiments out of which we obtain causal knowledge; they explain data; they focus research by identifying theoretical and practical issues; they systematize comparative study across space and time; they reveal formal analogies between problems that on their surface are quite different; they even help assemble data" (Keyfitz, 1971).

Projection of a population in future is the manifestation of facts and assumptions that we make. While analysis of population data in the past enables us to comprehend the population dynamics; the knowledge of the current data helps us to understand and foresee the future course of the population change. Thus with the knowledge of present facts on population and assumptions regarding the future course of change projection provide a link between the past, the present and the future. Hence the population projection virutally becomes result of speculations which are based on the trends in demographic indicators established by the past.

9.1 Methods of Population Estimation and Projection

Population estimates (intercensal, post censal and future projection) can be obtained by a variety of methods. The methodology especially for future projection may vary according to unit of population projection, say national or sub-national. Nevertheless, they can be broadly categorized into following three groups :

(1) Mathematical Method

(2) Component Method

(3) Economic-Demographic Method.

The mathematical methods of population estimation, or projection (hereby only projection term will be used) techniques have long history and they are still frequently used for local population projections but not for projection of State and national populations. With increasing need and requirement of knowledge about the population characteristics for planning, these methods have been replaced by more sophisticated and elaborate methods known as component and economic-demographic techniques. It does not mean that simple methods of population projection do not produce accurate results. Rather these techniques are successful to produce – short to – medium term forecasts of the total population that are, at least as accurate as those produced by more sophisticated techniques. Nevertheless, the mathematical methods do not provide satisfactory results in projecting various characteristics of population such as school going population etc.

9.1.1 Mathematical Methods of Population Estimation and Projection

The population estimates in the ancient times were mainly based on the perception of researchers about the population growth in the past. A landmark in the history of population projection by mathematical functions was made by the work of P.F. Verhaulst who suggested that the population growth could be '*S*' type that, he named, the logistic. The logistic curve possesses the characteristics of proceeding from lower limit to a determinate upper limit. However, more detailed description of the curve as the law of population growth was given by Pearl and Reed (1920). In general, mathematical methods are nothing but fitting of curves to the observed data. But it may be remembered that the curve may fit observed data with greater accuracy and yet fail to produce the population for future with same accuracy if the population trends undergo drastic change. Here we illustrate the utility of the mathematical curves discussed in Chapter 1 for the population estimation and projection.

Let us recall the mathematical models discussed in Chapter 1. They are :

$P_{(t)}=P_{(0)}\,(1+rt)$...Arithmetic Growth Model, ...(1)

$P_{(t)}=P_{(0)}\,(1+r)^t$.. Geometric Growth Model. ...(2)

$P_{(t)}=P_{(0)}\,e^{rt}$...Exponential Growth Model ...(3)

$P_{(t)}=\dfrac{K}{1+e^{a+bt}}$...Logistic Growth Model. ...(4)

For projection, the population beyond time t, with arithmetic growth model $P(0)$ will still remain as base year population. For example, if 1971 and 1981 totals are used to estimate population growth from equation (1), 1971 population would remain base for projecting the population in 1991. So

$$P_{91}=P_{71}\,(1+20r)$$

Since r is defined as

$$=\frac{(P_{81}-P_{71})}{10P_{71}}$$

Hence after substituting the value of r in the equation, we have

$$P_{91}=P_{71}+2P_{81}-2P_{71}$$

$$=2P_{81}-P_{71} \qquad ...(5)$$

If we define annual absolute increament as

$$R=\frac{P_{81}-P_{71}}{10}$$

and use P_{81} as base year population, *i.e.*,

$$P_{91}=P_{81}+10R$$

$$=P_{81}+10\left[\frac{P_{81-71}}{10}\right]$$

$$=2P_{81}-P_{71} \qquad \ldots(6)$$

Here eqns. (5) and (6) are the same. If R is defined as annual absolute increase, one can use 1981 population as the base for projecting population of 1981 otherwise not.

In Geometric model there is no problem like arithmetic growth for the selection of the base year population

$$P_{81}=P_{71}(1+r)^{10}$$

Now, $$P_{91}=P_{81}(1+r)^{10}$$

$$=P_{71}(1+r)^{10}(1+r)^{10}$$

$$P_{91}=P_{71}(1+r)^{20}$$

The Geometric model can also be used to estimate or project the population of each age group. It should however, be remembered that if mathematical methods are used to project sub-national populations, total of the projected population may not be equal to the projected national population.

It may be mentioned that if population is projected for 10 years period using census population which are 10 years apart or for 5 years using census totals taken 5 years apart, there is no need to calculate the growth rate.

Using Geometric growth

$$P_{81}=P_{71}(1+r)^{10}$$

$$(1+r)^{10}=\frac{P_{81}}{P_{71}}$$

$$P_{91}=P_{81}(1+r)^{10}$$

$$=P_{81} * \frac{P_{81}}{P_{71}}$$

$$=\frac{P_{81}^{2}}{P_{71}} \qquad \ldots(7)$$

In the Exponential Growth Model

$$P_{81}=P_{71}e^{10r}$$

$$e^{10r}=\frac{P_{81}}{P_{71}}$$

so $$P_{91}=P_{81}e^{10r}$$

$$=\frac{P_{81}^2}{P_{71}} \qquad ...(8)$$

In Arithmetic or Linear Model

$$P_{81}=P_{71}(1+10r)$$

$$(1+10r)=\frac{P_{81}}{P_{71}}$$

or $$10r=\frac{P_{81}}{P_{71}}-1$$

so $$P_{91}=P_{71}(1+20r)$$

$$=P_{71}+20rP_{71}$$

$$=P_{71}+2\left[\frac{P_{81}}{P_{71}}-1\right]P_{71}$$

$$=2P_{81}-P_{71} \qquad ...(9)$$

It can be seen that the projected population size for 1991 using Geometric and Exponential laws would be same but linear model would provide different population size.

Example 1

If population of India as of April, 1 for 1971 and as of March 1, 1981 is 548 and 685 million respectively, estimate the population for 1978 and project the population for 1991 using three mathematical methods discussed above.

Solution.

It may be noted that the censuses of India of 1971 and 1981 are not exactly 10 years apart. So for estimation and projection of the population some adjustment has to be made. The intercensal period during 1971-81 is

$$9 \text{ years}+\frac{11 \text{ months}}{12 \text{ months}}=9.9167 \text{ years.}$$

Using Arithmetic Model

$$P_{81}=P_{71}(1+9.9167r)$$

$$685=548(1+9.9167r)$$

$$685/548=1+9.9167r$$

$$r=\frac{1}{9.9167}\left[\left(\frac{685}{548}\right)-1\right]$$

$$=0.02521$$

so estimate of population for 1978 (P_{78}) would be

$$P_{78}=P_{71}(1+6.9167 * 0.02521)$$

$$=548 * (1+6.9167 * 0.02521)$$

$$=644 \text{ million.}$$

For projection of population to 1991, we should use 1971 as base to maintain linear growth rate as consant between 1971-91. Nevertheless, we can assume that population would linearly grow after 1981 with observed growth rate 'r'

$$P_{91}=P_{81}(1+10r)$$

$$=685\ (1+10 \times 0.02521)$$

$$=858 \text{ million.}$$

Using Geometric Law of Population Growth

$$P_{81}=P_{71}(1+r)^{9.9167}$$

$$685=548(1+r)^{.99167}$$

$$r=\left(\frac{685}{548}\right)^{\frac{1}{9.9167}}-1$$

$$=0.02276$$

so, $$P_{78}=P_{71}(1+0.2276)^{6.9167}$$

$$\hat{P}_{78}=548(1.02276)^{6.9167}$$

$$=640 \text{ million}$$

and $$\hat{P}_{91}=P_{81}(1+0.02276)^{10}$$

$$=685(1.02276)^{10}$$

$$=856 \text{ million.}$$

Using Exponential Law of Population Growth

$$P_{81}=P_{71}e^{r9.9167}$$

$$685=548e^{9.9167}$$

$$r=\frac{1}{9.9167} * \log_e\left(\frac{685}{548}\right)$$

$$=0.02250$$

so,

$$P_{78}=548e^{6.9167 * 0.0225}$$

$$=640 \text{ million}$$

and

$$P_{91}=685e^{10 * 0.0225}$$

$$=850 \text{ million.}$$

Logistic Curve

In Logistic curve there are three parameters K, a and b which have to be estimated. For estimating three parameters, we need population figures at least from three cenuses. The Logistic curve can also be written as

$$\frac{1}{P(t)}=\frac{1+e^{a+bt}}{K}$$

$$=\frac{1}{K}+\frac{e^{a+bt}}{K}$$

$$=\frac{1}{K}+\left(\frac{e^a}{K}\right)(e^b)^t$$

$$Y(t)=A+BC^t \qquad \text{...(10)}$$

where

$$Y(t)=\frac{1}{P(t)}$$

$$A=\frac{1}{K}$$

$$B=\frac{e^a}{K}$$

$$C=e^b.$$

The equation (10) is known as modified exponential curve in which the first differences of $P(t)$ when plotted on a semi-logarthmic growth paper, lie on a straight line. It means that any time series data would follow logistic law if their reciprocal follows a modified exponential law.

The Logistic curve is useful for projection over a longer period than the simple geometric law; particularly if the past series have reached the point of inflexion. The difficulty however, is to select the countries and the period of observations (Shryock and Siegel, 1980). Like all mathematical curves, this curve is also mechanistic. Therefore, it is generally advised not to use this curve for long run projections. The logistic curve can not be used to project population with negative growth rate.

Example 2

Fit logistic curve for following data for Denmark and project the population for 1985 and 1990 :

Year	*Population*	$1/P_t * 10^6$
1925	3434555	0.2912
1930	3550655	0.2617
1935	3706349	0.2698
1940	3844312	0.2601
1945	4045232	0.2472
1950	4281275	0.2336
1955	4448401	0.2248
1960	4585256	0.2181
1965	4767597	0.2097
1970	4937597	0.2025
1975	5072516	0.1976
1980	5123989	0.1952

(*i*) Method using Sum of Reciprocals

$$S_1 = 1.1028$$

$$S_2 = 0.9237$$

$$S_3 = 0.8050$$

$$d_1 = S_1 - S_2$$

$$= 0.1791$$

$$d_2 = S_2 - S_3$$
$$= 0.1187$$
$$a = \frac{1}{r}[\log_e d_1 - \log_e d_2]$$
$$r = 4$$
$$= 0.1028.$$

$$\frac{1}{K} = \frac{1}{r}\left[S_1 - \frac{d_1^2}{d_1 - d_2}\right]$$

$$K = 7.00 \text{ million}$$

$$b = \frac{K}{c} \times \frac{d_1^2}{d_1 - d_2}$$

$$c = \frac{1 - e^{ra}}{1 - e^{-a}}$$
$$= 3.4511$$
$$b = 1.08$$

So the fitted curve is

$$P_t = \frac{7.00}{1 + 1.08\, e^{-0.1028t'}}$$

where $t' = \frac{t - t_0}{5}$

and $t_0 = 1925$

(ii) Method of Selected Points

In this method we select three points in such a way that they are equidistant and cover whole range of the observations. In the above example, the selected three points are 1925, 1950 and 1975. So

$$\frac{1}{P_0} = 0.2912$$

$$\frac{1}{P_5} = 0.2336$$

$$\frac{1}{P_{10}}=0.1976$$

$$d_1=\frac{1}{P_0}-\frac{1}{P_5}$$

$$=0.0576$$

$$d_2=0.0360$$

$$a=\frac{1}{r}[\log_e d_1-\log_e d_2]; \text{ here } \quad r=5$$

$$=0.0940$$

$$\frac{1}{K}=\frac{1}{P_0}-\frac{d_1^2}{d_1-d_2}$$

$$K=7.27$$

$$b=\frac{K}{P_0}-1$$

$$=1.12$$

so the fitted curve is

$$P_t=\frac{K}{1+be^{-at'}}$$

where $t'=\dfrac{t-t_0}{5}$

and $t_0=1925$

$$P_t=\frac{7.27}{1+1.12e^{-0.094t'}}$$

It may be seen that there is no substantial difference in the two sets of the estimated parameters. We therefore use parameters only from the first method for projection

so $P_t=\dfrac{7.00}{1+1.08e^{-0.1028t}}$

For 1985 $t=\dfrac{t-t_0}{5}$

$$=\frac{1985-1925}{5}$$

$$=12 \text{ years}$$

and for 1990 $t=13$ years

$$P_{1985}=\frac{7.00}{1+1.08e^{-0.1028*11}}$$

$$=5.33 \text{ million}$$

$$P_{1990}=\frac{7.00}{1+1.08e^{-0.1028 * 13}}$$

$$=5.45 \text{ million.}$$

9.1.2 Component Method of Population Projection

A cohort component or component projection method was developed almost at the same time as the mathematical methods. First time, P.K. Whelpton in 1928 used this procedure for projecting the population of the United States of America. In this procedure, each component of population growth-fertility, mortality and migration is projected separately. The last component is generally not considered in the national population projections. Over the last five to six decades, there have been various improvements not so much in methodology but in the projections of growth components. In case of India, this method was first applied in projecting the population at future dates based on 1951 census which was further extended to the states after 1961 census.

Before we discuss the method of population projection, we outline the steps involved in the projection of three components of population growth :

Mortality

1. Construct a life table from the latest available age-specific death rates separately for the males and females.
2. Analyse the past trends of mortality and estimate the annual change in mortality indicator like e_0^0.
3. Using the past trend, form assumptions about future value of e_0^0, preferably at 5 years interval.
4. Select suitable model life table to estimate survival probability corresponding to the projected values of e_0^0.

The projection of mortality indicator about mortality for future date can be done by

(*a*) Assuming no change in Mortality that has been observed in latest year, or

(*b*) Assuming the trends in mortality during the last 5 or 10 years to continue in future, or

(*c*) Assuming target value for mortality in distant future date and interpolating the intermediate values linearly or exponentially.

In the procedure (*b*) there may be a chance of reaching at unreasonably low level of mortality. Therefore it is preferred to assume improvement in mortality with decreasing rate of change over time. We may also borrow the experience of other countries in fixing the mortality level at future date.

Fertility

1. Choose fertility indicator to be used in projection. Generally three measures of fertility are taken into consideration—the period measure of fertility, the cohort fertility and the marriage parity interval progression ratio. Since the data are not available for most of the developing countries on latter two measures, the only period measures are used. The measure generally used may be *SAABR*, *GFR*, *GMFR*, *ASFR*, *ASMFR*, *TFR* etc.

2. Study past trend in the selected indicator in view of the overall development and government population policy.

3. Assess the possible future target of family planning from the past achievement.

4. Estimate the fertility indicator for future date. In this case, generally three assumptions namely medium, low and fast decline in fertility are made.

5. If we choose, fertility indicator relating to married women, we have to project also the proportion of women married in each 5 year age group for the future years.

Migration

At the national level, the role of migration in population growth is generally assumed to be zero (negligible) but in the projection of sub-national populations migration plays an important role. The projection of net migration is very difficult due to lack of time series data for the past. If data on age specific net migration are available for few years in the past, one can venture to project migration also. In the absence of data on age-specific net migration, overall migration rate is considered for projection. Which helps in getting increase in the total population due to migration. Some standard age pattern of migration may be used to adjust the projected population by age and sex in the future. Projection of migration especially by age may involve more error due to uncertainity in its age-specific volume as compared to other two components of population growth; namely, fertility and mortality.

Method of Component Projection

Let us denote the female population in age group x to $x+5$ at time t as ${}_5P^t_x$. Further denote 5-year survival probability as ${}_5S_x$. The projected female population at time $t+5$, ${}_5P^{t+5}_{x+5}$ in age group $x+5$ to $x+10$ can be obtained as

$${}_5P^{t+5}_{x+5} = {}_5P^t_x * {}_5S_x \qquad ...(11)$$

where $${}_5S_x = \frac{{}_5L_{x+5}}{{}_5L_x}$$

$$x : 0,\ 5,\ 10......$$

Thus $${}_5P^{t+5}_5 = {}_5P^t_0 * {}_5S_0$$

$$= {}_5P^t_0 * \frac{{}_5L_5}{{}_5L_0}$$

$${}_5P_{10}^{t+5}={}_5P_5^t * \frac{{}_5L_{10}}{{}_5L_5}$$

and so on.

By using equation (11), population would be projected to the next 5 years. If life table is selected for each 5 years interval in future for both the sexes, population can be carried forward. Thus the population so survived becomes 5 years older at the end of projection period. In this process, we have projected the population already alive at time t but in order to obtain 0-5 age population at the end of each projection period we have to estimate the number of births which would take place in each 5 years interval. For estimating the female children during t to $t+5$, we take age-specific birth rates (${}_5f_x$) pertaining to period (t, $t+5$) which is calculated by taking baby girls during the projection period. So the number of female births to the women aged x to $x+5$ would be

$$\frac{5}{2}\left[{}_5P_x^t+{}_5P_{x-5}^t * \left(\frac{{}_5L_x}{{}_5L_{x-5}}\right)\right] * {}_5f_x \quad ...(12)$$

$$x: A, A+5......B-5$$

Where A and B are the lowest and highest limits of the reproductive period. To obtain the population in 0−5 age group we can sum the equation (12) over fertile ages multiplied with probability of survivorship of female child from birth to the 0−5 age group.

Symbolically

$${}_5P_0^{t+5}=\frac{{}_5L_0}{2}\sum_{x-A}^{B-5}\left[{}_5P^t{}_x+{}_5P^t{}_{x-5} * \frac{{}_5L_x}{{}_5L_{x-5}}\right]{}_5f_x \quad ...(13)$$

when $l_0=1$

The projection of male can also be carried in the similar fashion. It is generally observed that birth by age−sex is not available. In such case, one can use sex ratio at birth to estimate the births of male and female children. For example, let us assume that *ASFR* (total birth) is available, then the total births can be estimated as (like equation 13),

$$B=\frac{5}{2}\sum_{A}^{B-5}\left[\ {}_5P'_x+{}_5P'_{x-5} * \frac{{}_5L_x}{{}_5L_{x-5}}\right] * {}_5b_x$$

where ${}_5b_x$ is *ASFR* for age group x to $x+5$.

The birth of male children and female children can be estimated as :

$$B^m=\left[\frac{SRB}{1+SRB}\right]*B$$

and

$$B^f=\left[\frac{1}{1+SRB}\right]*B$$

Now these births can be survived using male and female life tabels form the date of birth '*o*' to age group 0−5.

The procedure of projection described above can be arranged in the matrix form.

$$P^{t+5}=M\ P^t$$

where, *M* and P^t are defined on the next page

If matrix *M* is constant, then population after *n* cycles of projection will be as :

$$P^{t+n}=M^n\ P^t \qquad ...(14)$$

If rates are changing over a period of time, each 5 years period will have its own projection matrix and therefore above equation becomes

$$P^{t+n}=M_{n-1}\ M_{n-2}\cdots\cdots\cdots M_2\ M_1\ M_0\ P^t \qquad ...(15)$$

The numerical implementation of the projection is more easily programmed but is less economical with the matrix (since it involves many multiplications by zero) than with equation (12) and (13). But the theoretical properties of the projection process are more easily studied and understood in the matrix formulation especially when they approach to stability (Lopez 1961, Mc Farland 1969, Keyfitz, 1968).

where

$$M = \begin{bmatrix} 0 & 0 & \frac{{}_5L_0}{2}\left[\frac{{}_5L_{15}}{{}_5L_{10}} * {}_5f_{15}\right], & \frac{{}_5L_0}{2}\left[{}_5f_{15} + \frac{{}_5L_{20}}{{}_5L_{15}}{}_5f_{20}\right] & 0 & 0 \\ \frac{{}_5L_5}{{}_5L_0} & 0 & 0 & 0 & 0 & 0 \\ 0 & \frac{{}_5L_{10}}{{}_5L_5} & 0 & 0 & 0 & 0 \\ 0 & 0 & \frac{{}_5L_{15}}{{}_5L_{10}} & 0 & 0 & 0 \end{bmatrix} \text{ and } P^t = \begin{bmatrix} {}_5P^t_0 \\ {}_5P^t_5 \\ {}_5P^t_{15} \\ P^t_{70} \end{bmatrix}$$

It is to be noted here that in application, the population is generally projected using single index of fertility like *GFR*, or *GMFR* etc. In such cases, above matrix has to be suitably modified.

If *GFR* is available for mid period of each projection interval, the births can be estimated as follows :

Number of births during t and $t+5$

$$=GFR\left[\frac{W^{t}_{15-49}+W^{t+5}_{15-49}}{2}\right]$$

where W_{15-49} is number of the women in the age group 15−49, suffix on the top denotes the time t and $t+5$.

In case, *GFR* is available at time t and $t+5$, births can be calculated as below :

Number of births in the year t

$$B^{t}=GFR^{t} * W^{t}_{15-49}$$

Number of births in the year $t+5$

$$B^{t+5}=GFR^{t+5} * W^{t+5}_{15-49}$$

So the number of births during the projection period would be

$$B(t, t+5)=\frac{5}{2}(B^{t}+B^{t+5})$$

and number of female births will be :

$$B^{f}(t, t+5)=B(t, t+5) * \frac{1}{(1+SRB)}$$

where *SRB* is sex ratio at birth (Male to Female Births). To obtain the female population aged 0−4 at time $t+5$, we can multiply above births by survival probability.

$${}_{5}P^{t+5}_{0}=\left[\frac{{}_{5}L_{0}}{5}\right] * B^{f}(t, t+5)$$

where $l_0=1$

Similar calculations can be carried out for males and for more time periods. The calculation of births with other indicators are illustrated with examples below ;

Example 3

The female population of India by 5-Years age group as on 1st March 1981 is given below.

Age	*Female population* ('000)
0—4	46234
5—9	43802
10—14	40906
15—19	35947
20—24	30413
25—29	25466
30—34	21838
35—39	18968
40—44	16212
45—49	13532
50—54	10863
55—59	8588
60—64	6557
65—69	4807
70+	6653
Total	330786

Project the India's female population by age upto 1991 using following information :

(*i*) Sex ratio at birth is 106 males per 100 females.

(*ii*) *SAABR* in 1981 was 34.99.

(*iii*) *GMFR* in 1981 was 205 per thousand married women in the age group 15—49.

(*iv*) Proportion of women married in the age group 15—49 in 1981 was 0.8048.

and following alternative assumptions :

(*i*) Assume 2 per cent annual geometric decline in *SAABR*. or,

(*ii*) The annual per cent decline in *GMFR* is assumed to be 2.2.

or,

(*iii*) The projected proportion of married women aged 15–49 in 1986 and 1991 are 0.7925 and 0.7832 respectively.

(*iv*) e_0° for females during 1981-86 and 1986-91 are 54.31 and 57.07 respectively. or,

(*v*) Migration is nil.

Solution :

1. First let us predict *SAABR* for 1986 and 1991. Since annuel geometric declie in *SAABR* is assumed to be 2 per cent, one can estimate *SAABR* as :

$$SAABR_{1986} = 34.99\ (1-0.02)^5$$
$$= 31.63 \text{ per 1000 population.}$$
$$SAABR_{1991} = 34.99\ (1-0.02)^{10}$$
$$= 28.59 \text{ per 1000 population.}$$

2. Calculation of 5-years survival ratio from model life table for given e_0° :

$$e_0^\circ\ (1981-86) = 54.31$$
$$e_0^\circ\ (1986-91) = 57.07$$

The 5-Years survival ratios are interpolated as below (Table 9.1) from South Asian Pattern of new Model life tables of U.N. (1982).

Projection of population in 1986 and 1991 by multiplying the age wise population of 1981 and corresponding survival ratios (Table 9.2).

TABLE 9.1

Interpolated Values of 5-year Survival Ratios for Females, 1981-86 and 1986-91

Age group	*5-Year survival ratio corresponding to different values of* e_0^o					
	54	*55*	*54.31**	*57*	*58*	*57.07**
	(1)	(2)	(3)	(4)	(5)	(6)
Birth to 0— 4	0.8527	0.8588	0.8546	0.8706	0.8765	0.8710
0— 4 to 5— 9	0.9423	0.9458	0.9434	0.9524	0.9556	0.9526
5— 9 to 10—14	0.9871	0.9880	0.9874	0.9896	0.9904	0.9897
10—14 to 15—19	0.9905	0.9915	0.9911	0.9927	0.9932	0.9927
15—19 to 20—24	0.9879	0.9887	0.9881	0.9903	0.9910	0.9903
20—24 to 25—29	0.9861	0.9871	0.9864	0.9888	0.9896	0.9889
25—29 to 30—34	0.9841	0.9851	0.9844	0.9870	0.9879	0.9871

30—34 to 35—39	0.9809	0.9821	0.9813	0.9842	0.9852	0.9843
35—39 to 40—44	0.9766	0.9778	0.9770	0.9801	0.9812	0.9802
40—44 to 45—49	0.9696	0.9709	0.9700	0.9735	0.9747	0.9736
45—49 to 50—54	0.9559	0.9575	0.9564	0.9608	0.9624	0.9609
50—54 to 55—59	0.9312	0.9335	0.9319	0.9381	0.9403	0.9383
55—59 to 60—64	0.8925	0.8956	0.8935	0.9019	0.9050	0.9021
60—64 to 65—69	0.8375	0.8416	0.8388	0.8497	0.8538	0.8500
65—69 to 70—74	0.7624	0.7672	0.7639	0.7770	0.7820	0.7774
70—74 to 75+	0.5524	0.5564	0.5536	0.5689	0.4689	0.5650

* The values in this column are obtained as

Col. (3)=0.31 * (2)+0.69 * (1)

Col. (6)=0.07 * (5)+0.93 * (4)

TABLE 9.2

Projected Population of India, 1986 and 1981

Age group	*Population 1981 in '000's*	*Survival ratio 1981-86*	*Population for 1986 in '000's*	*Survival ratio 1986-91*	*Projected Population for 1991 in '000's*
0—4	46234	0.9434	48326*	0.9526	51413*
5—9	43802	0.9874	43617	0.9897	46035
10—14	40906	0.9911	43250	0.9927	43168
15—19	35947	0.9881	40542	0.9903	42934
20—24	30413	0.9864	35519	0.9889	40149
25—29	25466	0.9844	29999	0.9871	35125
30—34	21838	0.9813	25069	0.9843	29612
35—39	18968	0.9770	21430	0.9802	24675

40—44	16212	0.9700	18532	0.9736	21006
45—49	13532	0.9564	15726	0.9609	18043
50—54	10863	0.9313	12942	0.9383	15111
55—59	8588	0.8935	10123	0.9021	12143
60—64	6557	0.8388	7673	0.8500	9132
65—69	4807	0.7639	5500	0.7774	6522
70+	6653	0.5536	7533**	0.5650	8432**

*For these figures see calculations in the following pages.

**The population of 65-69 is projected to 70-74 and 70+ is projected to 75+ and then the population 70-74 and 75+ are added to get population for 70+.

(iv) Calculation of Births During 1981-91 and its Survivor

(a) Weights used in the calculation of *SAABR* are 1, 7, 7, 6 4 and 1 corresponding to 15-19 through 40-44 age groups.

Weighted sum of female population in 1981

=1*35947+7*30413+7*25466+6*21838+4*18968+1* 18532=650212

Weighted sum of female population in 1986

1*40542+7*35519+7*29999+6*25069+4*21430+1*18532 =75384

Weighted sum of female population in 1991

=1*42934+7*40149+7*35125+6*29612+4*24675+1* 21006=867230

$$\text{Births 1981 (in '000)} = SAABR\ 1981 * \frac{\text{Weighted sum of female population in 1981}}{1000}$$

$$= 34.99 * \frac{650212}{1000} = 22751$$

$$\text{Births 1986 in '000} = 31.63 * \frac{753834}{1000} = 23844$$

$$\text{Births 1991 in '000} = 28.52 * \frac{867230}{1000} = 24794$$

$$\text{Births during in '000 } 1981-86 = 5 * \frac{22751+23844}{2} = 116488$$

$$\text{Births during in '000 } 1986-91 = 5 * \frac{23844+24794}{2} = 121595$$

$$\text{Female births during } 1981-86 = 116488 * \frac{100}{206} = 56548000$$

$$\text{Female births during } 1986-91 = 121595 * \frac{100}{206} = 59027000$$

Female survival ratio from birth to 0-4 during 1981-86 =0.8546

Female population in age group 0-4 in 1986=56548000*0.8546
=48326000

Female survival ratio from 0-4 to 5-9 during 1989-91=0.9526

Female population in age group 5-9 in 1991=48326000*0.9526
=46035000

Female survival ratio from birth to 0-4 during 1986-91
=0.8710

Female population in age group 0-4 in 1991=59027000*0.8710
=514300

Calculation of Births Using GMFR

GMFR in 1981=205 births per 1000 married women in 15-49 age group.

Annual per cent change in *GMFR*=2.2.

Projected *GMFR* for 1986 and 1991 are as below :

Year	*GMFR*
1986	182=205 (1−0.022*5)
1991	162=205 (1−0.022*10)

Calculation of *GFR* for 1981, 1986 and 1991 :

Year	*GMFR*	Proportion Married Females (15-49)	*GFR*
	(1)	(2)	(3)=(1*2)
1981	205	0.8048	165
1986	182	0.7925	145
1991	162	0.7832	127

Total number of women in the age group (15-49) in 1981
=148844000

Total number of women in the age group (15-49) in 1986
=171091000

Total number of women in the age group (15-49) in 1991
=193501000

$$\text{Total number of births in 1981} = \frac{148844000*165}{1000}$$
$$= 24559260$$

$$\text{Total number of births in 1986} = \frac{171091000*145}{1000}$$
$$= 24808195$$

$$\text{Total number of births in 1991} = \frac{193501000*127}{1000}$$
$$= 24574627$$

Total number of births during 1981-86

$$= (24559260 + 24808195)* \frac{5}{2}$$
$$= 123418640$$

Total number of births during 1986-91

$$= (24808195 + 24574627)* \frac{5}{2}$$
$$= 123457060$$

Total number of female births in 1981-86

$$= 123418640* \frac{100}{206} = 59911961$$

Total number of female births in 1986-91

$$= 123457060* \frac{100}{206}$$
$$= 59930612$$

For estimating the female population in the age groups 0-4 and 5-9 in 1986 and 1991 one should follow similar procedure as described in the case of *SAABR*.

Example 4

In last example we have seen how the number of births are calculated for each 5 years interval using *SAABR*, *GFR*, and *GMFR*. Now let us do the same exercise when *TFR* is given for 1981, 1986 and 1991. Since 1981 is our base year, we have *ASFR* also for 1981 as given below :

Age group :	15-19	20-24	25-29	30-34	35-39	40-44	45-49
ASFR (1981)	90.4	246.9	232.1	167.7	102.5	44.0	19.6

Projected *TFRs* are observed as 4.27 and 4.04 respectively for 1986 and 1991 by assuming 2 per cent annual linear decline observed during 1971-81. Now *ASFR* for 1986 and 1991 can be estimated by multiplying 1981 *ASFR* by the ratio *TFR* (86)/*TFR* (81) and *TFR* (91)/*TFR* (81) respectively. Here assumption is that the age pattern of fertility does not change during 1981-91. In otherwords, *ASFRs* decline in same proportion for all the age groups.

The estimated *ASFRs* are :

Age	15-19	20-24	25-29	30-34	35-39	40-44	45-49
ASFR (86)	85.8	234.3	220.2	259.1	97.3	41.8	18.6
ASFR (91)	81.2	221.7	208.4	150.6	92.0	39.5	17.6

Now the births for 1981-86 and 1986-91 are calculated as follows :

Total births in 1981=0.0904*35947000+0.2469*30413000+0.2321*25466000+0.1677*21838000+0.1025*18968000+0.0440*16212000+0.0196*13532000=23254245.

Total births in 1986=0.0858*40542000+0.2343*35517000+0.2202*29999000+0.1591*25069000+0.0973*21430000+0.0418*18532000+0.0186*15726000=25557330.

Total births in 1991=0.0812*42934000+0.2217*40149000+0.2084*35125000+0.1506*29612000+0.0920*24675000+0.0395*21006000+0.0176*18043000=27585285.

Total births during 1981-86 $=(23254245+25557330)*\frac{5}{2}$

$=122028940$

Total births during 1986-91 $=(25557330+27584285)*\frac{5}{2}$

$=132854040$

Total female births during 1981-86 $=122028940*\frac{100}{206}$

$=59237345$

Total female births during 1986-91 $=132854040*\frac{100}{206}$

$=64492252$

Again 0-4 and 5-9 populations in 1986 and 1991 can be obtained as described in example 1.

Example 5

Let us take net reproduction rate (*NRR*) for projection of population in example 1. Assume that *NRR* of 1981 reduces to unity by 2001. Use e_0^0 and *ASFR* given in example 1 and 2 respectively.

In this case, we may take *NRR* for 1981 and one as in 2001 and interpolate *NRR* for the intermediate periods assuming linear or exponential pattern of change. The interpolated *NRR* is then converted into *TFR* and *ASFR* of 1981 is adjusted as in example 4 to obtain *ASFR* for other periods. The rest of steps are similar to example 4. However, it has been observed that linear or exponential change in *NRR* does not ensure similar change in *TFR*. It would therefore, be better to estimate the trends in *TFR* directly as given below.

We know that :

$$NRR_{2001}=1$$

$$GRR=\left[\frac{l_T}{l^o}\right]*NRR \qquad \ldots(16)$$

Where T is the mean length of generation which would be approximated by mean age of Child bearing. It varies between 26 to 31 years. The l_T can be estimated from some suitable life tables.

From equation (16)

$$GRR_{2001}=\frac{NRR}{l_T} \qquad l_o=1$$

If we assume $T=30$ then $l_T=0.85756$

Corresponding to $e_0^0=62$ Years.

o, $$GRR_{2001}=\frac{1}{0.85756}=1.17 \text{ per woman}$$

Now,

$$TFR_{2001} = GRR\ 2001 * (1 + \text{Sex Ratio at birth})$$
$$= GRR\ 2001 * 2.06$$
$$= 1.17 * 2.06$$
$$= 2.41 \text{ per woman.}$$

It means that TFR of 4.5 in 1981 declines to 2.41 in 20 years leading to annual decline of 0.1045 units linearly. This would give the TFR of 3.9775 for 1986 and 3.455 for 1991. One can also interpolate these values with exponential or geometric growth model. With exponen tial growth, we get following estimates :

$$TFR_{2001} = TFR_{1981}\ e^{20r}$$

or,

$$r = \frac{1}{20} ln\ \frac{2.41}{2.45} = -0.03122$$

So,

$$TFR_{1986} = 4.5 \quad e^{-5 * 0.03122}$$
$$= 4.5 * 0.85547$$
$$= 3.8496$$

and,

$$TFR_{1991} = 4.5 \quad e^{-10 * 0.03122}$$
$$= 4.5 * 0.73184$$
$$= 3.2933$$

After estimating TFRs, we can follow the procedure of example 4 to get the female populations of 0–4 and 5–9 age groups.

9.2 Sub-National Poulation Projection

The national population projection are required for determining the overall targets for various componets of the developmental plan. But the implementation of such plans largely depends on the projection of population by sub-national areas or by some socio-economic groups of population. The sub-national areas may be States, Districts, Tehsils, Towns, Rural-Urban etc. The planning for future requirements of the smaller areas for food, housing, education, medical facilities, transport and other amenities would heavily depend on the projected population. Therefore, such projections are most useful and critical for regional development planning which help in reducing the disparities among the different regions within the country.

There are a number of other sub-categories of the population which are recognized as of special importance in the demographic and socio-economic planning and consequently, in population projection. Some of these categories are ;

1. Labour force population
2. Rural—Urban population
3. Agricultural and non-agricultural population
4. Population by Educational attainment level.

Since agriculture is still the largest sector of the economy in most of the developing countries, projections of agricultural population are essential for the preparation of development plans. At the same time with faster growth in urban population rural-urban projections are also essential for planning future investments by the government. The development of educational planning also requires the more detailed and comprehensive projection of school enrolments and total populations by educational attainment.

The task of sub-national population projection is more complicated than national population projection. Even the reliability of projection for sub-national areas is comparatively less and the projcctions vary according to the type of area. However, as area becomes smaller and smaller, complexity increases as smaller units are frequently subject to boundary changes. Boundry changes and related statistics constitute another difficult factor which must be settled before the preparation of subnational poulation projection.

In the present section, we would discuss only those methods which are commonly used in the sub national population projection. There are a number of procedures for projecting sub-national population. Some methods may be dependent on national population (larger units) projection whereas some may be independent. The mathematical methods which are discussed earlier may be effectively used for projecting sub-national population and these methods are independent of the national population projection. There is another group of methods which may be termed as Ratio type methods. The main methods for projection are :

1. Ratio Method
2. Apportionate Method
3. *URGD* Method
4. Regression Method

Now we discuss these methods separately with illustration of their applications.

9.2.1 Ratio Method

As mentioned earlier, the mathematical methods are independent of the national population projection. Due to this, the sum of sub-national projected population does not equal to the national population already known or projected. In case of ratio-type method, this consistency is assured as the national population is taken into consideration while projecting sub-national population.

In the ratio method, the proportion of population in smaller area to national population is calculated for past census years and changes in proportion are examined. The simplest method may be to assume the proportion observed in the latest census to hold true for future dates also. Under this assumption, the population for smaller area can be obtained by multiplying national population already prcjected to the proportion for that area by the latest census. The implication of such assumption is that each sub-national area is growing with the same growth rate as that of the national population. This simple method may be quite useful in short-term projection.

Let P^t be the total population of a country at time t and P_i^t be the total population of ith area (State, district, etc.)

The ratio R_i^t is defined as

$$R_i^t = \frac{P_i^t}{P^t}$$

If we assume that the ratio R_i^t observed at the time of last census remains constant for next 10 years, and P^{t+10} is the projected population of the country at time $t+10$, then the projected population of the ith region is

$$P_i^{t+10} = P^{t+10} * R_i^t$$

The above assumption may not hold true because some regions may be growing faster than other due to disparities in development. So one has to take into account the changes in proportions over a period of time in the past and state the assumption for the future. Now let us assume that we have census data for 1971 and 1981. So the ratio could be calculated as

$$R^{71}{}_i = \frac{P_i^{71}}{P^{71}} \text{ and } \sum_{i=1}^{n} R^{71}{}_i = 1$$

$$R^{81}{}_i = \frac{P^{81}{}_i}{P^{81}} => \sum_{i=1}^{n} R^{81}{}_i = 1$$

if there are n regions,

For projecting R_i, for future date we can assume linear or ary other form of changes in R_i over 1971-81.

For linear change, R_i for 1991 can be estimated as :

$$\bar{R}_i^{91} = R_i^{81}\left[1 + \frac{R_i^{81} - R_i^{71}}{10} \times 10\right]$$

since $\sum_i R_i^{91} \neq 1$

in the above case we need to adjust the individual ratios. The adjusted ratio is as given below,

$$\bar{R}_i^{91} = R_i^{91} * \frac{1}{S^{91}}$$

where

$$S^{91} = \sum \bar{R}_i^{91}$$

and therefore the population for 1991 can be estimated as :

$$P_i^{91} = \bar{R}_i^{91} * P^{91} \qquad ...(17)$$

In case we have more than two censuses a straight line can be fitted to the ratios against time. With the help of fitted line, we can directly estimate $R(i)$ for future time. However, there is good chance that past trend in ratio may be stopped or reversed through government policy or circumstances of particular area. Nevertheless, for short-term projection it is always suggested that the rate of change in R_i should be taken with respect to the latest census.

9.2.2 Projection of Age-Sex Composition of the Sub-National Population

The projection of age-sex distribution of sub-national population is very complex not only due to non-availability of reliable data on fertility and mortality but also due to greater role of migration influencing population. Therefore, age sex distribution of sub-national population should be projected for short-term. All the mathematical methods discussed earlier can be used in the projection of age-sex distribution by using age-specific growth rate. The ratio-type methods can also be used under the knowledge of projected age sex distribution of the national population.

The simplest method may be the use of ratio of proportion of population in each age-sex group for sub-national to the corresponding proportion at national level. For example the ratio for 5-9 age group may be given as :

$$R'_{5-9} = \frac{P'_{5-9}}{P^n_{5-9}}$$

The above ratio for each age group may then be projected under one of the following assumptions :

(*i*) The ratio will not change.

(*ii*) The ratio will change according to the last intercensal period.

(*iii*) The ratio will change according to some other rule like ratio would approach to unity by some time in future.

Once the ratio is projected, one can get the proportionate distribution of a population by applying already projected proportionate distribution of national population. It may be remembered that the projected distribution may not add to unity and therefore they have to be adjusted Proportionate adjustment for all areas at each age to the national total at that age, and of the age-sex total for each area has to be done. This type of adjustment may have to be iterated for number of times until full or nearly full agreement is achieved. Thus method is known as method of iterative proportions or two-way raking. The final results are utilized as a basis for the projections at the next projection date by the same procedure.

There is another procedure in which two-way raking method is used. In the second ratio type method, the male and female population at each age in the national population are distributed by areas according to the areal distribution in the last census and the results of overall ages are then adjusted proportionately to the total population. The adjustment is again carried out for full or nearly full agreement of the marginal totals.

Example 6 :

Project the total population of three divisions of Uttar Pradesh namely Uttarakhand, Meerut and Varanasi for 1986-2001 using ratio method under the following conditions :

(*a*) When only two census figures are available.

(*b*) When more than two census figures are available.

(*c*) Use of two Census totals of 1971 and 1981.

Step 1

Estimate percentage of population in these divisions for 1971 and 1981 as follows :

$$R_i = \frac{\text{Population of Uttarakhand } (i)}{\text{Population of Utter Pradesh}}$$

The estimated figures are given in following table :

TABLE 9.3

Percentage of U.P. Population in Three Division of Utter Pradesh for 1971 and 1981

Division	1971	1981	*Annual per cent change* (R_0)*
Uttarakhand	0.97	0.94	−0.3141
Meerut	11.18	11.44	0.2299
Varanasi	10.78	10.97	0.1747

* Percent annual change for Uttarakhand

$$= \frac{0.94-0.97}{0.94+0.97} * \frac{2}{10}$$

$$= -0.3141.$$

Step 2

Using annual change, project percentage of population for future date in each division. The projection of percentage can be done as follows :

$$R_i^{t+k} = R_i^t\left[1+\frac{R_0}{100}\right]^k$$

where k is the projection period.

thus, $$R^{86}{}_{i}=R^{81}{}_{i}\left[1+\left(\frac{-0.3141}{100}\right)\right]^{5}$$

$$=.94(1-0.003141)^{5}$$

$$=0.93$$

The estimated proportion up to 2001 are given below :

TABLE 9.4

The Projected Percentage for Three Divisions of Utter Pradesh

Division	1986	1991	1996	2001
Uttarakhand	0.93	0.91	0.90	0.88
Meerut	11.57	11.71	11.84	11.98
Varanasi	11.07	11.16	11.26	11 36

Step 3

For estimating the Population upto 2001, the above percentages are multiplied with State (U.P.) total population which is taken from Expert committee on Population projection of the Registrar General, India for the period 1986-2001. The results are given in Table 9.5.

TABLE 9.5

The Projected Population of Three Division of Utter Pradesh

Division	1986	1991	1996	2001
Uttarakhand	1144307*	1241902	1357917	1457490
Meerut	14236168	15980953	17864156	19841743
Varanasi	13620949	15230353	16989054	18814875
State Population	123043800	136472700	150879700	165623900

$$*\ \frac{0.93 * 123043800}{100}$$

(*b*) Use of More Than Two Censuses

In this, we must carefully examine the trends in ratio over a period of time and assign the trends according to changes inthe past. Once trends in terms of annual change in ratios are fixed, the ratios and population can be projected as shown in the last example.

9.2.3. Apportionment Method

This is a mathematical method of estimating or projecting sub-national population. This was used by U.S. Bureau of the census in estimating State population. This method is same as Water method used by R.G. India (1987) in projection of districts population of India. The apportionment method is approximately equivalent to arithmetic method. The main difference between the two methods is that in the apportionment method, total of projected sub-national population equals to the country's population whereas it is not the case with the arithmetic method. Let us illustrate the technique with notations :

Area	*Population* *t*	*t+10*	*Difference*	*Proportion*	*Estimated Difference t+10 to t+20*
1	P_1	P'_1	$P'_1-P_1=A_1$	$B_1=A_1/C$	$B_1 * D$
2	P_2	P'_2	$P'_2-P_2=A_2$	$B_2=A_2/C$	$B_2 * D$
3	P_3	P'_3	$P'_3-P_3=A_3$	$B_3=A_3/C$	$B_3 * D$
•	•	•	•	•	•
•	•	•	•	•	•
Country	P	P′	$P'-P=C$	1	$D=P''-P'$

where P″ is the country's population for $t+20$.

For estimating population for each area at time $t+10$, we have to add figure in last column to population of respective area at time $t+10$. So for first area we have

$$P''_1=P'_1+B_1 * D$$

In general the above method can be written as

$$P_i^{t+20}=P_i^{t+10}+\left[\frac{P_i^{t+20}-P^t_i}{P^{t+10}-P^t}\right] * (P^{t+20}-P^{t+10})$$

$$P_i^{t+20}=(1+k)P_i^{t+10}-kP^t_i \qquad \text{...(18)}$$

where $$k=\frac{P^{t+20}-P^{t+10}}{P^{t+10}-P^t}$$

Here it may be noted that t and $t+10$ are actual census years where $t+20$ is the year to which population at the sub-national is projected. Here P^{t+20}, *i.e.*, national population is independently projected. It may be clearly seen that the ratio increase in population between two intercensal periods at national and sub-national levels are the same.

Urban-Rural Growth Difference (URGD) Method :

The URGD method is basically develeped to project Urban and Rural population when total is already projected. But the concept of this method can be exteneded to project the sub-national population when national population is known. Let us assume that urban-rural population are growing exponentially. Hence

$$P^t(U)=P^\circ(U)\ e^{rt} \qquad \text{...(19)}$$

$$P^t(R)=P^\circ(R)\ e^{r't} \qquad \text{...(20)}$$

where $P^t(\text{R})$ and $P^\circ(R)$ are the rural population at time t and o respectively. $P^t(\text{U})$ and $P^\circ(\text{U})$ are the urban population at time t and o respectively. r and r' are the exponential growth rates of urban and rural population respectively. The ratio of (19) to (20) above can be given as:

$$S(t)=\frac{P^t(\text{U})}{P^t(\text{R})}=\frac{P^\circ(U)}{P^\circ(R)} \quad \frac{e^{rt}}{e^{rt}}$$

$$S(t)=S(o)\ e^{(r-r')t}$$

$$\text{...(21)}$$

where $=r-r'$ Urban-Rural Growth Difference

It can be seen from the above equation that the ratio of two populations, also grows exponentially. The proportion of urban population to total population can be defined as :

$$U(t)=\frac{P^t(\text{U})}{P^t(\text{U})+P^t(\text{R})}$$

$$=\frac{S(t)}{1+S(t)}$$

By substituting the value of $S(t)$ from equation (21) we get :

$$U(t) = \frac{1}{1 + A\,e^{-gt}} \qquad \text{...(22)}$$

where $g = r - r'$ and

$$A = \frac{1}{S(o)}$$

Thus, if ratio of urban to rural population is growing exponentially, the proportion of urban population in total population would increase according to the logistic growth curve.

For projecting the proportion of urban population using equation (21), we may assume

1. Constant value of g at the level observed for the recent period. or,

2. The changing value of g.

The projection with constant value of g would come out to be too high as urban-rural growth difference can not remain constant but narrow down over a period of time. The error may be more for those countries where g is large and proportion urban is low. To overcome this problem, U.N. (1984) has derived a mechanism which ensures a decline in g as the level of urbanization increases.

With the empirical analysis of 110 countries around 1960 and 1970, U.N. (1980, 1984) provided the following linear relationship :

$$g_h = 0.044 - 0.028\,U(o) \qquad \text{...(23)}$$

where g_h : hypothetical value of the urban-rural growth difference,

and

$U(o)$: initial proportion urban.

The urban-rural growth difference at any point of time can be estimated as :

$$g^t = W_1^t g_o + (1 - W_1^t) g_h \qquad \text{...(24)}$$

The value of weights over time are given below :

Time Interval	1975-80	80-85	85-90	90-95	95-2000	2020-25
W_1	0.8	0.6	0.4	0.2	0	0

It can be seen from the above that more weight is given to the latest value of g but with time, g_h is given more weight.

We do not have any specific method to estimate these weights and hence these lead to the arbitrary weighting. This may introduce sudden shift in the growth rate which can not be explained. In the recent publication, U.N. has just shifted the weight, for recent periods.

The value of weights becomes as follows :

Time Interval	80-85	85-90	90-95	95-2000......	2020-25
W_1	0.8	0.6	0.4	0.2	0

Nevertheless, *URGD* is one of the most appropriate methods available for projecting urban population.

Example 7 :

Project the urban population of India for 1991 using the Urban-Rural growth difference (*URGD*) method from following information :

Census	Population		
	Total	Rural	Urban
1981	665287849	507607678	157680171
1971	533202110	425415114	107786996

Solution :

From the above information we get the annual rate of exponential change, which is discussed earlier. The exponential annual growth rates for period 1971-81 for Rural is 0.0177 and for Urban is 0.0380.

(*I*) With constant g

$$U(t)=\frac{1}{1+Ae^{-g*t}}$$

where

$$A=\frac{1}{S(o)},$$

here '*o*' refers to 1981.

To solve the equation (22) we have to first calculate A and then g.

Therefore

$$A=\frac{1}{S(o)}$$

where

$$S(o)=\frac{P^{o}(U)}{P^{o}(R)}$$

$$S(o)=\frac{157680171}{507607678}=0.3106$$

so

$$A=\frac{1}{S(o)}=\frac{1}{0.3106}=3.2196$$

and g=(Urban, Rural) Growth Difference.

$$=0.0380-0.0177=0.0203$$

By substituting the value of A and g in the equation (22), we get,

$$U(t)=\frac{1}{1+3.2196\,e^{-.0203t}}$$

when $t=10$

$$U(1991)=\frac{1}{1+3.2196\,e^{-0.0203*10}}$$

$$=\frac{1}{1+3.2196*0.8163}$$

$$=\frac{1}{1+2.6281}$$

$$=\frac{1}{3.6281}=0.2756 \qquad \ldots(A)$$

(*II*) We with changing g. Use U.N. linear relationship to estimate $g(t)$ as :

$$g_h = 0.044 - 0.028\ U(o)$$

where $U(o)$ = initial proportion of Urban.

$$g^t = W_1^t\, g_o + (1 - W_1^t) g_h$$

We first calculate

$$U(o) = \frac{157680171}{665287849} = 0.2370$$

substituting the value in the equation (23) we get,

$$\begin{aligned} g_h &= 0.044 - 0.028 * U(o) \\ &= 0.044 - 0.028 * 0.2370 \\ &= 0.044 - 0.0066 = 0.0374 \end{aligned}$$

Now substituting the values of g_h and g_o in the equation (24) for 1981-86 and W_1^t as 0.8 for 80-85 (weights are given earlier in the text).

We get,

$$\begin{aligned} g^{86} &= 0.8 * 0.0203 + [1 - 0.8] * 0.0374 \\ &= 0.0162 + 0.2 * 0.0374 \\ &= 0.0162 + 0.0075 = 0.0237 \end{aligned}$$

For 1991

$$\begin{aligned} g^{91} &= 0.6 * 0.0203 + [1 - 0.6] * 0.0374 \\ &= 0.0122 + 0.4 * 0.0374 \\ &= 0.0122 + 0.0150 = 0.0272 \end{aligned}$$

Substituting both the values of $g(t)$ separately in the equation (22) we get,

$$\begin{aligned} U(86) &= \frac{1}{1 + 3.2196^{-0.0237 * 5}} \\ &= \frac{1}{1 + 3.2196 * 0.8883} \\ &= \frac{1}{1 + 2.8598} = \frac{1}{3.8598} = 0.2591 \qquad (B.1) \end{aligned}$$

and

$$U(91) = \frac{1}{1+3.2196 * e^{-0.0272 * 10}}$$

$$= \frac{1}{1+3.2196 * 0.7619}$$

$$= \frac{1}{1+2.4529} = \frac{1}{3.4529} = 0.2896 \qquad (B.II)$$

To obtain the population of urban area for 1986 and 1991, $U(86)$ and $U(91)$ can be multiplied with the total population of India for corresponding period which is taken from the expert committee on the Population projections, Occasional Papers No. 4 of 1988, R.G. of India, New Delhi.

Urban Population in 1986

$$= 0.2591 * 761070100 = 197193263$$

Urban Population in 1991

$$= 0.2896 * 837249400 = 242467426$$

9.2.5 Regression Method

It is well known fact that the component of population growth -- fertility, mortality and migration are affected by socio-economic development. A number of methods have been developed which employ socio-economic variables directly in the context of ratio, component or correlation method or a combination of these methods. The regression method can be used to project the total population directly. Various forms of regression can be developed depending on the indicators of fertility and mortality selected in projection and availability of data. For example :

$$GFR = a + b\ FL5+$$

$$e_0^{\circ} = a' + b'\ FL5+$$

where $FT5+$: female literacy above age 5 years.

In this method, first independent variables have to be projected and then using the regression one can easily estimate the projected indicators. This is done under the assumption that there is no change in the structural relationship over time and space. This assumption may not be true in the long term. Therefore, this approach can be used only in the short-term projection. The regression approach has not been vary successful especially at the sub-national level because the association between the indices of vital rates and socio-economic indicators are not conclusive. The factors responsible for the changes may be different in different areas and periods.

9.3 Projection of Special Categories of the Population

In addition to sub-national population projections, projections for specific categories of the population like labor force, school going children etc. are also required. For each special category to be projected, the total population already projected is used. The sex-age category specific rates are first projected using either past trend or the patterns from similar countries at higher level of development or any other method. The projected specific rates are then multiplied with total population already projected. For detailed methodolgy of such projection one can see elsewhere [see U.N., (1971), for labor force projection]

Here we briefly discuss the method of projecting the Economically Active Population (Only labor supply).

9.3.1 Methods of Projecting Labour Supply

Labour supply projection are the product of two separate projections namely

1. Projection of population by age and sex and
2. Projection of age sex-specific activity rates.

The anticipated changes in the size and composition of the total population have a direct influence on labour force projections especially in long-term projections. If the projection is for a period of 10 years, changes in fertility rates need not be taken into account since all the persons who would enter in working age groups will have been born when projection is made. Projection of mortality and migration would play an important role. So the quality of labour supply projections would depend on the quality of population projection by age and sex.

On the other hand, changes in activity rates by age-sex are brought about by a whole range of economic and social factors such as

(*i*) the number and type of jobs created

(*ii*) school enrolment trends

(*iii*) age at marriage

(*iv*) number of children

(*v*) educational level and so on.

It is very difficult to ascertain the influence of all these factors on activity rates. Infact, the activity rates evolve gradually under the pressure of the various changes—social and economic. Further, it is difficult to get the reliable time series data for developing countries. Therefore, methods of projecting labour supply will vary according to the level of development of the country concerned, the quality of the statistics available and dominant occupations. There are four principal methods which are based on one of the following assumptions:

(*a*) The future trends in activity rates would be same as in the recent past.

(*b*) Current activity rates will be constant,

(*c*) Activity rates in future years will be same as those of other advanced countries or the same as current rates in the more developed area of the country under study,

(*d*) Activity rates will be the function of the economy, growth of the urban population, the development of the pension system, nuptiality and fertility rates.

9.3.2 Extr[illegible]tion Method

(a) Direct Extrapolation by Age and Sex

Let $A(x, t)$ be the activity rate at age x and time $t = 0, 1, 2,$ for given sex. Here 0 and 1 are the beginning and end of base period and 2 denotes the end of the projection period. Further the length between the period 0 and 1 is called base period and between 1 and 2 is called projection period. These two periods may be the same. If they are not same, some adjustment in projection has to be made. The extrapolation formula is as follows :

$$A(x, 2) = A(x, 1) * \frac{100 + \Delta A(x, 0,1)}{100}$$

$$= A(x, 1) \left[1 + \frac{\Delta A(x, 0, 1)}{100} \right]$$

where

$$\Delta A(x, 0,1) = \frac{A(x,1)}{A(x,0)} * \left[\frac{A(x,1) * U(x,1)}{A(x,0) * U(x,0)} \right]$$

or,

$$\Delta A(x\ 0, 1) = 1 + \left[\frac{A(x,1)}{A(x,0)} - 1 \right] \left[\frac{A(x,1) * U(x,1)}{A(x,0) * U(x,0)} \right]$$

and $U(x\ t)$ is the inactivity rate at age x and time t for given sex.

The quantity in the braket is known as correction factor. The correction factor is important generally in long term projection. If they are not used, we would get absurd result. In short-term projection it may not be necessary to use correction factor.

(b) Indirect Extrapolation by Age Sex

This method is recommended when activity rates are increasing gradually as may be the case in female activity rate. In this method, inactivity rates are extrapolated instead of activity rates. So we may get as :

$$A(x,1) = 100 - u(x,1) * d$$

where

$$d = \frac{u(x,1)}{u(x,0)}$$

Here again correction factor can be used in similar way as discussed in the previous method.

(c) Extrapolation by Cohort

In this case, the formula for extrapolation is as follows :

$$A(x,2)=A(x,1) * \frac{A(x,1)}{A(x,0)}$$

The above equation is based on the assumption that the pattern of change in activity rates of a given age group or cohort during projection period would be same as that observed during the base period. This method may be more useful in projecting the female activity rates.

Almost similar type of method is developed by International Labour Organization Office and interested readers are advised to see U.N. (1971).

Methods of the projection discussed in this chapter are certainly not exhaustive. There can be numerous new ways of projecting the future population. Nevertheless, the procedures discussed here are quite general and may be suitably modified to suit the specification for the future trend of population change. By no means projection of fertility and mortality trends beyoud 15 years will be so accurate. Once the second generation starts entering i. to the reproductive span, the prediction of fertility level and pattern becomes difficult as the babies born during the projection period are governed by different socio-economic and political conditions. Even the nuptiality pattern is likely to undergo change drastically. It will not be out of place to mention that projections are after all manifestation of the assumptions and the existing facts on population at the base period. Even if the total population at the subsequent census, does not tally with the projected one, it should not be seriously taken. While mathematical methods require only to be accurate with respect to the total population, the component methods of projection require to be consistent with respect to internal composition of the population at future date.

In the recent years, family planning programme under the government population policy is considercd to be one of the most important factors influencing fertility. Therefore it becomes necessary to consider family planning as an input in the projection of fertility trends for the future dates. The relationship between fertility and the family planning performance has to be established first and then after projecting future family planning progress one can assess the future levels of fertility. For details one can see Expert Committee Projection of population for India on the basis of 1981 census. [Census of India 1981 Occassional Paper No. 4. of 1988, Report of the Export Committee on the Population Projection. Office of the R G. India, Ministry of Home Affairs, New Delhi]. However the projection of fertility either based on past trends or on the basis of trends in family Planning performance (for example Couple Protection rate) may not be very different if long-term target (say NRR=1 by 2000) is already fixed. But in case of couple protection rate projection and its relation with fertility, one may consider the commensurate changes in general Marital fertility rates. In this index, we may introduce the effect of change in marriage pattern also.

In [illegible] years, [illegible] have [illegible] the government population policy is considered to be one of the most important [illegible] & [illegible]? Therefore [illegible] necessary to consider [illegible] planning [illegible] upon the [illegible] for the future [illegible]. The [illegible] and the [illegible] has to be established first and then [illegible] [illegible] one [illegible] the [illegible] of fertility [illegible] and [illegible] (Indian [illegible]) [illegible] No. [illegible] Population [illegible] Bombay [illegible] However the [illegible] of [illegible] fertility [illegible] [illegible] trends in fertility [illegible] (for example Census [illegible]) may not be very [illegible] [illegible] [illegible] for [illegible] of couple [illegible] and [illegible] fertility [illegible] fertility [illegible] the [illegible] [illegible] [illegible].

APPENDIX A

EVALUATION AND ADJUSTMENT OF DEMOGRAPHIC DATA

1. Introduction

Demographic data whether they are obtained by enumeration, registration, sample survey or any other means are affected by various type of errors. The evaluation of data therefore becomes important in order to get reliable estimate of population size of a particular group or area and also reliable estimate of population growth. Investigation into accuracy of the data is prerequisite to any attempt at determining the reliability of the estimates. With the evaluation, it is not possible to make necessary compensating adjustments. It is not possible to have errors free data but what one should attempt is to minimise these errors. Thus, an evaluation or appraisal of the data is a prerequisite before they are utilized and interpreted.

There are two types of errors in the data: Coverage errors and content errors. Coverage deals with the completeness of enumeration or registration whereas content pertain to qualitative characteristics like age, sex, marital status, etc., of the enumerated persons. The term "errors of content" refers to instances where the characteristics of a person counted in a census enumeration or in the registration of a vital event are incorrectly reported or tabulated. Coverage errors are of two types. Individuals of a given characteristics might have been missed by the census enumerator or erroneously included twice. The first type of coverage error represents gross under-enumeration of given characteristics and the balance of the two types of coverage errors represents net under or over enumeration of a given characteristics.

The errors involved in the collection, processing and analysis of data can broadly be classified under the following two heads: Sampling errors and Non-sampling errors. Sampling errors have their origin in sampling and arise due to the fact that only a part of the population, i.e., sample has been used to estimate population parameters and draw inferences about the population. In a complete enumeration survey such errors do not exist. Sampling biases are due to the following reason:

(i) faulty selection of the sample,

(ii) substitution, and

(iii) faulty demarcation of sampling units.

Non-sampling errors primarily arise at the stage of observation, ascertainment and the processing of the data and are then present in both the complete enumeration surveys and the sample surveys. Thus, the data obtained in a complete census, although free from sampling errors, would still be subject to non-sampling errors whereas data obtained in a sample survey would be subject to both the types of errors.

2. Errors in Age Data

Demographic data tabulated by age may be affected both by errors in the reporting of ages and by variations in the completeness of enumeration or of recording of vital events for the different age groups. It means there may be errors of coverage, content, or a combination of both. Thus, in case of census data, at some ages there may be comparatively large numbers of persons who have been completely missed in the count. On the other hand, the some other age groups may contain some who should not have been counted or who have been counted twice. Also at any age, deficiency is produced by persons erroneously reporting at another age. Errors in age data may include:

(i) under-enumeration of young children (omission);

(ii) net count at the older ages; and

(iii) under-enumeration at the early adult ages.

This may happen due to the:

(i) misstatement of age (around attainment of majority, around age 65 years, and overstatement toward extreme of life);

(ii) a preference for ages ending with certain digits; and

(iii) ages unknown or not stated.

3. Evaluation of Age Data

In many populations, with a high level of literacy, most of the people are not aware about their birth dates or birth dates of the other family members and their ages. They simply cannot provide any idea about the ages of family members. When family members present at the time of interview, very often, even the interviewer make guesses of their ages and records them. However, in many instances, when it becomes impossible to guess the age, investigators records the age in the category "not stated." Many censuses have a large percentage in this category. There is also a tendency to report age into certain preferred ages or as a number ending with certain digits as 0, 5 or 2.

All errors discuss above distort the sex-age data. The sex-age distribution of the population reflects entire demographic dynamics of a given area and hence before using it for any purpose, as far as possible, it is necessary to make it free from all possible type of errors. It is quite obvious that age data when presented in a single years would indicate larger errors and fluctuation in volume as well as in proportion at different ages. This can be seen when single year returns are plotted on graph. In this type of presentation, ages are taken on X-axis and absolute number of proportions/percentages at different ages are indicated on Y-axis. Age data is generally presented in 5-years age groups as 0-4, 5-9, 10-14 ... 70+ or 80+. In such presentation, many type of errors get either eliminated or reduced. Data quality may also be reduced by taking different kind of age grouping such as 1-5, 6-10 .... etc., or 2-6, 7-11 ... etc. It is well known that population in 0-4 is always under enumerated and 5-9 has tendency of over enumeration. In 0-4 there is omission of children in addition to over-reporting of ages. There are, other than graphic representation, many measures of errors in age data that are discussed here briefly.

3.1. Whipple's Index (W.I.) of Concentration

This index is developed to measure the preference or avoidance of particular digits. Usually, it measures the extent of preference for ages ending with digits 0 and 5. The index is calculated as a ratio of persons aged 25, 30, 35, 40, 45, 50, 55 and 60 to one-fifth of the number of persons in the age group 23-62. In other words W.I. can be given as:

$$W.I. = \frac{P(25) + P(30) + P(35) + P(40) + P(45) + P(50) + P(55) + P(60)}{\frac{1}{5}\sum_{i=23}^{62} p(i)}$$

Where P (i) denote persons aged i.

The choice of the age-range 23 to 62 is largely arbitrary but found suitable in most of the cases. In computing the index of heaping, the ages of early childhood and extreme old age are often excluded, since they are more strongly affected by other types of errors of reporting than by preference for specific terminal digits.

Under the assumption that the number of persons either increase or decrease linearly as age advances, the expected value of Whipple's index ranges from 100 to 500. When the age reporting is accurate (no heaping or avoidance at any ages), then we expect the sum of persons with ages ending 0 and 5 to be exactly $^1/_5$ th of total number of persons in the age group 23 to 62 giving index value as 100. On the contrary, if we imagine the other extreme case when all people report their ages in ages ending with 0 and 5, then in such a situation, the index will be 500. However, if there is dislike or avoidance for the ages ending 0 and 5, then the index will vary between 0 to 100.

Whipple's Index is very effective measure of age accuracy as far as digit preference is concerned and can be easily computed. Its main drawback however, apart from measuring only digit preference is that it measures the preference for only two digits 0 and 5. Digit preference may be the function of culture and believes of the population which may vary from community to community.

3.2. Myer's Index

This index was developed by R.J. Myer in 1940 and reflects the preferences or dislikes for each of the 10 digits from 0 to 9. The method is based on the assumption that the number of persons by age varies linearly, i.e., the age distribution is in an arithmetic progression, i.e., from age 0 onwards, the number of persons of subsequent ages decrease by the same number. This may be true only in stable or stationary population.

The method involves the estimation of percentages of population totals for ages ending in one particular digit to the total population. For example the method determines the percentage of population for ages ending in any digit; say, 0, i.e., (10 + 20 + 30 + 40 + ...) to the total population. However, the estimation is not done in a simple way as is done in the case of Whipple's Index. The first step is the computation of a '*blended*' population in which ordinarily almost equal sum are to be expected for each digit. If this is true, the blended totals for each of the ten digits should be closed to 10 per cent of their grand total. Second step therefore is to compute deviation of each sum per cent from 10 per cent. Myer's Index is the sum of these deviation irrespective of their sign. This is calculated for ages above 10 only. The step in calculation is illustrated in Table A.1.

Table A.1 Steps in Calculation of Myer's Index

Step 1

Terminal Digit	*Persons (Male or Female) at Ages*									*Sum for Ages*	
	10-19	*20-29*	*30-39*	*40-49*	*50-59*	*60-69*	*70-79*	*90-89*	*90-99*	*10-99*	*20-99*
0											
1											
2											
3											
4											
5											
6											
7											
8											
9											
SUM											

Step 2

Terminal Digit	Ages 10-99			Ages 20-99			Blended Sum	% Dist"	Deviation from 10%
	Sum (1)	Coeff. (2)	Product (1+ 2) (3)	Sum (4)	Coeff. (5)	Product (4 × 5) (6)	(3 + 6) (7)	(7)/TOT (8)	(8) - 10 % (9)
0		1			9				
1		2			8				
2		3			7				
3		4			6				
4		5			5				
5		6			4				
6		7			3				
7		8			2				
8		9			1				
9		10			0				
SUM							Total	100.00	Absolute Sum

3.3 United Nation's Secretariat Method[1]

The United Nation's Index (sometime referred as Joint Score) combines measures of accuracy of the census age returns by age group for males and females separately with the measure of accuracy of sex ratio of different age groups. The quality of age returns by age groups is evaluated by means of age ratios from census data. An age ratio is the ratio of population of a given age group to the half of the sum of populations in the age group preceding and following age groups, expressed as per cent. The age ratio of five year age group ${}_5P_x$ is expressed as follows:

$$\frac{{}_5P_x}{\frac{1}{2} * ({}_5P_{x-5} + {}_5P_{x+5})} \times 100 \text{ ... (A)}$$

For example, Age ratio of 25 - 29 age group =

$$\frac{P_{(25-29)}}{\frac{1}{2} * (P_{20-24} + P_{30-34})} \times 100$$

It is assumed that the population in the three consecutive age groups should form a nearly linear series; and hence age ratios should be close to 100. The deviation from 100 indicates the extent of misreporting in the age group and the sum of deviations for all age groups (irrespective of sign) gives the summary measure of accuracy or misreporting of age data. Similarly, the index considers the sum of differences (irrespective of sign) in reported sex ratios of consecutive age groups from the first to the last age group as a measure of the accuracy of observed sex ratios. It is based on the assumption that these age to age changes in sex ratio should approximate to zero. Calculation is illustrated in Table A.2.

---

1. U.N. 1952. Accuracy Tests for Census Age Distributions Tabulated in 5-year and 10-year groups. Population Bulletin, No. 2, pp. 59-79.

Table A.2 Calculation of U.N. Secretariat Method

Age Group	*Sex Ratio (M/F)*100 (1)*	*Successive Difference (2)*	*Age Ratio**		*Deviation of Age Ratio from 100*	
			Male (3)	*Female (4)*	*Male (5)*	*Female (6)*
0-4	SR_0	—	–	–	–	—
5-9	SR_1	$SR_1 - SR_0$				
10-14	SR_2	$SR_2 - SR_1$				
15-19	SR_3	$SR_3 - SR_2$				
.	.	.				
.	.	.				
.	.	.				
70-74	SR_{14}	$SR_{14} - SR_{13}$				

* As defined in equation (A)

(1) *Mean Sex Ratio Score (SRS)* $= \frac{1}{13} \Sigma\, col^n 2$

(2) *Mean Age Ratio Score for Male (ARSM)* $= \frac{1}{13} \Sigma\, col^n 5$

(3) *Mean Age Ratio Score for Female (ARSF)* $= \frac{1}{13} \Sigma\, col^n 6$

*U.N. Index = 3*SRS + ARSM + ARSF*

The United Nation's have developed criteria for judging the census age sex data as accurate, inaccurate or highly inaccurate, depending on the estimated value of the index. It is as follows:

Table A.3

Value of Index	Judgement
Below 20	Accurate
20 - 40	Inaccurate
Above 40	Highly Inaccurate

3.4 Evaluation of Age Data for Younger and Older Age Groups

So far we have discussed the evaluation of age data for population above age 10. The nature of errors in the age data in younger age groups is quite different from that in adult ages. The age data for adult ages is mostly affected by errors due to deliberate age misreporting as well as digit preference errors; however, the data in the younger ages get affected more by omission. Generally, it is observed that there is gross underenumeration of children aged 0-4 and the age group 5-9 is overestimated at the cost of 0-4 age group. In the absence of omission, population in 0-9 is said to be comparatively accurate.

Best way of evaluating the youngest age groups is to estimate the birth rates from age returns for ages 0-4 and 5-9 and 0-9 by the reverse survival method and compare them with the actual levels of birth rate (in many cases, the exact levels of birth rates may not be known, but atleast the possible range of birth rate may be known). The more or less matching of the birth rates suggest reliability of age returns. Another way of evaluating age data in younger age is to calculate birth rate from the population aged 0, i.e., P_0. This can be done when IMR is available for the study population.

Generally it has been observed that there is over statement of ages by persons above age 60 to 70 and this tendency increases with age. When we present the data as 70+ or 80+, the error is minimal but analysis of aged persons in 80-84 and 85-89 may be inflated. In such situation analysis of sex ratio among aged may be in error depending on the pattern of age reporting by sex. The adjustment of age data at these ages are generally done assuming stable population condition.

4. Methods of Adjustment for Age Sex Data

4.1. Methods of Adjusting Age Data At Younger Age Groups

As mentioned earlier, the number of children reported below age 10 are the survivals of births which occurred 10 years prior to the census. In a population, with fairly reliable birth statistics, it is possible, to correct the age groups (0-4) and (5-9) by using the survivals of births 10 years prior to the census. However, in most of the cases, where the age data are quite distorted and of doubtful quality, data on births also suffer from under reporting. If we have fairly reliable estimates of birth rates and mortality rates from some source, independent of age-distribution, then only we can adjust age data in 0-4 and 5-9 groups as:

P^{adj} (0-4) = Births (During last 5 years prior to census)* 1/Survival ratio from births to (0-4).

P^{adj} (5-9) = Births (During 5 to 10 years prior to census)* Survival ratio from birth to 5-9.

The survival ratios can be obtained from the appropriate life table. In case omission rate is available, this can also be used in adjusting population at younger ages.

4.2. Adjustment of Age Data in Adult Ages (10-74)

Theoretically, the method applied for adjusting age data should depend on the degree of inaccuracy, so that fairly accurate statistics would be modified only slightly while less accurate data would be more radically transformed. However, from the point of view of simplicity, only one smoothing procedure for age group in the age range 10 to 74 years is described here. This formula is appropriate for use where the data are markedly inaccurate. It is derived from a simple parabola and has been widely used for relatively simple work.

The formula employs five terms; that is; in order to adjust the figure for one five-year age group, data for the two preceding and the two following age groups also be inserted in the formula. If the age statistics are tabulated by five-year age group up to age 85, by such formula, adjustment can be done for all age groups up to 10 to 74. The adjustments of ages below 10 and above 74 have to be done separately.

The formula referred to as United Nation's smoothing formula is stated as follows:

$$A = \frac{1}{16}\left[-S_{-2} + 4S_{-1} + 10S + 4S_{1} - S_{2}\right]$$

Where, A is adjusted number of persons in a five-year age group for which the reported number of persons is S;

S_{-2} and S_{-1} are the reported number of persons in the two preceding five-year age groups; and

S_1, S_2 are reported number of persons in the two following age groups.

In many instances, a formula involving just three terms referred to as the 3 point formula is used for adjustment. The formula is based on the assumption that a straight line fits the best to any three consecutive points (i.e., population totals of the three consecutive age groups). The formula is:

$$A = .25 * S_{-1} + .5 * S + .25 * S_{1}$$

Where, A is the adjusted number of persons in a five-year age group for which the reported number of persons is S, S_{-1} and S_1 are the reported number of persons in the preceding and the following age group respectively.

With the adjustment of data, total population so estimated may come out to be higher than that of enumerated population. There is need for adjusting the total by a correction factor as the ratio of enumerated population to adjusted total population. Population in each age group has to be multiplied by the correction factor.

5. Dual Recording System Based on Sample Registration Areas and Surveys (Chandrashekar and Demming's Method)

In this section, we will briefly discuss the procedure to estimate the coverage of two independent systems for collecting information about demographic or other events, based on the assumption that the two system of data collection are independent of each other. When the result of two systems — six monthly survey in the sampled area and continuous vital registration in the same area are matched, it is possible to obtain a numerical estimate of the degree of completeness of both the systems and hence to estimate the true total number of events. From the matching we get the following information:

C = Number of events recorded in both registration and household survey;

N_1 = Events recorded only by registration;

N_2 = Events recorded only by the survey; and

X = Events missed by both systems (not known):

	In registration system	*Not in registration system*	*Total*
In survey	C	N_2	S
Not in survey	N_1	X*	
Total	R		N*

*Estimate.

It is clear that $(C + N_1)$ is the total number of events registered and $(C + N_2)$ is the total number of events collected by the household survey. Naturally, there is a possibility that a few events could have been missed by both the registration and the household survey. Our main objective is to estimate X i.e., number missing from both the system. If the chance of detecting an event is independent of not detecting that event for both the agencies, then we have;

$$\frac{C}{C + N_1} = \frac{N_2}{N_2 + X} = \frac{C + N_2}{C + N_1 + N_2 + X} = \frac{C + N_2}{N}$$

On rearranging and simplifying, we can get,

$$X^* = \frac{N_1 N_2}{C} \qquad (B)$$

Where, X* is an estimate of X.

This simple formula of Chandrashekar and demming has turned out to be very useful in evaluating vital registration in many cases where dual recording system is being followed.

We have thus,

$$N = C + N_1 + N_2 + \frac{N_1 N_2}{C}$$

This may be written as:

$$N = \frac{(C + N_1)(C + N_2)}{C} = \frac{RS}{C}$$

Where, R denotes the number of events recorded by registration and S denotes the number of events recorded by the household survey.

The validity of the above estimates depends on the fulfilment of the following main conditions:

(i) The matching procedure successfully identifies all true matches, and conversely, only true matches are identified as matches.

(ii) All events identified in either of the two systems are true events, i.e.. occurred in the population under investigation and in the appropriate time period.

(iii) The two systems are independent, i.e., the probability of an event being omitted from one system is not related to the chance of the event being omitted from the other system.

There are many other techniques to evaluate the response to question "births during last year" and also the completeness of civil registration data. Some of these procedures are discussed in chapter 8 and can be used in evaluation and adjustment of demographic data.

Bibliography

Agarwala, S.N. 1962, *Age at Marriage in India*. Kitab Mahal, Private Ltd., Allahabad.

Agarwala, S.N. 1972, *India's Population Problems*. Tata Mc Gram-Hill Publishing Company Limited, Bombay.

Arriaga, Eduardo, E. 1968, New Life Tables for Latin American Population in the Nineteeth and Twentieth Centuries, *Population Monographs*, Series No. 3, University of California, Berkeley.

Barclay, G.W. 1958, *Techniques of Population Analysis*, John Wiley and Sons, Inc. New York.

Beard, R.E. 1964, *International Congress of Actuaries*, 3.

Beard, R.E. 1971, Some Aspects of Theories of Mortality, Cause of Death Analysis, Forecasting and Stochastic Process, in W. Brass (ed.), *Biological Aspects of Demography*, Tylor and Francis Ltd., London.

Bhende, Asha A. and Kantikar T. 1985, *Principle of Population Studies*, Revised Edition. Himalaya Publishing House, Bombay.

Brass, W. 1968, Methods of Analysis and Estimation. In W. brass, et. al. (eds), *The Demography of Tropical Africa*, Princeton, Princeton University Press.

Brass, W. 1971, On the Scale of Mortality, in W. Brass (ed.) *Biological Aspects of Demography*, Taylor and Francis Ltd., London.

Bogue, Donald, J 1969, *Principles of Demography*, New York, John Wiley and Sons Inc.

Bourgois Pichat, J. 1951, "*La mesure de la mortalite*" *infantile* Population.

Bourgois Pichat, J. 1952, "*Analyse de la mortalite'-infantile Bulletin demographiques* (*Nations Unics*), 2.

Carrier, N. and Hobcraft J. 1971, *Demographic Estimation for Developing Societies*, A Manual of Techniques for the Detection and Reduction of Error in Demgraphic Data, London School of Economics.

Chiang, C.L. 1968, *Introduction to the Stochastic Processes in Biostatistics*, John Wiley and Sons, Inc., New York.

Cho, L.J. 1973, The Own Children Approach to Fertility Estimation : An Elaboration, *In International Population Conferences*, IUSSP, Liege, Vol. 2.

Coale, A.J. 1955, "The Calculation of Approximate Intrinsic Rates", *Population Index*, 21 (2).

Coale, A.J. 1957, "New method for Calculating Lotka", the Intrinsic Rate of Growth in a Stable Population", *Population Studies*, 11 (1).

Coale, A.J. 1972, *The Growth and Structure of Human Populations : A Mathematical Investigation*, Princeton, N.J. : Princeton University Press.

Coale, A.J. 1981, Robust Estimation of Fertility by the Use of Model Stable Population, *Asian and Pacific Census Forum*, Vol. 8 No. 2. East-West Centre, Honolulu, Hawaii.

Coale, A.J., and Demeny, P. 1967, *Regional Model Life Tables and Stable Population*, Princeton, Princeton University Press.

Coale, A.J , and Trussell, T.J. 1974, Model Fertility Schedules, Variation in the Age Structure of Childbearing in Human Population, *Population Index*, Vol. 40, No. 2.

Coale, A.J., and Trussell, T.J. 1977, Estimating the Time to which Brass Estimates Apply. *Annex* 1, in *Population Bulletin of the United Nations*, No. 10.

Dandekar, V.M. 1955, Certain modified forms of Binomial and Poisson distribution, *Sankhya*, Vol. 15.

Duncan, O.D. 1957, "The Measures of Population Distribution", *Population Studies*, 11 (1).

El. Badry, M.A. 1961, Failure of Enumerators to Make Entries of Zero, Errors in Recording Caildless Cases in Population Censuses, Journal of *American Statistical Association* Vol. 56.

Feeney, G. 1975, Estimation of Infant Mortality from Children Surviving Data, *Asian and Pacific Census Newsletter* Vol. 3 (2).

Feeney, G. 1980, Estimating Infant Mortality Trends from Children Surviving Data, *Population, Studies.* Vol. 34, No. 1.

Fix, E. and Neyman, J. 1951, A simple stochastic model of recovery, relapse, death and loss of patients, *Human Biology*, Vol. 23.

Gibbs, J.P. 1966, "Measures of Urbanization", *Social forces*, 45 (2), University of North Carolina Press.

Goodman, L.A. 1961, Some Possible Effects of birth Control on human Sex Ratio, *Annals of Human Genetics*, Vol. 25.

Goodman, L.A. 1961, Statistical Method for The Mover-Stayer Models. *Journal of the Americal Statistical Association* Vol. 56, No. 2.

Greville, T.N.S. 1943, Short Methods of Constructing Abridged life tables, *Record of the American Institute of Acutuaries*, 32, Reproduced in U.S. Brueau of the Census, Handbook of Statistical Methods for Demographers.

Hajnal, J. 1953, Age at Marriage and Proportion Marrying, *Population Studies* Vol. 7, No. 2.

Halley, E. 1693, An estimate of the Degree of the Mortality of Man Kind, Drawn from Curious Tables of the Births and Funerals of the City of Breslen, *Philosophical transactions of the Royal Society of London*, Vol. 17.

Henry, L. 1953, Fecondements theories des measwres de la fecondite Naturalle, *Revve de L. Institute International de Statistigue* Vol. 21.

Hobcraft, J.N. and Chidambaram, P. 1982, Advances in the P/F Ratio Method for the Analysis of Birth Histories, *Population Studies*, Vol. 36, No. 2.

Johnson, R.C Elandt and Norman L. John son 1980, *Survival Models and data Analysis*, John Wiley and Sons, New York.

Kendall, D.G. 1949, *Stochastic Processes and Population' Growth*, Journal of the Royal Statistical Society, B.

Keyfitz, N. 1966, The life Table that agrees with the data *Journal of the American Statistical Association*, Vol. 61.

Keyfitz, N. 1968, The Life Table that agrees with the data II *Journal of the American Statistical Association*, Vol. 63.

Keyfitz, N. 1971, Models. *Demography* 8. (4).

Keyfitz, N. 1977a, *Introduction to the Mathematics of Population (with revisions)*, Addison Wesley Publishing Company, California.

Keyfitz, Nathan. 1977b, *Applied Mathematical Demography*, John Willy and Sons, New York, London.

Kitagawa, E.M. 1964, "*Standardised Comparisons in Population Research*, Demography, Vol. 1.

Krishnamoorthy, S. 1974, Effects of sex P. reference and mortality on family size, *Demography India*. Vol. 3.

Kuznets, S and Ernest Rubin. 1954, Immigration and the Foreign Born, *Occasional Paper* No. 46, New York, National Bureau of Economic Research.

Land, K.C. and Rogers, A. 1982, Multidimensional Mathematical Demography. *Academic Press*, New York, London.

Lee, E.S. 1966, A Theory of Migration, *Demography*, Vol. 3, No. 1.

Ledermann, S. 1969, *Nouvellers Tables—Types de Mortality*, Paries Press Univer_titaires de France.

Lewis, W.A. 19:4. Economic Development with Unlimited Supplies of Labour, in *The Manchester School of Economic and Social Studies*, Vol. 22.

Lopez Alvars, 1961, *Problems in Stable Population Theory*, Office of Population Research, Princeton University.

McDonald, J. 1973, Sex Predetermination : Demographic Effects, *Mathematical Bioscience*, Vol. 17.

McFarland, David. 1969, On the Theory of Stable Population : A New and Elementary Proof of the Theorems under Weaker Assumptions, *Demography* 6.

Mishra, B.D. 1981, *An Introduction to the Study of Population*, New Delhi : South Asian Publishers Pvt. Ltd.

Mitra, S. 1970, Preferences Regarding the Sex of Children and Their Effects on Family Size under Varying Conditions, *Sankhya* Series B, Vol. 32.

Neyman J. 1949, *On the Problem of Estimating the Number of Schools of Fish*, University of California, Publications in Statistics, Berkeley, California.

Palloni, A. and Heligman, L. 1985, Re-estimation of Structural Parameters to Obtain Estimates of Mortality in Developing Countries, *Population Bulletin of The United Nations*, Vol. No. 18.

Pathak, K.B. 1973, On a Model for Studing Variation in the Family Size under Different Sex Preferences, *Biometrics*, Vol. 29, No. 3.

Pathak, K.B. 1977, On the Sex Ratio of Children Born under Different Sex Preference and Stopping Rules. *IIPS Newsletter*.

Pathak, K.B. and Saxena, P.C. 1979, On the Time Required for Attaining tne Desired Size and Sex Composition of the Family, *Canadian Studies in Population*, Vol. 6.

Pearl, Reymond and L.J. Reed 1920, On the Role of growth of the Population of the United States since 1970 and its Mathematical representation, proceeding of *National Academy of Sciences* 6.

Peron, J. 1971, La Construction de tables de mortalite's abre' gee s : Comparisons de trois methods usuelles, *Population*, Vol. 26.

Perrin E.B. and Sheps M.C. 1964, Human Reproduction : A Stochastic process, *Biometrics* 20.

Pollard, J.H. 1973, *Mathematical Models for the Growth of Human Populations*, Cambridge University Press.

Potter, J.H. 1977, Problems in Using Birth History Analysis to Estimate Trends in Fertility, *Population Studies*, Vol. 31 No. 2.

Potter, R.G. and M.P. Parker. 1964, Predicting the Time Required to Conceive, *Population Studies*, Vol. 18.

Preston, S.H. 1983, An Intergrated System for Demographic Estimation from the Age Distribution, *Demography*, Vol. 20, No. 2.

Preston, S.H. and Bennett, N.G. 1983, A Census based Method for Estimating Adult Mortality, Population Studies 37 (1).

Preston, S.H. and Coale A.J. 1982, Age Structure, Growth, Attrition, and Accession ; A New Synthesis, *Population Index* 48 (2).

Ranis, G. and Fei, J.C.H. 1961, A Theory of Economic Development, in *American Economic Review*, Vol. 51, No. 4.

Ravenstein, E.G. 1885, The Laws of Migration, in *Journal of The Royal Statistical Society*, Vol. 48, No. 2.

Rele, J.R. 1967, *Fertility Analysis Through Extension of stable Population Concepts*, Population Monograph Series No. 2, University of California, Barkeley.

Rele, J.R. 1987, Fertility Levels and Trends in India, 1951-81. *Population and Development Review* Vol. 13 (2).

R.G. India. 1987, District Level Population Projections 1981-91. *Occasional Paper No. 2 of 1987. Census of India 1981*, Ministriy of Home Affairs, New Delhi.

R.G. India. 1977, Life Tables, *Census of India 1971*, Series I., Paper 1., Ministry of Home Affairs, New Delhi.

Sjaastad, L.A. 1962, The Cost and Returns of Human Migration, in *Journan of Poplitical Economy*, Part 2.

Sharpe, F.R. and Lotka, A.J. 1911, A Problem in Age Distribution, *Philosophical Magazine*, Vol. 21.

Sheldon, E.B. and W.E. Moore. 1968, *Indicators of Social Change : Concepts and Measurement* : New York, Russell Sage Foundation.

Sheps, M.C. 1963, Effects on Family Size and Sex Ratio of Preferences Regarding Sex of Children, *Population Studies*, Vol. 17.

Shryock, Henery S., Jacob S. Siegel, and Associates, *The Methods and Materials of Demography*, Vol. 1 and 2, Washington, D.C. : Government Printing Office.

Siegel, J.S. and C. Horace Hamilton. 1952, "Some Consideration in the Use of The Residual Method of Estimating Net Migration" *Journal of the American Statistical Association*, Vol, 45.

Singh, S.N. 1963, Probability Models for the Variation in the Number of Births per Couple, *Journal of American Statistical Association*, Vol. 58.

Singh, S.N. 1964, On the Time of First Birth, *Sankhya* Series B, Vol. 26.

Singh, S.N. 1968, A Chance mechanism of Variation in the Number of Births per Couple, *Journal of American Statistical Association*, Vol. 63.

Sinha, U.P. 1987, Overview of Indian life tables prepared by Census Actuaries, in P.C. Saxena and P.P. Talwar (eds). "*Recent Advances in the Techniques for Demographic Analysis*, Himalaya Publishing House, Bombay.

Smith D.P. 1974, Generating functions for Partial sex control problems. *Demography*, 11.

Speare, A. JR. 1971, A Cost—Benefit Model to Urban Migration in Taiwan. *Population Studies* Vol. 25, No. 1.

Spilerman, S. 1972, Extensions of the Mover—Stayer Model, *American Journal of Sociology*, Vol. 78 No. 3.

Stewart, J.Q. 1947, "Empirical Mathematical Rules Concerning the Distribution and Equilibrium of Population," *Geographical Review*, 37 (3).

Stolnitz, G.J. 1956, *Life Tables from Limited Data* : A Demographic Analysis, Office of Population Research Princeton University.

Stouffer, S.A. 1940, Intervening Opportunities : A Theory Relating to Mobility and Distance. *American Sociological Review*, Vol. 5.

Stouffer, S.A. 1960, Intervening Opportunities and Competing Migrants. *Journal of Regional Science*, Vol. 2.

Sullivan, J.M. 1972, Estimation of Infant and Childhood Surviving Probability from Children Surviving Data, *Population Studies* Vol. 26.

Todaro, M.P. 1969, A Model of labour Migration and Urban Unemployment in less developed Countries, in *American Economic Review*, Vol. 59, No. 1.

Trussell, J. 1975, A Re-estimation of the Multiplying Factors for the Brass Technique for Determining Childhood Survivorship Rates, '*Population Studies*' Vol. 29, No. 1.

United Nations. 1949, *Methods of Using Census Statistics for the Calculation of Life Tables and Other Demographic measures*, By G. Mortara, Series A., Population Studies No. 7.

United Nation. 1953a, *International Migration Statistic*, Statistical Papers Series No. 2, Statistical Office of the United Nations, Department of Economic Affairs, New York.

United Nations, 1953b, *Sex and Age of International Migrants for Selected Countries*, 1918-1947, Population Studies, Series A, No. 11.

United Nations. 1955, *Age and Sex Patterns of Mortality: Model Life Tables for Underdeveloped Countries*, Series A, Population Studies No. 22.

United Nations, 1967, *Methods of Estimating Basic Demographic Measures from Incomplete Data*, Manual IV., Population Studies No. 42, ST/SOA Series A/42, New York.

United Nations. 1971, *Method of Projecting the Economically Active Population*, Manual V., Population Studies, No. 46, ST/SOA/Series A/46, New York.

United Nations, 1977, *Demographic Yearbook*, New York.

United Nations, 1970, *Methods of Measuring Internal Migration*, Manual VI, Population Studies, No. 47, ST/SOA/Series A/47, New Yourk.

United Nation. 1980, Patterns of Urban and Rural Population Growth. *Population Studies* No. 68, New York, Dapartment of International Economic Affairs, United Nation.

United Nation. 1982, *Model Life Tables for Developing Countries*, Department of International Economic and Social Affairs ST/ESA /SERA/77, New York. ST/SDA/ Series A/47, 1970, New York.

United Nation. 1983, Indirect Techniques For Demographic Estimation Manual X., *Population Studies* No. 81, ST/ ESA//SER. A/81 New York.

United Nation. 1984, Population Projection : Methodology of the United Nation, *Population Studies*, No. 83, New York, Department of International Economic Affairs, United Nations.

Yule, G.U. 1924, A Mathematical Theory of Evolution Based on the Conclusions of Dr. J.C Willis F.R.S., *Philosophical Transactions of the Royal Society* B, CC XIII, 21-87.

Zaba, B. 1981, *Use of the Relational Gompertz Model In Analysing Fertility Data Collected in Retrospective Surveys*, CPS Working paper 81-2. London School of Hygiene and Tropical Medicines.

Zipf, G.K. 1941, *National Unity and Density*, Bloomington (Indiana) Principia Press.

Zipf, G.K. 1946, The P_1P_2/D hypothesis : on the intercity Movement of Persons, *American Sociological Review*, Vol. 2.

Zlotnik, H., and Hill, K. 1981, Use of Hypothetical Cohart in Estimating Demographic Parameters Under Conditions of Changing Fertility and Mortality, *Demography* Vol. 18, No. 1.